Journals 1939-1983

STEPHEN SPENDER

Journals 1939-1983

Edited by John Goldsmith

faber and faber

LONDON · BOSTON

First published in 1985
by Faber and Faber Limited
3 Queen Square London WC1N 3AU
This corrected paperback edition published in 1992

Printed in Great Britain by
Clays Ltd, St Ives plc

© Stephen Spender, 1985

A CIP record for this book is available
from the British Library

ISBN 0–571–13617–6
ISBN 0–571–13922–1 (Limited Edition)
ISBN 0–571–14591–4 (Paperback)

2 4 6 8 10 9 7 5 3 1

To Muriel Gardiner

Contents

The Journals

Contents

PART II / 1974-1983

Illustrations

Illustrations

Illustration acknowledgements

The author and the publishers are very grateful to Henry Moore, OM, CH, and to David Hockney for permission to reproduce their drawings. They also wish to thank the following for photographs: Mrs Michael Astor, Ida Kar, Spender/Edmiston Studio, Lucilla Sherrard, Humphrey Spender, Natasha Spender, Matthew Spender, David Plante, Eva Rubinstein, Mark Gerson, Joseph Bohmer, Frances Charteris, C. A. de Barry, Bee Gilbert. Cecil Beaton's photograph is reproduced by courtesy of Sotheby's, London. All uncredited photographs in the book are by Stephen Spender.

Introduction

This volume has been selected by John Goldsmith from journals, mostly handwritten, kept by me intermittently between 1939 and 1983. With his agreement I have sometimes added passages which he omitted, sometimes cut those which he included. Also, since his editing, I have found two journals unseen by him: one of a lecture tour which I made in America in 1948, from which I have chosen a few pages; the other of drafts for a verse journal which I made in Connecticut in 1970, most of which I have included here.

The volume falls roughly into two halves: the first, of journals kept before the mid-seventies; the second, those kept since 1974. Those in the first half are varied, having been kept for different reasons and purposes. 'September Journal', with which this volume begins, is a very personal *cri de cœur* written at a time of great public, and greatly exaggerated private crisis in my life: the outbreak of war and the collapse of my first marriage. I reprint selections from it here because the recollections of pre-Hitler Germany it contains contrast with the account of Germany in 1945 in my 'German Diary'. This was kept as background material for a book, *European Witness* (1945). The Indian and Japanese journals were written as notes for articles that never got written, as were the interviews with J. B. Yeats in Dublin and with Guy Burgess in Moscow. The Journal I kept in Washington in 1965 when I was Poetry Consultant at the Library of Congress was an attempt to retain a few coherent impressions from the rush of events in my life at that time.

I only discovered recently the notebook, referred to above, in which I attempted to write a journal in verse. Some of these sketches I had already developed to a point where they seemed publishable; for example, *Auden at Milwaukee* and *Art Student*, both of which have appeared in print. Looking over other sketches which I had abandoned as failures I found that, by making the effort to remember the scenes they tentatively described, I could complete accounts of Auden's remarks at a dinner given him by Tom Driberg in a London hotel, a tea at Mrs Longworth's in Washington in 1970, and a comparison of our poems between Robert Lowell and myself at his studio apartment in New York – without falsifying the casual journal form.

In the mid-seventies Alan Ross asked me to write a journal to appear periodically in the *London Magazine*. I welcomed the invitation because it provided me with an excuse for writing a personal record on which I could draw. In fact this did not work out because I found that in what I wrote I was censoring or tailoring my impressions with a view to their publication. The thought of how these things would look in the magazine was never far from my mind, and I was incapable of not thinking about this. Nevertheless, Alan Ross's suggestion – for which I am grateful – had set me off writing a journal, which I have continued to do, with many interruptions – some of them pretty long – since 1975. The essential of the journal for me is that I can put down whatever I like without consideration of fulfilling the expectations, or catering for the taste of, an editor or a reader.

'But after all,' the reader may protest, 'here you are, publishing your journals.' The answer to this objection is, I think, that the journal writer, like the poet, is haunted by the ghost of a reader; but a ghost is very different from some palpable flesh-and-blood reader whom the writer imagines looking over his shoulder with his expectations, standards and demands. The writer of the journal need only set down what is interesting to himself, his own truth, and much of this will conform to no standards of publication that he is aware of at the time. Much of it will be, indeed, unpublishable.

I had, indeed, no intention of publishing these journals though hoping, doubtless, that some day after my death, someone would read them and find them interesting. However, one day when I was lunching with my friend Mark Bonham-Carter, I mentioned to him that I had many volumes of journals written over many years; and he asked if he might see some. A few days later I sent him six or seven volumes. He read them and suggested that a good deal of the material could be published, adding that I should on no account edit it myself. This led to John Goldsmith, who had just edited brilliantly a volume of Roger Hinks's journals, being asked to edit them.

I am grateful to Mark Bonham Carter for his suggestion, and grateful, too, to John Goldsmith for what he has done – grateful also that I have been allowed to do my own additional editing, and glad that this publication has not been postponed till after my death, for the good reason that as a mass of writing the whole thing was in such a dreadful mess it might well have been beyond all rescue.

I also want to thank my wife, Natasha, for her great assistance and a forbearance which will probably be evident to many readers.

S.S.

Acknowledgements

I am grateful to the English Department at Emory University, Atlanta, Georgia, where I spent the first semester of 1985 and edited the final version of the journals. The typing was immaculately and speedily done there by a charming and enthusiastic trio of ladies (Carole Anderson, assisted by Lee Ann Lloyd and Trudy Kretchman) who also contributed many helpful comments on yellow labels – (for instance 'Are there really larch trees in Florida?'). Their stylish help made the whole enterprise more enjoyable.

'September Journal' is extracted from *September Journal*, first published in *Horizon* in October 1939, reprinted in *The Golden Horizon*, an anthology of work appearing in the magazine. A reprint based on the original holograph journal which is in the Bancroft Library (University of California at Berkeley) appeared in *Letters to Christopher* (Black Sparrow Press, San Francisco) and also in *The Thirties and After* (Macmillan).

'German Diary' is selected from notebooks which I used as the basis for *Rhineland Journal*, published in *Horizon* in May 1945, and also for *European Witness* (Hamish Hamilton, 1946), extracts from which are included in *The Thirties and After*.

The entries for 10, 11 and 14 November 1965, appeared in *The Thirties and After*. Some of the 'Washington Diary' was published in the magazine *Art and Literature* in 1966. The entry for December 1956, describing the first meeting of T. S. Eliot and Igor Stravinsky, appeared in the *Sewanee Review* (winter 1966) which was reprinted later as a separate volume, *T. S. Eliot: the Man and His Work*, edited by Allen Tate.

'Auden at Milwaukee' appeared in a volume which I edited, *W. H. Auden: A Tribute* (Weidenfeld and Nicolson, 1975).

In the 1975 Journal there are a few paragraphs providing the basis for the journal which I published in the *London Magazine* at that time.

Part I

1939-1970

Commentary
1936-9

September Journal *was written at the outbreak of war. The hysteria of the public disaster was for me compounded by a private disaster of my own, the breakdown of my first marriage. This accounts, I think, for the very different tone of this journal from the ones that follow.*

Inez and I had married within three weeks of our first meeting in Oxford at some assembly for Spanish Aid in December 1936. Almost immediately after our marriage I went to Spain, and then became involved in rescuing my friend, Tony Hyndman (called Jimmy Younger in World Within World*) from prison and the possibility of being shot as a deserter from the International Brigade. Inez and I separated in the summer of 1939, when she went off with the poet and sociologist, Charles Madge.*

The war had the effect on many English people who had lived partly abroad of making them think about the pre-war Europe they had known. Cyril Connolly, for example, wrote much in the early numbers of Horizon *about the south of France. I had lived in Germany, Berlin and Hamburg, before 1933, and I thought about young Germans I had known then, in the last days of the Weimar Republic, and of the reactions of some of my German friends to Hitler's coming to power. Evidently at first some of the tired, sensuous, sun-loving Germans, once admirers of 'new styles of architecture, a change of heart', saw in the clamorous rejoicing of 1933 and 1934, when the Nazis first came to power, some kind of release from their own personal preoccupations, and perhaps the realization, in a somewhat unexpected form, of populist socialism. They were soon disillusioned. At least one of these young Germans I had known was executed for his participation in the Stauffenberg rising against Hitler in 1944.*

September 1939 was the time of the 'phony war' during which Peter Watson, Cyril Connolly and I planned the magazine Horizon. *Our three names were on the letterhead of* Horizon, *which was originally published from my flat in Lansdowne Terrace, Bloomsbury, where I was living alone after the break-up of my marriage. I did not permit my name to appear as editor, as I feared that doing so would offend John Lehmann, since I was also on the board (which never met) of his magazine* New Writing. *However, perhaps understandably, this restraint did not help matters. The year 1939, I should have realized, was no time for 'appeasement'.*

In 1936 my brother Humphrey and I had bought the 'Great House' in Lavenham, where he and Lolly (Margaret Spender), Inez and I had spent many weeks or weekends. Soon after my stay there in September 1939, it was requisitioned by the army. After the war, when Lolly had died, and Inez had departed, Natasha, Matthew and I spent a summer there, after which it was sold.

1

September Journal
1939

3 September

I am going to keep a journal because I cannot accept the fact that I feel so shattered that I cannot write at all. Today I read in the papers a story by Seymour Hicks of a request he gave to Wilde after his imprisonment, to write a play. Wilde said: 'I *will* write a wonderful play with wonderful dialogue.' As he said this, Hicks realized that Wilde would never write again.

I feel as if I could not write again. Words seem to break in my mind like sticks when I put them down on paper. I cannot see how to spell some of them. Sentences are covered with leaves, and I really cannot see the line of the branch that carries the green meaning.

It so happens that the world has broken just at the moment when my own life has broken ...

The best thing is to write anything, anything at all that comes into your head, until gradually there is a calm and creative day. It is absolutely essential to be patient and to remember that nothing one feels is the last word; all feeling passes over me and as far as the life of the emotions goes there is only one rule: to wait.

I must put out my hands and grasp the handful of facts. How extraordinary they are! The aluminium balloons seem nailed into the sky like those bolts that hold together the radiating struts of a biplane between the wings. The streets become more and more deserted, and the West End is full of shops to let. Sandbags are laid above the glass pavements over basements along the street. Yesterday afternoon I was standing at the bottom of Archer Street outside the P.O. when a little dappled pony attached to a milk cart seemed to go completely off its head. It whimpered, kicked the front of the cart violently with its hind legs, trying to break all the bottles, and occasionally it started swinging around, forcing the cart against the curb. The milkman was in a telephone box, phoning presumably for assistance. People stood round staring neither with amusement nor annoyance, but a kind of faint sympathy as though the pony was expressing just what they were feeling.

4 September

The King broadcast a speech last night which was badly spoken enough, I should have thought, to finish the Royal Family in this country. It was a great mistake. He should never be allowed to say more than twenty words. His voice sounds like a very spasmodic often interrupted tape machine. It produces an effect of colourless monotony, except that sometimes after a very slow drawn-out passage words come out all jumbled together at the end of a sentence. First of all one tries to listen to what he is saying. Then one forgets this and starts sympathizing with him in his difficulties. Then one wants to smash the radio. Later there were [Arthur] Greenwood and [Archibald] Sinclair. They talked about gallant Poland, our liberties, democracy, etc., in a way which raised very grave doubts in my mind. Greenwood even talked about fighting the last war to end war. Personally, I prefer Chamberlain's line to all this sanctimoniousness, which is that he has done his best to give Hitler everything but feels that now he can give nothing more.

The communists say that this is an imperialist war, and, to the usual extent, they are right. But in the old days of about a fortnight ago when they labelled fascism the aggressor, they were still more right. Really it is a war between an imperialism, which is certainly a bad system but which still contains the possibility of change, and an imperialism turned into a kind of madness by Hitler. From an imperialist point of view this war really is unnecessary even to Hitler. He really wants war just as dictators have always wanted some kind of historic climax to their lives.

5 September

Doubtless my own contempt for my father's public speeches is what undermines my faith in political arguments. When I start a train of argument it is like the trains on the Berlin underground which strut confidently above the streets on their raised viaducts, surrounded below by the black tenements which seem to ask whether after all everything is going quite so well as the passengers in the train, flashing through slums, seem to think.

I shall try to recover Germany as it was in 1928-32, when I lived there for several months of each year. The people I knew there were not like the present rulers of Germany, not like the SS men, not like the army. Germans have a greater capacity, I should say, than any other people for invoking the idea of peace – *Ruhe*. To us and to the French, peace is a negative state when we are getting on with our business and private lives and are not at war. But to the Germans a state of peace is something positive and breathing and constructive, as opposed to a state of war. The positive idea of peace permeates a great deal of German romantic literature and music. Works like the slow movements of Beethoven's Fourth Symphony are hymns of peace. They summon up a vision of a landscape exhaling peace. *Dämmerung* is a peaceful word, and words like *Heim, Heimat, Friede, Ruhe*, are loaded with a greater weight of emotion than the corresponding words in other languages ...

Perhaps it is that the German landscape is particularly peaceful. I think of the Rhine at evening, the Harz mountains, the shores of the Alster at Hamburg with the heavy scent of lime blossoms on a summer evening.

I have a German relative who is the wife of a U-boat commander. They lived in Kiel, which has just been bombed. She plays the piano very well. Recently she came to London and she played an early Beethoven sonata to us at my grandmother's flat. After she had played the slow movement, her face was streaming with tears. 'Excuse me,' she said, 'but the music is so full of peace.'

Ten years after the war, Germany was full of peace, it dripped with peace, we swam in peace, no one knew what to do with all the German peace. They built houses with flat roofs, they sunbathed, they walked with linked hands under the lime trees, they lay together in the woods, they talked about art. Above all, everything was new and everyone was young. They liked the English very much and they were sorry about the war. They talked about the terrible time they had had during the inflation.

This was in Hamburg. I used to bathe, and I went to parties of young people. I had never enjoyed parties before and never have since, but these were like living in the atmosphere of a blue-period Picasso. Everyone was beautiful, and gentle, everyone was poor, no one was smart. On summer evenings they danced in the half-light, and when they were tired of dancing they lay down in the forest, on the beach, on mattresses, on the bare floor. They laughed a great deal, smiling with their innocent eyes and showing well-shaped teeth. Sometimes they let one down – sometimes the poorer ones stole, for example – but there was no Sin. I am not being ironic. There really was no sin, like there is in this kind of life in England.

Of course, it was all very superficial; it has all been blown away now. I could not dance. I could not speak German. I stood rather outside it. I think now of the sad émigrés who were the exquisite confident students of the Weimar Republican days. Perhaps it was all fictitious, but now in letting the mirage fade from the mind, I get very near to it because everything in Germany is inclined to be fictitious. The German tends to think of his life as an operatic cycle emerging from a series of myths. There was the War, then there was the Inflation, then there was the period of Youth and the Weimar Republic, then there was the Crisis, then there was Hitler. Every German can readily explain him- or herself in terms of What We Have Been Through.

Perhaps we should not laugh at this for isn't really a passive attitude towards life a tendency which we see everywhere, and which provides us with the connection between public events and the breakdown of all standards of private morality? Aren't the dumb oxen, heroes and heroines of modern fiction, doing exactly this?

This passive attitude to life, the tendency to consider oneself a product of circumstances and environment, gives one the connection between the breakdown of external standards and the private standards of people. A young man – John Cornford – fighting in the Spanish War wrote a poem to his lover beginning: 'Heart of the heartless world.' He was either optimistic or very lucky. I know a truer line would have been: 'Heartless one of the heartless world.'

I was 20 in those days, and I was caught up mostly with the idea of Friendship – *Freundschaft* – which was a very important part of the life of the Weimar Republic. This, if it was frank, was also very idealistic. It was not cynical, shamefaced, smart, snobbish, or stodgy, as so often in England. It was more like Walt Whitman's idea of camaraderie. I admit that I do not feel at all easy about this now, but I set it down for what it was. Two friends, young men, faced the world together: they camped, they travelled, they were happy in each other's company. There was usually a certain casualness about these relationships, a frank admiration of beauty. The Germans had a reputation at that time of being homosexual, but I think it would be truer to say that they were bisexual, though there were of course a few of those zealots and martyrs who really hate women, whom one finds everywhere. But what the young, free, handsome German looked for in the world was a reflection of his own qualities in either man or woman. It was part of the myth that he should 'travel light' and have no responsibilities.

A life in which people are exercising sexual freedom without, apparently, anyone suffering or paying for it in any way is very attractive. One wonders how it is done. In this case, I think it was done at the cost of making everything exist on exactly the same level. The new architecture, the Bauhaus, the social equality, the most casual affairs, marriage, an abortion, a party, were all just the same – they were a pack of cards all of equal value, precariously constructed – so that when one fell the whole house came down.

I stayed in Hamburg with a young Jew, E, whom I got to dislike far more than, in retrospect, I think he deserves. He had, as I thought, an attitude towards the life around him as though he were watching it from outside and at the same time living it vicariously. He had a dead, expressionless face, and he listened to what his friends said half as if he were criticizing it, half as if he were thinking, 'This is life! I am living it!' Whilst the others were participating in each other's lives, giving and taking, living and enjoying, he in some way remained an outsider, watching and willing to pick up any scraps of their lives thrown his way. He was the only one of the people I knew there who was rich, but he was notoriously stingy. The fact that he had a sophisticated, a collector's, attitude towards this life which I was in love with irritated me. Amongst other things, he collected his own feelings and would murmur of his 'affair' with so-and-so or so-and-so, five years earlier on, like a possession he kept in a drawer.

The young Germans took him much less seriously than I did. 'You see he is a Jew. He can't help it,' they would laugh. Being partly Jewish myself, I didn't feel quite easy about this. I told them my mother was of Jewish extraction. They laughed again and said politely, 'Oh no, it isn't possible, we don't believe you!' But I had never noticed a Jew being so consciously a Jew as E.

Actually, I think they knew far less about E. than, after a few weeks, I did. They regarded Jews as outsiders, without knowing much about them. But they made Jews conscious of the fact that they were Jews.

Again and again I had experience of the Germans' ignorance of Jews. Later, when Christopher (Isherwood) and I were staying in Insel Rue-gen, and when the Nazis were doing exercises every evening in the woods and the 'movement' had become a serious menace, I got to know one or two of these young men. They were not gay, irresponsible, intelligent, like the Hamburg set. They were heavy, stupid, but friendly and well-meaning. They seemed perfectly content to lounge around all day sun-bathing, listening to the band, going to the dance hall in the evening and having their girls in the pine trees afterwards among the hungry mos-quitoes. But actually their fun lacked lightness. For instance, when they sunbathed they would build little forts for themselves on the beach, set up a flagpost, hoist a Nazi flag on it and gaze up in reverence. Whilst they were lounging round listening to the music, they seemed always to be waiting for a patriotic air and when one was played they would stand to attention.

I was with two of them on some occasion when I suddenly lost my temper and said, 'Ich bin ein Jude!' They laughed incredulously. 'You, a Jew? Impossible. Why, you're the perfect Nordic type,' said one of them. 'You're tall, you have blue eyes, fair hair, Scandinavian features,' said the other. 'That's why we know and like you.' This revelation astonished me. 'Then what do you think when you meet a Jew?' I asked. 'We want to kill and destroy the pest,' they said. 'We want to crush him and knock him down.' 'Then knock me down!' I said. 'Here I am. I am a Jew. Please knock me down.' They looked at me, dazed by this wolf in Nordic clothing. I felt quite sorry for them. Then I got angry. 'I don't believe you have any idea what a Jew looks like,' I said. 'You imagine a monster, when really you have to deal with a human being. I don't believe you know what you are talking about, and your heads are stuffed with stupid hatreds and lies.' Probably I didn't know enough German to say all that, but I worked myself up into a great rage and rushed home to laugh with Christopher about it.

On another occasion someone made friends with me in the train specifically because I was of the Nordic type and, indeed, now I know exactly the kind of warm response that a Nordic appearance arouses in some Germans. How can one understand the tremendous interest in appearance of a military race? A uniform face, in a uniform phy-sique, dressed in a uniform, and marching. In a way the Hamburg set who wanted girls to be like boys and everyone to have a lovely face on a perfect body showed their craving for uniformity too.

Certainly 1929 was the beginning of the slump and the end of the efflorescence of the Weimar Republic.

6 September

I want to go on about Germany, about my landlord's Berlin, about Curtius,* but I feel too tired, I can't go on. The first thing about any war is that everyone is tired, countries at war are countries of tiredness – fatigue becomes a spiritual experience, an illumination. Fetters of habit fall away, and one enters into a more easy relationship with one's fellow beings, an exhausted state of communion. The wrong words that come into one's mind, and that rigid discipline of wakefulness would reject, are suddenly the right ones. Everything flows freely and nervously, one does not even respect the heavy weight on one's eyes because one sees so much light.

I remember again the water, the flowing line of the hills, the rich harvest quality of Germany. E. took me all over the place. His relationship with me was a sustained kind of mental seduction. He had a little car, and when he wasn't watching the road his eyes were watching for the effects on me of the storks on North German villages, of monkeys masturbating at the Hagenbeck zoo. We visited some friends of his called Harman who had a house in the Harz mountains. Like everyone else, they had lost their money and all they had was the property itself and, I suppose, the salary of Professor Harman. The whole family, grandfather, son, daughter-in-law, a grandson, two daughters, and a brother and sister who were fellow students of Manfred, the son, were there. Manfred had pinched, vague features of a pallid, distracted beauty which drew me to him. He was very much worried about sex. At night he would walk with a vague expression into the bedroom of Fräulein Bindler, the sister of the student. She received him into bed, but was afraid of having a child. I am sure that everyone knew about this, and in some comforting way thought it was right, or at all events just accepted it. He was also concerned with other problems – philosophy, poetry, art – and walked round the uncared-for garden earnestly discussing André Maurois's† *Life of Byron* with me.

* Ernst Robert Curtius (1886-1956). Professor at Bonn University. His main works are *The Civilization of France, European Literature and the Latin Middle Ages* and *Essays on European Literature*.

† André Maurois (1885-1967). Biographer of Shelley, Byron and Disraeli.

Several years later, after Hitler's rise to power, Manfred came to visit me in London. Earnest and pale as ever, he had a mission: he wanted to convert me to Nazism. 'Of course, there are things I do not like about the Nazis,' he said. 'I do not agree with their views on literature and art. I do not sympathize with the persecution of the Jews. I do not accept their explanation of the Reichstag fire. But all the same they do have a faith.' Here his fists clenched and his eyes burned with questing mystery. 'They have restored to us our belief in Germany and in life. Some of them are idealists. There is a great deal of socialism in their Germany.' I raged as I had done before. I said, 'If I were a German, as I might well be, I would now be either in a concentration camp or else deprived of any means of earning my living. You can't expect me to be fair. I don't care about your reasons . . .'

This was an unnecessary piece of self-righteousness on my part, because I heard later that Manfred became disillusioned about the Nazis and was one of those unhappy, pained, gentle creatures who represent the heart of another Germany, and do not understand what is happening to them. I have touched a deeper chord than I knew here, for have I not met two or three of them? Don't I know very well the peculiar whiteness and stillness of their eyes which seem to have been drained of pigment? These poor ghosts are really beautiful in a sexless way, because, if one is a young man of another country, an exile in one's own, one cannot expect to be virile. How closely I press upon a secret! Why am I always attracted by these desolate spirits? There was one I met on the Hook of Holland boat once, shortly before Hitler's rise to power. He was the son of a general. And now that at least four names crowd on to me, I remember that many are aristocrats and often close to the higher ranks of the army. This boy was called Horst. He had a round face with very well-formed features, delicate lips, light blue eyes, and brown hair of an almost feathery lightness. He was very quiet and polite, and he had some small, out-of-the-way interest – playing the flute or making musical instruments or something. There's really nothing much more to it than that. He had a scholarship at Oxford and I used to call on him there; we went for walks and I introduced him to Isaiah Berlin. But he never in the least became part of the life at Oxford. He was always just as gentle, just as isolated, and gradually one saw beneath the surface of his interest in the musical instrument – or whatever – to a restlessness that never ceased. Isaiah Berlin saw him several times and then confessed to me that the sustained gentle sense of his unhappiness was too much: he no longer cared for him.

Another such was surely Jowo von Moltke, who wandered about Europe looking at pictures. They all had some mild objective interest which was obviously not their life, but which covered their refusal ever to speak about Germany. Perhaps, like Manfred, when the Nazis first came to power they flamed with momentary hope which soon disappeared as they reverted to their former interests.

But the most remarkable case was the young aristocrat I met in Isaiah Berlin's room only a few months ago. He was a Prussian and his name was Jobst. He had the fine looks of all those well-bred Germans, though in his case something seemed to have gone wrong. There was the blond hair, blue eyes, the well-defined bones, and strong jaw, and yet in spite of its fine structure his face seemed to have collapsed. Perhaps his mouth when in repose was almost too rich and well formed, and when he moved it seemed to become distorted, the lips to disappear. He was tall and strongly built, but his movements were so nervous and the veins of his hands stood out so much and were yet so fine, that he had the appearance of being pulled the whole time by hundreds of strands of fine cord. We talked about music, for which he had an immense passion, but the idea of Germany hung over us because he was going back there next morning.

We stayed up till three o'clock, Isaiah and Jobst talking without stopping. I got very sleepy, so sleepy that I lay down on the sofa and attempted to doze from time to time. But the spirits of Horst, of Manfred, of Harman, of Jowo von Moltke were pacing the room and would not let me rest. He did not really attempt to apologize as he said, 'Excuse me for keeping you up, but we shall never meet again.' 'Oh nonsense,' said Isaiah. 'No, no, it is not nonsense. We shall never meet again. I know it. This is my last day of peace.'

Next morning, he turned up again before breakfast. 'I have not slept,' he said. 'I went to bed at three, lay down for three hours, and got up at six.' 'Why did you get up at six?' I asked. 'Because it is my last morning, and I shall never see all this again.' He held out his long, expressive, nervous right hand. Other people called, but even when Jobst was silent, it was really impossible to escape from his drama. He did not rest. When he stopped pacing round the room, he knelt down with those speaking hands of his touching the carpet. The worst of it was that he was not an actor. He was by nature a quiet, scholarly person with a rich inner drama. Seeing him act was as unexpected and shocking as, say, seeing one's father cry.

9 September

Yesterday morning while I was waiting for a bus, some soldiers passed down the road singing, 'It's a long long way to Tipperary'. An un-shaved ragged old tramp wearing the ribbons of several medals so loosely attached to his coat that they were almost falling off, said to me, 'They're singing now, but they won't be singing when they come back. Hearing 'em sing reminds me of when I went to fight in the trenches. We went out singing, but we didn't sing for long.'

There is very little cheering this war. There is no talk of victory. It is a war simply to avoid defeat, and to end the suspense of the last few years with war always hanging over us. The most hopeful thing is this complete lack of desire for a resounding triumph. Get rid of Hitler and then let the Germans do what they like is what people seem to think.

10 September

> The best lack all conviction, while the worst
> Are full of passionate intensity.

W. B. Yeats, who wrote these lines, himself became a fascist sympath-izer. He was prepared to accept the worst; he wanted strength at any price.

Why were the gentle and kind people I knew in Germany tired or weak?

The tiredness of our generation consists of exploring unimportant and superficial ideas of the idea of freedom. Freedom, the young people in Hamburg said, is sexual freedom primarily, then freedom to enjoy yourself, to 'wander', not to make money, not to have the re-sponsibilities of a family or the duties of a citizen. Freedom is one long holiday. They were tired. What they wanted, in fact, was a holiday.

I felt uneasy about discussing these things in a Left Book Club manner, suddenly identifying myself with the Workers in order to sneer at the people whom I met for coffee, and dismissing my own past as though I have renounced it finally. The fact is that my own sexual life is very unsatisfactory. I have just had a first-class failure in my personal life, and I am so full of regret and bitterness that I dream of nothing else.

If a human relationship becomes more important than anything else in two people's lives, it simply means that there is a lack of trust between these two human beings. A relationship is now a way of entering into a kind of dual subjectivity, a redoubled and reciprocal egotism; it is an alliance of two people who form a united front to deal with the problems of the objective world. The problem of married people is not to become absorbed in each other, but how not to become absorbed in each other; how, in a word, to trust one another in order to enter into a strong and satisfactory relationship with the outside world.

A great cause of weakness with people today is putting less important things before those that are important – for example, personal relations before work and an objective philosophy of life, sex before love. People who put personal relations before their tasks in society becomes parasites on each other, form mutual admiration societies, agree to do nothing that will give one a social advantage over the other, and prevent each other from doing so. People who put sex before love perpetually flee from one marital relationship to another because, for them, sex has become in itself a thing dissociated from personal relationships. They have an image in their mind of 100 per cent sexual satisfaction, and when they are in love they are continually asking themselves, 'Am I satisfied?'; they are continually tormented by the thought that perhaps they are not. For them love, at first an opportunity, soon becomes a trap, preventing them from enjoying the possibly greater delights that they might get elsewhere.

Satisfactory personal relationships exist when the people who enjoy them have a satisfactory relation with society. In the same way, satisfactory sex exists within love and it can be attained through love, which means patience and loyalty and understanding.

Another cause of weakness is not to admit, but to pursue our failures blindly. There is such a thing as real failure in personal relationships and in sex. How easily, then, that which symbolizes failure, the poor substitute improvised for love, becomes the most important thing in life! How people build it up and call the scars of failure their dazzling successes! Masturbation, homosexuality, following people in the streets, breaking up relationships because one has failed in one's own, all these compensatory activities form a circle of Hell in which people can never rest from proving that their failures are the same as love. Yet the lives of countless men and women show that the great compensation lies in recognizing failures as failures, substitutes as substitutes, making the most of the rest of one's life. In fact, the great artists and figures in literature have almost without exception been failures in life. By this I mean that their relations with their fellow beings were at some point unsatisfactory, that most of them were fully conscious of this, and that their honesty in admitting a defect restored to their lives a sense of scale which hopelessly neurotic people lack.

The artist realizes that art is not a complete life, otherwise he would really be self-sufficient; he would be cut off from the world and there would be happy, unreal artists creating a truly pure art. Some people, who are not artists, or who are bad artists, think that art is like this, a world completely cut off from the world, where aesthetic experience is everything. These are the virtuosi of art and of appreciation, spirits which have flowed completely into an aesthetic medium, without the friction of living their lives.

The young aristocratic sons of German militarists whom I call 'weak' were trying, without much conviction, it is true, to use the appreciation of art as a complete way of living, and as an escape from their despair about Germany. But this does not work. You go to the concert and music offers an interior life of sounds inside your head which is as complete as anything you have experienced. You read a play of Shakespeare and you enter into feelings completer because more explicit and final than anything your own life may provide. 'This is real for me; everything else can be put aside and forgotten.' But it can't. The felt life in the work of art is only intense, and often painful, because it actually touches the life of deep and terrible experience. In art there is real conflict, real breaking up and melting down of intractable sensations which seem expressionless lumps until they have been transformed by it. A work of art doesn't say, 'I am life. I offer you the opportunity of becoming me.' On the contrary, it says, 'This is what life is like. It is even realer – less to be evaded – than you thought. But I offer you an example of acceptance and understanding. Now, go back and live!'

12 September

Today I applied for a job as a translator in the War Office. Yesterday I had a printed slip from the Ministry of Information saying that my name was on a list of writers who may be used later. But I don't think I have a chance as I am told that that ministry is very overcrowded with applicants. Nor do I think the War Office will want me, as there must be many translators far better qualified. I feel that perhaps I ought to be doing stretcher work or filling sandbags or something and perhaps later I shall volunteer for one of these. But as long as I can write and read a good deal each day, I am not really bothering. What I would like most is to complete three books: this journal, a novel, and a book of poems, before I am called up.

Lunched with Joe Ackerley* who was depressed, having dined the evening before with someone high up in the Ministry of Information. He said that our achievement so far in the war was to have bombed a Danish village, shot down two Belgian planes, shot down one British plane during the last air-raid alarm, and lost five other planes which simply dived into the sea during the raid on the Kiel canal.

I want to remember all I can about Ernst Robert Curtius.† I do not remember the details, only the feeling of our first meeting. I think that perhaps there was a cool meal with fruit and wine laid on a table with a white cloth spread over it. There were bay windows opening on to a balcony, and a pleasant freshness of the forest at evening filled the room. Everything, I think, gave me an impression of coolness. That first evening I talked freely and indiscreetly to Ernst Robert about my life in Hamburg.

He listened to me with amusement, yet affectionately, laughing at me as well as with me. In my deepest friendships – with Auden, with Christopher Isherwood, and with Curtius – I have been conscious of being thus taken 'with a pinch of salt' ... Sometimes it is disconcerting to be laughed at when one is serious, but as long as it is done affectionately one is grateful to people who enable one to see oneself a little from the outside. From the first, Ernst Robert's attitude to me was one of gentle raillery, and I think that because he saw so far beyond me and at the same time loved me, I owe more to him than to any other older person.

Being anxious to impress him, I talked about literature, and especially about Dostoevsky, whom I was then reading. I was very interested in madness, partly because at school and Oxford I had been taught to regard myself as mad, and because Auden who, when he was an under-

* J. R. Ackerley, literary editor of the *Listener*. Author of *Hindu Holiday*, *My Dog Tulip*, *We Think the World of You* and *My Father and Myself*.
† See footnote p. 29.

graduate, was anxious to maintain a certain superiority over his contemporaries, and had always treated me as a lunatic. Experiences like my cerebral excitement on train journeys, my excessive credulity, my lack of complete understanding with even my best friends so that I always felt they stood to some extent outside me, bore out my theory of my own madness. Above all, I was, like everyone, in search of that ecstasy which is so lacking in our civilization – that ecstasy which is the justification of every kind of adventure and unscrupulousness in private lives.

During the next few days, I walked with him in the Black Forest. We went swimming together. We drank beer every evening. He criticized Dostoevsky; he told me to read other things than the Russians, particularly the French. I showed him the poems I had written and, to my surprise, instead of reading them with the patronizing superiority of one immersed in great literature, he read them with evident delight, and made translations of them which were (later) published in the *Neue Schweitzer Rundschau*. He listened to my accounts of my life in Hamburg, and scandalized me by treating this life which I thought so highly of simply as pornography in which he was unashamedly interested. To him it was pornography; it was not, as it seemed to me . . . ecstasy.

15 September

I spent most of yesterday and the day before typing this journal out and writing a review of Dylan Thomas's *Map of Love*. I shall try to work this journal into a book with several levels of time, present and past, which I am able to move in as I choose. During these first days of the war, and first days of the breaking up of my marriage, I tend to live in the past, partly because the present is so painful, partly because it is so fragmentary and undecided. We live now in a kind of vacuum in which the events on which we are waiting have not yet caught up on us, though our hour is very near. We have seen this whirlwind in China, in Central Europe, in Spain, in Poland, and now we are next on the list. If I let my mind drift on the present, I have terrible daydreams. Last night, walking the streets in the blackout, I had one of an aggressive alliance between Germany and Russia, which would not only destroy the whole of the rest of Europe, but divide it utterly on questions of ideology. Another of my unpleasant daydreams is a growing fear that this is only the first in a series of wars. This fear springs from the following reflections. Supposing the Allies win the war, what kind of peace will they make? The answer is that they must either repeat the mistakes of the Treaty of Versailles, or else they must establish Germany as a strong power under military dictatorship.

I do not think these speculations are of much value; it's better to get back to the little world I have some concrete understanding of, and the only point in giving rein to the nightmare is to preserve a sense of proportion. To show I am aware of the fact that the life of myself and mine is like Lear's hut on the heath in the thunderstorm, and filled with madness from within and outside ...

I know at least a dozen people who are worse off than I; so I should not complain. The whole of Europe is filled with people violently separated from those they love, whose homes and children are torn from them, who search for their possessions in a heap of ashes. Compared with these brutal realities, my luxury marriage and luxury separation seem an extravagant game of people who are millionaires in the way they spend their feelings.

18 September

Today I met Pares* in the street. We discussed the Russian coup, and he said that the whole situation made him wish to have to go, in order that he might then be able to examine all the relevant documents and discover what has really happened between Hitler and Stalin. He is right. When our lives are threatened, the most sensible thing is to start living as though one could see beyond the darkness of the tunnel into the light outside. However much one becomes involved in the struggle from day to day, one must have a long-term view of the final issues for civilization and also for reconstructing people's personal lives. Politics alter from day to day, and therefore lack continuity; for this reason private life and personal standards become very important because they have a continuity that one mustn't allow to be broken by outside events.

The communists argue that by making a pact with Germany the Russians have broken the Axis and robbed Germany of her Allies. If one applies the same argument to Russian intervention in Spain, one could say that by supporting the Republic the Russians provided a

---

*Richard Pares (1902-1958), historian. Fellow of All Souls College, Oxford, and later Professor of History at Edinburgh.

triumph for Franco by splitting up the supporters of the Republic in capitalist democracies. But at the time this was not the reason the communists gave for Russian intervention.

19 September

With Curtius I was in contact with the Germany of Goethe, Hölderlin, and Schiller. That is an Apollonian Germany, a Germany of the sun, not the Dionysian Germany of Hitler who rouses himself from a torpid dullness into a wild frenzy.

Curtius was an egotist of the liberal, Goethe tradition. His life was organized with an enlightened selfishness; he did not take more than he could take, nor give more than he could give. He would not put himself out, even for his best friends, if he thought that his own resilience was going to be depressed by their needs. One could say, perhaps, that he was a fair-weather friend. Once, when I was hard up, I wrote asking him if he could introduce me to people in Berlin to whom I could teach English. He wrote back about other things, ending his letter with the curt, 'leider kann ich keine Verbindungen für Ihnen in Berlin schaffen'.*
I myself have a tendency in my relationships with people never to refuse anything and often to undertake far more than I can undertake. I know how this leads to a feeling of resentment which affects one's relationships with them, and to a fear of making new acquaintances, who may plunge one into new commitments. He remained happy and light and broad and objective. He would lose this by identifying himself with others in their needs.

I do not mean that he was unsympathetic, but that he was unself-sacrificing because what he had was of too great an objective value to himself and to others to sacrifice. He did not enter into their lives because his generosity lay in the freedom with which they could enter into his.

If one realized this, he gave a great deal.

Once when I was staying at Bonn, I went into Cologne for a night and got into an extremely unpleasant scrape. I liked going to very squalid places, and I went to a hotel near the railway station in the lowest part of town. When I got into bed, I didn't notice that the lock of the door was on the outside instead of the inside, so that the guests in this hotel were like prisoners locked into their rooms instead of

---

* '... unfortunately I am unable to make any contacts for you in Berlin.'

guests who could lock out intruders. In the middle of the night, the door was flung open and a man came into the room who put his hands to my throat and threatened to throttle me unless I gave him my money. He was much stronger than I was, and I was undressed, so I asked him to pass me my clothes. He did this, and I gave him my money. It amounted to about 60 or 70 marks, which he did not seem to think enough, so he said he would take my coat as well. I protested about this, but it did not seem much use, so I asked him to leave me a mark at least to pay my fare back to Bonn. He flung a mark down on the marble-topped table beside my bed, and ran out of the room. I lay in bed staring into the darkness and listening to the noises from outside of whores talking and screaming, and a continuous sound like water running away in the darkness. I felt as though I had reached the goal of something horrible and mysterious in my life, as though it were unfolded from my own flesh and was part of me. I did not resent the theft because I thought of it as something I had let myself in for. I did not blame the thief at all, for what had happened seemed an automatic consequence of my choosing this kind of life and, in short, I felt completely passive, as though a whole process which I had called into being by my own actions were now happening to me, and I knew that I would never escape from it. Because I knew this, it was very difficult for me to resist, but at last I realized that I must do something; so I sat up in bed and shouted for the landlord. A few minutes later, he and two or three other men came into the room, switching on the light and standing round my bed as though I were an invalid, seriously ill, and they were four specialists whom I had summoned. 'Why are you making such a noise in my hotel?' asked the landlord. 'I shall call the police.' 'For heaven's sake, do call the police,' I answered, feeling that I was now prepared for any kind of disgrace. 'I would like to speak to them very much.' This seemed to make him hesitate, and he said quite kindly, 'Why, what do you want then?' 'Someone in your hotel has just stolen all my money,' I said. 'This is a disgrace,' said the landlord, 'I won't have things like this going on in my hotel. Why should you come here and bring this disgrace on me?' 'It isn't my fault,' I answered. 'I am very sorry. I don't mind my money being stolen, but I must have my coat and an assurance that all my clothes won't be stolen, else I won't be able to go home.' 'Nothing else will be stolen,' said the landlord honourably. 'I can assure you of that.' 'Well might I at least have my coat back?' I asked. He nodded to one of the other men who left the room and returned a few seconds later with my coat. Then he said, 'Goodnight,' reassuringly, and they left the room.

I felt that nothing else was likely to happen, but I could not sleep and continued to lie with my eyes open in my waking nightmare. At last it was dawn. Then for the first time it occurred to me that I had been made to pay my bill before taking my room. Therefore, there was not the slightest reason why I should stay any longer. It surprised me to realize that I was free and that nothing final had happened. I quickly put on my clothes and ran downstairs and out of the hotel, without anyone stopping me. I ran until I came to the river. Outside it was cold and raw. In the grey light the cathedral and the bridges and the modern exhibition building had a photographic quality. Suddenly I started laughing. I had a gay sensation of release, and from hating and feeling ashamed I was suddenly pleased.

After an hour or so of waiting, I went back to Bonn. When I had rested and changed, I called on Ernst Robert, partly to borrow some money from him. When he saw that I was upset, he took me for a walk by the Rhine. Full of shame again, I told him my story. But to my surprise, instead of being shocked, disappointed or upset, he started laughing; putting his arm round me, he patted my shoulder.

While I have been writing this last page and a half, I have had the wireless on, playing Hitler's latest speech. His voice varies from a cavernous rumbling to the peaks of an exalted hysteria from which he shrieks like a raucous beast of prey, until the whole chorus of his followers breaks into a thunder of triumphant hatred. Undoubtedly there is something disintegrating about that voice, that applause, and everything they stand for. The cities of one's mind seem to be bombarded, as though a threat could make them fall to pieces. He speaks of a new, terrible secret weapon which, if the English oppose him, he will use. When he does this, I feel as though the world could be destroyed by pressing a button, and he were a madman who had access to this button and was about to press it.

26 September

I have not heard from Inez since I saw her, nor have I written to her; I thought I would let her be the first to write this time. Although it is desolating not to hear, I think it is better than crushing myself by writing about three letters which would have the effect of alienating me from her. I had better realize the full extent of her indifference, or I will live in a condition of illusion in which I feel insecure. If she wants me for any reason, I shall doubtless hear from her, but the fact that I want to hear won't ever bring any kind of response. The sooner I realize that, the better. One is isolated if the response one does get from a lover is only a reflex action from one's own love that one invests in her. I mean one letter for three written to her; still I would like to forge this complaint in one of those kisses which again seal up one's security.

Last week I bought a printing press for £5, which was being sold second hand at a bookshop near here. I have taken it to Bobby Buhler's* flat, and we hope to print small books of poems, stories, etc., by unknown poets with it.

On Thursday I lunched with Tom Eliot. Friday George Barker dined here. Spent the weekend with Leonard and Virginia Woolf.

All these people whom I met last week were concerned with the work they are going to do during the war, and their attitude toward it.

29 September

In the afternoon I went to Bobby Buhler's. Another painter, Basil Johnson, was there. He is the first person I have met who is very warlike, though he was only funny about it. He said he disliked all this; we love the Germans and we only hate Hitler propaganda. He is quite prepared, he said, to hate the Germans, though until now he has never thought about them, etc., etc. He wants to join up, and is very sick of having nothing to do. He was sacked from ARP work, because when a Duchess came round to inspect their unit, she stopped at him and said, 'What do you do all day, my man?' He answered, 'Play cards.'

Met Cyril (Connolly) and spent much of the evening discussing his project for a magazine.† He seemed rather vague about what it would cost – I think it may be more than he imagines. We spent a long time thinking of names, all signs of the zodiac being discussed. The most favoured names were *Sirius*, *Scorpio*, *Equinox*, *Centaur*, though we really aren't satisfied with any of these. I said I would give him any

* Robert Buhler, R. A. Painter. Did portraits of Stephen and his sister Christine, and a pastel of his second wife, Natasha.

† This was *Horizon*.

amount of help but did not want my name used as it has been used too much in this sort of way.

This morning came the news about the Russo-German mutual assistance Pact over the wireless. Although I expected this, I felt shattered when I actually heard it. We are living at a time when we see the forces behind events, and the direction which may take years to be revealed, with a blinding clarity. The question does arise: what are we fighting for? Though this is not quite in the form the Germans put it to us. We aren't fighting for Poland.

30 September

The Times this morning answers my question by saying that we are fighting for the independence of a new Polish state with an entrance to the sea, and, I suppose, the loss of the bits of Poland which have already gone to Russia.

Yet, if the whole of Eastern Europe is held between the nutcrackers of Russia and Germany, it becomes absurd to talk about fighting for the sovereignty of all these little reactionary states which, anyhow, have been the cause of so many wars. There may be no military alliance between Germany and Russia; they may even hate each other. But whether they love or hate each other, they are now clinched, and no amount of wishful thinking can pretend that they won't destroy any (country) between them that comes in their way.

The English communists have now twisted again and say we should make peace and accept what they call 'the Russian terms'. I think that they are probably insincere in this. What they want is what Russia wants, i.e. to let the war go on, while dissociating themselves from it and using it as a process for getting their own ends.

Yesterday I lunched with Peter Watson* and Cecil Beaton, who Peter says is like me in some ways. I do actually see a certain resemblance because there is something ascetic about his appearance and character, in spite of his affectations.

At six o'clock, Cyril and I had a long conference about the magazine. I pressed that there should be features on the subject of Culture and War, so that we should be able to keep a constant criticism of how broadcasting, publishing, music, art are going.

---

* Peter Watson. Collector and friend of artists. Co-founder with Cyril Connolly of *Horizon* magazine, of which he was the art editor and benefactor. He inherited a fortune from his father, who manufactured margarine.

Earlier on, Cyril talked a bit about the war. He said that we were all wishful thinkers about Russia, that Stalin sympathized with Hitler as a 'strong man', and detested the British Empire and the line of British Cabinet Ministers from whom he has recovered so many states.

The blackout time gets a few minutes earlier each evening, so one notices more than ever the drawing in of the autumn evenings. Actually, the weather has been particularly fine lately. The streets glitter a biscuit yellow all day. The crowds waiting at the bus stops for the few buses give the town an air of festivity. The sandbags on the pavements, the strips of paper on the windows, the balloons in the air, are sufficiently new in the bright sunlight to be interesting and almost gay.

When I drew the blinds, I felt the autumn chill in my bones, and because of the decision I have taken, which is really simply a recognition of existing facts, I had a sudden sense of the desolation of the world. Above all, the world should be home, it should be somewhere where everyone has his place, is surrounded by the simple machinery, the task, the house, the furniture, the companion, the river, the trees or the streets which assure him that he is loved. Everyone should be rooted. This is the simplest thing in life: it is the cocoon that surrounds childhood, it is the simple security of the flesh and the kiss and the fireplace and the setting sun which brings him home. The hands that destroy this homeliness, whether in children or grown people, are ripping the child in all of us that never leaves the womb, away from the womb, and tearing the belly of the mother into ribbons. No one should want anything except to find his place in life, the centre of his potentiality to love and be loved.

Yet if love is the essential thing in life, lovelessness is the fiend and the madness which enters certain bodies and tears the life surrounding them into shreds. The depredation of the loveless and homeless who seek power over their fellow beings can be seen everywhere today. The world suffers from the worst and least necessary of mental illnesses – homesickness. The papers are filled with photographs, and have been now for years, of those who have been driven out of their homes – the endless rustle of shuffling peasant feet through the dust all night along the road outside Malaga. The family with their possessions piled on a cart outside a burning Polish farmhouse. The widow searching amongst the ruins of her house for a souvenir. They are driven from the little hole which surrounded and comforted them into the elemental world of alien stones and light. Most homeless of all, little shreds of minerals from distant countries that have nothing to do with them are driven through their flesh. The whole universe of death enters their bodies – a fragment of a bomb, a bullet.

After that in the world today is the desolation of ideas. In times of war and revolution, the great comfort has always been that in place of home there is the idea. One goes out into the street and finds people friendly, everyone is a brother or a sister of everyone else because England is threatened. Patriotism, revolutionary fervour, can knit people together into a spasmodic unity. But today, for hundreds of people, even that consolation is denied them. There is confusion of ideas. Many no longer can fight with any conviction for their country, because it represents the Past. And the idea of the future, Revolution, is so compromised that only the most ideological thinkers wish to fight for that either. Suddenly the world appears a desert. There is no woman, there are no children, there is no faith, there is no cause.

The moon shines above the London streets during the blackouts like an island in the sky. The streets become rivers of light. The houses become feathery, soft, undefined, aspiring, so that any part of this town might be the most beautiful city in the world, sleeping amongst silt and water. And the moon takes a farewell look at our civilization everywhere. I have seen it in Valencia, Barcelona, and Madrid, also. Only the houses are not plumed, feathery, soft there. The moon was brighter and they seemed made of white bone.

I had lunch with Eliot a few days ago at the club. The stupid thing is that I can hardly remember anything of what we said. I remember that we had Port-Salut cheese, which he chose. We each had a half of draught beer, so we were very abstemious. He smoked his French cigarettes. He was very gentle and courteous, as he always is, and more than that he talked with a great deal of freedom, was not at all 'the great man'. At lunch I said that it might be a good thing to start a new magazine now. He agreed, but asked whether I thought we could get any subscribers. I said, not till January, I suppose. He asked me what I was doing, and I said, I think, writing my posthumous works, and that I wasn't taking an official job. He said, 'I think it's very important that as many writers as possible should remain detached and not have any official position.' I mentioned that I had sent in my name to the Ministry of Information and the War Office, but had had no reply. He had done ditto to the Foreign Office and had also had no reply.

He said he had designed a cover for his children's book about cats.

'I don't know whether it's altogether successful. I find that in drawing it seems purely a matter of chance whether I get the expression I want on a cat face or not. So I have to make a great many drawings, and hope that sooner or later I'll strike in the expression I want.'

About writing, he said that it was very important that one should, at all costs, go on writing now. 'It doesn't seem to me to matter very much whether one isn't able to do anything very good. The important thing is to keep going. Probably it's impossible to do excellent work while things are so disturbed.'

I mentioned that I hadn't been able to work, so had started this journal. He said, 'Yes, that's an excellent idea. Just writing every day is a way of keeping the engine running, and then something good may come out of it.'

He talked a little about Joyce. 'If he wrote anything now, it would have to be so entirely different from *Finnegans Wake* that one can easily imagine the necessary reorganization of his whole way of thinking would be too much for him.' I said that perhaps he might write something simple, as, indeed, it is in parts of *FW*, but that it would be difficult to imagine him using a simpler vocabulary. Still more so abandoning his linguistic discoveries.

I said how necessary I felt it to be lucid in poetry when the world was so confused. Eliot said he thought the poetic drama might be a way of attaining lucidity, because, I suppose, it puts one outside oneself, whereas the poem tends today to be an introspective monologue. He praised my *Trial of a Judge*, but said I couldn't have presented the same situation in that way today. I said I was attracted by but also sick of public events being dealt with in a public manner in plays. We agreed that the problem was to write about a smaller theme – perhaps family life – which had all the implications of what is going on in the world outside.

We talked about writing poetry. I tried to explain my difficulties. I write entirely from ear and from my own inner sense of what the poem should be. That is to say that from the first few lines, which occur to me suddenly as a 'gift', I work the rest out simply by writing and rewriting, so as to develop the logic of what I have to say as fully and clearly as possible. I dream that one might attain a great freedom in this way. But there are disadvantages in this way of writing which is the method of the *vers librist*. In the first place, it concentrates entirely on expression, and is only poetry in so far as the thought happens to be poetry. Whereas if one chooses a form which is in itself poetry, like any of the well-known traditional forms, the traditional use of the form tends towards poetry, to which one conforms. In other words, accepted forms tend toward an objective realization of what form requires if it is to be successfully used, whereas my way tends towards subjective needs and standards. On the other hand, contemporary writing which fits into traditional standards does not really interest me. Eliot agreed with me about this, and he seemed also to agree that Auden's virtuosity in using accepted forms, while it certainly saves him from extremes of subjectivity and also, to some extent, from obscurity, has evaded the real problem – which is to discover new, recognized, generally acceptable forms suited to the requirements of today.

Another consequence of my way of writing is that I have no predisposition towards any particular medium. I have a prejudice in favour of poetry, a romantic feeling about the poet, a desire to achieve immortality, a desire to condense what I have to say in the shortest and most memorable phrase possible. But really my only qualification as a writer is that I have something to say. That is, my situation as an individual human being seems to me interesting and potentially, if it is fully realized, to contain implications reaching out into the whole of contemporary life. Thus the view of some communist writers that today one can only write about the workers and from their point of view seems to me to be not only nonsense, but also inhibitive and destructive to literature – at all events, until after the workers' revolution when, presumably, working-class writers will write about workers. The important thing is to write about what one knows and realize it as fully as possible. If one lived in the depths of the country and felt that the only point in existence was to live in the town, the real centre of one's life, if one were to realize it in writing, would be one's vision of the town. But this life would be unreal, fantasy imposed on the reality of one's life in the country. To come to town and try to be the most conventional of urban writers would be to destroy one's imaginative gift. Yet that is the attitude of communist critics towards bourgeois writers whom they want to become workers. The fact is that the interest of the bourgeois writer who becomes a communist is the penetrating insight he then gets into the life he already knows, which is now no longer isolated but implies the life of the workers beyond it. There are no negative situations – everything implies that which is complementary to it.

This is a digression, not what I said to Eliot. What I did state was my difficulty: that owing to my preoccupation with what I have to say rather than the means of saying it, I could, theoretically at all events, write in any medium. It is a question of expressing 'the situation' in one form or another and then, by writing and rewriting, working out the logic of the form. But the question is whether working everything out in this way one isn't working always back to the same centre, expressing the subjective in subjective terms according to subjective standards. For example, if there were some accepted form of excellence recognized by the age – such as the heroic couplet in the eighteenth century – one could judge one's performance by the standard attained in this.

Eliot said that an objective form might be the poetic drama, because here one had to meet one's audience half-way and adopt to some extent their standards. I agreed, but this of course raised the question of whether the poetic drama was a suitable form for the drama today. Unless this is so, poetic dramas published as books are just a waste – if they are good as poetry. Eliot also said that he wasn't sure whether he didn't feel as I did about writing poetry. I asked him if he didn't feel that perhaps the trick of his poetry wasn't to make the reader identify himself with Tom Eliot and enter in his subjective mood. Then how could one be sure at a later time, when the situation of his poetry is no longer such as people can now enter into, that his poetry won't be seen from the outside – much as we see the work of the 1880s for example. He agreed that this was a problem.

I was very glad to have put my difficulty in writing verse before him, and to find that he understood it. That is all I remember of our conversation, though I dare say we speculated about the war.*

1 October

Wrote this diary last night and read about half of Isaiah Berlin's book on Marx.

19 October

So it seems that I have made no entry in my diary for eighteen days, and the time is approaching when there will be such a congestion of

* See Virginia Woolf's diary, Volume 5, p. 268. 'Tom talked about Stephen's diary. Pages of S's conversation "for I can't remember what T.S.E. said" – were sent to T.S.E. He's benevolent and tolerant of the young.'

material that I will not know where to start and will give it up altogether. Here I am on the track of one of the main forces which inhibit
writers from getting on with their work - the accumulation of unful-
filled tasks and projects and ideas, which finally so confuse one that
one prefers forgetting one's inspiration and waiting for something new
to dealing with this excess of material.

Let me sort things out a bit, make a list of my ideas, and try to find
some solution to the problem of having a superfluity of subjects. What
have I done during the past few weeks? What are the ideas which I
have had in mind all the time but which seemed too difficult to undertake? Just as if one was being dragged round in a whirlpool in the
centre of which there was an iron post to catch hold of, the difficulty
of catching hold of it might be so great that finally one would become
grateful to the very speed and rush of the waters which pulled one
away and so spared one from making the effort!

That eighteen days can become lost, a mere torrent of movement
and distraction and running round! What I've had at the back of my
mind all the time is that I ought to write an account of my weekend
at the Woolfs, which I still see as a kind of raft where I was for a few
days. Then after that there were five days at Humphrey's* flat, most
of which I spent on typing out my novel, although I still haven't
finished doing that. Then there was the weekend at Isaiah Berlin's at
Oxford. Since then, I have been in London staying first at Humphrey's
then at the Buhlers', where Bobby and I spent most of our time
printing. During all this time I have seen many people, made many
arrangements, and the last part of it has been overshadowed by something which I cannot write about, and which really had the effect of
making me lose all desire to be married or not married, or to live at
any particular place, because it was so close and yet so much worse
than anything that has happened to me personally.†

It wasn't only this diary I wanted to write, but also my novel and
a long Eclogue, which I started at Isaiah's. Perhaps now this will be
possible. I have notes in a brown book for about a dozen poems I want
to get on with. Yet nothing drives poetry out of one's head so much
as big projects, like a novel or anything sustained. Perhaps one day I
shall give up the idea of writing any books altogether, and just write
poems. Also, note that I have two short stories in mind. In addition

* Humphrey Spender, my brother.
† My sister-in-law, Humphrey's wife, was extremely ill with Hodgkin's disease.

to this, there is the work on *Horizon*, which I enjoy. There are also one or two things that I wanted to write about in this *Journal*, apart from meeting with people. One is solitude. The other is the attitude of writers to contemporary life in an amoral age. Also, I've decided to do an account of the background of Christopher's Berlin stories.*

When I think of these things, I am tempted to get up and go out for a walk. If I decide to do one of them I am only drawing my own attention to the fact that I am not doing the other. Happiness would lie in doing them all, and having a full life as well. I'll try to do them all. The result may be a sense of failure, but the consolation will be that at the end of a few months I find I have after all done something. Perhaps I should try to evolve a shorter way of writing things in this *Journal*, simply in order to spare myself a certain amount of physical labour.

20 October

It must now be three weeks since my weekend at the Woolfs. They live in a very pleasant house at Rodmell near Lewes. The view from the garden looks across to the downs near Newhaven. There is a plain between the garden and the downs where the railway runs to Newhaven. The other side of the house is the village, so that on one side the country is open and spacious; on the other, it is a closed-in valley. I like this effect very much. The Woolfs have a large pond in their garden with water lilies and goldfish.

I arrived in time for tea. After tea, we went out on to the lawn and played a game of bowls. I had beginner's luck, and I think I won the first game, though I never succeeded so well afterwards. Virginia and I walked about the garden talking about writing, which she said she wanted to discuss with other writers. She was pleased that I kept a journal because she said she found it was the only thing she could do, too. She thought that every day an occasion arises in which one sees things in an entirely new and different way, that these moments of transformation are one's grasp of reality. This is the experience which she tries to catch hold of in her journal.†

She talked also about the danger of creating a literary personality

---

*Collected in *Goodbye to Berlin*. I never wrote the projected account of their background.

† There is an ironic account of our conversation in VW's diary, Volume 5, pp. 237-238.

for oneself. Her dislike of self-importance links up with her dislike of the egotism of successful men. She said that the mistake of ambitious women was to try to compete with men on their own ground, to become men. Women had a life of their own which they could develop without being diminished by men.

22 October

We came to Lavenham.* In the afternoon, we picked mushrooms in the fields. In the evening I played some gramophone records, Beethoven's opus 127 Quartet and the last movement of opus 132. This last movement seems to me the most mysterious and religious of all Beethoven's ideas. It has a line which exists amongst the arid, harsh surrounding instruments like a view of a distant, blue range of mountains beyond a rolling desert. At times the rocks shut out this refreshing vision, but it always exists beyond them, and at moments one is immersed completely in it, until finally as one at last turns away it recurs. Wonderful the passage at the end where one thinks the movement is finished, and it is repeated very quickly in between final chords so that when the chords do close there is a suggestion of it again, a suggestion that this pure, limpid fountain runs for ever.

25 October

Yesterday I worked hard all day. In the morning wrote some of my novel and a poem for Humphrey. Also wrote to Wystan (Auden), Wells, Kathleen and William† about *Horizon*. At five o'clock, went to the Buhlers and set up type. Eve pregnant. Bobby not very well and rather preoccupied with his health, I thought. Had a drink with Cyril to discuss *Horizon*, particularly J. B. Priestley's letter offering us the serial rights of his play.

26 October

Wrote all the morning, lunched with (Geoffrey) Grigson at the Café Royal. As soon as he saw me, he said, 'I say, is Cyril seriously going to call his magazine *Horizon*?' 'I think so,' I said, already rather damped. 'Anyhow, what's your objection?' 'Well, magazines called

---

* I shared with my brother Humphrey and his wife Margaret a house at Lavenham in Suffolk.

† H. G. Wells; Kathleen Raine, poet; William Plomer, poet and novelist, godfather of my son, Matthew.

Horizon never last for more than two numbers.' 'What other magazines have been called *Horizon*?' 'I don't know, but it's a metaphor and a pretty trite one. It suggests flatness, the flatness of the dead.' 'Well, it's been quite well received by everyone we've told about it.' 'Oh,' said Grigson, 'it wasn't so well received last night at a dinner party at Henley. Betjeman and Piper were there. In fact, to be perfectly frank, there was quite a lot of laughter about *Horizon*.' 'Well,' I said, 'as a matter of fact, I thought of *Horizon*.'* This mollified him somewhat. Then he said, 'By the way, who is doing the publishing and the distributing?' 'Witherby's,' I said. 'Witherby's?' he repeated, incredulously. 'Yes.' 'How delightful, how charming. It's such an original idea that it really has quite an appeal.' He looked graver and added, 'Of course, there are disadvantages in publishing in London. It will cost you at least 15 per cent more, I should say.' I explained that Witherby was a friend of ours. Geoffrey now became helpful and said he would let me have his subscription list for the now defunct *New Verse*. He also gave me various hints about the importance of set-up and paragraphs in a magazine. I am very grateful for these and shall remember them. However, he had soon started again on a new tack. 'You may not believe it,' he said, looking slightly embarrassed, 'but I've always put you on a bit of a pedestal. So I was very disappointed at a remark by you in the *New Statesman* which I thought beneath you, the other day.'

Afterwards we joined Cyril and went through the *Horizon* discussion again. Later Cyril said to me, 'We bow our heads. We accept Grigson's sneers, and thank him for them. But we might have pointed out that if *Horizon* is a dead title, *New Verse* is dead and done for. And if a metaphor is flat, nothing is so positively sickening in a title as the adjective "New".'

Advantages of living alone. Increase of energy and creativeness because I can indulge without qualms of conscience in the brutal selfishness of being a writer.

When I am living with someone, I am always reproaching myself for not paying enough attention. This means that all the time I feel under a certain constraint. It also means that I attach far too much

---

* My recollection is that while we were worrying about the title I was reading André Gide's journal and kept on coming across the word *horizon* which I then suggested as the title. Some years later I told Cyril this. He looked at me quizzically and said, 'If you go on remembering hard enough you'll find you remember every good idea we ever had, Stephen.'

importance to other people's whims and moods, which make me feel guilty of inconsiderateness. I feel that pleasures which people might, in fact, easily sacrifice, are mysteriously important, and this makes any decision, like living in the country or demanding that my wife should stop having an 'affair', etc., very difficult. In fact altogether there is a lack of confidence in any behaviour within a possessive relationship. The effect of this is not to lessen but rather increase the egotism which I am trying to repress in myself.

It is really rather disturbing to write this. I do not even entirely understand what I am trying to explain yet. But what it comes to is that when someone I am with whom I am accustomed to think of as happy is unhappy, I experience a feeling of deep apprehension, guilt, a sense that nothing is ever going to be better now, because I have discovered that everything is wrong. At the same time, a corresponding distress of my own is revealed by my companion's unhappiness, and soon I feel that it is I who am making her unhappy. In certain cases, I even manage to persuade her that this is so.*

I can only imagine that these feelings have something to do with my mother being an invalid. When we were children, our mother was often well and even gay. But nevertheless, the fundamental fact about her was that she was ill – or so we were told. The happiness of a summer day was fragile – a raised voice, a quarrel with my brothers or sister, and then the headaches would begin. 'You have given Mummy a headache', etc. I never trust anyone I am with not suddenly to break down and reveal some fundamental physical or mental disability.

But it is not only unhappiness that distresses me deeply, but also tiredness, laziness, and other weaknesses in people. I don't mention this, but I freeze with horror. When I was 16 and used to go home on the tube from my grandmother's house on Sunday evenings, a thing that irritated me almost beyond bearing was if my sister or her companion, who were with me, yawned. The fact was that I was very tired myself, but it was impossible for me to relax even so far as to yawn, and the fact that I was with someone who yawned, unthinkingly, not accepting the necessity I saw of never revealing that one was tired, maddened me.

I know I am giving myself away far more than if I owned, for

* Cyril once said to me: 'You feel guilty about leaving people but you're very good at making them leave you.'

example, that I had committed a murder. The real crimes in post-war society are sexual incompetence and Puritan traits of character. If one is guilty of these, none of the punishments of domestic life is bad enough. One's wife and friends soon find out and proceed to adopt a really merciless attitude in which they are completely justified.

However, now that I am alone, there is no reason why I should not be frank. It is as though a special set of rules applies to my own life which does not apply to other people. These rules were put into my head by my father, whether he was conscious or not of it. He was furiously ambitious for at least two of his sons, and particularly for me. I hated his kind of journalistic ambitiousness, but I was only able to wriggle out of it by substituting an even more difficult ambition of my own. Instead of being a fake great man, I wanted to be a real great writer. I have resisted my own ambition by sabotaging it for years. But the only relief for me now is to give way to the desire to write endlessly. What is so difficult to understand is that there are people who are not ambitious, either in a publicist or a truer sense; they just enjoy themselves and are content to be ignored. It does not seem fair. I learned from my father that it was silly to want to be Lloyd George, but how can I learn that it is silly to want to be Beethoven or Shakespeare? I shall have to be all I can be in order to learn this.

One day I might meet some adult person who understood and forgave what I feel. Meanwhile, though, it is better to be alone. Then my moods are my own, and they don't upset anyone else, and I can give way to my intolerable ambition. I still haven't explained this right.

27 October

Ten thirty pm. Today has been a grey day. I worked in the morning, I suppose, though I hardly seem to remember what I did. At lunch there was Brian Howard,* rather silly, I thought, with his feminine way of tilting his head up as though under a cloche hat, and looking at you through half-closed eyelids. He had a friend dressed entirely in corduroy. I saw Cyril before lunch and felt rather uneasy with him. Before tea I went to the *New Statesman* and got some books to review. A letter from Sally Graves† was there, saying I had better accept the

* Brian Howard, aesthete, poet, anti-Fascist, the model for Anthony Blanche in Evelyn Waugh's *Brideshead Revisited* and Ambrose Silk in *Put Out More Flags*.

† Sally Graves, later married Richard Chilver and became Principal of Bedford College, London, and Lady Margaret Hall, Oxford.

situation about Inez, and go on with the divorce. This, just because it was about her, upset me, as it did when I heard she had visited Lolly* the other day. I think it probably would be best to go on with the divorce, but (a) I have other things to spend my money on now; (b) if she asked me not to do it, I am sure I would give way, even now. The fact is that I don't believe any longer that I shall marry or even love anyone else. Those sort of feelings don't seem to have any future for me. I have a sense of loss and, in spite of myself, I still feel cruel and vindictive; one of the things I most resent about the whole business is that it produces in me many feelings that I am ashamed of. Well, I'll try writing a bit of my novel.

16 November

I have given up the idea of writing events from day to day here. It is best to write reminiscences and meditations and fragmentary soon-lost illuminations which occur to one just before one is going to sleep, or on a walk or in the bathroom, when a whole sequence of things is as clear and yet featureless as a face remembered in a dream.

When I was a child I used to try thinking of something perfectly familiar, like my mother's face or a postage stamp. I could imagine it so clearly that it seemed even more vivid than the real image. But I could only think of it as a whole impression. When I tried to imagine the features separately or to relate the proportions to each other, I realized that I could never draw them from my mental image, which immediately I took up a pencil to do so, faded.

The very rigid mental image of a sequence of words, just as one is taking one's socks off to go to bed, is like a view of mountains from an aeroplane. They lie there making a single, complex but comprehensible form. But one hoards the sense of distance for fear of being lost if one were down there amongst the verbs and nouns.

But that isn't the whole problem. It's not just the lack of courage and patience that one fears, but that the descent into language actually puts one wrong. The words suggest their own sequences, partly dictated by the rules of language, partly by clichés, and one's reading, partly by habits of thought, which are themselves clichés. One repeats the same mistakes, one finds that instead of hauling down to earth the singular vision, one is just writing what one wrote before.

* Lolly – our family name for Margaret Spender, Humphrey's wife.

How I fear that I will fall again into the grooves of words which instead of expressing what I see, drag me along their lines away from it! I leave long gaps between my poems in the hope that the last one will not influence the next, and perhaps I will create finally the real image that I saw.

Yet it's not just a matter of willing and working. It's a matter of letting oneself go. Somewhere there's a fountain of words wanting to say the things I can say, only directly I set myself to will them out of me, the fears, ambitions, habits of thought, prejudices, demands of style form a barrier between me and what is perfectly clear.

Commentary
1940-5

In June 1940, during the Blitz, Horizon *was evacuated for a few weeks to a house on the cliffs near Salcombe in Devon. Peter Watson paid for this, as he did for everything that concerned* Horizon. *From the cliffs at night we could see air raids on Plymouth, the black sky seemed a background to fires and bombs and shells, shaken like spangles out of it, and criss-crossed by the straight lines of searchlights.*

Nothing gave us a greater feeling of unreality than being evacuated from London, where everything was happening, to the countryside at a time when it was difficult to think of anything except the war. Cyril kept going up to London. I stayed in Devon, thinking that I was keeping things going at the 'office'. Then one day Peter complained to me that he had rented this house and could never use it for himself because it had been taken over by the staff of Horizon. *That was the end of being evacuated.*

That autumn I taught for a term at Blundell's School in Devon, which I hated, for the same reasons I suppose that I had hated being near Salcombe. At the end of the term I resigned and joined the National Fire Service in London. I did keep a short journal of Christmas at a Fire Service station, which I used for my autobiography World Within World.

On 9 April 1941 I married the concert pianist Natasha Litvin. We had a lunch party at the Etoile Restaurant in Soho, followed by a drinks party in the studio of Mamaine Paget (who later married Arthur Koestler). Cecil Beaton took a photograph of this party. Among the guests were Cyril Connolly and Lys Lubbock (later to change her name to Connolly by deed poll), Janetta Sinclair-Loutit (now Janetta Palardé), Sonia Brownell (later Sonia Orwell), A. J. Ayer (in Guards Officer uniform), Guy Burgess, Ernö Goldfinger, the architect, and his wife Ursula, Louis MacNeice and Nancy Coldstream (then married to William Coldstream but later to marry my brother Michael, who was at that time an officer in the RAF and a pioneer of photo-interpretation. Michael died in an air accident in the last week of the war.)

Soon after I joined the Fire Service Natasha and I took an attic flat in Maresfield Gardens, Hampstead. It was over the flat occupied by Ernst Freud, the architect, and his family, and a few doors away from the house of his sister, Anna Freud. She was running in Netherhall Gardens a nursery for children who were, in one way or another, war victims. We helped raise money for it and in turn she invited Natasha, when Matthew was expected, to learn baby care in the Netherhall nursery.

The war was a time of entertaining friends – survivors, fire-watchers, non-combatants, or soldiers on leave. Benjamin Britten came to see us on his return from America, and also our older friends, Forster, Eliot, Elizabeth Bowen. Our social circle seemed to centre on Horizon.

In late 1944 I was transferred from the NFS to the Foreign Office, though that seems rather a grand name for a subsidiary branch of Political Intelligence, situated at Bush House in the Aldwych. We were compiling information about the history of Italian fascism, as background material for the British force occupying Italy. Nothing secret.

Our son Matthew was born in March 1945, during one of the worst nights of V2 missiles, and the following week we moved to 15 Loudoun Road, a house which we still occupy.

In May, not long after VE Day, Auden visited us there. He was en route to Germany as a member of the team which formed the US Strategic Bombing Survey (known as Uzzbuzz) for finding out the reactions of Germans to having their cities bombed. When, answering the door bell, I saw him standing on the doorstep in his American officer's uniform which, since he was not built for uniforms, could not but look bizarre on him, I burst out laughing. This was not just on account of his appearance but partly through pleasure at seeing him; partly also through a kind of mental flash-back to the thirties when he would dress up very self-consciously in a new outfit – hat and suit and stick perhaps – partly for the amusement of his friends. He said: 'What are you laughing at?' and I realized that this was a different Wystan from the one who had left England. He then said 'You have a son' as he crossed the threshold.

That first evening was rather strange, perhaps because after the criticism of him in the press for having left England in the summer of 1939, Auden was on the defensive. Looking at our baby he pronounced 'All babies look like Winston Churchill', dismissing Matthew like an incident which had been closed. He examined our bookshelves, asking us what we had read since 1939. He complained about the cold in London houses and wore his overcoat throughout dinner. He said – and this was true enough – that compared with

Germany, where he was about to go to see the real thing, England had suffered no war damage. As he left we lingered on the doorstep for we still felt exhilarated at the sight of un-blacked-out London. Wystan, looking up and down the street of two- and three-storey houses, commented: 'Gee, New York is a wonderful city.' Louis MacNeice, Auden's fellow guest, watched all this through a wary eye.

On Auden's return from Germany we gave a party for him and his friends in Uzzbuzz. These included old friends – Jimmy Stern and Tony Bower – and a new one, Nicolas Nabokov the composer, who was later to be Director-General of the Congress for Cultural Freedom, and to play a considerable role in my life until his death in 1978.

Early in 1945 I applied to become a member of the so-called Civilian Military Forces – of the Control Commission – occupying Germany. My private reason for doing so was to go to Bonn and concern myself with the fate of my friend from pre-war days, the great scholar and teacher and critic, Ernst Robert Curtius of Bonn University. I managed to get myself commissioned to make a report on the attitudes, during the war and under the Occupation, of German professors and intellectuals. For this I had to be granted a dispensation to talk with them; for it had been decreed by the authorities that there should be a policy called 'non-fraternization' (meaning 'non-speaks') between occupiers and occupied, English and Germans.

Cyril Connolly asked me to write a journal about my meetings with the German intelligentsia for Horizon *(published as* Rhineland Journal) *and Hamish Hamilton asked me to write a book* (European Witness *1946). I kept a journal on which the* Horizon *piece and the book were based, which contained much that seemed unpublishable at the time.*

As soon as I met Ernst Robert I told him I was going to publish my German impressions, but that before doing so I would show him anything I had written about him. On returning to London I found in the circumstances then pertaining that it was impossible, without great delay, to send him my text. Cyril was very anxious to publish it immediately, so, thinking that there was nothing in it unfavourable to Curtius I published Rhineland Journal.

Had I been more considerate I would have realized that although Curtius was an anti-Nazi (and presumably would not have minded this being written about him) he would not have wished his deep disillusionment with the German people to be published. He could not, of course, in any circumstances have taken action against a journalist publishing reports which were entirely favourable to him, but he took the line that it was only because he was a member of a defeated people, living under an occupying power, that he had no legal recourse against me. Believing this, he wrote protesting his helplessness to the Archbishop of Canterbury, T. S. Eliot and others. They seemed bemused, rather, by these communications, and did not raise any objections with me. Perhaps they thought that, after all, the attitude of Curtius to the events of 1933-45 was a matter of public interest and, if presented sympathetically, overrode his objections.

My second journey through the British zone in 1945 was for the purpose of reopening libraries that had been closed for denazification. I had to go into the political backgrounds of librarians, as well as the contents of the books. Between these journeys I went for a month to Paris. This was a time when, after five years of interruption on account of the war, followed by the liberation of Paris, relations between the French and the English were like a family reunion, indeed a love affair.

One day, later in October, when I was stranded by the side of the Autobahn where my car had yet again broken down, a car stopped to offer help. By an extraordinary coincidence one of its occupants was Natasha. Having made her début as a concert pianist in 1944 she was now touring Germany giving recitals, mostly at RAF bases, but also to the survivors of Belsen. We drove together to Berlin, staying at the Hotel Bristol, just off the Kurfürstendamm. Having lived nearby (at the Nollendorfplatz) in 1931, as soon as we arrived I set off to explore the neighbourhood of ruins, only to find myself unable to recognize anything except the Gedaechtniskirche (which to this day is preserved as a ruin and a landmark). Next day we toured Hitler's bunker, with singed books on modern architecture still by his bedside, and the Chancellery with the great candelabrum collapsed from the ceiling and hanging barely a couple of feet above his desk with its surface of petrified wood, now in fragments, of which I took some pieces as a souvenir.

My sister-in-law Margaret (the wife of my brother Humphrey) died on Christmas Day, 1945. Shortly before her death she saw these relics of Hitler on the chimneypiece, without being told what they were. She refused to touch them, looking at them for a moment only and saying with an expression of horror, 'They're evil. You must throw them away.' Which I did.

2

German Diary
1945

6 July

Got up at 6 a.m. At Air Transport 7.30 a.m. Our plane was delayed about three hours and did not take off until midday.

Bad Oenhausen. First impressions of Germany. People do not look at one, or, if they do so it is without expression. They have such a shut-off way of behaving that it is quite curious to see them hailing and talking to each other. It is like watching them from behind a glass screen.

The landscape – very beautiful. Like an eighteenth-century pastoral engraving tinted with watery blue-greens and yellow-golds of fields with a flat sky of greyish cloud behind. This fairy-tale German landscape – little squashed painted houses like cream buns and a sinister breadth and depth of green in the meadows: waving fields of corn or grasses and above them a sky shaking spears of cloud.

When I arrived at Bad Oenhausen I could get in touch with no one. Everyone at HQ having afternoon tea.

At 5.30 p.m. I went to see Brigadier Williams. He listened attentively to my account of my mission (to interview professors) and said he thought it a good idea. Asked me to come back in a few weeks' time and report to him.

He told me how stupid our behaviour was in some respects. E.g., we are about to convert the Museum of Homburg into a NAAFI. He was willing to resign his commission to prevent this happening. He presented me with an historic document (in my personal history), a pass saying I might fraternize with Germans.

Wrote five pages of my play.* After that I talked for half an hour with a German refugee who has been fraternizing. He had the impression that

---

* *To the Island.* Produced at the Oxford Playhouse by Frank Shelley in 1951 for the Festival of Britain.

the Germans are very malleable and disillusioned, and waiting above all for some kind of lead. They cannot understand the policy of non-fraternization, as they want to be told how to act in some way, how to think, what to think, etc. Also they do not see that not being allowed to talk with the English is a punishment.

Before bed walked in the Kurgarten, which is beautifully trimmed and tidy in contrast to gardens I saw in France. Wandered into church, requisitioned by the British chaplain, where some soldiers were playing the organ, one of them very well. A town occupied by an army looks like a deserted shell of grey inhabitants watched over by khaki ghosts.

8 July

Lunched with Goronwy Rees* (a colonel). After lunch we motored through the country and then to headquarters. We passed many fantastically beautiful villages. Gabled, painted houses, almost lost amongst creepers and vines. The German villagers out on Sunday walks. Neatly dressed, old women in starched dark-looking clothes, one or two men in black suits and top hats. A few of those I met said, 'Guten Tag' and were polite in a subdued veiled kind of way. Goronwy very much his old gossipy talkative self, despite his Colonel's uniform.

11 July

Arrive at Bonn after incredible adventures.

The Rhine with the destroyed bridges over it has a certain grandeur. The girders of the largest bridge with sections of the structure attached to them slope diagonally into the water. Effect of an aeroplane diving at an angle into the river. The water seethes and froths over them. These destroyed bridges with their swooping girders ending in frayed ribbons of steel, splinters and shreds, make the whole landscape seem turbulent. And as foreground to this dramatic scenery of destruction, there are the dark dogged crowds of people with their bags and bicycles surging in utter silence over the temporary bridges. Beyond the bridge the cathedral, solitary, almost undamaged, surrounded by ruins of buildings which seem to have been scratched and torn down by gigantic claws: scooped and tattered cliffs torn by tempests.

---

*Goronwy Rees (1909–79), journalist and novelist. Fellow of All Souls College, Oxford. Close friend of Guy Burgess from the 1930s. After Burgess and Maclean fled to Russia he published articles stating that Burgess had tried to enlist him as a communist agent, an offer which, Rees maintained, he declined.

Almost as soon as I got to Bonn, I called on Ernst Robert Curtius. He seemed moved to see me. He took me into his library, once a beautifully furnished room, now cavernous and dark, with no carpets, little furniture, dirty walls and few books. Ilse, his wife, was there, for they use the library now as their living room. I explained that I had come to Bonn to enquire into the intellectual life in this university city. He said that there was little intellectual life, but the important thing was that I would talk to people and get to understand what was happening in Germany.

He started talking about the war and its effects on the University. He said that his pupils had gone to war not really wishing to win. They fought for their country but they had on their back this monster, the Nazi Party. Anybody who maintained that it was possible for Germans to stop the war happening after 1937 should study the effects of government by terror, propaganda, lies, and a perverted psychology.

I remarked that I had met several simple-seeming Germans who did not think that Germany as a whole was responsible for starting the war. 'Of course,' he said, 'it is absolutely clear that Hitler began the war. There is no doubt about that at all. In spite of all Goebbels's propaganda, any person who says otherwise is either completely ignorant or lying.'

'The trouble with the Germans', he went on, 'is that they have no experience of political freedom. Right up to the last century they were governed by ridiculous little princelings; then they came under the influence of the Prussian militarists. They have never freed themselves from servile attitudes of mind. The German people must learn the significance of political freedom. You English cut off the head of a king several hundred years ago. The basis of your freedom is that revolt against a tyrant exists as a possibility in your minds. The Germans have never risen against a tyrant. They always submit.'

The Curtiuses complained bitterly against their American 'liberators'. Some of these complaints seemed understandable, others were such that one would have expected Germans who undoubtedly always hated Hitler, to hesitate before making them: for example, that the American forces were lamentably slow in occupying the Rhineland. They missed many opportunities, they were bad soldiers, they were incompetent, etc.

He counted it one of the greatest misfortunes of the citizens of Bonn that they were 'liberated' from Hitler by an American army. Apparently, the Americans were about to cross the bridge across the Rhine into Bonn, in the autumn of 1944, when, most unfortunately, one of Hitler's hastily conscripted army of teenagers and old men called 'werewolves' fired a shot: upon which the Americans withdrew and did not return for another three months, during which the citizens of Bonn suffered terrible hardships. 'It is very hard to be defeated by an amateur army,' sighed Curtius.

Other complaints seemed more reasonable. 'The American policy in areas they seize was simply to occupy them and otherwise do absolutely nothing.'

Another complaint was about the Allies' policy of non-fraternization. How could we expect to influence the Germans if we were not allowed to speak to them, nor they to us? Did we not realize that Germans had been completely isolated from ideas coming from outside for thirteen years and that now, if we refused to give some sort of lead and communicate our humanity to them, they were left in a vacuum? Curtius drew attention to the contrast between our propaganda and our actual behaviour.

On Wednesday morning I called on Curtius again. There was a section of *Finnegans Wake* lying on his desk, and for some time we discussed James Joyce. The book of fragments from *Work in Progress* was inscribed 'for E.R.C. from J.J.' and it contained notes on the text made by E.R.C., taken down from J.J.'s conversation.

We talked of James Joyce and also of Sylvia Beach* whom I had met recently in Paris. I told him that at the beginning of the war Sylvia had employed a beautiful 17-year-old Jewish girl. The Germans had asked Sylvia to give her notice. Sylvia pointed out that she, Sylvia, was an American citizen and that she did not recognize anti-Jewish laws. The Germans then sent Sylvia to an internment camp and the Jewish girl to a camp in Poland. Nothing was ever heard again of the girl.

Curtius touched my arm and said: 'When you spoke of guilt last night what I wanted to tell you is that we are guilty. The German people are guilty of these frightful crimes and they can build nothing new unless in some way they repent and rid themselves of them. We train a domestic animal by shoving its nose in the mess it has made.

---

* Sylvia Beach (1887-1962). Original publisher of Joyce's *Ulysses*. American proprietor of the Left Bank Paris bookshop, Shakespeare and Co.

1. Stephen Spender, Hamburg, 1930
(self-portrait)

2. W. H. Auden at twenty

3. Auden, Spender and Isherwood, Insel Ruegen, 1931

4. Sally Bowles (Jean Ross)
Berlin, 1931

5. Christopher Isherwood
in Berlin, 1931

6. Isherwood and his friend 'Otto', Insel Ruegen

7. Nazi street meeting in the thirties (Photograph Humphrey Spender)

8. Rehearsal by the Group Theatre of 'Trial of a Judge', 1938
(Photograph Humphrey Spender)

9. (*above left*) The author,
photographed by
Spender/Edmiston Studio

10. (*above right*) Muriel Gardiner
(Buttinger) (Photograph
Joseph Bohmer)

11. Cuthbert Worsley, Stephen Spender,
Tony Hyndman, Helen Gibb
(Photograph Humphrey Spender)

12. Drawing by Henry Moore, 1934

13. Helen Gibb, Derek Kahn (Blaikie), Inez Spender, Margaret Spender, with Winifred Paine behind her chair. Taken at Rogate 1935/6 (Photograph Humphrey Spender)

14. Wedding party in the studio of Mamaine Paget, 1941. The guests included Cyril Connolly, Lys Lubbock, Sonia Orwell, A. J. Ayer (in uniform), Guy Burgess, Louis MacNeice and Ernö Goldfinger (Photograph Cecil Beaton, courtesy Sotheby's, London)

15. In uniform with Paul Eluard and Nusch, Paris, 1945

16. Destroyed bridge over the Rhine at Cologne, July 1945

17. Ernst Robert Curtius, 1930

18. Jean-Paul Sartre

19. Karl Jaspers

20. André Gide

21. Auden with Natasha Spender, Venice, 1949

22. Isaiah Berlin in Salzburg

23. Reynolds Price in Rome, 1965

24. Maurice
Merleau-Ponty
in Geneva

Well, the Germans must be made to know and feel these disgusting things done by Germans.'

The Curtiuses invited me to lunch. At first I refused, but they pressed me so strongly that finally I accepted. Lunch consisted simply of boiled potatoes and boiled cabbage. Nothing else. Curtius said: 'You see, we live on a Tolstoyan diet. We always used to speak with admiration of the simple life. Now we have it.'

16 July

Bonn is affected with a plague of midges. Last night I went for a walk along the Rhine, before sunset. At dusk, on my return, the midges formed a cloud along the river.

A feature of the hotel here are four Belgian dancing girls and a very dago young man, also a Belgian, I suppose, who has sideboards, and the profile of a character in a pornographic photograph. In a tacit way, this quintet forms the centre of the life of the hotel as pollen and stamen form the centre of a flower.

After meeting Professor von Beckenrath, the economist, I met next Professor Clos, geologist. The opinions of men such as Clos, von Beckenrath, and Curtius are those which one would expect from highly cultivated Europeans. Their testimony is most valuable, but open to question when they assert that many young people here are untainted by Nazi teaching and propaganda. Curtius, in any case, would hardly say this. He is deeply pessimistic about the Germans and more profoundly disgusted by their behaviour than his colleagues appear to be. Nevertheless, he would argue that there are German books and teachers who would use these books and there are programmes of education which could be returned to, with certain modifications. In this he has not really altered greatly the position he took in 1933 when he published a book *Deutscher Geist in Gefahr* [*German Spirit in Peril*] which is a strong attack on the Nazi influence on education in the universities, and which contains an eloquent defence of the past German academic tradition.

Nevertheless, some of these anti-Nazi professors hold opinions which they share with other Germans. One is resentment of the French whose occupation of this part of the Rhineland they regard as a bitter insult inflicted on them by a defeated people. Another is their conviction that Russia will eventually either occupy the whole of Europe or have to be fought by the Western powers.

A naval officer who has just come here from Hamburg tells me that the workers there recently took a holiday. They said that they were celebrating the birthday of their new king, George VI.

It is assumed by almost all the people with whom I have spoken here that the zones are semi-permanent and that Germany is finally split up.

One afternoon I walked into a bookshop, and noticing a rather intelligent-looking young man who was also looking at the books, I got into conversation with him. He said that he was a writer, painter and law student at the University, and he invited me to his studio to see his pictures. Technically they were slightly better than Hitler's but otherwise much the same.

Walter Jostin, a man of about 55 years, is a translator of Shakespeare who has never succeeded in getting into the University. He spent much time before the war promoting his own translations and trying to get others stopped. He said to me that in order to understand the cultural situation in Germany I must realize that after the First World War Germany was flooded with Jews who seized all the most important positions in the world of art, music and letters. Orchestras were run by Jews, films were made by Jews, the critics were Jews. Almost as bad as the Jews were the Catholics, especially in Bonn where they controlled the life of the University. The Protestants were also bad but 'a little more patriotic than the Catholics'. He told me that he had not been a Nazi Party member 'because as translator of Shakespeare and writer of essays, I could not be a member of a political party'.

20 July

All yesterday I was terribly depressed and homesick. If I heard a baby cry, it reminded me of Matthew. Saw Ernst Robert who has translated poems of mine called *Spiritual Explorations*.

On my way to the Curtiuses a young man stopped me. He had a square bony head with eyes of different colours and expressions in each, the look of a beggar in a blue-period painting of Picasso. He said that at the age of 17 he had been arrested and sent to the concentration camp of Esterwege (he had papers attesting to this). He had been there for six years. He was now 23.

I asked him to call on me at five at my hotel. He arrived at four thirty when I was having tea in the lounge. I could not offer him tea so I sent him up to my room. He was now better dressed as he had

[66]

borrowed a suit. He told me much about the Gestapo and the life in the concentration camp. He said that his aim, when he settled down, was to write a book called *Human Beasts* about his experiences. I asked him to describe this to me and, to my astonishment, half closing his eyes, he recited the opening pages of some lyrical prose depicting the wicked godlessness of humanity. He had written all this in his head. He also recited some nightmarish details of his examination by the Gestapo. They put him in a cell like a bath which was constantly filled with water which he had to pump out in order to prevent himself from being drowned. The most curious of his stories was that when he had been beaten up in a cell, a Nazi who seemed more human than the others threw a wooden football – a kind of toy – into the cell for him to play with.

This morning I went with Ilse Curtius to the French Zone where Ernst Robert had been evacuated during the worst of the bombing. On our way there we passed an enormous column of prisoners. These unshaved, ragged men with haggard deeply lined faces, shuffling along the roadside, were the caricature of a defeated army. A defeated army is, indeed, its own caricature. Many of them carried sticks, not walking sticks, but longish poles which looked oddly like shepherds' crooks. On his back each carried a bundle containing his possessions, and under the bundle a largish round tin. They were immensely impressive, an image of judgement, like a show that happened to be real, put on to illustrate despair, a poem written by their lives, true beyond any possibility to invent.

21 July

Spent the whole day in Cologne.

At the Rathaus I was shown almost immediately into a room where the mayor, Konrad Adenauer, and Dr Kroll were sitting. Adenauer is a man with a long oval face and a little snub nose. He looks quite young and has the quick movements of a youngish man. Actually he is 70.

He remarked on my name because, as he said, at the end of the last war someone called Spender – and this, we decided, must have been J.A.* – had interviewed him. It is rather strange that, having recalled the name Spender over twenty-five years, he called me Mr Stenton during the rest of the conversation.

I explained to him my cultural mission and he responded at once

* See Appendix, p. 488.

[67]

that I had come to see him at a most fortunate moment because he had just been talking with Dr Kroll about this very thing, the reconstruction of the cultural life of Köln (Cologne). He explained to me, eagerly and seriously, that two things in the city were of equal importance. One was rebuilding the city. The other was reconstruction of spiritual life ('geistliche Leben'). He said that the Nazis had laid German culture absolutely flat and that fifteen years of Nazi rule had left Germany a country in dire need of spiritual things. He thought this was specially true of Cologne, and that here it was possible to do something. In his view only the best education, the best newspapers and literature, were good enough.

He said that his own observation told him that the young of 15–25 showed an unexpected interest in cultural values. 'Our children are like a dry sponge waiting to immerse themselves in knowledge.'

The Americans were wrong in their attitude to the German universities and schools. The really important problem was not that of children under 14, but that of the young of 15–25 whose minds were not so much distorted and perverted as confused and ignorant. They should be provided with education – and soon.

He was greatly concerned with the problem of newspapers and he told me of an idea which he was turning over in his mind. The Burgermeister of Frankfurt had told him that it should be possible to start up the *Frankfurter Allgemeiner Zeitung* again in October. Adenauer thought this very important and he considered that in the Rhineland there should be a newspaper closely working together with the *Frankfurter* but with a more 'Christliche' policy. He therefore proposed a newspaper called the *Kölnischer Zeitung* which could have an arrangement of cultural interchange with the *Frankfurter* but a different editorial policy reflecting the ideas of people living in the Rhineland.

I went to see Dr Melchior who lives in the Marienburg district. He spoke very warmly of Adenauer and said what an opportunity there was for him now to re-create Cologne from which he had been thrown out of office in 1933. I left Melchior and went to see Professor Kroll who also lives in Marienburg in a pleasant house, only slightly damaged. He has books, a grand piano, excellent gramophone records, Piranesi engravings on the walls. He has an appearance vaguely recalling Goethe in old age – a rather dyspeptic Goethe. When I asked him about his plans as cultural leader of Cologne, he said: 'What plans? Which ones? I have so many.'

Conversation at the mess about requisitioning: 'If the shoe were on the other foot, the Germans would do worse to us than we do to them.' Anyone who argues that two blacks make a white evidently has a bad conscience. After we had drunk each two large gins and orange, two brandies, and, between us, three bottles of hock, my companions started talking about the war. They all admitted that the army life had a simplicity and camaraderie which they liked very much. One of the officers said that there is no imaginative literature which comprehends our life. He said that the happiest days of his life were spent in the Western Desert.

7 September / *Buckeburg*

Left Croydon at 7 a.m. yesterday, having breakfasted at 4 a.m. Arrived at Hamburg, instead of Buckeburg, at about ten. It was two (by German time) when we left Hamburg, and arrived at Buckeburg at two thirty.

I lost my haversack *en route*. I have been having a fit of leaving things in taxis, aeroplanes, etc. recently, and it is very distressing, quite apart from being a great nuisance. What upsets me most is that I lost the packet of vitamins, coffee, etc., I was bringing to the relatives of a refugee friend out here. I blame myself for this, but I also lost my own toothbrush, razor, etc., which are almost irreplaceable. To obtain shaving things as a civilian military officer one cannot go and make purchases at the Officers' Stores.

Yesterday morning I read through my briefing for opening libraries. In the evening I dined with Ashley Dukes,* an energetic, most likeable man. He invited me to go with him to Berlin to see the theatres.

8 September

Lunched at the mess. Ashley Dukes there. Again most agreeable. After lunch set out in the Humber provided by PID for Benrath bei Düsseldorf. Called at Bad Oenhausen *en route* to cash a cheque. Went through the Ruhr: Dortmund, Bochum, Kathingen, Wuppertal, Düsseldorf.

It seemed miraculous that the car survived the journey through these towns of the Ruhr. Glass and rubble in the roads, tram rails sticking up

---

* Ashley Dukes (1885-1959). Dramatist. Directed at the Mercury Theatre, which produced *Murder in the Cathedral* (1935) and *The Ascent of F6* (1937). He was Adviser on Cultural Affairs in the British Zone of Germany from 1945 to 1949.

out of them like tank traps, holes, and everywhere appalling surfaces. All these towns are in ruins.

Benrath is a charming place on a part of the Rhine where the river banks are flat and an industrial landscape looms in the distance. Opposite the Officers' Mess, there is a Schloss built on an artificial lake. It is so baroque, like the setting for *Figaro*. There are huge gaps torn out of the front of it, and parts of it are gutted by fire. But most of the exterior retains its charming painted pinkness, which looks so well and yet absurd – like a Dresden china shepherdess – amongst the chestnut trees and ruins.

I met officers of the Film and Publications Division. Amongst them a young parachutist dropped behind the lines before D-day who was captured by the Germans and imprisoned in Buchenwald. Of forty people shot he was one of two who escaped.

Drinks at the bar before dinner, excellent claret with dinner, liqueurs. Then we adjourned to a bar in the town. Here the officers became very animated. There was a screen dividing the end of the bar from the restaurant. They kept on lifting one another up to peer over this screen. The young Wirt of the bar, who looked like a sucking pig, followed these proceedings anxiously with an abject smile on his face. I wondered how often, with the same grin, he had watched drunken SS officers endangering his property.

Went to bed at eleven having managed to borrow a razor, but with no shaving brush or toothbrush or toothpaste.

The Germans here seem aloof, not friendly like the Rhinelanders. A young officer told me that the Catholic Zentrumspartei in Cologne is a large-scale racket and that the whole administration is corrupt. The entire Civil Government can be bribed with cigarettes. He said that Adenauer was an old fox, but that he was an able administrator. He spoke highly of the Social Democrats as the only honest people in Germany – too honest to get anywhere. He said that thousands of people would starve and die this winter. Therefore, although the administration was corrupt there should on no account be elections until the spring, because it would be a catastrophe if Adenauer fell.

10 September

One of the officers told the following story to demonstrate the pedantry of German doctors. In 1929, in Leipzig, he had to undergo a major operation. He was put on the operating table and given an anaesthetic.

This did not make him unconscious, because, as is well known, people who drink a lot take more than the average amount of time to 'go under'. 'While I was lying fully conscious on the table I saw the surgeon approach me, having wiped his knife on the sole of his boot. I said, "Hi, what are you up to? I'm conscious." The surgeon replied, "You are not conscious. You cannot possibly be. You have been given 30 cc of anaesthetic, which is exactly the amount required to send a man your height and weight into oblivion." At this, as I was fighting drunk, I got off the table and assumed a fighting posture. Thereupon, three nuns set on me. One held my left, another my right arm, while the third sat on my feet. The surgeon then attacked me with his knife, and I fainted.'

In the evening went to a concert given by the Symphony Orchestra of Düsseldorf. They played a Mozart symphony and Beethoven's Pastoral Symphony to an audience of British soldiers. Nothing has made a sadder impression on me than this orchestra of pale, sad elderly men playing, with great feeling, but no zest or energy, to the Army of Occupation among the ruins of their city. The flautist, in particular, was a pathetic old man who played with a pure tone but a slight tremolo.

After the concert I met Humphrey Jennings* and a man called Martin Wilson. They are in Germany to make a film of Military Government. Of course, the officers to whom they told this said: 'My God, that's the end. A film of Military Gov. – my God.'

Everything about Humphrey Jennings irritates me, beginning with his Adam's apple, his flapping ears, his pin-head face, and his bumptious expression, which looks odd in a man who now has white hair. He talks an appalling kind of Anglo-American film-world slang in which he mixes up Americanisms such as 'oh boy oh boy' with cockney slang such as 'Bob's yer uncle'. He combines the gestures of a GI with those of a stage Frenchman.

Jennings told a story supposed to demonstrate the irresponsibility of the Germans. He said that he saw a woman go to a tap in the main street in Essen, to get some water. The tap would not work. She turned to Jennings and said, 'Kaputt.' Jennings pointed to another tap some yards away. 'Das ist auch kaputt,' she said. Then she shrugged

---

* Humphrey Jennings (1907-50). Painter, maker of documentary films, anthologist. The impression I formed of him does him less than justice. See Peggy Guggenheim's *Out of this Century: Confessions of an Art Addict*.

her shoulders and looked all around her at Essen, and said, 'Alles ist kaputt.' Jennings seemed to think that she ought to have commented that everything was broken down through the fault of the Germans.

I observed that if one was living from day to day without water, in a cellar – and with very little food either – one probably would not keep on moralizing about it. After this the conversation turned to the press. Jennings said how lousy all the war correspondents were. I said that they did their best and that often their editors would not print their stuff. I added that I had travelled home with a correspondent who complained that his newspaper would print nothing about the desperate conditions in Berlin. Someone remarked that oddly enough nearly all the *Daily Express* journalists were socialists. To annoy Jennings, I said: 'We all find it difficult to believe Germans who now say they were never Nazis when they were in fact members of the Nazi Party, yet none of us is surprised to learn that journalists on the *Daily Express* are socialists. The Germans were forced to say that they were Nazis. No one forces socialists to work for the *Daily Express*, and yet they do so.'

Jennings said that the war correspondents were fools who had missed the most wonderful stories. For example, that of Hugeln, the mansion of the Krupps family near Essen, which was pure *Citizen Kane*. The Krupps family live in this mansion where they have a table which seats a hundred. The tablecloth requires a special machine to wash it. He said that he had been shooting a scene in the Law Court of Cologne. While he was doing so, he became aware of an unpleasant smell of burning. He discovered that the smell was caused by several families who were living in cellars burning cheque books and old records of the Palace of Justice, with which they cooked their meals.

He said that the British public has no realization of these conditions. His attitude that everyone except the director of his film unit is a bloody fool annoys me. All the same he is a live wire and part of my irritation arises from jealousy and competitiveness. Went to bed still thinking of the Düsseldorf Orchestra, and depressed by Düsseldorf and by the cocksureness of Jennings.

11 September

The HQ of Military Government at Düsseldorf is situated in a huge modern redbrick building of several blocks round three sides of a square. Inside are beautiful stone floors, staircases with walls covered with a bistre-coloured synthetic stone which has a high polish. In offices there are chromium fittings, furniture of polished walnut. I called at once on Wing Commander Walsh, who seemed pleased to see me. He summoned the Mayor and the two Chief Librarians to his office. Before the Mayor arrived he said: 'When the Mayor comes in don't stand up or shake hands with him. I don't believe in being friendly with them.'

Nevertheless, he said that he was keen on opening all the schools and libraries as soon as possible.

The Mayor gave us his opinion about Dr Peters and Dr Reuter, librarians respectively of the Bibliothek and the Landes und Stadt Bibliothek. He said that Dr Peters was no Nazi, though he had been a member of the Party. He did not think that we need throw him out of his job. He said that Dr Reuter was an old and honourable man whose character was above suspicion. He said that about 60,000 volumes in the libraries of Düsseldorf had been burned. He added that the libraries had been or were in course of being purged of Nazi literature.

Dr Reuter then arrived and I went away with him to his library. Dr Reuter is a thin, elderly, spectral-looking German, thin-lipped, pinch-nosed, leaden-eyed, sallow-skinned, yet he has something vaguely dignified about him, and a certain kindness shows behind his rimless spectacles. He wore a raincoat which hung on him as on a coathanger. His ears were stuffed with cotton wool. He showed me many things in the library, including a bust and manuscripts of Heine. There was the last letter written by Heine to his mother in 1855.

Dr Reuter said that just as he had preserved Jewish books under the Nazi regime, so now he thought it was necessary to preserve Nazi books, as they were of historical interest. Also, in the long run, they were the most valuable weapon against the Nazis.

I am told that a German employed in the *Kölnischer Kourier* had offered his resignation some days ago. When asked why he wanted to leave he said: 'Because I am on Adenauer's black list.' He maintained that Adenauer kept a black list of employees in the Civil Government who supported politics other than those of the Christian Democrats. He said this was difficult to prove about Adenauer, as people were too frightened to speak.

When we were going through Cologne, my driver remarked, looking at the ruins: 'One gets pretty callous when one has seen people blown up in front of one's eyes every few minutes. At Normandy the only thing that really upset me was running over a kid. I couldn't help it. She ran out into the road right under my wheels.' He told me that his father was a chauffeur and that he himself had driven a car from Brighton to London when he was 10.

At 3.30 p.m. I called on Major Brow, a Yorkshireman who has taken the place of the CO who has been away for six weeks. Major Brow seemed strong and sympathetic, egoistic but kindly, in the manner of Yorkshiremen. After this I saw the Mayor who looked like all the German mayors I have seen, bald and rather silly, with a wrinkled face like the inside of a walnut.

After that I went to see the Curtiuses. Ernst Robert, who has been complaining ever since I first came to Bonn that the Nazis requisitioned a wardrobe from his house, now suggests that his wife and I should go together to the Office of Civil Affairs and claim it for him. This I refused to do. Curtius told me that the town Mayor had paid him a visit and addressed him as though he were some kind of underling. I felt a little like making one of the stock replies the British make on such occasions such as 'Well, you lost the war, didn't you?' or 'How can you complain when you belong to a guilty race?' However such replies are not really the clever argument that we imagine them. They are simply crude applications of the formula (that we refuse to consider any German an individual) to the particular instance.

Rumours in Bonn – if the war had gone on another week, Hitler would have been in a position to use the atom bomb, which the Germans had in readiness. A variant of this: 'After all, Hitler was a good man. He had the atom bomb but he was too humane to use it.'

One of the waiters in my hotel told me that the whole Rhineland would shortly become part of the French Zone; the other, that the Rhineland is on the point of becoming an independent republic. The first, a rumour arising from fear; the second, from wishful thinking.

After tea, I visited the Curtiuses, as arranged. Walked along the Rhine with Ernst Robert, who talked about French literature. He was the foremost authority on this at Bonn University (and perhaps in Germany) before the war. He said that in *Phèdre* the character of Hippolyte was 'cut out of paper'. The whole tradition of French tragedy now seemed to him mechanical and absurd. He did not see what virtue there was in the much boasted 'psychological insight' attributed to French writers. French poetry of the seventeenth century could not compare with Crashaw, Donne, etc. He would give the whole of Racine for a few lines by Donne. There was no *Tom Jones* in the whole of French literature. The Francophile English critics such as Lytton Strachey and Clive Bell were absurd. Strachey had even succeeded in liking Voltaire's tragedies.

He went on to say that he could not admire Greek tragedy either. But he admired Homer. It always seemed to him ludicrous to read on the title page of a programme the word 'Tragedy': thus establishing an understanding between spectator and author that the hero was certain to be killed. He had heard that China was a civilization without the sense of tragedy – and this struck him as very appropriate. The works he now admired were *Don Quixote,** Shakespeare's Histories, Virgil. He said he could understand that I was at present enchanted by French charm, and it was quite right that I should absorb everything that intrigued me. He himself had done all this twenty years ago. But when one was old, in the last five or ten years of one's life, one had to cast aside that which one did not really live by. He went on to say that he had translated my *Spiritual Explorations* poems because he admired them as poetry. But nevertheless they implied only despair. All the same he realized that I myself did not realize the implications of this, and even the reader did not feel it because I was so creative and so productive that my own creativeness gave me a kind of optimism.

I said that nevertheless perhaps the fact that although I had written five or six books in the last years I did not really want to publish them, showed that I really agreed with him.

He said that he thought the only solution to Europe's problems lay in Christianity. I said that I found it very difficult to dissociate Christianity from Christians, Christian thinkers, Christian institutions, and that nearly all of these repelled me. Even with Eliot, the whole emphasis of his thought lay in his insistence on a rigid and authoritarian orthodoxy, on the ritualistic and dogmatic side of the Church; and although I saw the reasons for this, I could not accept it myself. Curtius replied that Eliot was an Anglo-Catholic and that to him was as meaningless as his having declared himself to be a royalist.

This conversation took place walking along the Rhine. After this we walked to the Koblenzerstrasse and waited for a tram. On the other side of the road beyond tramway and railway lines there was a row of very

---

* At this time Curtius thought that the greatest European literature was Spanish.

ugly nineteenth-century houses, each of them having its own special ugliness at variance with the others. Curtius said: 'If it weren't that we were accustomed to such things, in our true selves we simply wouldn't accept the idea of a row of houses like that. We are hemmed in on every side by the conditions in which we live. And yet we long all the time for a greater freedom, a realization of some quite other potentiality within ourselves. But within the conditions of human existence such a release is impossible. I am therefore quite sure that death will prove to be the greatest possible release and realization of ourselves.' I did not say anything to this, but gave him a cigarette, and lent back against the railings of the Koblenzerstrasse. Of course, I understood what he felt, and I myself feel exactly the same, yet I thought: 'I know nothing about all this, so I refuse to express an opinion.' Then he went on: 'When someone asked Bergson what he anticipated after this life, Bergson replied: "J'attends ma mort avec la plus grande curiosité."' And he added, thoughtfully, 'I think Gide must have a great fear of dying.' He told me an anecdote illustrating Gide's fear of lunching in a cemetery. Then my tram arrived.

Curtius made a fuss about his wardrobe again today. It has become a major issue between him and the Occupation. He asked me once more whether I could not approach the authorities about it. I said I would do so, but when I asked Captain Craven who is Administration Officer, he said that he spent his time surrounded by weeping women whose houses were requisitioned, so I felt I could not bother him with Ernst Robert's wardrobe. It strikes me as very curious that Ernst Robert, who, after all, still has his house and books and most of his furniture, should make so much fuss about this, especially since he has the receipt and is certain to get the wardrobe back.

Scenes in Bonn. Trains go with passengers on the roofs, and on the sides of the carriages, and between the buffers. People cling like flies to the sides of trains. Goods trains also carry people sitting in trucks on top of heaps of coal.

Cafés are open (there is no coffee, however), there are a few cabarets, concerts, a performance of *Faust*. There are queues outside the one cinema open to civilians.

14 September

Car still broken, so I asked Military Government if they would let me have another car, which they did.

It was a most beautiful day. When I came back from Cologne in the afternoon, the view of Bonn across the plain with the Rhine between Cologne and Bonn, and the mountains beyond Bonn, might have been the north of Italy. The mountains were a transparent violet colour slightly misted below and etched in outline above, against the sky. Bonn with its few spires and rather low houses was also seen in silhouette. In the foreground the rich plain, multicoloured, formed a dense carpet in which the light seemed to shine through from below.

At Cologne I got in touch with Mayor Adenauer, who told me that the Chief Librarian was Dr Schwerin. I found Dr Schwerin at a large Catholic charitable institution. He said that the Military Government had already given him leave to open several of the libraries in Cologne, which he had done. He himself was a Catholic, who had been in the concentration camp at Buchenwald. He could also guarantee the integrity of all his officials working for him.

15 September

Car still broken down so I wrote and read most of the day. Dr Lelbach, Librarian of the University, visited me. He said that in a village in the French Zone there were 130,000 books belonging to the University which he wanted moved back to Bonn. I shall send Mil. Gov. a note about this.

Went to tea with Curtiuses. A professor of history was there and he and Curtius discussed the curriculum for the coming semester. They have to limit their teaching to the available books. It is very curious to hear them talking about books that have been available in England during the past five years. It is like hearing people talk about events which may or may not have happened on another planet. Nothing makes one realize more how completely Germany is cut off from the rest of the world.

Dined with a French *aumônier*, whom I met some weeks ago in Oenhausen. He is getting in touch with the Catholic clergy here. A Palestinian Jewish soldier joined us and talked a lot. Asked by the *aumônier* what he thought of Germany, he said: 'I think of Germany what I think of this soup.' (The soup was particularly bad tonight.) He said that in Baden-Baden there was a camp of 35,000 Jewish prisoners who had been moved from their concentration camp. He said they were almost as badly off now as under the Nazis. The *aumônier* disputed this but both agreed that conditions were bad and that the prisoners were demoralized. 'Il y a beaucoup d'immoralité,' said the *aumônier*. I asked him what immorality. He replied: 'Il y a beaucoup de jeunes hommes et de jeunes filles et évidemment . . .'

16 September

Car still out of order. The latest diagnosis is that the carburettor needs to be replaced.

Went this morning to Beethoven's house. A charming house, with a nice courtyard. Only Beethoven's family, of course, inhabited it. He was born in a very small room which is now occupied by a very large bust of him. So large, indeed, that if the whole body of Beethoven were blown up to the same proportions there would be no room for him in the humble space in which his mother bore him. This somehow seems symbolic of his reputation.

The Museum is very boring. Dozens of very bad portraits of the master, or copies of bad portraits. It is difficult to think of anyone who has inspired so much bad portraiture as Beethoven. His ear trumpets which, before the war, were a great feature of the Museum have now been hidden in the 'Beethoven treasure' containing memorabilia considered too precious to risk being destroyed in air raids.

The manuscripts are interesting, because they vary so much. Beethoven surely put some of the passion of his music into his actual handwriting. For instance the curved lines over the bars of the *Leonora* Overture are like lines freely drawn. The manuscript of the opus 111 Sonata has an abstract intensity, and one could admire it as abstract expressionism. I would have liked Picasso to see it.

Met my driver at breakfast and walked with him to the garage outside Bonn where the Humber is being repaired. I talked quite a lot to him because I worry about him having nothing to do. He said he was getting very browned off as all he had to do now every day was go to the garage and watch them at work on the car. He said they had tested every part of it and replaced all those that seemed deficient. Theoretically the car ought to be in perfect running order, but in fact it went on behaving exactly as it had done a week ago. He said he thought the trouble must be the carburettor, which cannot be replaced.

He told me that he had quite a time in the evenings and that now he had a nice girl, aged 18.* I asked: 'Do you take precautions so that you

---

* The policy of non-fraternization had by now been dropped.

won't get her into trouble?' He looked astonished and answered: 'I never touch her, I wouldn't think of doing so, that wouldn't be any pleasure for me nor for her, sir.' I was rather dazed by this reply. He told me that he thought it would be very wrong, in times like these, to leave a girl with a baby. He said, 'It makes me very angry, sir, sometimes to read in the newspapers and see what they imagine our fellows do when they fraternize out here. As a matter of fact, very few do what they think at all. I myself wouldn't dream of it. Yet even my girl at home thinks the same thing.'

He told me that one night he and another chap had gone to a fair with their girls and that on their way back they ran into some Germans who were attacking some other German girls who had been fraternizing with our men. So they had a free fight with the Germans and saw their girls home as well as their own girls.

17 September

Went to Wuppertal by way of Cologne, through some villages and small towns, seemingly unaffected by the war. Charming architecture: half-timbered houses looking much neater than our English Elizabethan ones. They had blue-grey fish-scale roofs. After dinner, I went to the Curtiuses. They told me that Wuppertal had two of the worst raids of the war. Until very near the end it had not been raided at all and then in two raids it was wiped out. The people did not know how to behave in a raid and rushed into the streets. In this raid liquid phosphorescent bombs were dropped for the first time. People were sheeted in flame. Some of them jumped into the Wupper in an effort to put the flames out, and they drowned.

I noticed that every single large residential house on the hillside outside Wuppertal had been destroyed. The Curtiuses said that a feature of the Wuppertal raid was that single aeroplanes had flown over these houses, dropping bombs and destroying them one by one.

19 September

Went to Aachen. As they had thrown out a great many books from the shelves I took away with me copies of some of the works of Goebbels which I read when I got back to the hotel. Goebbels is a hypnotic writer for young people. He communicates the excitement of the Nazi movement extremely well. The causes of what is now called German guilt are exemplified completely in the works of Goebbels and

Hitler. Guilt lies in being captivated by the speeches of Satan, and in the lack of a sense of values whereby to criticize them. The diaries of Goebbels and his book *Kampf um Berlin* could only appeal, one would think, to readers of sensational and quite unsubtle crime stories, or sadistic fairy tales. The crime-story side is the perpetual hunt of a ruthless scientifically minded Nazi detective for the communist or Jewish criminal who must be destroyed, even though (before Hitler came to power) the police are on the 'criminal's' side and acting against the detective. In such crime stories the detective is no saint and does not pretend to be one. He uses methods which he attributes to his opponents. Above all he is 'scientific' and theory-ridden, though he also has a contempt for ideas (other than his own). The illustrations in these books repay study. Drawings of Nazis fighting communists and Jews are exactly on the level of those in boys' adventure stories or for the works of Karl May. Goebbels whole-heartedly admires the works of the illustrator Mjohir, whom he regards as master of a 'gott-be-gnadetes Kunstlertum' [God-given artistry].

The fairy-tale side of the Nazi myth goes deeper than the *Boy's Own Paper*, amateur-detective side. In this, Hitler is the fairy prince or Shining Knight in Armour whose acts are perfect. Communists and Jews are the wicked dragons, the forces that are considered subhuman. Here again though, as in fairy stories, there is much room for all-devouring vengeful cruelty. No bones are made about this in the Nazi books I read.

Another aspect of this writing is baseness, vulgarity, *Gemeinheit*. The Nazi writers have a repulsive habit of letting the cat out of the bag, letting the reader, from time to time, share their guilty secrets (incriminating the reader), especially when they are talking about propaganda and 'the masses'. Goebbels will tell you quite openly: 'Propaganda . . . in politics the goal is only one thing: the winning of the masses. Every means which serves that goal is good. And every means which eludes this goal is bad.' (He tells the reader, who is being hoodwinked, this.)

After this, and after similar passages in *Mein Kampf*, it is very difficult to maintain that there were Nazis taken in by Nazi propaganda. For this was a conscious and deliberate and self-declared form of deception, by people who said, 'We are now going to deceive you.' The label POISON was written on the bottle.

Then there is the Nazi 'philosophy': which, again, simply plays up to the desire of certain Germans that ideas should look 'deep', 'difficult' and 'mysterious'.

The most appalling and also the most enthralling thing about Goebbels's writing is its note of total confidence, a confidence which does not come just from the man himself, but from the certainty that there are thousands of Germans who want just this kind of thing. The same impersonal overpowering confidence throbs through Hitler's speeches. The certainty of evil.

20 September

Did very little all afternoon except stroll around, write letters, and think. Later, at seven, went into Düsseldorf, to the headquarters of the *Rheinische Revue*. Without meaning to do so, I attended an editorial conference. In the course of a very heated argument one had the most bizarre impression of the way in which the press is run. Apparently a brigadier in the neighbourhood can ring up the editor of the *Rheinische Revue* and say abruptly: 'I see that your newspaper has not got a serial story in it. The hallmark of every decent newspaper is that it runs a serial.' Is that why they were printing, in twenty instalments, Conrad's *Typhoon?*

21 September

Went to Dortmund and Essen. In each of these places I found the library was either opened or just about to be opened.

22 September

As my car has not arrived and as I failed to borrow another, I accepted Colonel Dilke's invitation to attend conferences about the German press at Essen and Wuppertal. Once again I was impressed by Dilke's skill in handling a meeting, listening to everyone and explaining his own point of view. The meeting at Essen consisted of a social democrat, a communist, a Christian Democrat, a Centre Party man, an Evangelical pastor, a Catholic, the Mayor, and one or two others. Only the communist really commanded respect. He did not have to give any account justifying himself, since he had actively opposed the Nazis throughout his career, had been sent to a concentration camp, etc. He said that the communists honourably and in good faith supported the occupying forces. Colonel Dilke asked me whether I would like to ask any questions so I said I would like to know at what point the communists intended to return to communism and introduce policies into their programme other than that of simply co-operating with the occupying powers. He said he believed that sooner or later the struggle between capitalism and the proletariat, which for the time being was overshadowed by the overwhelming conditions of the defeat, would return and that the communists would then again take part in the struggle of the proletariat against capitalism.

All the delegates looked hungry and careworn except for two very fat and comfortable-seeming Roman Catholics, one of them a priest, the other a delegate of the Zentrumspartei.

T. S. Eliot sent me his *Four Quartets* to present to Ernst Robert Curtius. They contained a touching inscription to the effect: 'This was my own copy, the only one left of the first edition. I send it to my friend E. R. Curtius' – words to that effect.

24 September

Morning, went to Düsseldorf where Wing Commander Weber had arranged for immediate opening of the library. Visited a large printing works.

At lunch in the Mess, the officers discussed the order sent 'freezing' their demobilization. Obviously this was a very great blow to them but on the whole they accepted it with patience and good humour. The most notable reaction was ragging one another about how glad the wife would be not to have her old man back. I could see though that the letters they would now receive from their wives were not the least of their fears.

Amusing, though, to think that this country is administered largely by a service every member of which is now praying that he will leave in three, six, nine months – at most within a year.

26 September

This morning attended one of Colonel Dilke's meetings for editors. Three or four times repeated the same little procession of grey bent unsmiling faces asking permission to start the *Solinger Anzeiger*, the *Wuppertal Rundschau* or whatever. Two social democrats from Essen turned up and said they would not co-operate with the publishing firm which had been chosen there. They brought with them a copy of an illustrated paper printed by this firm in 1934 to celebrate the first joyous year in Essen under the Nazis. To judge from the photographs of happy crowds celebrating this occasion in the newspaper, it looked pretty well as if everyone in Essen was compromised.

Dilke and another officer started writing down humorous verse. Dilke shows a considerable gift in imitating translations from the Chinese. In the evening a major who had come from Berlin was in the Mess. He was depressing about Berlin. He said the Russians still continue to loot and rape. It was not safe to go out in Berlin at night. The level of existence in Berlin was so low that few people there thought of anything beyond where they were going to get their next meal.

28 September

An assistant librarian at Aachen said to me: 'We understand perfectly what you require with regard to our library. We shall take all the Nazi books down from the shelves and lock them up in a separate room where they will be read by no one except students who may be given access to them for their purely historical studies. We are perfectly used to doing this since formerly we took down from the shelves all the books by socialists and Jews and kept them locked up in a special room where they were only accessible to students writing anti-socialist or anti-Semitic studies.'

29 September

Spent most of today reading Ernst Jünger's *Feuer und Blut*. This is one of the best war novels I have ever read. It is also one of the most deeply shocking. It describes a single dramatic event – the activity of one section of the Germany army during the German attack on the Allies of March 1918. The action is described as though its organization were a well-designed piece of engineering – which is, I suppose, how it was. The drama lies in the entry of human feeling into such a piece of machinery. The book is shocking because it is written by a man who believes whole-heartedly that war is an exalted mystical experience. In it, there is practically no sense of a just cause for which the Germans suppose themselves to be fighting, apart from that of proving that they are better, in the sense of being better as soldiers, than their opponents. French towns and villages, and the English enemy, exist simply as objects and persons to be destroyed by Germans to test their heroic virtues. Even the torn-up landscape ruined by the Germans only causes Jünger to exclaim: 'As yet no poet in his dreams had ever beheld this fiery landscape.' The Germans dream that 'the enemy will be thrust to the ground with one gigantic blow' – the same old dream. At the same time when three-quarters of the company are wiped out by a mortar and there is a scene of horror, lyrically described, Herr Jünger reflects what a cruel place the world is, instead of reflecting that the war-makers have made it cruel. His mystique of war is such that he cannot believe that it is 'fair' that those who share the mystery should be defeated. The Germans put into war the faith that can move mountains, so how is it that they can lose? The fact that they lost the war is 'Misgluck'.

30 September

Bonn. Afternoon, tea with the Curtiuses. Evening, went to the Guards Division theatrical show which was a play called *By Candlelight*. This is about the butler of a Viennese baron who one day puts on his master's evening dress instead of his own livery and makes love to a fair visitor whom he takes to be a baroness but who turns out to be a lady's maid who has borrowed her mistress's clothes for the evening. A strange play to put on after May 1945 to an audience consisting mostly of privates who had voted a Labour government into power.

1 October

Bonn. This morning I met a student called Auerbach, and went for a walk with him. He said he would take me to his favourite hiding place in Bonn. It is a deserted landing stage on the Rhine. We discussed Ernst Jünger. Auerbach said that Jünger was not solely a nationalist writer, he was also regarded with some favour by the communists because he expressed a ferocious radicalism which was a meeting place of nationalists and communists. I said that Jünger was diabolic and that *Feuer und Blut* was a masterpiece written from Hell. Auerbach said: 'I cannot disapprove of that. Jünger is a devil. And I have so much understanding of devils that I cannot disapprove of diabolic books.'

When he said this I felt a strange sympathy for him. 'What do you mean by a devil?' I asked. 'A devil is a person who is aware of himself as a unique part of existence. To him the fact that he exists and that he is part of the human condition is more important than that he belongs to the society. Most people consider themselves part of their social environment, their job, their class, etc. A devil, in his heart, despises the whole social and political structure around him.'

Auerbach said that he despised the Nazis because they were not honest devils. There was, indeed, a diabolic side to Hitler which he admired, because Hitler really did see through bourgeois society. At the same time, Hitler was not really honest with himself, nor was he true to the more diabolic of his friends – Roehm and his storm-troopers. A true devil recognizes in the world other devils, people who recognize the truly chaotic nature of human life, and who despise all fixed forms of institutions. They are willing to destroy all the outward forms of society. They may put towns and whole countries to flame but they remain loyal to each other. The Nazis failed by this test.

I said that I was ten years older than he and that although I certainly understood the ferocious nightmares that he was talking about I did not feel that the whole of society should be sacrificed to the perhaps quite justifiable contempt for it of a few people who thought them-selves more truthful than the majority. Suffering was also real; and it was the duty of people who realized that social forms and institutions had little relation to the truth nevertheless to try to mitigate suffering.

Auerbach had no sympathy with this. He said: 'I have noticed in your poems that you sometimes write simply about your own experi-ence of yourself as an individual isolated in the universe. When you do this, you write as though you realize that the only aim of life should be to achieve one's own existence and to disregard everything else. All institutions and all political programmes set up a kind of routine – nations, parties, business, machinery – that absorbs people's lives into it and makes them think of themselves as part of a structure. All this has nothing to do with the truth – which simply is that one is living and is going to die. All talk of right and wrong is the attempt to make the individual loyal to something outside his own existence. Therefore it is untruthful.'

2 October

Hanover. *En route* I visited Dortmund, Bochum and Essen. Rather miserable about my job, as owing to the lack of transport my researches into libraries have been far from thorough, and my statistics incom-plete. Whilst I was in Dortmund seeing the Oberburgermeister, he exchanged one cigarette for two cigars, which seemed good business to me.

As we approached Hanover it was evening and the ripe fields glowed against a darkening sky as though they had absorbed all the light of the past day like a sponge and were now exhaling it. I sat about most of the day waiting, not knowing quite where to go. I read Palgrave's *Golden Treasury* and was taken aback by Wordsworth's 'Ruth, or the Influences of Nature', which, I thought, reveals much more of human nature than Wordsworth usually reveals. A nature of evil influences! In fact, to use the student Auerbach's language, nature (or Wordsworth) is here the devil. Wordsworth is enraptured by his picture of the youth from Georgia's shore:

> Nor less, to feed voluptuous thought,
> The beauteous forms of nature wrought
> Fair trees and gorgeous flowers;
> The breezes their own languor lent;
> The stars had feelings, which they sent
> Into those favoured bowers.

This is the language of a fantastic and tempting condition of experience in which everything else is sacrificed to ecstasy – as a drunkard sacrifices everything to alcohol.

I remembered that I had a note in my pocket from someone in Paris for Ernst Jünger who lives only twenty minutes away. Accordingly I got into the car and went to his house. It is a charming parsonage, built in farmhouse style, next to a church. I was shown into a comfortable sitting room with leathern armchairs, and lined with books. Herr Jünger came down and greeted me. He was smallish, dressed in tweeds. He had the kind of lined, tanned active-seeming features under a head of silver-white hair which makes one think that a man looks young for his age.

He said: 'I have two friends upstairs with me. Would you mind joining us?' The two friends were Klaus von Bismarck and Herr Weimann, a dramatist. Klaus von Bismarck looked, indeed, Bismarckian with cold grey-blue eyes and a pale complexion. Weimann was swarthy, dark-haired – a leathery, wrinkled, kindly face. Frau Jünger, who looks fifteen years younger than her husband, was also there (at least, I assume she was Frau Jünger).

They were all seated at a table with coffee, some breadish-looking cake, some slices of bread covered with a meat paste. There was a fire in the room, which seemed pleasantly warm after the chilliness of the Officers' Mess.

Jünger asked me if I was going to Paris again. I said yes. He said that there were one or two commissions which he would like me to undertake for him. He had left in Paris some cases of champagne. There was a Mrs Florence Gould with whom he would like me to speak, in order that they might be forwarded to him.*

I said it was unlikely that I would see Montherlant as he was somewhat compromised as a suspected collaborator. Jünger said testily: 'That is an unreasonableness which the French must get over. They must really learn to be a little reasonable.' I said that since I was travelling in France in a semi-official capacity in any case I was not completely free to see people who were compromised.

Jünger talked expansively about his friends in France and said that he expected to be back in Paris in a year's time, seeing them again.

They all agreed that during the latter part of the war Germans had realized the disaster which they had brought upon themselves. 'In a way,' said Herr Weimann, 'there are advantages in living among these ruins. Although it is nice to have possessions, one is freer without them. Now we are free we have the possibility of a great spiritual revival . . .'

Jünger showed me downstairs and through the garden to my car. While we were alone I said I had read *Feuer und Blut*. I added that while I considered it a masterpiece it had also greatly shocked me. Jünger said, 'Yes, but it is real. It is about something extremely important to me, one of the realest things in life.'

I asked him if he had now changed his point of view. He said certainly he had done so but that this had been a necessary stage of his development. 'At 20 a man is a warrior, and I was 20.' He said that in the 1914–18 war he had won the highest military honour. This war had been very different for him but in it he had also won the Iron Cross – this time for saving a man's life.

4 October

Started out at nine thirty. On my way I stopped the car to get out and take a photograph of Ernst Jünger. He was friendly and courteous, and pleased, I thought, to be photographed, since he asked me to send him

* Mrs Florence Gould, the millionaire American art collector and hostess who lived in Paris. At the end of the notebook in which I wrote my German journals there is a list of those people in Paris to whom Ernst Jünger wished me to give his greetings. They are Mrs Gould, the novelist Joseph Breitbach, Henri de Montherlant, Mme Bousquet (also a hostess), André Gide, Jean Cocteau, Marcel Jouhandeau, and, lastly, Leo Toad, whom Jünger wished to send the last instalment of his memoirs, for him to translate.

copies. I also got him to sign my copy of *Auf den Marmorklippen*. I did not tell him that I had been given this by the Librarian of the Aachen Public Library, since they were uncertain there whether or not to keep it on their shelves and said that, in any case, they had more copies of it than they could deal with.

Outside Celle the car developed its old trouble of spitting and cutting out. The driver managed to clean the carburettor and then it started again but did not go more than 40 mph. I seem to have acquired a whole philosophy from this car. From it I have learned that it does not really matter whether one arrives at one's destination at the expected time, that one can miss meals and engagements, that one must be patient and that sometimes the vacuum produced in one's plans by a delayed journey leads to the greatest revelations, the most significant encounters. The journeys recorded in this diary have been guided not by my will but by the car's, which caused me to spend days in Bonn when I should have been interviewing librarians of the Ruhr. The many meetings with Curtius are due to the car. So was the introduction to Ernst Jünger and Klaus von Bismarck.

We managed to push on to Hamburg where we arrived too late for my driver to have lunch at his Mess but not too late for me at mine. The Atlantic Hotel is, apart from the Officers' Mess in Paris, the most grandiose Officers' Mess I have been to. It also contains very good-looking officers.

After lunch I went to a charming suburb of Hamburg where each house seems lost in its own small wood or grassy field. Here I had tea with Klaus von Bismarck and Herr and Frau Ellbrechter, K. von B's hosts.

K. von B. said that ever since we had met yesterday he had been thinking about a remark I made about the necessity of making Germans Europeans. He said that this might seem difficult at present because Germany had incurred so much deserved hatred. At the same time he felt that the very depth to which she had fallen might provide her opportunity. Also there were advantages in losing everything, not only one's land, even one's books. He had lost irremediably his properties in East Prussia, but he felt freer and more capable of action as a result of doing so. What he believed in was bringing together in Germany people who still believed in principles and Christianity. He thought that Germany was capable of religious revival and this might be achieved through the effort of individuals.

[88]

5 October

Hamburg. Another day in which I was frustrated by the car and also, to some extent, by my driver, with whom I am annoyed. Natasha sent a message to Bad Homburg to say that she would be at Lübeck this afternoon. But a message did not arrive from him till five, to say that he was at the workshops. Accordingly, I neither had my own car nor was able to arrange to get another one. I ought to have realized a long time ago that my driver is a Kafka-ish character, one of those 'assistants' from *The Castle* who alternately help and hinder.

Called in the morning on Sefton Delmer at Radio Hamburg. He was buoyantly working in a furore of secretaries, visitors and telegrams. He has such a padded appearance that he looks as if he was wearing under his clothes a life-jacket, in case he should be hurled into a sea of troubles.

Before this I breakfasted with Dick Crossman* who has been in Berlin and is on his way home. Congratulated him on being an MP. He was critical of the administration although he admitted that he thought that in the areas of transport and economics it was doing a good job. It is, he said, in politics, news, education and intelligence that we are weak. Nevertheless our zone in many ways contrasts favourably with the others.

At noon, Dick Crossman and I called on Dr Wolf, Rector of the University. He seemed a man remarkably lacking in distinction. It was difficult to interview him for he had no views on any subject whatever. He said that he was a liberal and that the problem of Germany was to form a large middle party of the centre and SPD. Dick pointed out, rather boisterously, that this was absurd, since, if the socialists were socialists, they would not form a single group with the conservative Zentrumpartei. And if the members of the Centre Party had decided to join the socialist party they had better be socialists.

Dr Wolf made a half-smile (he does nothing by wholes). Dick and he started talking about the Weimar Republic and Dick said, unlike the leaders of the French Resistance, the leaders of the Weimar Republic did not have the courage to refute the charge of being traitors, which was hurled at them by the nationalists. In their hearts they accepted the charge that they were traitors. Dick and I were arguing

* Richard Crossman (1907-74). Socialist journalist and politician. Editor of *The God That Failed* (1953). Author of the *Diaries of a Cabinet Minister*.

that Germans must both accept responsibility for the past and move forward into a new political future.

Dr Wolf was critical of our newspapers. At the same time he shrank from the suggestion that German political parties should have their own newspapers. It was too soon. 'Why too soon?' asked Dick. 'Well, everything is too confused.' 'How can you clear up confusion without debate?' roared Dick. 'How can you clarify without clarification?' 'Ah, that's just the difficulty,' said Dr Wolf, 'it's all so difficult.'

An officer of my acquaintance who had driven with Dick Crossman here from Bünde took me aside and said, with charming *naïveté*, 'At Bünde the Colonel said to me, "This chap Crossman is terribly left-wing. He may write an article for the *New Statesman*. Almost anything may be expected of him. If I were you I wouldn't answer all the questions he asks you." ' The officer solved this problem by sitting in the front seat with the driver and leaving Crossman in the back seat. The fact that we have a Labour government has scarcely penetrated the officers at Bünde HQ.

Dined with Humphrey Jennings. He was ebullient. 'Boy, what a day. Gee, what shots. I've never seen anything like it.' A Belgian joined us and Jennings got going in a corresponding kind of French version of his Hollywood English. With every other sentence he banged the table and exclaimed, 'Je suis foutu.'

I have not seen much of the destruction of Hamburg as I have only been in the residential part of the town around the Alster which is pretty well intact. Hamburg is certainly as beautiful as I had remembered it to be. The lake was a dazzling blue with a silky softness, which made it seem a pool of sky with sails drifting through it. The night was even more beautiful – with a starry sky above a coal-black wedge of houses with a very few scattered lights gleaming in them, and then the reflection of the Plough plunged into the misty web of the lake.

6 October

My driver reappeared this morning. He said the car had been re-prieved. He had called for me at the hotel at three. I said I was here at three. He said it might have been later than three when he called. He seemed very upset and offered to drive me at once to Schleswig. I said this was impossible as I had to lunch with Sefton Delmer.

I ought to have been more severe with him. Sometimes I wonder whether I am so mild through weakness, timidity, conviction, perversity or what. I think it is a mixture of these things, and added to them, above all, the desire not to disturb the relationship in which the driver reveals so much about himself to me. I feel that I am looking into a very delicate mechanism and I do not wish to disturb it. The same with everyone I meet.

Commentary
1946-53

On returning from Germany I was invited by Julian Huxley to join the Preparatory Commission for the newly founded organ of the United Nations, UNESCO, of which he had been appointed the first General Secretary. I became Counsellor to the Section of Letters, whose head was the slyly entertaining poet, Anton Slonimsky, who later returned to his native Poland where he became President of the Polish Writers' Union. In this capacity he did a great deal to protect and defend the freedom of writers. When UNESCO moved to Paris I went to live there, but resigned in 1946 when the General Assembly failed to re-elect Julian Huxley as a result of his lack of support by the American delegation, already influenced by McCarthyism. Julian was suspected of being 'soft on commies' employed in the secretariat of UNESCO.

After the summer of 1946 – our last at Lavenham – Natasha and I attended the first of the annual international meetings between intellectuals called 'Rencontres de Genève', held in Geneva. This provided the occasion for the first post-war meeting between the French and German existentialists. Merleau-Ponty, who was an atheist, was leader of the French; Karl Jaspers, a Christian, led the Germans. Jaspers infuriated the French by asking them whether the most prominent French existentialist, Jean-Paul Sartre, would accept the Ten Commandments.

This was the post-war period of international conferences and other meetings between European intellectuals. These junketings were much criticized. However they fulfilled a real need felt by writers, teachers, scientists and artists at that time to exchange ideas after the complete breakdown of communication between them during the war years. For the French it was also a continuation of the pre-war meetings, held at Pontigny, between intellectuals of diverse views, Catholic, agnostic and communist.

When the conference ended, Dominique de Grunne, whom we had met during that week, took us to stay for a few days at the Chalet Waldegg in

Gstaad, where our hostess was Hansi Lambert. She became one of our closest friends until her death.

I first went to America in 1947, at the invitation of Harold Taylor, then President of Sarah Lawrence College in Bronxville, outside New York. Under Harold Taylor the college had a starry faculty, including Mary McCarthy, novelist, Robert Fitzgerald, poet and translator, Horace Gregory, poet, Joseph Campbell, anthropologist and author of books on mythology, Rudolf Arnheim, psychologist of art, Robert and Helen Lynd, sociologists and co-authors of the famous study Middletown, *Mark Slonim, Russian historian, and Randall Jarrell, poet and critic. Natasha and Matthew (then aged two and a half) went with me to Bronxville.*

At the end of the academic year, in the summer of 1948, we went on a tour of the American west and south-west (beginning in the north-west with Seattle and Portland, Oregon). We visited Christopher Isherwood in Los Angeles, then went to San Francisco, and ended up in New Mexico. In Taos we met Frieda Lawrence and her lover, Angelino (whom she later married), Dorothy Brett* and Mabel Dodge Luhan.† Neighbours of Brett in the desert were William Goyen, whose story The White Rooster *Cyril Connolly published in* Horizon, *and his friend Walter Berns, later to become a Professor of Economics at the University of Chicago.*

That summer, after Natasha and Matthew had returned to England, Frieda lent me the ranch, which was 2000 metres above Taos. Before going there I had returned to New York. Leonard Bernstein, hearing that I was going to the ranch to write, offered to drive me to Taos if he could also be there, as he too wished for solitude in which to write his ballet, The Age of Anxiety. *Lennie's brother Bertie, then aged 17, accompanied us, and many years later described the journey in an article in the* New Yorker. *After less than a week Lennie found the solitude of the ranch intolerable, and returned to New York. I stayed on for six weeks alone, writing* World Within World *and visited every three days or so by Bill Goyen or his friend Walter, sometimes accompanied by Frieda.*

In April and May of the following year I went on an extensive lecture tour, lasting several weeks, in the south and Mid-west, including Lexington,

---

* The Hon. Dorothy Brett, a painter and friend and disciple of D. H. Lawrence since 1915; eccentric and deaf. Author of *Lawrence and Brett*, a vivid evocation of Lawrence.

† Mabel Dodge Luhan, heiress to the Dodge fortune, who invited the Lawrences to Taos in 1922 and gave them her ranch on the sacred mountain above Taos. Married to an American Indian, Tony Luhan. Wrote an envious account of Frieda's relationship with Lawrence in *Lorenzo in Taos*.

Charlottesville, Minneapolis and Chicago. Many people I met were worrying about the McCarthyite campaign against communists and other leftists being conducted on the campuses.

I met Allen Tate and his wife Caroline Gordon for the first time in May 1948, in Chicago. In the same year Poems of Dedication *was published, and also an essay on my attitude towards communism, in* The God That Failed *edited by Richard Crossman, for which Ignazio Silone, André Gide, Richard Wright, Arthur Koestler and Louis Fischer had also written essays. It may be that the invitation which I received in 1953 to co-edit with Irving Kristol a magazine published by the Congress for Cultural Freedom was a consequence of my essay in* The God That Failed. *The Congress for Cultural Freedom had resulted from an international conference (which I had not attended) held in Berlin at the time of the airlift.*

In the spring of 1951 Natasha and I went for some weeks to Greece and saw Delphi and other places I had not been to since 1934. World Within World *had been published and chosen as Book of the Month by the Book Society. With the proceeds we took rooms for the summer at a small hotel at Torri del Benaco. This peaceful interlude, during the summer of the Festival of Britain, was interrupted by the furore caused by the disappearance of the 'missing diplomats' Burgess and Maclean. Owen Seaman, a journalist from the* Daily Express, *came to Italy to interview me about this.*

A few months previously, in May, Auden had come to stay at Loudoun Road. One afternoon, when he happened to be out, Burgess (whom I had not seen for several years) telephoned, urgently wanting to speak to him. Getting me instead of Wystan on the line, Burgess said 'I'm so glad you answered because I want to tell you how much I agreed with everything you wrote about communism in your autobiography. It expresses the dilemma of a generation.'

Auden did not return the call. (Many years later when I saw Burgess in Moscow he explained that his purpose in making the call was to ask Wystan whether he could borrow his house in Ischia. His idea was that, having taken Maclean to Prague, he would leave him there while he himself went to stay in Auden's house until the trouble blew over.)

Remembering this conversation I told a reporter from the Daily Telegraph, *who had telephoned me in London before we went to Italy, that I did not think Burgess would have made this comment if he had been a communist agent. Soon after we arrived in Torri I received a letter from John Lehmann stating that if I knew what he knew on the authority of a lady we both knew I would never have made such a statement. Wishing to demonstrate my ignorance I showed Owen Seaman John's letter. He asked me whether he might borrow it for a few moments in order to telephone the contents to his office. Stupidly, thinking that all the letter proved was my ignorance, I said he might do so, provided that he did not quote from it and returned the letter to me. The next day the letter appeared, photographed in the* Daily Express. *Much later I received an apology from the editor of the* Express, *Christiansen (see p. 173). Meanwhile John Lehmann, reasonably, was furious with me.*

In a press interview many years later I explained that I did not suppose that if Burgess had got through to him Auden would have lent him his house in Ischia. Auden wrote to the newspaper saying that he would certainly have done so – Auden's dislike of Burgess's politics did not affect Burgess's claims on his friendship.

In 1953 I was invited to become Elliston Professor of Poetry at the University of Cincinnati. This chair was founded as a result of a bequest left to the university by a local journalist, George Elliston, an eccentric lady regarded by all who knew her as almost a pauper (she accepted $25 from a friend on her deathbed), who had for many years been hoarding a sum sufficient to make this endowment, thus fulfilling her life-long ambition to support poets and poetry. My predecessor was John Berryman, and among later Elliston professors were Robert Lowell, John Betjeman and Robert Frost (who made it a condition of his appointment that he appear in Cincinnati for one weekend only).

As I had been a self-confessed communist for a matter of a few weeks at most in 1937 the American Embassy did not at that time have the authority to grant me a visa. The University of Cincinnati had to appeal on my behalf to the State Department in Washington for what was called a 'waiver'. My case took so long being decided that I might never have got to Cincinnati had it not been for the generous intervention of Senator Robert Taft, who wrote to the State Department on my behalf. Taft was so far to the right that he regarded Senator McCarthy as a vulgar upstart. Later when we met in Cincinnati he told me that he did not care what extremist political party teachers belonged to so long as they did not teach its ideology to their pupils.

Cincinnati proved hospitable to us. Not only were the people there kind and friendly, they also wished, I think, to show the pride that people in this city, with its many inhabitants descended from the German high bourgeoisie, take in its culture. Perhaps, too, they were still a bit provoked by the very uncharitable account of their moeurs *contained in Frances Trollope's book* The Domestic Manners of Americans *(1832). In it Mrs Trollope drew on her experiences in Cincinnati to illustrate her complaints about the crudeness of American manners. It was surprising how often Mrs Trollope's book was mentioned to us. Sometimes we felt that the city had never quite got over her portrayal of its social life. Our experiences there were, however, entirely of good manners, and some of the friends we made in 1953 have remained friends for life.*

While I was in Cincinnati Irving Kristol* flew over from New York to discuss with me the project for a political and literary magazine to be sponsored by the Congress for Cultural Freedom, and to be co-edited by him and me. I was to be informed later by Julius Fleischmann, a millionaire who lived at Indian Hill, outside Cincinnati, and who entertained us often, that Encounter *was paid for by his own foundation, the Farfield Foundation, through the CCF. He did not add that these funds were channelled from the CIA. And when I enquired later whether this was so, from his office, its director violently denied it.*

---

* Irving Kristol, writer, editor, social scientist, co-editor with me of *Encounter* (1953-8). Now co-editor of *The Public Interest*.

3

Journal
1948–53

1948

7 April / *Syracuse, New York*

Everywhere this week when I have met members of faculties at universities, there has been much talk of communism. As Margaret Marshall* said to me in NY: 'One of the things we notice is the great increase of fear among us.' The expulsion on political grounds of three professors from Washington University has made a great impression.

I was struck by the desire to help, to do what is right, to be constructive among people I meet here – e.g., a long discussion here about ways in which teachers could help by sending books to Europe.

17 April

Stayed the weekend with Sam (Samuel Barber) and Gian Carlo (Gian Carlo Menotti) and Kinch (Robert Horan)† at Mount Kisco.‡ Gian Carlo expounded to us his faith, which is that everyone will at the moment of dying experience a great illumination when the significance of his entire life will become clear to him. 'Beethoven must have realized on his deathbed the significance of being Beethoven. The sum of life is discoverable within every moment of being,' Gian Carlo said.

20 April / *Johnson City*

Amazing how utterly absorbed the South is in all the old politics. Hatred of the Yankees, the Negro problem, struggling with poverty, consciousness of the 'hillbilly country', the 'old Kentucky home', etc. It seems a very foreign country. It also has a mysteriousness that I find lacking in the North. One of my hostesses here said yesterday:

---

* Then literary editor of the *Nation*.
† Robert Horan. Originally a ballet dancer, who later became a poet of great promise, never fulfilled. Friend of Samuel Barber and Gian Carlo Menotti.
‡ The composers Barber and Menotti shared a house at Mount Kisco, NY, called 'Capricorn'.

'Of course, they must be making a mess of the German Occupation like they made a mess when they occupied us after the war.' She said the Yankees had put 'Negroes in charge of Whites', and she talked about the carpetbaggers.

At dinner my neighbour, the very intrepid Dean of Women, told me that Johnson City is 'dry'. East Tennessee has 'local option'. She said that in the mountains there are people who make 'moonshine', a very potent whisky. Formerly this used to be made of corn which fermented slowly but now it is made so as to ferment much faster and, in consequence, is poisonous to drink. She said that the 'moonshiners' regard themselves as an old and respectable business. 'They resent being confused with bootleggers.'

She said that the chief local moonshiner had recently been sentenced to six months in gaol. He appealed to the Governor of Tennessee for pardon. It was explained that the Governor could not pardon him while he was free. So he spent a day in gaol and was then pardoned.

Johnson City has adopted a town in Scotland, near Dundee. She said that the committee responsible for this want it to be a personal arrangement: to establish contacts between individuals and to make this an act of friendship and not of official charity.

I went to lunch with the Rotary Club. The appearance of the members confirmed my impression that the old men play a prominent part in the life of East Tennessee. They were vigorous jolly old men, singing a western ballad and wearing their Rotary Club badges with an air. At the end of luncheon two new members were introduced and given badges. After that a local doctor made a speech attacking socialized medicine. He criticized it on several grounds: (a) bureaucracy; (b) expense; (c) that it was German, if not Russian; (d) that it was un-American. He said that in Germany it had proved inefficient so that after thirty-four years of socialized medicine, German medicine was backward. He said it was too early to judge the results in England but he drew attention to objections that had been made.

28 April / *Lexington*

My host said: 'The Northerners regard the South as a colony' and he provided examples to illustrate this thesis. Then he spoke about the movement of the Southern Agrarians – John Crowe Ransom, Allen Tate, etc.: a conservative movement, regional, opposing the industrialization of the South, paternal towards the Negroes.

20 May / *Kansas City*

Mr Channon, Chairman of the English Department, told me that he had tried to be in touch with the three professors who had been expelled from Washington University for their communist views. He had written to two of them enquiring about their position and indicating that he would like to help them. Neither had replied. He said he was sure they had not done so because they were afraid that their mail was being watched by the FBI. One of them was soon going to come to Kansas City in order to explain to a group of professors his point of view regarding their expulsion.

At Lexington an English instructor told me that in a student vote as to whether or not they approved of Negro students coming to the University, students in the English Department had the highest number of votes in favour, those in scientific disciplines the lowest. And an art teacher who had examined caricatures done by eight schoolchildren near here told me that all eight of them had chosen themes illustrating the idea that America should go to war with Russia.

27 May / *Chicago*

Dinner party where there were Allen and Caroline Tate (Gordon). The Tates were very friendly and we got on well though they made some extremely pointed remarks in the course of the evening. Told me that Hart Crane was always drunk during the last two and a half years of his life. He used to sit composing poetry to the music of an old-fashioned HMV gramophone. From time to time he would walk across the room and put a pinch of salt down the horn of this machine. Said that Robert Lowell, who is almost in the position of being their adopted son, is pretty well insane. Conflict between Lowell and his parents. When Lowell was 16 or 17 his father found him in his room with a college girl: a row followed in which Lowell knocked his father down. Now he is looked after by his silly (according to the Tates) mother. Allen dislikes *Partisan Review*. They told me several stories about Wystan and complained that he lectured them a lot about America and the Americans. I said people made rather absurd complaints about Wystan, e.g. that he exploits his situation in America. 'That's exactly what he does do,' said Allen, laughing hard over his drink.

He said in a way that was and was not serious (his usual way of taking the sting out of remarks which otherwise might seem hostile) that the British sent over here writers whom 'we American writers' have to put up with. 'You have no idea', he said, smiling most amiably, 'how we hate you. We hate all the British, but most of all we hate Auden, MacNeice and Spender. You are much cleverer than us and we can't forgive you for it. You come over here and everything is made easier for you than it is for us.'

This declaration of war was made in such a way that really it was a declaration of peace, of taking me into his confidence. Allen obviously enjoys gossip of this taunting kind. It was a very cordial evening. By being declared, the Anglo-American hatred had receded almost into abstraction.

The dinner was rather strange. Living in a lavish apartment, our host was a lawyer interested in poetry. However he hates modern poetry, and announced that he held T. S. Eliot to be on a level with Coventry Patmore.

I complained that American critics had no good word for unintellectual poetry. Tate said that though they might wish to praise work which they themselves liked just because it was pleasing, they would not do so, for fear of pandering to popular taste. This conception of critical obligation seemed to me rather demanding. But when our host began to repeat again how much he hated Eliot, and that he only liked poetry which he could understand, I began to see what Allen meant.

[NOTE: *I have put the following entry for 27 April last because it seems to sum up my impressions of this six-week American tour in 1948:*]

27 April / *Lexington*

Before going to bed I bought two newspapers. The news: Chinese Reds race towards Shanghai; Harry Pollitt* besieged in Plymouth. The British editor, Archibald R. Johnstone, quits *Britansky Soyuznik* and becomes a Russian citizen. My sympathies are with Pollitt, who is a brave man. I read with great interest about Johnstone. In his statement he says: 'The time has now come for every person to decide with whom he stands.' Then follows a lot about Attlee, Bevin, Morrison and Co. being 'tools of America' and of the Soviet Union being 'the cause of peace'.

* Harry Pollitt (1890-1960), General Secretary and subsequently Chairman of the British Communist Party. He was largely responsible for raising the English (Clement Attlee) battalion of the International Brigade.

What distresses me is having to reflect that Russia, although certainly not 'the cause of peace', is, nevertheless, a cause. It has a faith to offer to millions of people all over the world, even though communism might destroy the liberty of all except a few political leaders. But America is not 'a cause' in the same way. It is just America by itself with the American way of life and opposition to un-American ways, and tremendous waste, and broadcasting and press and movie industry – not to mention two political parties – which advertise a brand of materialism which is an insult to people not directly involved in American ideas and interests. There are few Americans who realize what agony it is to be asked to choose between loss of liberty according to the communist pattern and possessing liberty at the American price, which is that of having the standards and standard of living that are American. Probably Americans are right to see the great virtues that match the weaknesses of their system. But not to see how America does not speak for the world at present – in fact that it could only do so by hearing the voice of the world – that of its poorest populations – is a fatality which affects even America itself.

Perhaps this is exaggeration. There is the Marshall Plan, there is American private generosity, and there are many good Americans. But all this does not make up for the great weakness that America judges others by *her* values, *her* interests, which prevent her from either understanding or being understood by the rest of the world.

1950

13 March / *Dublin*

Yesterday, the University Librarian, Dr Park, took me to call at the Portobello Nursing Home on Jack Yeats, the painter, brother of W. B. Yeats. He takes a room here all the winter. His room was bare – three chairs, a table, with bottles of whisky and brandy, luggage piled up on top of a cupboard, a wash basin. Nothing on the walls except a conventional calendar with a coloured photoprint of two horses. Jack Yeats was up to receive us. He is bald, has a long, countryman's face, very pale after a winter indoors, with eyes bright as chips. He is 88. He asked us what we'd drink; Dr Park said sherry, I whisky. He poured at least a quarter of a tumbler into my glass, and while he was pouring Dr Park his sherry, I poured half my whisky back into the bottle. Some of it went over the edge of the neck and, sliding down, made a damp ring on the tablecloth. 'Ah,' he said, 'you've been pouring back your whisky. Nothing is ever poured back that doesn't notice.' At first the talk was rather sticky, but soon he was telling anecdotes of his father whom he called 'the governor'. He said 'the governor' spoiled his paintings through having too long a working day and painting when he was tired. 'It was all very well for the Pre-Raphaelites, who painted in every leaf and every brick, they could devote whole days to painting leaves and bricks. But my father was aiming at a kind of effect on which you can only concentrate for two or three hours a day, so he spoiled his work. Then he was very delighted because he learned from Orpen how to cover a canvas with sheets of paper, and then peel the paper away together with the body of the fresh paint he had put on, leaving only a thin, shadowy painting on the canvas. In this way he could start a painting all over again several times. And he would spend two or three pounds on paints in no time.' Jack Yeats said that the whole family was made by his father to learn to draw and paint. His brother WB did some very wild things at art school, but could have done some very fine work had he gone on. Later in life he had chalks and did some interesting drawings. JBY said his father's idea was true ... if in drawing you got beyond the stage of drawing symbolically (a disc for the head, sticks for the arms and legs, etc.), then even if you never took up pencil or brush, you went on drawing things mentally all your life, and in that way learning more about appearances and anatomy.

In the evening I dined at the University Club with Dr Park (and his 23-year-old daughter acting as hostess), Mr and Mrs Dougan, Mr Hadow, and Mrs George Yeats.

Mrs Yeats is an elderly, robust, somewhat stocky lady, wearing glasses with thick lenses – the sort of person who is described as a 'body'. She struck me as extremely intelligent, alive and friendly, with a very independent existence of her own, no nonsense about her, and definite irony. I asked her about John B. Yeats (the Yeats father), and she told me that he left home after his wife had died and when his daughters were middle-aged, because there was a feeling in the air that he ought to be looked after, and he did not wish to be. 'He wanted to go on being untidy and not have people putting his things away in drawers.' So he went for six months to America, and stayed there for twenty years. He wrote a great many letters. He had a desk in the room where he was painting, and would often get up in the middle of his work, and sit there writing one of his letters. Jack Yeats and his daughters had stacks of John B. Yeats letters that had not been published. Mrs Yeats said that when they were young there was a disagreement between the old man and his sons, because he was domineering and insistent on the exact way in which everything should be done. I said, 'All the same, to judge from his letters to your husband, the disagreement was of a kind that is fruitful.' She said that yes, this was so, as long as it was confined to correspondence. When he was actually on the spot it amounted to interfering and could be tiresome.

1951

1 November / *London*

Afternoon, went to the Hall School gym class ... The gym instructor, in his white clothes, gave instructions. Matthew, age $6\frac{1}{2}$, was in the second row, and I noticed that he never heard any orders. He just guessed, or copied what the other boys were doing. 'Hands on hips!' roared the instructor, Matthew put his on his head. Then they had to climb up a kind of gate of six bars, passing through the gap between the top two bars, and coming down the other side ... One of the boys got stuck trying to crawl between the two top bars. He waited half-way through, shaking and trembling. All the other boys started laughing at him, until they were stopped by the instructor.

In a blessed moment while I was half attending to these things, half reading my newspaper, I could understand the state of mind of all these little boys so completely that the gap between me and them seemed paper-thin. I could easily be the Spender who did not attend, or the boy who got stuck, or the other boys who jeered at him. I was only *pretending* to be the middle-aged man reading his newspaper.

And on the way home in the bus where I sat with Matthew, one of his little friends who was seated directly in front of us suddenly turned round, pointed at me with butting finger, and said, 'Spender, is that old, white-haired man with spectacles your daddy?' 'No,' said Matthew with perfect self-possession. When we got off the bus and were at a safe distance from his little friend I asked Matthew why he had said I was not his father. 'Because you aren't,' he exclaimed passionately. 'You aren't like what he said you were.'

30 November

I managed to get a ticket to the dress rehearsal of *Billy Budd*. The stalls at Covent Garden were full of the Harewoods, the Clarks, Willie Maugham, Rose Macaulay, William Plomer, Joe Ackerley, John and Myfanwy Piper, Desmond Shawe-Taylor, etc. Benjamin Britten conducted. The curtain went up on a cloaked figure, the narrator – Peter Pears.

It is interesting to compare this opera, with its masterly libretto, with the Auden-Stravinsky *The Rake's Progress*. Stravinsky's score has a wonderful purity and a profound heartbeat which is lacking in the contorted and neurotic *Billy Budd*. All the same, Britten and Forster build in the first two acts a massive picture of life in the navy in the early nineteenth century, with its barbarism. This use of opera to make a vast painting is something I have not seen before. The music is dense with the heaving and howling of the sea, sound of whistles and foghorns and tolling bells, the feel of the mist, the constant changes of atmosphere. In the last two acts the narrative really gets going. What is most impressive, though, is the elation with which Billy revives spiritually when he is confronted by death. At the end, when the old sea captain takes over the narration, and says, 'I am an old man, these things happened long ago' and that somehow they are involved in a future that endures, one feels that Forster is writing his own testament.

In the interval I talked with William Plomer who said, 'The world's number one exhibitionist is standing over there' – alluding to Willie Maugham. After the second act I sat next to Forster who, wrapped in a greatcoat, and with a satchel at his feet, like a warming pad, was completely absorbed in contemplating his own work. 'Deeply moved by my own words', he said, 'and enjoying my first experience in the theatre.' A man standing in the gangway just beside me said in a loud voice to his wife, 'If you see a man who looks like an old grocer come up for the day from the country, that is E. M. Forster.' The old grocer seated two feet away did not appear to have heard him.

I feel elated and purified by the gloomy yet exhilarating *Billy Budd*, which has the quality of a great white snowy night shining through a mist. It takes me back to the Stravinsky-Auden *Rake*, in which I recognize more originality, more purity, more courage perhaps. But the two works are complementary and it is strange that this year has seen the production of two operatic masterpieces.

4 December

Dined with the very effete French aristocrat, Ann de Biéville, who can sometimes be very amusing. He told me that he had just been to Oxford, where he had lunched with A. L. Rowse. Rowse had told him how he hated and despised human beings – idiots, fools, hideously ugly, contemptible, etc. Ann said, 'Oh, but my dear, what a terrible time you must have every morning, shaving.'

10 December

It is six days since I wrote this diary. So now it must consist of notes only. On 5 December, Eliot, William Plomer, Rose Macaulay and Veronica Wedgwood* came to dinner. Eliot came rather early and, on doctor's orders, left rather early. He was in a very good mood. Dinner and drink were excellent. I can remember nothing serious about the evening. Rose talked about her early memories. Eliot said he could remember being fed out of a bottle. Rose said, 'In that case you must have been weaned very late.' Eliot said, 'Now, now, Rose, you're making me look ridiculous, in public.' Eliot also said, quoting the Russian press about him, 'I am a reactionary, anti-Semitic, pornographic hyena.'

The next morning I got up at six and went to Paris for a meeting at UNESCO.

These two days I had the strangest feeling about my French friends – Yves Gallifret† and Jacques Legris,‡ for example. When you get to know certain French people well, you feel that they have in them such a perfect fusion of mind and senses that it seems their nerves and blood and muscles are penetrated by their intelligence. You don't find yourself dividing them into soul and mind and animal. All that they are flows through all of them with great sweetness.

14 December / *Paris*

A period of frightful weather. On Thursday (in London) we gave a dinner party – an evening of dense fog. There is something very

---

* Dame Veronica Wedgwood, OM, historian and writer.
† Yves Gallifret. Professor of Perceptual Psychology at the Collège de France.
‡ Jacques Legris. A member of the Free French Air Force in England during the war.

unnerving about this, like a party during an air raid. Jamie* and Yvonne Hamilton, June Osborn,† Sonia Orwell and John Morris‡ came. Sonia got rather drunk. Her conversation, when she is drunk, is a mixture of extraordinary pretentiousness and baffling revelations about herself. Pretentiously, she was delivering a school prefect's lecture to Jamie Hamilton, to the effect that it was a great mistake to publish books on American politics because 'nothing looks so shabby as that little row of books we all have in cupboards, from the 1930s'. As self-revelation of her feelings, she provided a description of Cyril's (Connolly) poverty ever since his marriage this summer, since when he has been ignored by nearly everyone and sometimes had nothing to eat for a day or two at a time . . . At a party Sonia will attack someone with a virulence which goes beyond the decencies of the particular gathering, and suddenly seems like a person armed with a hatchet in a drawing room. She is obsessively interested in her friends' marriages – especially in those that don't succeed.

She said that one night when Simone de Beauvoir was in London, and in the Gargoyle Club, criticizing English men, someone asked, 'Do you find any English man attractive?' Simone de Beauvoir was just about to answer no, when Lucian Freud walked into the room. At which she said, 'Tiens' and walked off with Lucian.

Altogether I consider Sonia the most puzzling person I know. What, I think, everyone finds disconcerting about her is an incredible outrageousness constructed over some kind of underlying changeless virginity. Her marriage with George Orwell brought all her characteristics into the open . . . I think that her own sense of her virginity has in some way been outraged, despite the fact that George was in hospital. Also she found herself incapable of really loving him, even for the short period of a few weeks before he died. Perhaps she found a whole lifetime of demands being made on her in the few days she had with him – demands which she sometimes refused. At this time she often pressed me to see

---

*Hamish Hamilton (Jamie). Founded Hamish Hamilton Ltd in 1931. He published the original edition of *World Within World*. Together with his wife Yvonne, a genial host, clubman and friend.

† June Osborn (*née* Capel), widow of the pianist Franz Osborn. Married Lord Hutchinson in 1966.

‡ John Morris travelled much in India, about which he wrote several books. He became Director of the BBC Third Programme when it first started. A not very daring promoter of the cause of culture, cruelly teased by his friend E. M. Forster, who referred to him as 'the pudding'.

George in hospital (as, I suppose, she did with other friends). I would have been glad to do so, quite apart from this, but, in fact, only managed twice. One of these times, she came in at about six, and found George talking to me about the death of D. H. Lawrence. George said that D. H. Lawrence died because his philosophy of life had become absolutely untenable. The proof of this was that one could not imagine Lawrence having any plausible attitude towards events if he were living today. 'Oh, do let's stop talking about this. Let's talk about something cheerful,' said Sonia, suddenly like a bossy hospital nurse. Then she explained that she had to go to a cocktail party, and would not be back that evening. Orwell protested faintly, but she put him off, in her bustling way.

22 December

All this week, we have been simply bogged down by Christmas. This part of winter becomes every year more like a dark tunnel one enters about 15 December, not to emerge until after New Year. Christopher Isherwood rang me Friday morning, just arrived from New York. He is staying at the Alexandra Hotel, Harrington Gardens, where his mother and his brother are with him.

Christopher and I spent Friday afternoon together, looking at bookshops where he loaded himself up with books. He told me of the great success of his play (*I am a Camera*). Stravinsky, Marlene Dietrich, and God knows who else were there the first night. During the intervals Christopher stood in the foyer, meeting everyone, thinking that he would never have a success like this again in his life, so resolved to make the most of it.

1953

17 January

It has been one of the foggiest, darkest, most disagreeable winters I remember.

On Thursday I went to the luncheon given in honour of John Lehmann at the Trocadero. Rosamond [Lehmann], Rose Macaulay, T. S. Eliot, E. M. Forster, William Plomer, Cyril Connolly, Joe Ackerley, Laurie Lee, Alan Ross and about twenty other people were there, including Arthur Koestler, who arrived late and found himself sitting at the end of the table with a group of people all of whom hated him. Food and drink were inferior and the room itself dull and un-interesting. During the meal, Cyril [Connolly] got rather indignant because the waiter – through not having heard what he ordered – brought him the worst instead of the best wine on the list. After some altercation I heard Cyril say: 'Well, you can leave it if you like, but I won't drink it!' Like a child saying, 'So there!'

Really it was not at all boring, there were so many interesting and nice people. (Louis MacNeice and William Sansom* now come to mind) ... but everyone behaved as though he was being consciously at once disappointed and a disappointment. The speeches further en-forced this impression. Henry Green got up and said that when he began arranging this meal, forty-nine (I think) people were invited and of these, much to his surprise, thirty-seven accepted. If there were only thirty-two present, this was because five had suddenly been struck down by flu. He thought it was a jolly good show, and a surprising tribute to John Lehmann. With this he sat down. Then Eliot got up, looking bowed and old, leaning forward with his hands on the table-cloth and staring down at the table. With infinite gravity he said that he shared three occupations ... or should he say professions? ... with John Lehmann: as poet, businessman and publisher. He was quite sure that whatever happened ... and he didn't have any air of knowing in particular what would happen ... that John would carry on with one of these. Then he sat down. John then got up and said he didn't know what to say ... (always a good beginning). He had found himself thrust forth, thrown out on to the world alone, as he thought: and then he had observed that he was surrounded by friends. Support came from (or on) every flank. (At this point his metaphors became military, and there were references to reinforcements, flak, etc.) He then said that as an editor he always had a feeling of being haunted: he was haunted by articles, stories and poems which came flooding in on him, haunted by ideas for articles and poems suggested to him. He also had to send out a great many rejection slips, by the consciousness of which he was haunted also. (We all shuddered, Cyril putting on an expression as though he were stuffed with John's rejection slips.) Then John said that when he began editing he had thought he was going to be the instigator of a great new movement, a new literature, new poetry; that

---

* William Sansom (1912-76). Novelist and short-story writer. During the war we served in the same section of the London Fire Service. Author of *Fireman Flower* (1944).

everything would be wonderful. But we had all turned out very differently from what he had expected. He then went on to say that in the minds of some people he was thought of as a headmaster who thrashed us all, like Dr Keate of Eton. His speech ended with a peroration in which he managed to introduce the names of most of Henry Green's novels. He didn't want us to think ... he said ... that he was going to 'pack his bag'. He wanted to assure Mr Green that he intended to go on *living* and that he thanked him for his *loving* if not his doting care. There would be no turning *back*, etc. This peroration spared us to some extent the utter bewilderment caused by John's addressing Eliot, Forster and the rest, as though they were raw young cubs whose efforts had proved disappointing.

Cyril cheered up considerably in the course of the meal, and he, Harvey Breit (from the *New York Times*) and I went to Brown's Hotel together, where I stayed till five. Cyril's explanation of John's speech was that it was prepared for another occasion, as a headmaster's oration to a school for writers and potential contributors to one of his organs.

Thursday was a really terrible day. After all this I went to a meeting of Julian Huxley's Idea Systems Group, where people discussed nothing but how much money would be needed to set up an Institute of Research. Every idea Julian has, of a kind that anyone else would write a book about, doing his own research, Julian turns first into a committee for turning it into an institute. I can never enter into these discussions without imagining a dreary redbrick building with a quadrangle consisting of damp mud and sand, and rain falling everywhere, inhabited by scholars from Chatham House.

30 January

The last few days have been spent in crazy business about my visa.

Meanwhile I have spent a lot of time reading to prepare my lectures for Cincinnati. I am very excited about my general theme, that it is the tendency of modern literature to be visionary. I am so excited about this idea that I can hardly write about it. As Christopher Isherwood once said to me, 'My novel is so terrific that I cannot put pen to paper.' Read Rimbaud, Breton, some Laforgue, Bowra on the Symbolists and Wilson's *Axel's Castle*, Starkie on Rimbaud, Klee on modern art, *Letters* of Ezra Pound.

I don't think that Ezra Pound is a very intelligent man. He has a serious, craftsmanly attitude towards poetry, but his letters are nearly always badly written, and finally he tries to make a virtue, of what are really the vices, of a very egoistic, abrupt style. He is generous, and what the French call an 'animateur'. His general ideas about poetry are negative, barren and dry. Poetry must be concentrated and hard, he says, but very little else. In 'Hugh Selwyn Mauberley', he puts a nineties-ish regret for classical values into a terse and effective modern idiom. He contrasts a tawdry present with the past of archaic Apollos, and he does this in a stanza which is new and catchy – cute – and which, if used by other poets, could become as obvious as the 'clerihew'. He started off with the nineties and his achievement really is to have supplied the nineties-ish mood with a contemporary idiom. He came gradually to find this inadequate, and the economic theories of fascists and of social credit supplied him with a philosophy, and also the machinery of his own personal tragedy. All the same, the thread of an economic motive through human society, and the division of economics into good (the theories of Douglas)* and evil (usury) is no satisfactory substitute for a moral vision.

5 February

I got my visa on Monday by an abrupt release of all obstructions whereby officials sometimes baffle one.

The journey eventless, except that we were delayed for an hour at Boston by engine trouble. Landing early in the morning at Boston made a startling impression. The whole city seemed covered in dust, and, being not fully awake, I started wondering whether an explosion had taken place before I realized that of course it was snow.

At New York there was no difficulty at the Customs at all. I went to Harcourt Brace where the directors, Eugene Reynal and Robert Giroux, seemed like cagily welcoming cherubs. They asked me about my lectures in Cincinnati, which I said I wanted to do as a book, and listened with a look of 'that won't sell a thousand copies' as I outlined my theme. I wound up rather lamely: 'I suppose my idea that the central impulse of modern literature is an isolated vision, amounts to an attack on Eliot's critical theories.' 'Oh that's OK with us,' they said, producing the *Collected T. S. Eliot* they've just done – which is

* Major C. H. Douglas (1879–1952) was, after the First World War, a proselytizer for the theory of Social Credit, a form of state socialism without tears. Douglas was a great influence on Ezra Pound.

the size of a small suitcase – 'Every time anyone attacks Eliot we just sell another thousand copies of this.'

The premises of Random House resemble an Old World brownstone mansion, with a drive-in leading off Madison Avenue.* You go in and see a girl sitting in the chilling marble entrance hall at a vast rounded desk made of some expensive substance like ebony. She is telephoning a friend. You sink into one of about six vast leather couches and gaze across the hall at glass cases in which books published by Random House are displayed like expensive ladies' handbags. Finally the college girl behind the desk disengages herself, gives a calculated jump from her chair, says, 'Oh, I say Mr Spender, but Mr Cummins will be dying to see you' and invites me to walk up to the room of my editor on the first floor. You get to the top of glorious marble stairs and you see about six doors all wide open, each leading into a room richly carpeted, filled with white light like an immense ice-cube, book-lined, and with a vast desk. Seated behind each desk is a director of Random House. Mr Cummins, my editor, welcomes me. His room has an unutterable look of emptiness and the air in it seems to stream through the conditioning machinery with a thin pure sound such as you hear when you are under gas at the dentist. After a few moments you are unconscious of everything but this sound. Mr Cummins said: 'Now, do you have a new volume of poems?' 'I shall soon,' I lied, thinking that the very idea of my publishers would purge me of all poetry. Yet I think that really I don't want to run the gauntlet of publishing a volume of poems ever again. Then I think that this is abysmal cowardice. I am taken to meet a director, then another director, and then I run down the flight of marble stairs into the great pure fresh air of Madison Avenue, which I breathe in like a sea breeze.

6 February / *Cincinnati*

Flight to Cincinnati. As we landed the wing of the aeroplane seemed immense, as though it were scraping across the lights of the city and the dark landscape of the airfield pricked out with abstract patterns of light. Next morning I was interviewed by the Cincinnati press, an occasion of some anxiety, since the University runs the risk of attacks from the press for communist or even liberal views. The interviews, as they appeared in the papers, were almost entirely concerned with

* Random House has now moved from these premises.

the question of my having been a communist, but otherwise were nice, all except one in, I think, the *Cincinnati Enquirer*, which, with the kind of meanness one expects from the *Daily Express*, reported that after I had said some things to which they couldn't take exception, 'President Walters* intervened and prevented any further questions about Mr Spender's communism.' The papers are, incidentally, terrifying: obsessed with whether it would be a good thing to attack the Chinese mainland, calling the communist bluff and so on.

American professors are an oppressed, overworked, underpaid, and now also a politically suspect class. Socially, their position is about that of English doctors in my great-grandfather's day, who were expected to call on their rich patients via the back door.

At luncheon in the cafeteria, the Dean and Dr William Clark† told me how it was now almost impossible to teach Marxism or anything about it. I said I thought it must be difficult to explain certain American writers ... Edmund Wilson, Dos Passos, etc. ... without reference to Marx. 'It is', said Clark, 'and I can only explain this background in a fragmentary or indirect way. Personally I think the present attitude is a great mistake.' (Clark by the way is an ardent Republican.) 'It seems to me that it is necessary to know the ideas of your opponents.' They said there was an almost complete neglect now of Russian language and Russian literary studies, because people were afraid either to teach or to learn about them. They told me that in Cincinnati during Henry Wallace's‡ campaigns in the Presidential Election of 1947, photographs had been taken of people attending Wallace meetings. Subsequently efforts were made by the anti-red groups to identify the faces of people in these photographs in order to persecute them.

I spent most of today going through thirty-four manuscript poems from my prospective students. I eliminated twenty and am left with fourteen students, eight men and six women. I shall meet these on Monday ... After working all day, came back to my room and cooked myself some supper and have been reading ever since.

---

* President of the University of Cincinnati.

† Chairman of the English Department at the University of Cincinnati. He was a member of a local political party striving for integrity in politics, called the Chartist Party.

‡ Roosevelt's Vice-President and later a candidate for the American Presidency.

7 February

Went into Cincinnati – the centre of the town – with its streets cut straight across one another and numbered in the grill pattern of a Midwest town. The newest hotel in the town has achieved the ambition implicit in its surroundings, to have eight storeys with no windows in them at all; just blind walls, surmounted by a pillbox restaurant.

I opened one of the books I ought to read ... Nietzsche's *The Birth of Tragedy*. Instantly my eye struck phrases like: 'What self-experience, what stress, made the Greek think of the Dionysian reveller and primitive man as a satyr?' And I could read no more. An almost intolerably clear picture filled my mind of a little screen of small and delicate cypresses (like trees in a drawing of Botticelli) along the roadside leading from the little modern town of Delphi up the mountainside. Through these trees as though suspended between their hair-thin branches, you can see a temple in the valley below on a kind of lawn, among grey-green olive trees. The mountainside steps down to this by a series of terraces where there are squat, black-trunked olive trees. And just a little further along the road, there is a place where the Castalian Spring gushes out through the rock-shelves of the mountain into a wide shallow bowl. And there is a great plane tree whose branches hang right down into the valley. Here, overlooking the valley, you see fold on fold of olives, with the river gleaming below leading to the sea. There is Parnassus to your left and to your right the other mountain where you climb tier on tier of temples till you come to the remains of the stadium, higher up than all the other shrines. When I had come back from India once, I went to Delphi on a shining star-lit night and I noticed how with star and moonlight brilliant on tree-like columns, there seems a geometric relationship between stars and temples, as though there were lines drawn between the stars illustrating the heavenly signs, as depicted in old globes of the heavens.

There is comfort and reassurance in being able to remember things vividly – to count them over again and again in one's mind. For instance the glaring white streets of Corinth, the flyblown cafés opposite the sea, the shops full of oranges and other fruits. The very first time I went into Corinth, the streets were crowded and from a balcony of one of these low, almost Moroccan houses, there was a mad orator speaking in a voice that seemed to direct the crowd listening to him below. Now I imagine hundreds of things in Greece. That place in the mountains where we climbed up the hillside to a holy cave. You dipped a glass down into a well and drank sacred water. The beautiful little church of Daphne outside Athens with the immense tall cypresses like twisted candlesticks on each side of the porch, and with the Byzantine mosaics inside.

Then Sunion: clean-cut white lines, the temple of Neptune, jutting out above the Aegean at the extreme eastern edge of Greece. The sparkling sea all round us, and the pillar on which Byron carved his name.

I am torn by the tragedy of Europe. Everything points to it and has always pointed to it, and I wonder whether we have not known about it far longer than we think ... longer than my own lifetime. Just as Baudelaire in 1850 writes of the horror of the world being Americanized (which we think of as quite a recent idea) so perhaps we were born in the shadow of the decline of Europe. Certainly Nietzsche knew all about it by 1870. The grotesque idea occurs to me that the kindness of Americans to us is like the kindness of people to invalids.

8 February

This morning on the radio I heard a discussion about the kind of government Christ would establish on earth. It sounded extraordinarily like the present American administration. It would be completely righteous, democratic, but all-conquering. It would control all the administrative offices of government, and would be directed by human agents who would resist evil, which was on the increase all the time. Christ would remain invisible, like agents of the FBI.

10 February

Two days ago a student came to interview me for the campus *Recorder*. The magazine is a student affair, but the University is so vast and plays such a role in this town that it has the status of a local newspaper, and therefore has to be treated with caution. The reporter was a freshman, a Jewish boy in some kind of uniform, with a thin narrow face, big nose, dark eyes, fresh complexion, and glossy hair. He reeled off at me the following questions: What was the first poem you had published, for which you were paid money? This was the only one I could answer. If there was a meeting of your fellow poets – your colleagues – and they were talking about you, what would they think of your work? What do you consider your greatest achievement? Now,

Mr Spender, when you write a poem, what sort of message do you have in mind that you are trying to convey to your reader? What do you expect to achieve in life by writing poetry? Do you expect people to convert to something? How did you get your appointment to this university? Mr Spender, we've all heard something about you having belonged to the Communist Party, and we would like you to make a statement about this for the *Recorder*.

To add to the confusion of these questions, he knew absolutely nothing about poetry or politics, or about anything else, so far as I could make out. The only one of his questions I might have answered was: What was my greatest achievement? – because it occurred to me very forcibly when he asked this that it was being the father of Matthew and Elizabeth. But I did not want to say this, so I simply had to admit that I did not imagine that my fellow poets – if they deigned to discuss me at all – would think much of me, and that I thought nothing about messages, and couldn't express what I thought about achievements. I then told him the old, old story about my communist affiliations. I always have to remember that this is a recital of a crime, like, 'When I was in Sing Sing ...' Fortunately I insisted on seeing the interview before it was published.

Two hours later the typescript came to me ... incredible. It started off about communism, explaining that I joined the CP because the Secretary of the British Party had told me that in exchange for my signing a membership card he would publish an article by me giving my views on the Spanish Civil War. 'As Mr Spender was at this time a young writer and lecturer wishing to have his views appear anywhere where they could get published, he accepted this arrangement.' The article was terribly ill-written and would have disgraced a boy of 10. I took it to Dr Clark who showed considerable signs of alarm, as he said he thought it was not only unpleasant for me, but would upset President Walters if it were published. The next morning Clark and I went to see the editor of the *Recorder*. He was a gaunt youth, at once hard as nails and rather amiable. Trying to explain to him why we wanted the article changed was the most exasperating piece of diplomacy ... but very revealing ... in which Academic Age tries to put its point to Youth with an Eye to the Main Chance.

The editor said that Al was a smart lad in his opinion, and he'd asked him to go out and get from Mr Spender just facts, plain facts, because those were what they wanted to plug the *Recorder* with ... I pointed out that the so-called facts were all wrong, and the editor said that this did not matter, what they wanted was FACTS, right or wrong. Besides, he added, there also had to be a new Angle, different from that of the papers in town. He then revealed that they wanted a NEWS Sensation, and that Al's article was to be the leading news item, with 3-inch-deep headlines about the ex-communist poet on the campus. Dr Clark pleaded, 'But surely, the students will already have read all this?' To which the editor replied incontrovertibly, 'Our readers never read.'

One of the things that amazed me about this interview was the way in which student and professor negotiated as completely equal powers. Indeed I had the strong impression that we were throwing ourselves on the young man's mercy. Dr Clark larded his speeches on my behalf with praise for the *Recorder* and its achievements, and he spent over an hour covering and re-covering the ground in order that the student editor would not feel that he was being asked by a professor to 'climb down'. I couldn't help comparing in my mind an interview as I supposed it would be between an Oxford vice-chancellor and the undergraduate editor of a magazine under similar circumstances. The point is that fundamentally there would be more feeling of mutual regard and respect between the vice-chancellor and the undergraduate even though the undergraduate would probably be sent down. The idea that students are the equals of their teachers is simply hypocritical, and results in the genuine dislike and distrust between students and faculty.

15 February

Will have been here fourteen days tomorrow. Have only received one letter from home since I've been here. It is a low-water mark like 3 a.m. I feel I haven't appreciably lessened the time. Being away so long is to miss one-sixth of Lizzie's life and one-fourteenth of Matthew's, and in addition to missing home, I feel anxious. All the same, I am working well and hard.

A further thought about my interview with the *Recorder*. One of the questions I was asked was: Is writing poetry satisfactory to your ego? I had forgotten to note this gem in my previous entry. Now in no other country would a poet be asked such a question. Sometimes I have the feeling that in America no instinct or intuition is taken for granted. Everything is questioned and explained, with the result that there is a kind of low-level rationalization or intellectualization of every kind of behaviour. No one is happy until the whole of life has been translated into pseudo-scientific jargon. Yet this may be an advantage to Americans in the long run, because it is part of a process of cutting out European roots. In Brazil, for instance, no one would ask these questions. But in Brazil, where everyone is a poet, there are no poets, whereas in America where even poetry has been rationalized, there are a few poets, and certainly some very good novelists.

16 February

Today was a much happier day, in which a lot of things went well. First of all, I had a letter from home. Secondly, I heard that income tax is not to be withheld on my salary. Thirdly, I heard that Sunion did at one time have a frieze: a fact which makes a lot of difference to a poem I have been writing. Fourthly, my Creative Writing course went very well.

My students, who consist of fifteen first-year students, and people from outside the university, including two journalists and two house-wives, are really very nice. They appear to make the mistake of imagining that they are going to be turned into great poets. I am not teaching them as Berryman* taught them last year, and as – from what he told me – Auden teaches his pupils, making them write in strict verse forms. Instead I'm trying to make them visualize and imagine things. So I set them as an exercise to write a poem or prose poem on the subject of a glass of water. One or two of them did this, and others wrote about other things they had attempted to see. Then we went through all their poems criticizing them for imagistic, visual qualities. One of them had written a poem about a Siamese cat. It began with two lines which were about 'limpid shadows trailing scarlet ribbons' laid before the figure of an Egyptian goddess – the cat. I asked him to come up to the blackboard and do a drawing of the limpid shadows trailing scarlet ribbons. He did so, showing that he intended two mice laid in sacrifice before the cat. Another student objected that the cat may have killed the mice herself in which case they could not be victims of ritual sacrifice to a cat-goddess. This is the kind of thing that is excellent with American students. They don't get offended if you tear their work to pieces, and they are interested in the structural side of things.

* John Berryman.

I'm very much against teaching form before you teach vision and concreteness. In fact, I think it is evident that the Imagists were the only 'school' who have taught anything in this century. I'm going to try to teach them to concentrate, visualize and write clearly.

21 February

My second lecture seems to have been successful. It was on Rimbaud and as I had to talk quite a bit about his life people were interested, and imagined they were listening to talk about poetry. In part they were, and although it seems doubtful how far one should mix up the biographies of poets with their poetry, a lecture may draw the audience into an interest in the poetry through presenting the life, just as poetic drama does. Anyway Rimbaud's life is almost inseparable from his poetry. I myself am deeply interested in the lives of writers and it would be wrong to pretend not to be.

After the lecture, a man aged about 30 came up and said we had met once at Greenwich Village, at a dinner – I forget where or with whom. He started hurriedly explaining that he was at present occupied in being male nurse to some friend of his who was in an alcoholic stupor somewhere in Cincinnati. I asked him to lunch on Friday. As Friday approached I remembered the strong smell of alcohol on his breath and began to wish I hadn't arranged this meeting. He arrived – a quarter of an hour late – and I took him to one of the restaurants in the shopping centre above the campus. He had short black hair, streaked with grey, rather bristly all round his head, and intense eyes. He told me his alcoholic friend was still in a stupor, that one of his toes had gone gangrenous and that he had procured him – with great difficulty – some drugs. I felt vaguely guilty because I thought perhaps lecturing about Rimbaud involved me in this. He said he would not eat anything, and ordered a bock. He drank a bottle, then ordered another bottle. He talked about himself in a detached rather self-satisfied way. 'You must think I'm rather irresponsible,' he said complacently. 'Not at all,' I said, very much to my own amazement. 'I just think that all this is extremely boring.' He looked shocked and said, 'I suppose you wonder why I am thrusting all this on you.' 'Yes, I do wonder.' 'I suppose the fact that one is extremely and immensely lonely isn't in the least an excuse or a justification,' he said. 'No, not in the least.' I took up the check and paid and went out. I don't really feel sorry that I behaved like this. It is the first time I have ever triumphed over someone else's assumption that I was going to be sympathetic. Being a wedding guest who refuses to listen to a dypso-maniac ancient mariner is not an altogether unpleasant sensation, I found.

I went to a party given for Jenny Tourel, who is singing with the orchestra here this week. She is very black and white, with thick features, enormous onyx eyes, frizzy black hair and a pale complexion. She must have been very beautiful when she was young. She told me how when she was in Israel this year, as soon as she got off the aeroplane at Lydda Airport she was met by three officials who asked her what language she intended to sing the Mahler song-cycle in. 'German,' she replied. They then explained that they had been ordered by the Foreign Office to inform her that she could not do this. 'What language do you expect me to sing in?' she asked. 'Hebrew or English,' they said. She said that maybe she should fly back again and not stay in Lydda. At this they suggested that she might sing so that the words were unintelligible. She said that she would sing in German or not at all.

Just before the concert, as she was standing behind the stage, she heard a member of the orchestra say to another one – in German – that after the concert she was going to be arrested if she sang in German. She went on to the stage very nervously, sang the Mahler in German and was given an ovation. After the concert she went to a reception, and a very handsome man came up to her, explained that he was the chief of police and that he had come to arrest her. She laughed and said she would be delighted to be arrested by *him*. Then he explained that he had looked up the law and discovered that as this was a concert and not a theatrical or operatic performance, she could sing in German, since the law omitted to cover this point.

On the following evening I heard her sing the Mahler cycle – *Songs of a Wayfarer*. She sang this much more beautifully than some Rossini she sang afterwards, and which seemed to require a more chiselled type of voice. This work is quite beautiful but completely backbone-less, in the Viennese manner, which – like so many other European symptoms of decay – extends so much longer back in time than we think. On the one hand the music wants to be gay and carefree, on the other hand it is dominated by an overwhelming sense of defeat and death ... These two things never come to grips with each other, so that you get neither tragedy nor comedy, but pathos. What it does very effectively is to represent the mood of the Viennese, who are simply victims.

I had been taken to the concert by a lady psychologist, in the box of friends of hers whose names I forget. Afterwards we went back to the house of these friends and the dinner which followed did not break up until 3 a.m. At about 2 a.m. the lady psychologist told us that in the mental institution where she works in Cincinnati some of the patients who were suffering from lack of love were so without confidence that a scheme had been devised to 'pick them up' at the time when they were mentally 3 months old. This is done by making them lie down and relax completely, while a gramophone disc is played to them which has the necessary reassuring effect. She then said briskly, 'Although this is very successful with psychotics, it can also be used beneficially by normal people.' Before we knew where we were, we were all being ordered to lie down on the floor and relax completely. Then she put on the record. Crooning music was played and a gentle voice said words to this effect – 'Baby is in the cot ... Mother loves baby ... Mother pats baby ... Mother draws up the blanket over baby and tucks him in ... Baby feels so calm and loved ... Baby is so peaceful ... Mother works in the room while baby lies in the cot ... Mother comes over and feeds baby ... Mother draws the blanket over baby ... It is so peaceful ... Mother loves baby ...' etc.

This performance slightly shook my confidence in the lady psychologist. For one thing, if a gramophone record were a substitute for a mother, life would be much simpler. We were not drunk or anything. The incident was carried out in a perfectly sober, businesslike way.

4 March

I am beginning to think that the kind of analytic criticism which explains or 'explicates' every image in a poem as a symbol translatable into some meaning other than itself can cause students to get into dreadful muddles. Yesterday I gave a tutorial to Z, a very nice and intelligent student, from the Hebrew College. Z. is lean and tall and dark, with long hands and fingers, and thumbs that curve back. He arrived with a copy of a poem of mine in which there occurred the line 'build walls and towers'. 'Why do you write "walls and towers"?' he asked. 'And not just "walls"? Surely towers are built with walls so they must symbolize the same thing. Or do "towers" symbolize something special?' Then he pointed with a thumb at two or three of my lines, heavily scored by him, and said: 'Now just say something about these. Just let yourself talk' as though he was a psychoanalyst, and I his patient. Then we came to *The Waste Land*. He had not only Eliot's own notes but also notes he had made about the comments of the critic, translator and anthologist Kimon Friar, at the end of some anthology of modern verse. According to Z, Friar found contradiction of the symbolism in the fact that in the early part of *The WL* there is dryness, aridity, waterlessness, and rain symbolizes Good; whereas in the later part of the poem in the section called 'Death by Water', water symbolizes Bad, because it drowns Phlebas the Phoenician. According to Z, Friar's 'explication' of the contradiction implicit in the fact that the water which might refresh dry roots, can also, if collected in a pond, pool or lake, drown you, is that all the water symbolizing Good had got sucked out of the Waste Land and collected in a pool where it became the water symbolizing Bad. At this, I almost lost my patience, as I pointed out that water was notoriously a thirst quencher in which you could also drown. 'Yeh, but in this poem the dryness symbolizes the water which ought to revive the Waste Land not being there, so this symbol which is good in one place becomes bad in another, when it is drowning Phlebas the Phoenician.' Then, 'This looks like being pretty pregnant with symbols,' he said, pointing to a rather densely printed page of *The Waste Land*. We came to a line in which there is a dead tree ... 'Now what's the symbolism of the dead tree?' 'It's a dead tree,' I said. 'Yeh, but what does it being dead symbolize? What's it doing there being dead?' 'It just happened to be growing there – or dying there,' I corrected. He did not seem satisfied with this, so I added, 'It was in the Waste Land, so it died.' 'D'yer mean to say that you don't know?' he scowled suspiciously. 'Or do you mean to say that Eliot's stuck with a tree that doesn't symbolize anything?'

[NOTE: *Of course, Z. was right, the dead tree symbolizes the cross on which Jesus was crucified.*]

Am much behind with this journal, mostly on account of the illness I had as a birthday present from the gods, on 28 February which was my forty-fourth birthday. I woke up that morning with a slight pain which developed into a violent backache. As I had been invited by Myra Hess – who is giving a concert in Cincinnati – to lunch with her at her hotel, I hated to stay in. So at noon I staggered out of the house and got on to a bus. The bus was going in the wrong direction but it took me a long time to get myself together enough to do anything about this. Then I got out and went into a bus going the other way. I just managed to avoid collapsing in the bus and to get myself to bed. In the evening I managed to get to the concert and reassured Myra afterwards in the green room, as she was a bit worried. After this I stayed up a bit at the Clarks' house, and then when I got back to my room experienced a relapse. But by Sunday I was pretty well recovered, though a bit depressed over the weekend, and the thought of my class on Monday followed by my lecture on Tuesday weighs on me.

12 March

My life here has settled down to a routine of reading, writing, taking my class once a week, and giving my lecture. The class are very sympathetic, and oddly enough they seem to make progress. Poetry is for all of them, so far as I can see, a substitute for writing an essay or keeping a journal. It is possible to encourage them to express themselves more concretely and to tidy up the ideas they choose to write.

I have read an enormous amount since I got here. Probably I ought to write about this in a journal, but I feel that to write about reading is to make a commentary on thoughts which pour into me, and I feel it more important to write here about external things, people I meet, what they say and so on ... Reading this journal through it seems to me happier, and also less spiky about people, than I had thought it would be. Of course, doing little vignettes of people you meet right after you meet them, it is impossible not to caricature them, and select the things they say which strike you as absurd.

At parties I show symptoms of saying the kind of things which pop out of a British mouth among Americans after two or three highballs. Sometimes indeed one has the impression of being a batsman in a game in which everyone is waiting for you to hit up a nice catch. On one occasion the lob that came curving down was someone's remark that the French had no wish whatever to defend themselves from invasion and were a bunch of no-good cowards. I hit up my catch, which was: 'They happen to think that architecture is more important than people.' During the rest of the over I hit up catch after catch and was caught out time after time. I said that if you destroyed Venice and left the Venetians there would be no Venetians within a few years, whereas if you killed the Venetians and Venice was occupied by the Red Army, within a hundred years there would be Venetians again. Venice would have civilized them. 'We don't attach that amount of importance to dead buildings in the US,' someone said. 'We think more about life, and our ideals.'

A conversation like this is utterly unreal, especially as even if neutralism is right one cannot admit to being a neutralist without appearing to be inviting the enemy to invade one's country. My point of view was a reasonable though unreal one; theirs was reasonable but meaningless. If you cannot see the importance of architecture, and if you really think that starving people stumbling about ruins (like those I saw in Germany after the war) are great idealists and living exemplars of democracy, you have no sense of realities. Really arguments on these lines run rapidly into an impasse. Both sides are talking dust and ashes. Luckily people I talk to here have a sense of this, so they were not really annoyed with me.

George Ford* told me that Raymond Aron, who has recently been to Washington, went back to France deeply disturbed and published some pronouncement somewhere that in part he had to concede in the argument he had been having with certain French writers who say there is political persecution in America.

'All things can tempt me from this craft of verse.' Yesterday it was a request from the Paris Committee of the Congress for Cultural Freedom, that I should edit, together with Irving Kristol, a magazine, and also take over some of Nicky Nabokov's† work while he is in Rome. This is disturbing, because my idea of that Paris office is of a nightmare. The thing to do is to try and think of alternatives. It is easy to think, 'It will be distracting, I shouldn't do it.' But all work is more or less distracting, and if I have been fortunate here at Cincinnati, I must think of that as an exception. Another job in an American university might not be so agreeable and give me so much time. Allen Tate, for instance, seems to be leading just as distracting a life here as I would in Paris. In addition to which there are aspects of this kind of life which I hate for my own reasons and which may be bad for my family: being away five or six

---

*Canadian scholar, author of several studies of D. H. Lawrence and Dickens, who taught at the University of Cincinnati.

† Nicolas Nabokov, cousin of Vladimir Nabokov; composer, and a Director of the Congress for Cultural Freedom at this time.

months in a year, I mean. The editing job would probably mean being half in London, half in Paris, which would be much better. The main consideration is that freelance journalism is the most completely distracting thing of all, because it means I have no regular income. Given a job, I have enough energy to do the job and do my own work. The disadvantages of Paris are not the job itself but the worries connected with it, to which I am very susceptible – otherwise I would not be put off from writing for two days by attacks on my public reputation, like one by Roy Campbell which recently appeared in the *Times Literary Supplement*.

Anyway I have written a letter to Paris accepting the editorship in principle but asking for a clearer definition of what is meant by 'Nicky's duties'.

The material I have had to read about Yeats in the last few days has also rather disturbed me. It makes me feel that now I know quite a lot of things superficially but nothing really well or systematically. Yeats at a certain moment in his life took hold of himself and systematized his ideas. I think I know why. He had to shed the skin of his Irish Celtic Twilight background, but he could not grow roots in the life of human beings because he was rather inhuman himself. People to him were not people he understood, but personalities he had theories about. What he really believed in was fairies and Irish myths. He therefore substituted seances for fairies, and finally, when he discovered that his wife had gifts as a medium, used her unconscious as his own private line to those 'spirits' in the other world who dictated to him his own mediumistic system. His means of interpreting life was through a logically constructed supernatural machinery.

Yeats invented a private mythological system because he couldn't accept the Church. I feel in a worse position than Yeats, because while I see that the complications of inventing a private system have increased since his day, I believe that the reasons for rejecting the Church still hold. The Church has more truth to offer – or more sense should I say? – than any private system of mythology, but it has nothing to say about contemporary history, because materially speaking it is part of that history (a state institution), although spiritually speaking it rejects, or should reject, modern life altogether. When it attempts to relate Christianity to life, it can only offer feeble palliatives. The reality on which an imagination like Eliot's can still construct is death, the idea of eternity. When Eliot writes about life, he is merely a well-disposed reactionary trying to temper conservative individualism with a little Christian charity. All Wystan really says is that our bad conscience is a Christian conscience. The effect of cultivating a bad Christian conscience has been to free him of interest in social problems.

15 March

America: a country which is entirely different from every other by dint of being more the same. Existence is reduced to a common denominator. Mystery is stripped from everything. All people of all other countries have something in common, which is the sense of mystery. The European, the Latin American, the Asiatic, the African, know that religion, sex, and poetry are things which cannot be explained. In America not only is everything explained, but sometimes you get the impression that nothing exists except the explanation. Analyse American existence to the ultimate essence and what you get is an explanation or a fact. This is all contained within the concept 'The American Way of Life' – which is basic to Americans. Dissect an American mind, and finally you arrive at an odourless transparent thin concept. Sometimes I think that this analytic way of looking at or 'explicating' things applies to their view of everything, even of nature. You drive through the country and the trees say we are American trees. Some of the animals give off appalling smells, but this is simply a problem to be solved by giving the animals deodorant pills.

American learning is always haunted by the idea that there is an 'explication' which is the ultimate reality. A symbol symbolizes something, which is something else, but at a certain point the regression stops and there is the 'truth'. Nothing simply is, inexplicably so.

When Americans become Catholics they take a gamesmanship pleasure in the more impenetrable mysteries of Catholicism. They do this because there are no mysteries for them, but conceptual tangles give them a kick. This is true even of someone like Allen Tate.

In Allen's new book, there is a passage in an essay called 'The Symbolic Imagination' where he quotes a scene in which St Catherine of Siena (she described it in her journal) holds in her hands the head of a martyr which is about to be chopped off. The axe falls and St Catherine writes: 'When he was at rest my soul rested in peace and quiet, and in so great fragrance of blood that I could not bear to remove the blood which had fallen on me from him.'

Allen comments: 'It is deeply shocking, as all proximate incarnations of the Word are shocking, whether in Christ and the Saints, or in

Dostoevsky, James Joyce or Henry James. I believe it was T. S. Eliot who made accessible again to an ignorant generation a common Christian insight, when he said that people cannot bear very much reality ... St Catherine had the courage of genius, which permitted her to *smell* the Blood of Christ in Niccolò Tuldo's blood clotted on her dress: she smelled the two bloods not alternately but at one instant, in a single act compounded of spiritual insight and physical perception.'

It all reads like a description of a cocktail to me. No one except an American writer would calmly connect this action of St Catherine with Christ and the Saints, Dostoevsky, T. S. Eliot, James Joyce and Henry James. Of course the question here is whether Allen is treating the struggle of writers with their material as living problems of the same order as St Catherine's or whether he is treating her smelling of the fragrance of the blood as a literary problem. I wouldn't like to judge this. Perhaps the American taste for violence is really the endeavour to discover a mystery.

Commentary
1954-9

The first number of Encounter, *as the magazine was called, was published in October 1953. The magazine was anti-communist in policy, but it was not McCarthyite, and its pages were open to political debate of Left as well as Right. The title was meant to indicate its openness to clashing views. An article chosen by Irving Kristol (probably the liveliest in the first number) by Leslie Fiedler on the Rosenberg case caused considerable offence on account rather of Leslie Fiedler's lack of sympathy for the two spies, than his belief that they were guilty, which they were. Fiedler's critics took no account of the fact that at the end of the article he gave it as his opinion that the Rosenbergs should not have received the death sentence.*

The article that put Encounter *on its feet appeared a year or so later and was of a very different kind. This was Nancy Mitford's famous essay on 'U and Non-U'.* The great success of this was the result, almost, of an accident. Irving and I had decided to commission a series of articles on themes such as the intellectuals, the social classes, the rich and the poor, in several countries (like other similar editorial projects this did not come to much) and in accordance with this plan I asked Nancy Mitford to write about the English upper class. In thanking her for her article, I pointed out to her that it was 1,000 words too short. She wrote back to say that she was guiltily aware of this, and that, returning it, she had found an easy way to add the necessary number of words – simply by expanding on a pamphlet written by a Professor Ross and published, I think, in Iceland, called 'U and Non-U'. Our fortunes were made by the obscure pamphlet of the obscure professor.*

I liked Irving Kristol and it was a blow to me when he left Encounter *at the end of 1958 to take a job on Max Ascoli's* The Reporter. *Before Kristol left, for a few numbers Dwight MacDonald joined the editorship and I had hopes that he would replace Irving as my colleague. But instead of this the*

* 'The English Aristocracy' by Nancy Mitford, *Encounter*, Vol. 5 No. 3 (September 1955).

Congress for Cultural Freedom transferred Melvin J. Lasky, the brilliant editor of the most senior of their magazines, Der Monat, *to* Encounter.

Being the literary editor of a magazine that is political as well as literary is always frustrating because the political, which is immediate, tends to push out the literary which, being supposedly immortal, can in the view of the political editor wait upon eternity. I found myself rejecting contributions that I liked because I could not face postponing their publication indefinitely.

In March 1956 I attended a remarkable meeting held in Venice and sponsored by the European Cultural Association – the first of its kind, I think, since de-Stalinization – between Soviet and Western European intellectuals. The Russians were very weakly represented by the feeble and ineffective Fedin, a dear old museum director from Leningrad called Alpatov, and a third man whom Ignazio Silone immediately denounced as a police agent supervising the other two, and asked that he should leave. The Polish representative was Jaroslav Iwaszkiewicz, an immensely intelligent, profoundly cynical novelist, a kind of Polish André Gide. Two of the French representatives were Jean-Paul Sartre and Merleau-Ponty. The debates were quickly reduced to absurdity by Jean-Paul Sartre putting forward the view that discussion between the Russians and ourselves was meaningless because we were inhabitants of incommunicable ideological worlds. They talked out of the context of their proletarian culture, we out of the context of our bourgeois one, and so deeply conditioned was each in its particular way of thinking that there could be no communication between these opposites. Merleau-Ponty protested that while in the main agreeing with Sartre, he did think that certain thoughts could pass like smuggled letters à travers the ideological impasse, allowing an occasional message to get through. While Sartre and Merleau-Ponty argued about this, the two old Russian survivors of the Stalinist system sat helplessly by, not a proletarian thought in their heads, occasionally murmuring how grateful they were to be in Venice, though dutifully regretting that it was not the playground of the proletariat, as a Russian Venice would be. I wrote a satiric novella about this meeting, Engaged in Writing *(1958).*

In 1956 we were lent the Red Brick Cottage, which was in the garden of Bruern Abbey in Oxfordshire, the home of Michael Astor, who had become a great friend. We spent weekends and school holidays there until the early sixties. It was a beautiful and peaceful place in which to work, and to enjoy life with the family.

In early 1957 I went to India, and in the summer of that year I attended the International PEN Conference in Tokyo as guest, together with Angus

Wilson, of the Japanese PEN. After the conference was over, Alberto Moravia, Angus, a Japanese friend of mine called Masao and I travelled for a week together. At the conference I had met another Japanese friend, Shozo, who was later to become my translator. I longed to return to Japan, and did so in 1958, partly to lecture for the CCF and partly as a freelance, travelling all over the country and paying my way by giving lectures. The fees were so small that sometimes I had to lecture two or three times a day. Shozo accompanied me, acting as my interpreter.

In 1959 I took six months' leave from Encounter, *in order to fulfil the appointment as the Beckmann Professor at the Berkeley Campus of the University of California. Natasha, Matthew (aged 13) and Lizzie (aged 8½) were with me.*

4

Journal
1954-8

1954

30 August / *Paris–Rome*

Lunch in Paris with Denis de Rougemont* and François Bondy.† 'I have the idea of writing a travel book in the third person.' Denis: 'You will be the first person to do that since Julius Caesar.'

Flew from Paris to Rome.

Grey as lead slate and nothing to be seen until suddenly there was a clearing in the clouds and the cabin was filled with light from the Lake of Geneva. At the far end of the lake, above Montreux, the landscape was lost in dull grey cloud, until high above this there were the peaks of snow mountains, as though drawn on white paper, a montage on a grey paper.

Crossing the Alps – the Dents du Midi do look incredibly like teeth – like great white molars stuck up there.

Just on the edge of Italy, high up in the Alps, a little lake like a peacock's feather with a concrete dam at one end, looking from the air like the ivory fastening at the bottom of a fan.

The Italian side of the Alps always seems like a sloping southern garden in which roofs and towers ripen like peaches.

Douceur de vivre – one thinks looking down from the aeroplane on Italy – inseparable from the idea that it is the dead who have made this for us. We will soon belong to that which is most empty about it – the mere fact of its being of the past. This kind of happiness is inseparable from unhappiness.

In Rome, the lines of aeroplanes at the airport, seen against a background of hills, are like diagrams scratched upon the surface of those age-long textures.

---

* Author of *Passion and Society*.

† Swiss journalist, at this time editor of *Preuves*, the magazine in Paris of the Congress for Cultural Freedom.

Rome–Athens

Eating a luxurious and rather hasty meal 10,000 feet up, one has the real feeling of modern travel. That the travellers are on stilts and going at speeds which have no relation to those on the ground. Inflated balloons, stuck-up giants poised above crawling, microscopic flies, we are.

Society

Most members of high society are easily influenced people, too intimidated to challenge the rules.

Whoever cannot change the hidden gold of his most intimate life into its currency of gossip insults society.

Whoever is deeply interested in some topic which he either talks about or else is withdrawn about, is, socially, a bore.

All subjects like illness, death, and religion, are excluded unless (as sometimes happens, through a great *tour de force*) they can be made amusing, and a little shocking. A, describing the cremation of his third wife.

But society serves an ideal, which is exactly that of transforming our private lives into the terms of its own circle. If hard, it has no place for self-pity. It has its own standards.

In fact, society may be the one true survival of a classical way of life in the modern world. For all society is basically the same, putting names before everything else, hostile to seriousness, hard, glittering, sacrificial. Its great merit is that of being external and objective, as though all its members had transformed themselves into the styles of a fashion display. The aim is the show.

It fights the tendency to be subjective, though it sacrifices everything else to this, it does create a style.

3 September

In Rome I spoke about the idea that the freedom exercised by an artist could be reduced to the element in his work of his individuality, where his lines are the objective truth yet are subjective and unique to him. I said that in music tune is line, so that when composers were disciplined by society for not using tunes in their music, they were being attacked for their 'lines'.

Nicky (Nabokov), acting on behalf of the Congress for Cultural

Freedom, met some composers and asked them how they could be helped in their work. He offered to have their scores read abroad, and said that those approved by the committee would be performed. He said that he would have composers' transparent paper sent to them.

I realized again at Beirut, when I met our Lebanese representative, that what the Congress should do is help intellectuals in a practical way, give them materials, make it possible for them to form associations if they need these, help them to publish.

Aeroplane: Beirut to Karachi

Little boys and girls rush up and down the gangway between the seats, waving their arms like trapped butterflies.

4 September / Singapore

At airport message from Hugh Gibb.* He came to Raffles Hotel. We went to his room at the Cockpit. Far from being the playboy he is in London, Hugh is very much the on-the-spot journalist here. He told me some interesting things. All the Chinese in Singapore want an English education, but we cannot provide this. We are making a great effort to build 129 new schools. This seems an incredible figure. On the other hand, the Chinese have a competing policy of inviting back the 'foreign Chinese' and then sending a percentage of these back (on their British passports) as trained communists to Singapore.

6 September / En route Djakabor-Darwin

Islands which remind me of 'on the coast of Coromandel'. From the air I noticed one with a little headland of cliff covered with jungle, this island surrounded by a bright yellow ribbon of sand. On one side a bay with surf pinned to the sand, seeming not to move, on the other, a cove with only a very thin line of surf and the sand a colour like pale raw wood, under the transparent water. The island, seen through flocks of cotton-wool clouds, seemed suspended in space where sky and sea were a single blue. What shells one imagines on the beaches, what natives, what life!

'Boys innocent as strawberries' Thomas; 'Adagios of islands' Hart Crane; 'Emily-coloured primulas' Edith Sitwell; I had an interesting conversation about these phrases with a young don at Sydney

---

* Family friend, brother-in-law of Margaret Spender. At this time working on films on the Far East, some with Tom Harrison, the anthropologist.

University. They are within the writer's memory, but not exact. They *appeal* from poet to reader rather than communicate: appealing in the hope that they will light up a similar memory in his mind. They are rhetorical, not precise in effect.

The countries of prose and the countries of poetry: this contrast struck me the moment I arrived in Darwin.

For entrance into the countries of poetry, you would not be ashamed to have 'poet' or even (for some countries) 'dervish' or 'astrologer' written in your passport. There is a poem by Rilke, in which he calls a beggar standing on the Pont du Carousel in Paris the centre of the universe around whom everyone and everything flows; this interpretation of a social reality would not do in the Anglo-Saxon countries, which are – supremely – the countries of prose, where poets *qua* poets are simply outsiders. For a century or so poets accepted this situation, rather proud to be outsiders – dressing differently, saying things like: 'Vex not thou the poet's mind/With thy shallow wit.' They had their status – calfbound editions, and the best of them became a kind of pseudo-aristocracy. Alfred, Lord Tennyson.

But only recently have the poets really re-established themselves in the countries of prose, and they have done this by a very interesting trick. They have pretended to be analysts dissecting contemporary life with their special symbolic method. Since this requires some justification, they have enlisted criticism on their side, often writing for themselves the criticism which establishes the credentials of their poetry. Criticism is the prose analysis of poetic analysis of life. It explains what the symbols mean. Modern criticism can say a great deal about analytic poetry, which deals in ideas, but nothing to any purpose about a Walter de la Mare or a W. H. Davies.

But the poets are even cleverer than this. They not only produce an analytic product which can be analysed, they also extract from it an irreducible poetic substance. When I was an undergraduate, T. S. Eliot came to Oxford and was asked what he meant by the line: 'Three white leopards sat under a juniper tree.' He replied: 'Three white leopards sat under a juniper tree.' By this he may have meant that the three leopards symbolize nothing, or that what they symbolize is not subject to prose analysis.

In the prose countries, something is felt to have gone out of life. Hence the attraction of the 'primitive'. Hence, too, psychoanalysis is looked on hopefully because it does discover, in the subconscious, instinctual life forces which, without having to defend themselves as rational, simply exist. Still, psychology cuts both ways, because it shows that these forces can be analysed. And from the idea of analysis extends the conquest of larger and larger areas of unconscious existence by scientific consciousness.

27 October / *Kandy*

To Kandy, through a landscape of thick coconut palms, banana trees, etc. on either side of the road. Occasional openings in which we saw the paddy fields – rice like bright green stems whose tops emerge above the sheets of glassy water in which they grow. Grey, sultry sky. Oxen, little calves kneeling along the roadside where they are tethered. Villages of shops like shacks with one side opened completely on to the road. Crowds of people in their bright clothes or their brown nakedness. Then, nearer Kandy, hills surmounted by boulders upon which trees densely cluster, waving fans and plumes against the sky.

29 October / *Madras*

Managed to escape my hosts for just an hour, to write my notes.

Yesterday. Rose 5 a.m. Went to airport and caught 6.45 plane to Madras. Arrived here ten thirty. Had a moment of sheer horror when I saw a large crowd gathered beyond a barrier, armed with wreaths of flowers and posies. When I approached they burst into clapping. I forced myself to smile, and then a man, walking just behind me, stepped forward and had a wreath placed over his head.

I was met by a delegation. The men looked terribly scruffy, with dirty clothes, dishevelled grey hair, and stomachs protruding under their costume. There was a writer who looked like an Indian dressed up as E. M. Forster dressed up as an Indian in the days when Forster wore a walrus moustache. As soon as we got into the car, Mr Vasan started talking about the Indian cinema. At the hotel there was the press, asking questions only about politics. I tried to say things that dissociated me from the official policy of the Congress here. After a brief lunch, a visit to a millionaire who pays for the university. He told me that all that mattered was the English language. He looked like a mufti, or the head of a harem, with soft features, a round bald head, and endless loud soothing sentiments. Then I was whizzed off to the radio station and did a broadcast. Then I was whizzed off in rapid succession to two other places and delivered lectures to audiences utterly stupefied by the combination of heat and me. As I was, also.

We ended the day at a hotel called the Oceanic where there was a dinner of twenty different dishes vying with each other in (to me) inedibility. During this meal and in the course of the afternoon, I felt conventional feelings of disgust about Indians and India. Sometimes they sit in their robes, which look like those one is given to wear in a Turkish bath, vibrating their knees towards and away from one another. Then betel-leaf chewing – in which you twist your mouth about and from time to time reveal a great lolling carmine tongue – takes a lot of getting used to. After our dinner, we went up to the roof of our hotel, which was covered with insects the size of bats. We went downstairs to the lounge, but even here immense beetles, akin to the creature into which the young man was transformed in Kafka's *Metamorphosis*, kept flapping into the room and flopping on to the floor. One got into the sandal of a distinguished writer in Tamil.

This morning visited the Minister of Education at his house. Was received in a large dreary room with a clock like a railway clock on one wall, photos of Nehru and Gandhi pinned on other walls, and a stone floor. The only thing I liked was the stone floor.

30 October

Yesterday an even madder day. After the meeting with the Minister of Education, went to the Christian College. Made two speeches. Then was taken to the Arts College where I gave a lecture. Then was taken to a film studio where there was an immense reception – wreaths, bouquets, etc. Then to the British Council where I gave another lecture. After this dinner with pale British Council characters, putting up a brave show in the banter with which they chided their Indian guests.

31 October

Tea at 'Chitra'. Host, Narayan Swami. This turned out to be an attempted frame-up by bankers and brokers. As soon as I arrived I was handed a printed sheet with information about an institution called Democratic Research. The sheet said the purpose of this was anti-communism. At the end of the tea Narayan Swami got up, welcomed me, and asked me to make a speech about Democratic Research. I refused to let him get away with this, saying that I had never heard of

Democratic Research but felt that as an aim it was unexceptionable provided it was objective and did not attempt to make propaganda.

My programme involved me in spending the next two nights in trains, with numerous engagements in between. When we got to the station at Madras, two other poets who had come to see us off suddenly decided to make the same journey. We all crowded into the sleeping compartment – five of us. One of the poets, with a relaxed feminine face, and with jewelled ear-rings studded in each ear, was no sooner in the car than he produced from his pocket a version in Tamil of my poem 'Ultima Ratio Regum', which he proceeded to chant in the voice of a watchman from a muezzin tower. When he had finished he repeated the performance, this time with pauses so that the second poet, who had eager eyes behind spectacles with heavy black rims, could translate it from Tamil back into English. An English poem of about twenty-four lines had come out in Tamil as one of the longer border ballads.

The night passed in this way. After a time the sheer kindness of their intentions and their solicitousness made me enjoy it.

Chidambaram. Lectured to about 2,000 students through the buzz of their conversation. Returned by night to Madras. Flew to Cochin. There I was met by a bevy of six altogether charming students who carried me right through the day. The head of the Jewish community showed me the synagogue.

2 November / *Cochin*

Poems are statements, more or less simple, but with everything in the poem related to the core of statement.

Art is the objective function of using devices to realize the statement in rhythm, imagery, etc. When we say 'artless' we mean that occasionally, without art, or without apparent art, an artistic, i.e. made-with-objective-artistic-tools effect has been produced. The statement should arise from unconscious depths, the art can be as deliberate and conscious as is required.

2 and 3 November / *Trivandrum*

Arrived here supposedly for one day, but found I was completely fixed up with a programme for two days.

My guide here is a lean dyspeptic young man who chews some fibrous stuff which he carries round wrapped up in little papers. He decided, without consulting me, that we must go down to the Cape and spend the night there. We left after my lecture, arrived about ten forty-five, spent a very restless night in a room which was like a lounge in the hotel, open on all sides, got up at dawn, and then drove straight back to Trivandrum where I had to address two girls' schools. This is the kind of crazy arrangement people make for you here. The country – which I could see coming back today – was lovely. Near the Cape, palm trees standing so tall and separately in the fields, with behind them odd-looking volcanic mountains, the shape of pine cones. Flat sheets of water everywhere, wooden villages, oxen, and all those endless processions of people who trail along Indian roads.

Question from a young university lecturer: 'After the God that failed, did you find the God that succeeded?' No.

Went to a ceremony near the Maharaja's palace outside the temple. We sat on the roof of a small one-storey lodge in front of a house which, I suppose, was part of the palace. We looked down on to the road immediately below us, where, to our left there was a platform with, at the back of it, a screen of branches and leaves. My neighbour explained to me that this shrubbery was supposedly inhabited by an evil spirit and that the Maharaja would emerge in a procession from his palace and then shoot it. Until he did so no one must make any noise in case the evil spirit should be forewarned and try to escape.

Soldiers stood on guard, some of them carrying pennons, some shields and spears, and some in modern battledress. One elephant, his back covered with a great red cloth on which two ebony servants sat, and with a rattling chain tied to one leg, sauntered along the road and turned into the temple.

The scene was lit up by torches held by soldiers posted at intervals along the road. Before the processions began, some men below us dipped the ends of their three-branched torches into oil and then lit them, so that the screen of leaves on the platform was illuminated. Just as this happened, those of us who were on the lodge roof stood up for the Maharaja's mother and her three daughters who joined us to watch the procession. The three daughters, the oldest about 25 and the youngest about 11, were very pretty. They wore gold necklaces with large rough jewels in them. The Maharaja's mother was very Queen Motherly and made agreeable conversation with me about the weather.

Then the procession, which was a great muddle of white and

coloured uniforms, emerged from the palace. With all its colours bristling in the light it looked like a peacock's tail dragged along the ground, and we waited for it to unfold and reveal more splendours. Meanwhile, a few priest-like figures waited rather nervously near the evil spirit's altar. The procession below us now stopped, with three or four men who were in front holding up what looked like golden screens. A trim figure, dressed in a white gown, stepped out and walked forward in a curious crab-like sideways manner towards the altar, looking up at the royal family as he did so. He almost ran forward to the leaf screen where one of the priest figures offered him a bow. He then stooped down and, holding the bow about six inches away from an unripe green coconut, which the Evil One was supposed to inhabit, he transfixed it with an arrow. At this a cry went up, and the Maharaja (who reminded me of the Dauphin in G. B. Shaw's *St Joan*) trotted off, moving in the same sidelong way towards the temple.

When the procession had disappeared into the temple, the soldiers who had been holding the crowd back from the ceremony let go, and hundreds of children leapt with whoops and yells towards the screen, tearing off leaves and branches which they took home as treasured sacred relics.

4 November / *Bangalore*

In the morning lectured on T. S. Eliot to honours students at Trivandrum. After this flew across a landscape at first flat green plains, then wooded mountain, to Bangalore. Lectured. Dined with Mr and Mrs British Council. When I returned home at ten thirty the streets were completely empty. No one but a policeman going round in a little three-wheeled yellow car. The air here is cool and dry and pleasant.

7 November / *Bombay*

Arrived yesterday. Quiet afternoon. At dinner, met with the boy poet Dom Moraes.* Aged 16, dark, thin, silent, absorbed, with long lean hands clutched together over his bony knees, cutting into the arms like knives, a sudden frank, luminous, most excellent smile.

8 November

At lunch found myself at table with six women, none of them attractive

---

*Indian writer, who subsequently wrote, in English, volumes of poems and an interesting memoir, *My Son's Father*.

and two of them immense. They all gulped down quantities of vegetarian diet (which included baked eggs) taking up their plates and going to the table where there were dishes to refuel. The mountainous woman next to me with pagoda-like ear-rings and a great belt of flowers in her hair, while devouring rice, told me that she was a film censor. 'They are always trying to get away with things,' she said with a voluptuous shudder. 'I wouldn't like to tell you of the things I have cut out.'

9 November

Dom Moraes came to breakfast. He is extremely advanced in every way. The awful embarrassment of having a mind of 20 or 30 when you are 16. We went through his poems, which are very good. I made one or two suggestions about rhythm and language. He listened attentively but said something which showed he is so much inside his own poems he cannot get outside them. He talks about stories he wrote when he was 11 or 12 just as an older writer might speak of his work five years ago. He asked if I remembered going to his father's house in 1952. I remembered the occasion, but not meeting him. 'I asked for your autograph,' he said. Then he added: 'I was watching you, leaning forward with my face cupped in my hands, and then I noticed that you were in the same attitude. I thought, how curious that the only two people who are poets in this room should sit leaning forward with their faces cupped in their hands.'

14 November

Since my last entry have been to Poona where I gave two lectures. Spent the night in a dirty room in the Poona hotel. Lovely country, with canyons, and then the plain with the river flowing through it.

On the 12th went to see Manipura dancers. A boy who did a dance while playing a drum strung horizontally in front of him was wonderful because his movements were so rapid and complicated. The women were very slow. The extreme length of Indian performances is boring. And the women's dancing – though they do all these things with their hands – is flatfooted.

What was much more interesting was hearing the poets recite their own poems yesterday. Of course I could not understand the meaning of the poems, but the recitations had that kind of unity and intensity which make a performance wonderful. The listeners, a group of writers

I had addressed, showed their approval by saying wah! (bravo) when they approved a phrase. When this happened, the performer made the slightest acknowledgement. At such moments, as with the short invocations of prayer which precede any performance, India has extraordinary grace. The applause was not an interruption. It was interwoven with the poet's gestures of giving out his work and taking in their reaction, like breathing in and out.

Suddenly India had become Spain, where there is just such an enthusiastic interconnection between poetry and public.

In meeting Jayaprakash Narayan,* what most struck me was that he did not pretend that the Boodah movement was irresistible, attractive or easy. In fact he stressed most of all the difficulty of it. Ultimately its success – he said – depended on voluntary workers and there were not as many of these as when Gandhi was living, and it was dishonourable for young men to go into British Government service. The actual distribution of land was perhaps the most difficult part of their problem. It involved sending advisers to each village where there was land to distribute and spending at least a week helping the villagers to arrange the distribution themselves. Sometimes the portions of land are very scattered, and the formerly landless ones will find that they have pieces of land in all sorts of different places. Then they must attempt to persuade (often unsuccessfully) other villagers to exchange and rearrange their properties. Sometimes the new landowner will discover that he has been given more than he can manage, and of course he will have reasons for wishing it to be situated in one particular place rather than another.

Thus the movement is getting round to distributing about a tenth of the land which has been pledged. And it is difficult to think of a way in which the process of redistribution can be hurried.

JN wants a form of co-operative system in which the peasants will have separate smallholdings worked independently, but will sell their produce jointly for the whole community. JN describes this scheme as modified Marxism: from each what he is able, to each according to his need.

Recently a mill-owner of Bombay had handed over a whole mill to the movement with the idea that all the profits go to the movement. 'Surely that raises the whole question of the wages paid to the worker in the mill?' I asked. 'Certainly that is a very difficult question,' said

* Leader of the Boodah movement for distributing land among the peasants.

JN, who seemed not so much weighed down by, as swimming through, difficulties. 'On the one hand we want to pay the workers the best possible wage, but on the other hand we want to make it clear to them that the profits of the concern are going to the landless peasants. Also, in present circumstances, we have to relate the wage they are paid to that which other workers in similar jobs are paid. We have to explain this to them and get them to co-operate.'

He said that he hoped the movement would spread even beyond India, though he was sure that in other countries it will have to take a different form.

When he talked his eyes wrinkled with a curious expression, which was a smile and yet not a smile. I thought a lot of this look on his face, the laughter beyond laughter. It was a look of light, the look of one who sees all the difficulties but does not let them weigh on him.

1955

18 May / *London*

Lunched with Chinese student, Tseng. He is intelligent, always laughing, rather ungainly, with something about him of a man much older. He talks all the time about painting. He told me he sympathized with the Government in China but thought it impossible for a painter or artist to work there now. He said the Government had tried to harness an idea of the remote tradition of the Past with that of a remote Future. He said that nearly all writers and artists had found it impossible to work in these conditions. They took to studies of archaeology and antiquity. He thought Chinese communism was more nationalistic than communistic and that it provided something which satisfied the people and would go on satisfying them for a long time. He has some idea that an Oriental artist like himself can connect with the European tradition through Giotto and Cézanne.

I read a great many manuscripts today. Nothing interesting. Went to an exhibition of young English painters which gives the impression that they simply have no idea what to paint, so cover large canvases with any objects in front of them.

Went to MacNeice party. Then did broadcast for French Service. Coming home found Raymond Chandler carrying on rather drunken conversation with Natasha. His point was that she was a great genius at her music and that I did not drive her enough to perform. I felt there was some truth in this and his drunken way of saying that art was the only thing worth living for seemed to throw light on what I had been feeling behind all the other things I had done the whole day.

The routine of the day, the routine of all the contributions sent in for me to read, the routine of the paintings I had seen: all this leaves one feeling completely unsatisfied.

19 May

I had lunch with a journalist from a Swedish women's newspaper who interviewed me. She asked me questions about Communism, the Labour Party and Religion. I found myself giving quite stupid, irrelevant answers such as that I thought the West had to acquire some of the religion of the East in order that it might win the war against communism. It is very easy to improvise silly theories in order to tease people, and thus to find oneself getting more and more cut off from any kind of reality.

Came home, but after a sleepless night due to drinking too much coffee, I did not do any work. Went to drinks with the Glenconners where I met Ivan Moffatt* who talked about Christopher Isherwood. The woman journalist, putting questions about religion and politics, and doing so in a quite foolish way, nevertheless made me think all the time about something quite different which I felt to be extremely important. In that way she was rather like Raymond Chandler last night when he was drunk and when saying rather stupid things in a monomaniac kind of way, he also kept on saying, 'Stephen knows quite well what I am talking about.' Reminds me of a tall young man, an American veteran, in an insane asylum for mental victims of American wars, who came up to me and said, 'We know one another very well. You know you have met me before' and I felt that I knew exactly what he meant.

20 May

Two nights ago I had a very curious hallucination, or fancy, not exactly a dream. I lay in bed and I thought, supposing that I had had an accident, that I had been unconscious and then that I had half awoken, and was either trapped in my car, or else in bed in hospital, quite out of my mind,

---

* A writer who works almost entirely on screenplays in Hollywood. Friend and colleague of Isherwood.

and that I then imagined I was in my bed at home lying awake. This fantasy became so intense that I could not see the slightest reason why it was not the reality. The fantasy became a vicious circle. In some way, this kind of hallucination is characteristic. Ever since I was quite young, I have been so conscious of time rushing past and of death approaching that often I have seemed to be living not so much in the present as in the future out of which I was looking back at myself in the present. It is as though what I was living was a memory of my own life after it was over. Another discomfiting feeling of the same kind arises often when I am in art galleries or reading about people who have lived in the past. Suddenly I think: these people are all dead, their portraits, their history, their stories are told. The fact is that they are all under the ground, and everything they have left behind them – their historic deeds, their art – only lingers on like a smell. People often talk about what is meant by history, why it has to be studied, and so on. I think it was in the National Gallery that the idea occurred to me very vividly that history is simply our way of getting to know the dead as though they were our contemporaries, and of forgetting how thoroughly dead they really are. That we should read about Charles James Fox, that we should follow his career, its ups and downs, his character, is just as much a game we play with ourselves, perhaps even more so than the game of fiction. I marvel at the historian's imagination more than at the novelist's or the poet's.

At present, my life seems to me very wasted. This simply means that I am not writing, and that I am even beginning to think of my writing as a kind of withered faculty, a muscle which has become atrophied. This is made worse by the fact that I am perfectly aware that the muscle was never in the first place fully developed. But things I do other than writing seem to take up a larger and larger place in my life. It is this that suddenly makes one feel that one is being reduced to the status of an amateur. Of course, it is rather difficult for very active people, however devoted they are to their poetry, to write poetry all their lives, and for that reason their lives get filled up with other things. Writing poetry is to spend three-quarters of one's time in a kind of controlled inactivity. It is this which makes me feel it would be much easier to be a painter or a composer than a poet. Painters can paint almost the whole time.

For a good many months now I have tried to interest myself in a writer left over from the 1930s, called A. A. is an alcoholic, and a bit mad. During the 1930s he wrote, with great rapidity, several surrealist poems which are alive and amusing. He has the moral superiority and contempt for others that goes with total concern with something that many people like him call 'life'. He is a real anti-bourgeois. He wrote an autobiography which was a perceptive account of his childhood. Unfortunately, when it got beyond childhood, it trailed off into his kind of philosophizing. He does not write well most of the time, though when he is really inspired (as happens) he has flashes of genius. On these occasions, his language does really seem to flow spontaneously out of his life and personality, without his appearing exactly to be exercising any kind of literary skill.

A. realizes that I am a sucker for him, and that we are in a peculiar moral relationship. He probably thinks that it is my vocation to understand him, and that I am failing badly in this. This gives him a certain power over me. At the same time I have never admitted to it. I treat him with reserve, acting out my role of a respectable, bourgeois, successful literary figure and editor. Yet, underneath, we know one another well. What each of us is probably looking for, in this elaborate game we play, is something that he can finally reject in the other's character. Perhaps I have at last found this, for today I discovered that while borrowing money for himself from friends, he is neglecting his wife and child. Ten minutes after I heard about this, the telephone rang and it was A. asking if I could send him money care of a poste restante, as he was being a tramp somewhere in the country – living the real life, of course. With a feeling of secret triumph I put down the receiver. A few minutes later he rang again and said we had been cut off. This gave me a certain satisfaction, because it showed that his intuition, which is very considerable, had this time failed. (Except that perhaps he did not really believe we had been cut off.) Now I explained to him that I put the receiver down on purpose because I had just heard that he did not help his wife and child, and therefore I did not wish to help him. This was really playing the role of a heavy father, a bourgeois, but with a deep moral justification, I thought. I expect A. really understands quite well that I was exercising my right to be harsh, just as he can exercise his to be pestering and tiresome. All the same, I don't see how his friends can go on supporting him indefinitely. Or I do see, rather. But like a great many other helpless people, he goes on living off others and will probably go on doing so always. The relationship of people who support other people, although they consider them to be practically hopeless, is one of conspiracy. In a world in which personal values are disappearing, this kind of conspiracy is disappearing also. A pity, really.

22 May / *Vienna*

I took the children, Natasha and Granny to Funtington* for the weekend. I left on Monday for Vienna. The children were wildly excited about the weekend. On Saturday they got up at six and came into my room at seven thirty each with a little bouquet of what they said were 'wild' flowers.

After breakfast we took them to Bosham to look at the sea. We stopped at a shop where they wanted to spend their pocket money. ('What do you want to buy?' we asked Lizzie. 'Anything,' she replied.) Matthew got out. Standing in the road, he said in a strained voice, 'Quick. Open the door. My finger is caught in it.'

He was so calm that at first I thought he was pretending. He sat in the back of the car, blood streaming from his finger, and tears in his eyes. 'Oh God, how it hurts. Oh damn, oh damn, oh damn.' We got him to the district nurse. She bandaged his finger and said he must go to hospital ... On the way he started singing hymns to forget the pain. Lizzie was very calm, obviously paying attention to Matthew at some level of her mind, tactfully serious, but getting on with her own interests. I did drawings with her in the garden of the hospital while Matthew had his hand examined, was given an anaesthetic and had part of the nail removed and X-rayed. Luckily nothing was broken.

When I got home I discovered another shock for Matthew. His tropical fish were swimming sluggishly as though the water had turned to jelly. One angel fish was flattened against the surface, another was only just moving its fins, like a sea anemone's tendrils. There it lay at the bottom of the aquarium. Someone had accidentally disconnected the electric plug and the water had got cold. Looking at this fish was like looking at Matthew's damaged finger and it brought to mind so many past episodes – his dog being run over, his canary being eaten by the cat in front of his eyes.

After working on the profile of Auden for the *New Statesman*, I got to bed at three and was up again at seven. With the result that I

---

* Funtington. The house of George Booth (1887-1971) and his family, who were friends of Natasha (and her mother) from her earliest childhood.

arrived in Vienna exhausted. Got to this hotel, lay down and slept for two hours before going to *Tristan*.

A performance of *Tristan* still seems like crossing the Alps. One wonders whether one would be able to rise to all the heights. Still more, whether the singers would be able to do so. It was well sung but the orchestra and conducting were poor, the sets undistinguished. The love duet was made soporific by the direction, but King Mark's long aria, which follows it, was poignantly nostalgic. Tristan was good in the third act. If Wagner had finished with *Tristan* he would have seemed the most original genius in the history of music. With the completion of the *Ring* he worked out his own vein and it does not seem so astonishing to us. But there is nothing in the world like the morbid poetry of *Tristan*.

26 May

In the morning I went to the Kunsthistorische Museum. There was a marvellous light, and I felt more strongly about painting than I have at any time since I went to the gallery in Melbourne. So often in galleries I seem to see nothing. Very impressed by a Guardi, *Miracle of St Hyacinth*. This picture of monks and priests rescuing other monks and priests from a shipwreck is composed almost entirely of forms that suggest the splintered wood of the broken-up ship and the jetty on which the rescuers are standing. The sea and sky are of a blue like a Cézanne. The hands of the rescuers, and also the rescued, are extended in shapes like loops or hooks; these curves are repeated throughout the picture. These extended arms are very distorted, most of them being twice as long as they would be in nature.

I had meant to go on with my long short story about the Venice meeting* but in fact I only typed out and rewrote the first chapter. However, I am not dissatisfied with this as the first chapter is in some ways the most important since it lays the foundations of the whole thing. At least two of the other chapters carry themselves, consisting mostly of reportage.

On Tuesday I lunched with Nicholas Henderson† and his wife. They are going to Chile, about which they seem quite depressed. Some weeks ago Nicholas suddenly fainted and the doctors have taken a serious view

---

* *Engaged in Writing.*

† Sir Nicholas Henderson. Then at the British Embassy in Vienna, later Ambassador in Paris and in Washington.

of his health ever since. The Foreign Office seems to think that Chile will be good for his health. The same evening (Tuesday, 22nd) I dined with the Thorbergs. Friedrich Thorberg is a journalist, Austrian by birth, but an American citizen, now returned to Vienna. He is a brilliant editor of his magazine *Forum*, which is a kind of sister magazine of *Encounter*. He is passionately anti-communist, and feels that we who live further West don't really appreciate the horrors of life behind the Iron Curtain.

On Wednesday I went to a performance of *Rosenkavalier* with Jurinac as Octavian. Reiniger was the Marschallin. The first act was good, but with the second the whole performance sank into depths of Viennese Blue Danube banality. The Sophie was in any case particularly bad, with a pointed face which she held downwards at an angle while she looked up at the audience with tilted eyes. Baron Ochs terribly overplayed the part. The stage was overcrowded with peasants and menials overacting.

Gradually the charm of Vienna influences me. (I was almost going to write 'gets me down'.) Many of the usual performances are undoubtedly excellent, especially the intimate operas at the Redouten Saal. But the atmosphere is of the second rate in everything. The people of Vienna inhabit the Old Imperial city like mice. The city was spiritually gutted when the Jewish intelligentsia left or were liquidated. The political parties have now grown so close to one another that there is no great difference between Left and Right, that is to say there are very few extremists on either side. There is almost no communism, and the fascism of Fey, Stahrenberg and such-like figures of the 1930s no longer has any representatives. It is provincial.

Vienna seems tremendously prosperous. There has been nothing like the present prosperity of Europe in my lifetime. This is a fact that is very difficult to take account of. Europe has become middle class – like us, that is to say.

27 May / *Brussels*

On Saturday afternoon I flew to Brussels to stay with Hansi.* On Sunday, there was a big party, consisting of the Prince and Princess de Lignes, the British Ambassador and his wife, the French Am-

* Baroness Lambert.

bassador, who is the son of Paul Claudel, and his Greek wife, a Mr Bentinck and his wife – both of them from London. Parties in Belgium tend to be boring, but this one was lively. Bentinck and the Ambassadors gave me a lot of advice about the Common Market – I want to run an article about it in *Encounter*. Claudel's wife talked about her husband being the son of a poet, and that she thought that it made his life extremely difficult to be in this position. There is obviously a feeling of unreality about it, like being Hamlet's father's ghost.

28 May / *London*

Got home to find a lot of work and arrangements waiting for me and I have to go to Paris and Rome on Sunday night. The effort to keep pace with my life seems to get more and more difficult, and this means that it is even more difficult to keep pace with ideas and work. Also Auden is coming to stay this week, and on Friday I have to give a lecture in Oxford. Then there's everything to do in the office.

I had a letter from the solicitors of Peter Watson asking for the addresses of Cyril (Connolly) and Sonia Brownell. I rang the solicitor and he confirmed what I had thought, that Peter had made bequests to Cyril and Sonia, but not to me. The last few months have been my first experience of living in a world in which wills suddenly count, and it is a very strange experience. Peter's is the only one I mind about, and all day I had a quite childish feeling of being very hurt, and left out. This was exaggerated by the impossibility of one's being able to do what with the living one can do, namely effect a reconciliation. It was like not receiving a letter from Peter and now knowing that I could not ever receive one. In the end, I felt that I did not want a bequest at all, but would have liked a line in his will mentioning my name.

Here is a subject for a short story: the dead conducting a campaign through their voices beyond the grave, letters left, remarks in wills, etc. Obviously people have some consciousness of this, when they announce to you that they are going to leave you something, thus preparing a kind of posthumous revenge.

Oddly enough, we have experienced this lately. Edith Sitwell, looking at Natasha a few days ago, said that she was sure that her (that is, Edith's) rings – the stones of generous size – would look very well on her fingers and therefore she intended to leave them to Natasha.* I have as it happens received two small legacies this year, one from a great-aunt whom I never knew, and one from Winifred Paine.† Both of these were useful, but neither of them meant anything emotionally. So here one has an interesting mixture of things: legacies which are just windfalls, messages or silences from the dead, and promises or threats from the living about the course of action they may or may not adopt when they are dead. A theme for Henry James.

9 June

Auden stayed with us for three days from the end of May till 2 June. The effect of returning to England to take up his professorship of poetry at Oxford is to make him revert to something like his under-graduate manner. He was entirely absorbed in his hopes and fears about Oxford. His conversation was mostly of the Senior Common Room at Christ Church, the problems caused by his not being allowed as an American citizen to take a job in England, and other such difficulties. One notices how he becomes completely absorbed in his own preoccupations, and hardly gets outside them. For example, pre-viously when he has been here he has been very nice to the children. This time they might just as well not have been there. When he is anxious like this, conversation consists largely in his waiting for an opening for him to hold forth on some topic. On the other hand, when he is on a congenial subject, or when he heeds some other point of view than his own, he becomes his old self. He was very helpful about the profile of him I wrote for the *New Statesman*, while at the same time maintaining an attitude of almost supercilious indifference to it. This is humanly hypocritical, since I am pretty sure that he takes a great deal of interest in his publicity and how he affects other people.

To see Auden reading something like this profile or any passage of a book one shows him is disconcerting. He reads at an enormous pace, grunting from time to time. He appears to take in at a glance the general tenor of the piece, and then to look for points that he approves or disapproves. There seems no room for any appreciation of shade or nuance that he has not already anticipated from the written.

We gave a dinner party for him at which there were Elizabeth

* She did not do so.

† An old friend who looked after my sister, younger brother and myself when we were adolescents.

Glenconner,* David Jones, Francis Bacon, Sonia Orwell, and Osbert Sitwell, whose illness – Parkinson's disease – is by now far advanced. He shakes so much that one cannot avoid noticing it all the time. When Osbert had gone (he left early) Auden remarked that the thing he hoped most for Osbert was that he should die very soon. This is understandable, yet like a lot of things Auden wishes for others, it seems a little too sensibly final. There is no margin for the possibility that Osbert may want to go on living, even under worsening circumstances. During dinner, Auden annoyed Francis by declaring that X was a crook. 'He just isn't straight about money, and I don't approve.' Here again he was right, but his dogmatic manner showed no realization of the feelings of Francis, who happens to be fond of X. Afterwards, when they had argued about it, he admitted that he liked X but the admission had the same quality of filing X into some category of approval or disapproval as the criticism. It was really one of those strangely unsatisfactory controversies between the prigs and the anti-prigs, in which both sides are both in the right and in the wrong, one through being very moralistic, the other amoralistic – and both being so on principle.

We gave a luncheon for Auden and the Austrian Ambassador and his wife, at the ICA [Institute of Contemporary Arts]. Auden and I were due to leave for Oxford afterwards. For some reason, he was determined that we should leave precisely at three. This was quite unnecessary as we did not have to be at Oxford until six. However, at about a quarter to three he started looking ostentatiously at his watch. At the same time he took no more interest in the conversation, evidently feeling that so far as he was concerned, the social occasion was at an end.

Driving to Oxford, he was amiable again. He told me he loved driving, but it also made him impatient, as he secretly felt that when he drove the roads ought to be cleared of all other traffic. He said that he associated driving a car with being an engine driver, so he passionately wanted a completely clear run in which green lights signalled him right through. We talked about Christopher Isherwood. I asked him whether he thought that Isherwood had any sense of having failed in his vocation as a writer, or any bad conscience about having abandoned it.† We speculated about how Christopher would answer such

* Wife of Lord Glenconner.

† At this time Isherwood was writing in Hollywood and for long had published no fiction.

a question. He would say that of course it was exactly the question that troubled him most, that he never thought of anything else, that he lay awake at night aware that he was wasting his talents in Holly-wood, etc., etc. But at the end of all these explanations, one would feel that he had somehow evaded the question. Auden said: 'After all, perhaps the truth of the matter is that what Christopher likes is lying in the sun in California and being surrounded by boys also lying in the sun. Maybe this is all he really wants from life.' He said he had never known anyone who had grown out of his past interests less than Christopher. He said that Christopher often hurt his older friends deeply by his neglect of them.

When we got to Oxford, Auden seemed quite unwilling to let me go, and wanted us to breakfast together next morning. This we did. He has a room in Christ Church, belonging to an elderly don, whose walls are covered with photographs and reproductions of the world's masterpieces: the Parthenon, the *Venus de Milo*, Renaissance pictures, and so on. The rooms are depressing. I think that Auden has a hard time in the Common Room at Christ Church, where several of the dons twit him about his being an American. He is half fascinated, but also half bored by the endlessly cliquey donnish con-versation. He was due to have dinner that night with Maurice Bowra, who was the chief supporter of his opponent Harold Nicolson for the Poetry Chair. Maurice, as it turned out, did not give a party for him, but simply invited him to the High Table. This seems a studied insult.

I was at Oxford because I had undertaken to speak to the Spanish Club. They had persuaded me that I had something interesting to say about Spain, but an hour before speaking I discovered that my mem-ories of Spain, from over twenty years ago, were extremely vague. However, I thought that I would be able to speak about the Spanish Civil War. This hope was somewhat damped by having dinner with the Secretary of the Club who explained to me that most of its mem-bers were supporters of Franco. After all these years, this confession still has the power to disgust me. The Secretary had a conventional fascist face: thin nose, a lip that seemed waiting for a small bristly moustache to sprout, a small mouth, and ears protruding from each side of his head like the handles of a jug. In my speech I explained that I knew only the Republican part of Spain. I talked about the Spanish poets I had met, and about translating Lorca. A Spanish don from Queen's College got up and said that if I supposed that all the members of the society were pro-Franco I was wrong.

On the way back to my hotel I encountered John Sparrow and Alan Pryce-Jones, about to enter the Warden's lodge at All Souls. They took me in for a drink and we sat up till 2 a.m. John started reading Maurice Bowra's poems. These, about our common friends, were brilliant parodies of contemporary style, from A. E. Housman and Thomas Hardy to *The Waste Land*. Many were scabrous and obscene. They showed a genius which I would not have suspected for M, dazzling as he is. That someone in his position should have written these poems, that they should be circulated and read by his friends, that he should have given them to the wife of the editor of a great newspaper, and that they should actually be known to members of the Cabinet, is amazing.

Rome

From Monday to Friday, 11–16 June, I was in Rome, for a meeting of editors.

At first I was rather bored with the idea of being in Rome and having to attend committee meetings. But somehow Rome permeated through the routine. One cannot take the smallest walk or taxi ride across the city without coming upon something – a church, a fountain, a statue – which seems to be an axle round which the whole of Rome turns. It is perhaps the Piranesi engravings which make me feel that every monument in Rome is one picture in a unique gallery, which reflects all the other such images. I have visited Rome fleetingly and infrequently over a number of years, but one takes up each visit at exactly the same point where one left off, and gradually constructs a complete picture of Rome in one's mind.

I managed to spend one morning at the Baths of Diocletian, looking mostly at Greek sculpture, and I went twice after midnight to the Coliseum. I have come to like the Coliseum at this hour better than at any other. From below, with the light shining on the interior of the walls, it is so vast; the windows in the tiered walls are like the entrances to an immense cavern. One looks across the great space in the building, in which lights glimmer. To enter the Coliseum at night one has to pass through a throat of pitch darkness at the entrance, before one stands in the arena. Below there are the catacombs, like tank traps.

16 June

I am interested in the different views of two different people of a third person: Auden, for example, in the minds of Stuart Hampshire and Lucian Freud – because I do not believe one ever understands the real person. All one sees is some facet of what someone else sees. The planes of the different facets suggest that one might project lines at right-angles from the planes, to reach a centre. Behind every explanation of a person's conduct there is always a 'Why?' The truth behind Auden's seeing everything in categories is that he does so for a reason: and the reason lies at the centre of his invisible existence. For instance, I myself often behave weakly. I am not strong because there is a reason for avoiding strength. Therefore anyone who described me in terms of examples of weakness of behaviour would produce a convincing portrait but he would leave out the essential fact that I might have acted in a dozen different ways from the particular one in which I do act, which is held characteristic of me. What is called the role.

Thus it always annoys me that novelists so often appear to believe in the consistency of their characters. When I see a novelist giving an exact portrayal of the behaviour of a person whom I happen to know – like Angus Wilson's portrait of Sonia Orwell* – I feel that he only sees Sonia in the role which she has cast for herself or which has been cast for her by her conditions. Sometimes I doubt even whether any such thing as character exists at all. Everyone is, as it were, completely amorphous but choosing at different moments to fit his action into certain forms. Every time a miser is mean he knows that he is choosing to be mean. He also knows that he could stop being mean. There is in his circumstances and in his conditioning something that perhaps makes it impossible for him in fact to stop being mean. Nevertheless he feels capable of this choice and the consciousness which is aware of choosing is the real self. Angus seems to think that there is something about his characters that can be judged success or failure by external criteria of judgement. This also seems to me wrong. I doubt whether we have any criteria at all whereby we can decide whether our lives are successful or failures. The concept of success really should not be applied to people. If anyone could decide it, it would be God, and presumably God would not think in terms of success or failure. One

---

* I unfairly assume here that Angus Wilson portrays Sonia Orwell in his brilliant and witty novel, *Anglo-Saxon Attitudes*.

does know of course that one has failed in particular instances. Perhaps, even, one's failure might seem tragic to oneself or others. But all this still does not prove that one has been a failure. For who makes this judgement? These disasters may have been necessary for one's fulfilment. Even the term fulfilment smacks too much of the idea of success.

1 July / *London*

I saw Augustus John tonight about the drawings he has done for his *Encounter* article on gypsies. I called on him at 14 Percy Street where he occupies the flat of his daughter Poppet. He had left all the doors open so I went right upstairs to find him sitting in a room all alone at a desk. I took him out to dinner at the Queen's restaurant in Sloane Square. He seemed relieved when I told him I had my car and I could drive him there. He said he hated dining in restaurants where he was not familiar with the waiters. He said several things which seemed to show that he did not feel at all at home in today's world. He said he hated London, and he hated where he lived in Hampshire. He also said several times that he hated settling down, and that he was thinking of leaving his family. We talked about Wyndham Lewis and he told me that when Wyndham Lewis went blind, he sent him a telegram imploring him above all not to give up his criticism of art. When he told me this I very nearly burst out laughing. It seemed such an ironic message to send. He was very fierce against communists and told me that one of his daughters had married a communist doctor with whom he could not bear to be in the same room. At the same time he seemed to have some strange ideas about Americans. He told me he could not tolerate the way they bombed Indian villages. He looked quite magnificent with his mane of hair and his filbert-shaped beard. At about ten I got up to go, but he said that he could not go to bed at that hour and he seemed very unwilling to break up the party.

I waited a further half-hour, and then explained that I simply had to work that evening. He talked quite cuttingly about his son, Henry, who had become a Jesuit and then left the Order. Henry John died as the result of a bathing accident.

12 July / *London*

Went yesterday to Oxford, at the invitation of a club called the Mermaid. The guests were Auden and myself. Our hosts were six or eight undergraduates. We first of all had drinks at New College in the rooms of an undergraduate who had also invited Jean Cocteau who was coming to Oxford to get his degree. We then went to a cellar-like room in Christ Church, where we dined. The dinner was rather late, and Auden as usual complained that he was getting hungry. I sat next to a tiresomely effeminate young undergraduate who wore a cloak lined with red satin and carried a cane. He talked in a camp way about his fiancée. There was a young Welsh tutor who made a set first at Auden and then at me in a Welsh way. At dinner, Auden was complaining about the extremely officious way the British authorities behaved to him with regard to his permission to work here. He talked in his usual categorical way, which is sometimes agreeable, sometimes illuminating, sometimes brilliant, sometimes funny, sometimes irritating. We talked about the question of whether or not, morally speaking, Dylan Thomas had committed suicide, Auden saying that he had done so. He then made a curious assertion that he had been able to tell exactly which of his preparatory school pupils would be killed in the war.* He even went so far as to say that in the cases of two sets of twins, he knew which twin of each set was doomed to die. Another odd thing he said was that Americans in their approach to biography demanded, and were right to demand, to know exactly what happened in people's lives. As Auden hates people to write about his life, I found this puzzling.

Before going to Oxford, I had lunch with Dom Moraes who was shy, concerned with whether or not I liked his poetry or thought he was a good poet, and was preoccupied with his own problems as always. While we were lunching, Lucian Freud arrived in the restaurant, the Perroquet, with his friend Charlie. They were both dressed like workmen, Charlie almost in rags, without ties. The restaurant was appropriately shocked. I thought: this is part of the war of the bohemians against the bureaucrats. Lucian is trying to demonstrate that I, in my dark suit, am a bureaucrat. However, he was amiable and gave me an article by Augustus John to publish in *Encounter*. He spoke unhappily about Auden, said Auden did not approve of him, but was in no position to judge his affairs, and that he does not want to have to justify himself. He told me that Auden complained about him, Lucian, now, but that after the war, when he came back to London, he had complained to Lucian about me, and had said there was no one in England he wished to see except him, Lucian.

*Auden taught at Larchfield Academy, Helensburgh, 1930-2, and at The Downs School, Colwall, 1932-5.

The attitude of the Oxford dons towards Auden fascinates me. What with Auden and Jean Cocteau, there is a kind of love affair going on between professors and poets. It seems to me bound to end in tears, that is to say by the poets writing nasty things about the professors despising the poets because they don't know anything. Stuart Hampshire thinks Auden inspired, a good poet, intelligent, but often, in what Auden himself believes to be his most serious opinions, frivolous. He thinks that Auden longs to be admired by the undergraduates, but that he feels awkward and shy at Oxford. He said his inaugural speech was partly very good, but in some ways false. He thought that the quotations which Auden introduced from Charles Williams were absolute nonsense. He said that Auden ended his inaugural by reciting magnificently a poem of Thomas Hardy (entitled 'Afterwards').

Cocteau was given a garden party at the French Institute. He explained to me that he had his red gown cut long enough to come down to his feet. He said he was painting some murals, and that Picasso was assisting and guiding him. Like Auden at Oxford, Cocteau also seemed uneasy and filled with a desire to please. Apparently he did not always succeed in doing so. Enid Starkie, for instance, asked him to a cocktail party where there was a don, a dour Scot, who simply observed, 'utter rot', 'complete nonsense', and 'it simply isn't true' to everything Cocteau said.

Dreamed all night about Peter (Watson), conscious of wanting to go on dreaming in order to have more time with him. He said he had wanted to give me something, and he gave me an oil painting by Jean Cocteau. The painting was inscribed by Jean to Peter and had a quotation from Keats. In the dream, I remember thinking that Jean did not do oil paintings, and also the quotation from Keats showed a French lack of understanding of Keats.

Now everything connects! On Sunday, on the *Brains Trust* programme on TV there had been a discussion of Keats's line: 'Beauty is truth, truth beauty.' Yesterday George Harris came into my office and said: 'Peter, I just can't get over Peter.' Harris is the little man who goes from stall to stall promoting the sale of *Encounter*. We employed him on *Horizon* and he became part of the life there. Harris told me Peter had invited him, only a day before he read about his death, up to his flat to hear his new gramophone. No one of us except Peter would have dreamed of inviting Harris to his home. How discomfiting the memory of Peter is, something like a reproach. Partly, no doubt, because he was like that: quite unsnobbish, completely generous, quite unvulgar.

What also connects is this very feeling of discomfiture. I think this is really due to my having done no work recently. Work is really the only drug that appeases. Although, at the same time, I admire people less for working than I did. The great workers, T. S. Eliot, Auden, seem to me more and more unsatisfactory as people. As one grows older one feels about one's friends that one wants them to be complete people, not specialized. Nevertheless, it is the workers whom I envy. Yesterday I had further cause for discomfiture. I had drinks with Sally and Paddy Kavanagh* and Paddy said that the profile of Auden in the *New Statesman* was characteristically like all profiles in the *New Statesman*. I laughed and said that I had written it. We were all embarrassed, but Paddy's statement suggested all sorts of lines of thought in connection with my feelings about Auden, my feelings about myself.

In August, Matthew and I were guests of Hansi Lambert on a yacht, on a Mediterranean cruise. After Corfu, we went to Corsica and then to Ischia.

2 September / *London*

Our first stop after Corsica was Ischia. The Port of Ischia is a bright fashionable resort with a harbour into which our large steam yacht could go. We got a taxi and I drove with Hansi and Lucy to Forio to see Auden. When we first called he was not at home and Giocondo, the young Italian painter who keeps house for him, told me he was on the beach, so we drove down to the Forio beach and little harbour where all the sand looks dull grey and all the houses seem to have their backs to the sea. Beyond this really rather shabby and dusty harbour of broken-down and dull hotels, there is a sprinkling of modern villas.

We did not find Auden at the beach so returned to his house in the Via Santa Lucia. Although Auden is so anti-Indian, in his surroundings he shows an indifference to appearance which reminds me of Indian writers. The ground floor of his house here consists of cellars, a disused garage, and derelict basement. Upstairs there are discoloured, damp-looking walls, and – apart from one painting by Giocondo hanging sideways on a wall – nothing higher than the tops of a few chairs. On tables are spread books, magazines, manuscripts, letters in disorder.

---

* P. J. Kavanagh, poet and novelist. Then married to Sally, daughter of Wogan Philipps and Rosamond Lehmann, who died in 1958.

Being extremely untidy myself, I have no difficulty in understanding untidiness. But the disorder of Auden's living shows an indifference to appearances which makes one think of someone blind to his surroundings. Apart from one or two paintings by friends, in all the times I have known him, Auden has never had or wanted to have a beautiful object. He has always lived in the manner of someone wishing to turn away from the things around him.*

Lucy and Hansi stayed only a few moments. Wystan and I sat talking. He told me he was doing a new libretto for *The Magic Flute*, which he has to have finished by September when it will appear on television in America. He sang snatches of it to me – very beautiful, some of the words, though, necessarily, pastiche and with many inversions. He said that the way he really would like to write would be in an idiom in which one could use phrases like 'love's lambent flame'. And he complained that to be a poet now was to attempt to write in an inevitable but almost impossible idiom. He quoted Valéry saying that if poetry did not exist no one would be able to invent today such a medium.

While we were talking, I smoked. After I had had three or four cigarettes, Wystan said: 'I only have this packet, and you are using up all my cigarettes.' Then he added rather grudgingly: 'Cigarettes are very expensive here: almost as much so as in England.' I said: 'Well I would go out and get a packet of my own, but unfortunately I have no lira.' He looked up as if he regarded this reply as inadequate, so I said: 'All the same I have one pound. If you give me the lira for it then I can buy myself a packet.' 'All right, I'll look up in the paper to find out the rate of exchange.' He looked up the exchange rates in the *New York Herald Tribune* and said: 'I'm afraid the pound is doing rather badly, my dear. I can only give you 1,700 lira for it.' We went out and changed the money and I bought a packet of Nazionale cigarettes.

This incident seems to me more an example of the 'absurd' Auden than of meanness. But if I had said: 'Now look here, Wystan, when you stayed with us six weeks ago, you drank up all our wine in the house' then we would have started on an irrelevant bickering in which he might

---

*When he was at Oxford, Auden had on a wall of his rooms a still life by his former schoolfriend, the painter Robert Medley. Later in New York he had the hand-coloured woodcut of Pythagoras leaning forward and measuring with compasses by William Blake.

very well have pointed out that in 1945 when he was with us he left more than thirteen bottles of champagne in the house over from a party he had given and that we drank the champagne. Moreover, when I asked him later whether I could not pay him for four tickets to *Rigoletto*, to which he took Hansi, Lucy and me, he would not hear of it.* All the same, not to protest, not to say anything on such an occasion, but just dumbly to go through an absurd farce seemed vaguely humiliating. I felt sure that if Christopher Isherwood had been in my place he would have objected, saying, 'Come off it, Wystan!'

6 October / *Berlin*

As Curtius declined the dedication to him of my early poems, I felt that perhaps he would not wish to see me when I was in Bonn. At first I thought it might be best not to tell him I was there. But when I got there, I realized that my reason for asking to go was that I wanted to see him and that perhaps my visit would, if he found out about it, and I had not told him, cause him pain.

So I asked a third party to telephone to Ilse and to explain to her that I thought Curtius would probably not wish to see me, but if he did wish to do so, I would like greatly to visit him.

At 9.40 a.m. the telephone rang in my hotel room and I heard Ilse's voice. She asked in German whether it was Herr Spender, and when I said yes, asked me whether I would come to tea. I explained that I had to go to Düsseldorf that afternoon, but that I could call immediately. After a moment's hesitation, she said: 'Good. Come now.'

As I walked through the Hofgarten and then the Koblenzerstrasse, I thought: 'I feel my heart lighten. I feel twenty years younger.' I realized that I had never walked down this street without a feeling of happiness when I was going to see the Curtiuses. I thought that whatever happened I should tell Curtius this. But then I thought that to say exactly the words which had come into my mind would be like acting lines I had written out for myself. But sometimes there are occasions when such thoughts should be remembered and said. And I felt that this was one of these occasions.

Still walking along the Koblenzerstrasse my next thought was that Ernst Robert had been ill and perhaps I should prepare myself to see

---

*Once, in the fifties, when Auden was staying with us at Bruern and he heard Lizzie talking a lot about horses, he suddenly produced £50 in notes from his pocket as a contribution towards buying Lizzie a horse.

him changed. But I knew there was no need for such preparation. I knew it was impossible for those whose wisdom and jokes one has shared to be inaccessible. There is no wall which cannot be penetrated by the sense of a seriousness which is also a joke.

When I got to Joachimstrasse – past the other streets I knew so well – I was a little disconcerted by the fact that I was not quite sure of the number of the house. For a long time, between 1939 and 1945, I had always thought of it as number 14. After the war I discovered this to be wrong: now I had it in my mind that the number was 16. But really it turned out to be 18, as I discovered by seeing the bust of ERC's grandfather through his library window.*

I rang the bell and Ilse opened the door, scarcely greeting me (but she cannot really be unfriendly, she can only act the whirlwind from time to time). Inside the house, I saw Ernst Robert waiting for me at the end of the corridor. I have the impression that by the time I had walked to the end of the corridor, he was seated at his desk in his room. Here I had a slight shock although it was the shock of the expected rather than the unexpected. On the desk open in front of him were two books: one was a volume of photographic pictures of Roman busts, the other *The Golden Horizon*.†

After his illness Ernst Robert has a certain difficulty in speaking – that is he speaks rather slowly. He seemed simply to be pointing at the page, which was open on my *Rhineland Journal*. I explained it was not my fault that this had been republished, as the editor had never sent me proofs of the extract which was printed, and he had promised me that he would not put in the parts which were offensive to Curtius.

Curtius said: 'All the same, you could take a *process*.' I explained that this would really have been quite impossible. I pointed out that I had always said to everyone that I was in the wrong about the printing of the *Rhineland Journal* without Curtius's leave and that I was extremely sorry about it.

He beckoned me over and pointed out with his finger certain words: 'He was my teacher (for he was really that).'

I really did not know how he meant me to take this; whether he meant that I had been boasting or lying in saying this, or whether he realized the sense in which I had meant it as true. I said: 'But you

---

* Many years later Ilse told me that before the war the number was 14, but after the war it had been changed to 18.

† An anthology of articles from *Horizon* which included *Rhineland Journal*.

were my teacher. I merely meant that you taught me a great deal – more than anyone else.'

Then I said: 'I know I should never have published the *Rhineland Journal*, but what I do wish you to understand is that what I wrote about you was written with no malice but out of love and respect. I really wrote about you because I wanted to write about you, as I still do. I write about you because you have always preoccupied me, and you will continue to do so.'

He shrugged his shoulders and said: 'This is the barrier between us.' Then, with a great movement of his hand, he said: 'Ja ... aber ...' I had the impression that the whole of our conversation was enclosed in a parenthesis between a 'ja' and 'aber'.

I said: 'When Ilse telephoned and said I could come to see you, I felt twenty years younger. I have never walked along this road to your house without a lightening of my heart.'

He said with difficulty: 'I also ... a lightening of my heart.'

After this, the conversation became much easier. The only trouble was that as he could not speak as rapidly as he thinks, I had to put forward subjects and see whether they were those he wished to hear or talk about. I recalled the very first time we had met in Baden-Baden: I reminded him that then he had warned me against my enthusiasm for Dostoevsky and told me to read Stendhal and Flaubert, which I had done. When I said this, I hoped he would realize in what sense he had been my teacher. I said the impression I had today of Germany was of a bright new glittering haystack in which I looked in vain for a needle of genius. Was there any genius, I asked. None, he said.

We talked a little about France, and he said he saw no one to take the place of Gide or Claudel. Then he said: 'Yes, there is that art historian ...' and he fumbled for his name. 'Malraux?' I suggested. 'Yes, Malraux. He is not a good novelist. But his history of art is interesting ... Yes, he was a communist and then he was ...' 'A Gaullist?' I suggested. 'Yes, a Gaullist and now he needs another religion so he makes one from a Pantheon of Art. Aber, aber ... I don't see it.' He shrugged his shoulders again.

He got up, looked for the poems of Baudelaire and turned up the famous one on great painters. He read out the last stanza very clearly.

'You see, already Baudelaire making a religion of art.'

When he sat down again, there was a pause and I told him that I had gone with Matthew on a yacht with friends in the Mediterranean.

'You were a communist, and now you go on yachts in the Mediterranean,' he said. 'Ja . . . ja . . .'

I said that when he first knew me, my life was perhaps better because I always lived in one bedsitter, and had very few needs. But I could not have gone on living like that. I also said that I would tell him what I could not really say in public because to do so would seem like a renunciation or a denial of my own past, and this was that I have never been in any real sense a communist. Today I did not dislike and resent the communists nearly so much as during the few days when I was one. Really only a matter of a few days, because I never joined any Party cell or paid any Party dues. In fact I quarrelled with them as soon as I joined.

He annotated, or filled out our conversation with references. I spoke of Jouhandeau, and he said he had first known his work in the 1920s. 'But when one is old one is uninterested in anything which is not helpful to one, one throws away what is unnecessary or ballast – so this bores me,' he said. But he looked up Jouhandeau's name in a reference book and remarked that he was born in 1888. I mentioned the name of Arthur Calder-Marshall, who had been with me in Bonn in 1932, and from this we turned to his friend Humphry House and thence to Gerard Manley Hopkins on whom Humphry House had written an introduction to the edition of his letters. Curtius got up and took down a volume of Valery Larbaud ('a greatly neglected writer') and drew my attention to an essay of Larbaud on Dolben, a young poet who had been a friend of Bridges and Hopkins.

He gave me a copy of his essays on European literature. I asked him to inscribe it. He took up a pen from a tray of pens and pencils, none of which seemed to work very well so I gave him my ball pen. He wrote on the flyleaf. I looked at the inscription he had written. It ran:

> Für s.s.
> Für wie lang!
> ERC

I smiled and said: 'This inscription seems to look at me backwards, forwards and sideways.'

Then he said: 'I would like to give you my great book but I cannot find the English edition.'

'Give me the German one. It will be good for my German to read the original.'

So he gave it to me, this time writing on the flyleaf only, 'To SS from ERC.'

I asked him to keep my ballpoint pen. He handed it back to me saying: 'It is very precious.' I put it down on the tray, and he let it stay there.

He said that shortly they would be going to Rome. 'I cannot bear this darkness. I need light.'

Shortly after this I took my leave: saying I must go, staying a few more minutes and then going. At the door, he clasped my arm affectionately.

It was not exactly that I felt I was forgiven, but I felt that what was unforgiven could not be forgiven and that a great deal else had always been forgiven and could not be unforgiven.

9 October

I have spent the whole of the past week in Germany, lecturing for the Deutsch-Englisch Society. I went to Frankfurt, Düsseldorf, Bonn, Kiel, and Berlin. Lectured on D. H. Lawrence and George Orwell.

This society is mostly for political, scientific and economic lecturers – so I met only stuffed shirts. The audience at Frankfurt was young and lively and asked good questions. At Bonn there were the British Ambassador, and a few deputies of parliament and people of that kind. I was given a luncheon at which the Head of Chancery from the British Embassy and a Parliamentary Deputy of Bonn were the only two other guests. Of course the German parliamentarian who had been my chairman used the occasion to tell the English diplomat everything he wished the Foreign Office to know, and the English diplomat was busily occupied in getting as much information from him as possible. During the past two years I have been to seven or eight German towns. Hamburg is a jack-in-the-box which disappeared for a few years and has now reappeared, looking, as nearly as possible, as it was before.

Before the war, Bonn was a charming university town, with a very pleasant marketplace, and beautiful university buildings with a large tree-shaded lawn of the Hofburg in front. All this is now being squeezed out by monstrous buildings like packing cases on the bank of the Rhine. These great crates are only tolerable so long as they look bright and new. When the rain soaks into their surfaces, they will be as heavy, depressing and stale as Regent Street. As though every spark of genius in modern art had been extinguished and a cheap caricature of modern idea left, German architects are now building in a vulgarized modern style.

Frankfurt has been more enterprising than most other German towns. It has not gone in for the banal restoration of a recent past; nor, like Düsseldorf, does it rely on 'planning' broad streets. The new buildings on the Altemarkt are built in a style that acknowledges the manners of those traditional ones which survived well enough to be restored.

In West Berlin there is an extraordinary mixture of styles, many of them borrowed from America with little that either seems new or shows any awareness of the past. The most successful is perhaps the simple, white stone-and-glass building of the Freie Universität.

In East Berlin I found the Stalin Allee strangely impressive with its inhuman masses like immense tanks on either side of the overwide street, as though they were moving down it to answer the West in two columns. The detail is hideous, but the masses are blocked in. The total impression is made.

In reality, the Stalin Allee is coated with yellow-coloured tiles like those in a lavatory. These vast, uncompromising surfaces have the fog-absorbent quality of buildings like St Pancras or Euston station in London, which are so much of their time and purpose that they seem to realize the atmosphere of a past London of pea-soup fogs. But the atmosphere of the Stalin Allee is not past.

The Western Zone has the conventional energy and ostentatiousness of a forward-pushing enterprise. The Eastern Zone is of a uniformed army among ruins.

The Russian memorials are all uncompromisingly hideous except perhaps for the statue of a mourning Russian peasant mother seated at the base of the cemetery and cenotaph for the Russian dead in Berlin. This brutish ugliness is rather impressive. The concrete prongs which form the American memorial for the pilots of the Airlift to Berlin are simply silly. They look like an unfinished project left over from a World Fair. The idea of an arch which rises from the ground and plunges into the skies may be a good one. However, it is carried out in the wrong material – concrete. It required some transparent material or perhaps metal suggesting machines taking off or the ribbons of trails left by aeroplanes in the sky.

X. is a very prominent and obvious member of the German Jewish community. He emigrated in March 1933, coming to London where he lived for the next twelve years. With the end of the war, he volunteered for Military Government, stuffed himself into a civilian military officer's uniform and returned to the British Zone as a propagandist for democracy and freedom. He is now frequently to be met in Berlin. To his other accents he has now added an English one when he speaks German. His conversation consists of saying how he detests the Germans and how he pines for Maida Vale. He tells stories of villages in the west where Hitler's toast is drunk in Rhine wine, while the band plays the 'Horst Wessel Lied'. Wherever he goes he encounters anti-Semitism.

X. makes me nervous. I ask myself why did he ever go back to Germany if he hates it so much, and what good he imagines he is doing by being there. It seems to me that his presence, his attitude, his sayings all breed anti-Semitism. If he were told this, he doubtless would explain that the Germans after their behaviour to the Jews do not demand any consideration. If he is not received as a friend, he is perfectly prepared to be a scourge. This I understand. But it seems surprising to me the Jewish community shows so little concern about its members who go back to Germany detesting and making themselves detested.

In Berlin, at a luncheon, I met George Kennan again, whom I think to be one of the most remarkable men in American public life. Kennan has a high-domed forehead, rather bald at the top, and very light blue eyes, which look shiningly out at the world, creased at the edges almost like those of a Chinese. Everything he says expresses awareness and disquiet: and yet he has a gleam and assurance about him which are more often found in the East than in the West. He expresses ideas of disillusionment, but with an expression of passionate belief. Another guest at this lunch was an Austrian playwright and poet, who has just written a play about the Fuchs* case, who kept on relating every subject of the conversation back to the thesis of his play. I mentioned that I had attended the Fuchs case, in order to cover it for the *New York Times* magazine. I had stood in court quite near to Fuchs, and when he was sentenced and asked if he had anything to say, I was probably the only person near enough to him to hear exactly what he

---

* The nuclear physicist and spy.

did say. This was to the effect that he thought that his worst crime lay not in any secret he had betrayed, but in the betrayal of his friends in England. I said that although there was no doubt a gulf between being a member of the Communist Party and actually betraying some military secret, from the point of view of some remote future it might seem that we exaggerated the wickedness of giving away a secret to an opponent who would discover it anyway in six months, if he didn't know it already. Kennan said: 'Yes. If there is one thing we have learned from these cases, it is that loyalty is perhaps the only absolute value!'

Thus the real evil done by espionage in cases like Hiss or Fuchs may turn out to be one that has no apparent connection with the offence committed. With a spy, we know that some definite secret has been given away; yet the spy's betrayal of colleagues and friends may have some far worse result than betrayal of the secret. For instance, Hiss handed over to the communists some documents of little importance. But the result of his action was McCarthyism in America.

Kennan said that while he was in Berlin he had been to see one or two of the political cabarets performed by young people in the Western Zone. While he sympathized with the political attitudes expressed in these performances, he confessed that they made him uneasy. In one cabaret there was a scene of Japanese fishermen who apparently only wished to fish quietly and not to have atomic bombs dropped on them. 'After all,' said Kennan, 'one can wish for Japanese fishermen to be able to fish in peace, but all the same the situation is not quite as simple as all that. One cannot forget that the Japanese story began not with the atomic bomb but with Pearl Harbor, and that there is a longer history than this cabaret pretends.'

12 October / *London*

Encounter gave a party at the Ritz for William Faulkner. Faulkner looks and talks like a gentleman farmer of the South. He is very conscious of this role, and insists he has no literary friends, reads no books, but just farms and knows the people of his village in Mississippi. He was politely uncompromising, and sometimes more uncompromising than polite. However, nothing happened of the kind that I heard about in Rome when Faulkner was introduced to various Italian writers, his hostess explaining to him what books they had written, and he replied that he had never heard of any Italian writers. Perhaps this was because I was rather careful to avoid introducing anyone as a writer. In fact I had brought Burns Singer* along in order that I might introduce him in his role not of poet but of poor fisherman. This did not quite work out. BS got very drunk in a way which seemed as tiresome to Faulkner as to everyone else at the party. Faulkner refused to be illuminating about anything but answered all questions in a flat, prosaic, straightforward way. One American, from the Embassy, went up to him and asked him how he liked Japan. Faulkner replied: 'It is a beautiful country but I think one has to be born there to appreciate the Japanese people. They talk English but it is not English. The Japanese people I do not understand.' One has to say this in a Southern accent to get the full effect.

I talked at a branch of London University called Queen Mary College in the East End. The discussion that followed afterwards was mainly around one thing: which is more beautiful – a statue of Michelangelo or an aeroplane? Hence, of course – is our civilization more, or less, creative than past civilizations?

I was amazed how many of them seemed to think a jet-bomber quite as beautiful as a cathedral. They were obviously unimpressed by arguments that machinery does not last, is as subject to changes of fashion as women's hats. The argument that modern industrialism produces a hideous environment did not interest them either. Someone advanced the view that what has been done in the past has been done and we should not judge our own achievement or even present state of existence by the past at all.

1956

5 July / *Bologna*

Here are some notes that I should have written in London.

Apropos of Yeats, Auden said: 'It is possible to be too untruthful in poetry. For instance when Yeats writes, "Once out of nature I shall never take/My bodily form from any natural thing/But such a form as Grecian goldsmiths made/Of hammered gold and gold enamelling" he is being too untruthful. No one ever has wanted or could want such a thing. Besides, it is not for him to decide what will happen to him.'

*Burns Singer, a Glasgow poet. I gathered from him that he was of Polish origin, a physicist as well as a deep-sea fisherman.

19 July

From the 3rd of the month until the 8th I was in Bologna. With its arcades, its two towers built by noble families in the centre of town, its church of San Stefano, which incorporates the buildings of six churches going back to Roman times, its orange and rust colour, this city reminds me of early paintings by Chirico.

In the hard light of midday summer it tends to shrivel up. It must be most beautiful in winter when the shadows are long. At night, in summer, it is electrically mysterious, with walls like stage scenery, and people looking like their own shadows moving under the arcades.

On 8 July, I went for two days to stay with Nicolas Nabokov in his château outside Paris. It was very pleasant to be alone with him and not in the usual tangle of committees and dinners. Each morning we worked hard at the scenario for the libretto of his opera about Rasputin.* What really happened was that he dictated to me the entire action of the opera, with all the scenes, all the positionings of characters on the stage, the outlines of every piece of dialogue, from the first moment to the last. He has a concreteness of grasping an idea from start to finish, which would be genius if it went with a corresponding grasp in every note of the music. I just hope that we may create one of those strange mad Russian works in which a Russian genius who has apparently been leading a dispersed kind of life suddenly pulls himself together and writes a near masterpiece.

I returned on 9 July to London, to take part in the PEN Club conference this week. Our activities were partly to organize a poetry reading conducted at the ICA by the MacNeices – Hedli and Louis, Laurie Lee and myself. This went off quite well. Much less happy was the International PEN discussion about the technique of poetry that I had to chair at Bedford College. This began with (someone's) speech about the problems of modern poetry. They were, that the poets, being asked by the public for loaves of bread, insist on giving them stones, with the result that poetry is not popular. A fat lady from Vienna got up and said that poetry should be simple. A lady from the South of Ireland got up and said that poets should sing.

On Wednesday evening I went to dinner at Claridge's with Jack Beddington,† who had invited various guests chiefly with the idea that

---

* *Rasputin's End.*

† A banker who supported the arts. In the 1930s he took great interest in the Group Theatre.

they should become interested in *Encounter*. It was an exceedingly good meal, and Jack was an excellent host. Apart from Bill Coldstream, Michael Ayrton,* and Christiansen, the editor of the *Daily Express*, I forget who was there. Knowing that Michael Ayrton is a great enemy of *Encounter* I tried to steer him off by telling him the moment I arrived that I greatly liked a sculpture of his which I had seen in the Leicester Gallery. He was quite pleased and then I got him on to various subjects that we could more or less agree about, such as the paintings of Wyndham Lewis exhibited at the Tate Gallery. Nevertheless, at a certain point in the meal he started telling me how much he had disliked the first number of *Encounter* and saying that he had scarcely read a number since, though he did occasionally pick one up. I found it impossible not to adopt a sarcastic tone, telling him it was very kind of him to have read *Encounter* at all. Rather to Jack's distress, we began to quarrel in an animated way, and I managed to be quite unpleasant – which I do not regret at all. The quarrel was stopped by guests changing places at the table. After the brandy Michael apologized for having been rude to me, and I said that I had to admit that if there was an objective observer, he would probably say I had been just as rude. However, I did not find that I could feel at all warmly to Michael. He seems to me quite clever, competent, yet somehow coarse-grained and obtuse in all he says and does. For instance, one thing he said was that political issues today were as simple as they had been in 1930. To say this, one would either have to be exceptionally perceptive or exceptionally stupid. Politically speaking, Michael is simply a reader of newspapers, some of which he likes, others of which he dislikes. He sides with *Tribune*,† and gives himself much credit for doing so. The thing that really annoyed me was his saying that the Spanish War was a perfectly simple affair despite the reporting by 'gloomy George'. I retorted that George Orwell judged matters by the standards of his own life, which in politics were as exacting as those of a saint, and I did not see that Michael showed, in *his* life, any standards of a kind that would justify his criticism of Orwell.

At about 2 a.m., Christiansen, Michael, Beddington and I adjourned to Jack's office in Brook Street. Ayrton now told Christiansen that the

---

* Michael Ayrton, painter, sculptor and writer, a great admirer of Wyndham Lewis of whom he did a fine drawing.

† *Tribune*, weekly periodical on left wing of the Labour Party. George Orwell was once literary editor.

Daily Express was an altogether disgusting and filthy paper from beginning to end. He said this was his opinion, and if called upon to do
so he would substantiate it: however, he thought it would be boring
for the company if he did so there and then and accordingly he would
invite Christiansen to luncheon to tell him about it. Part of Michael's
stupidity was that he did not realize how incensed Christiansen was
by this kind of boorishness. For a moment, Christiansen did lose his
temper, but immediately controlled himself. I said that I could not
agree with Ayrton although as a matter of fact I myself had a grievance
against the *Express*. I told Christiansen how a *Daily Express* correspondent had extracted from me a letter from John Lehmann about
Burgess, at the time of the Burgess-Maclean scandal, and had printed
a photostat picture of a paragraph in it, contrary to his promise to
treat it as confidential. Jack said: 'I see, Stephen, that you are still as
sensitive as you always have been.' Christiansen said: 'No, as a matter
of fact he is quite right. We behaved quite improperly about this and
I would like to apologize.' [See p. 96.]

29 July / *London*

I went to Stratford, to give a lecture. With the Memorial Theatre like
a mothers' meeting hall in a garden city, the neo-Georgian gardens
along the side of the theatre, the runabouts and charabancs, the little
preserves of Ann Hathaway's cottage, Shakespeare's church, the
Memorial Theatre museum, the whole of Stratford expresses dull
piety and a tastefulness worse than bad taste. The production of *The
Merchant of Venice*, with Emlyn Williams as Shylock, showed that the
obsession with tarting things up can go too far. Fearing that the
audience would be bored, the producer had evidently decided to introduce as much distraction into the play as possible. The climax of
this kind of nonsense was reached in the scene when Bassanio chooses
the leaden casket. The court nods and winks with delight, while Bassanio, after hesitating, offers his reasons for preferring lead to gold and
silver. So the court is made to share the secret of the casket, which
was unknown to Portia's suitors. One wonders why, in this case, the
Moroccan prince and the unscrupulous French monsieur did not discover it.

From Stratford, in frightful weather (the worst rainstorms of a July
which is the rainiest on record), I drove over to Warwick, Tewkesbury
and Worcester. At Warwick on Sunday, there was a communion

service going on in St Mary's Collegiate Church when I arrived. It was performed in a conscious slightly exquisite way by a slender, beautifully robed priest. I went into the chapel where there are the tombs of the Beauchamps, serenely crowned and lying in iron repose. After a time the priest came in, and told me things about the chapel. After this, he went back into the church and talked to the choirboys about the anthem they were practising. I heard him say, '... and when you see the letter "F" written after a word, it doesn't mean "feeble".' The choir seemed amused at this: I wonder whether this was because they thought of a good many things that leap more immediately to the mind than 'feeble' which 'f' might stand for.

The spirit of Derek Blaikie was very present with me, and filled me with a feeling of nostalgia, mixed with awe. I stayed with him when he had just left Oxford (in 1934) near Tewkesbury where his family had a country house. At the time his surname was Kahn: at the request of his rather dominating mother he changed it to Blaikie (and after this, Maurice Bowra always referred to him as 'the Aga Blaikie'). At home he wore a cloth cap and thought of himself as the squire of the village. He looked slightly oriental, with his Englishness superimposed, and this made him difficult to place. He might have been some narcissistic young Florentine with an embroidered cap, painted by Botticelli. When we were at his house, he drove me all over the countryside. We looked at country houses. He was some years younger than I (perhaps three: it seemed a lot at the time), and I never dreamed of him being attracted by me. But my failure to respond to him, and perhaps the fact that I was always conscious of those defects which troubled him greatly in himself – his grating voice, his coarse large hands, his general awkwardness – made me uneasy with him. He never forgave me for something he felt I should have given him. And, as happens in such cases, I wonder now whether I forgive myself. He was my shadow in some ways, becoming a communist soon after I did, but using his more ideologically righteous communism to reproach me with. When I was in Greece once he wrote me an immense letter attacking me for caring about the Acropolis, and not about the tobacco workers of Salonika. I took to thinking of him as crude and rather stupid, a blunderer, someone for whom I felt a joking contempt. He suffered from everything, and never did anything well. At the end, he became religious, studied theology and would perhaps have become a priest, had he not been killed in the war. His end was mysterious and I have never heard any details of it. I think of him often with that strange almost physical attraction one can feel for the dead. Yet if the past were restored, and one lived the whole relationship over again, the circumstances would either repeat themselves, or perhaps lead to a future still more painful. On the other hand, if there is something about someone dead which one loves apart from the *embêtements*, then perhaps one is not wrong to cultivate the remembered affection.

1 August

Went with Lucian (Freud) to *The Family Reunion*. As Lucian pointed out, the production was not good. There is something macabre, belonging to another world, in this play which ought to be more strongly brought out. The choruses should not just be represented as a freezing up of the actors into stylized attitudes which are like a slow-motion caricature of their worldly roles. They should be a transformation of the characters into roles belonging to another dimension of existence.

Yet, I wonder whether the fault does not lie in the writing. The choruses fail because they tend just to become generalizations of the kind of life which these characters live: 'And now it is nearly time for the news/We must listen to the weather report/and the international catastrophes.' This kind of self-satire seems more a comment through the mind of the writer on the superficial lives of his characters – who fall into 'types' in the choruses – than the self-revelation by them of their inner despair.

The acting of the play tends to become desultory because the different planes on which it moves are scarcely related. Harry is pursued (a) by the conviction that he 'pushed his wife over', (b) by the Furies who are driving him to salvation. The trouble is that dramatically speaking (a) ought to be more realistic. The pursuit by the *police* should be as *actual* as that by the Furies, though the spiritual flight could be the one which matters. As it is, Harry's guilt about his conviction of himself as a murderer seems a fuss about nothing. The scene in which the policeman appears seems contrived. The idea that Harry committed a real murder is tiresome too, because it obscures another possibility which might be the real alternative theme of the play. This is the possibility that his wife died as a result of Harry's behaviour – in which case the idea of actual murder is a false issue which leads also to a false acquittal.

The trouble with the play is that whereas it sets out to contrast two kinds of reality (that in which people destroy one another, and the lonely search for religious truth), it is really loaded from the start against the reality of life lived in this world. Eliot's characters are divided into the 'real' (i.e. Aunt Agatha and Harry who know what things are about) and the 'unreal' – the mother, the uncles and aunts. What the choruses fail to show is that the uncles and aunts also have some contact with spiritual self-realization – that they are also people who suffer and can be redeemed. All the choruses really show is how, at a certain moment, the spiritually unreal realize that they are so and that their preoccupations are meaningless. This results in the look of complacent spiritual superiority which is inseparable from Aunt Agatha's face. It was not really Gwen Ffrangcon-Davies's fault that one so longed to kick her.

[Soon after the war, lunching with the American writer Harry Brown,* we found ourselves fiercely arguing as to whether Eliot's hero is supposed to have murdered his wife actually, or only in his imagination. So fiercely indeed, that we took a taxi to Russell Square and called on Eliot at Faber's to settle the matter. He puzzled us by saying that he did not think it important to know whether the murder is real or imagined.]

15 September

I am in the amenity ward of Hendon District Hospital, having at last gone through a long overdue operation for varicose veins in my right leg. I started to develop these at the age of 16, when in the school OTC [Officers' Training Corps]; my knee breeches had a clip which fastened very tight over one junction of veins, causing them to congest. When this happened I was still at the stage of thinking that my own illnesses were interesting, and calculating that they might even be useful, as I wished to be disqualified from any consequences of the OTC. I watched my veins swelling with a kind of malicious pleasure.

Four days after the operation, I am up, and tomorrow I am going home.

The Summer Holiday

The summer was spent, as usual, with the Lamberts, only this time, instead of travelling, we stayed at two of their houses, first in Le Zoute

* Writer of novels and screenplays. Author of *A Walk in the Sun*. During the war he was editor and writer for the US Forces magazine, *Yank*, stationed in London.

and then in Gstaad. The children spent the first week of their holiday at a farmhouse in Sussex run by Mrs Anderson, a very energetic lady – a kind of large child herself who writes books about children. It is a rambling, broken-down house, red-tiled, steep-eaved, of uncertain period, with a garden that seems simply a smoothed-out piece of countryside, an English paradise, at once wild and very traditional.

I picked them up at the beginning of August and drove from Battle to Dover. The following conversation occurred. Almost as soon as we had left the house, Matthew talked about a boy who had told him some rhymes which he did not think I would appreciate. Lizzie looked very mischievous and said: 'Go on, Math, tell Dad. He'll simply love them.' While she sat listening with an expression of marvelling wonder on her face, Matthew recited some of the most obscene rhymes I have ever heard. I said I thought he had better not tell these at school or there might be trouble. He said airily: 'Oh I wouldn't dream of doing that. I'm perfectly aware of it.' I felt troubled myself. However, all I did was tell him that I thought perhaps it wasn't a good thing that Lizzie should know about such things. Matthew said he quite agreed. He told me that the boy who had passed these on had learnt them when he was acting in some film or other, from the engineers. He said the boy was not going back to the farm, so I mentally resolved to mention the matter to Mrs Anderson some time, but thought that apart from this it was better to do nothing.

At Dover, in the bar of the White Cliffs Hotel, Cyril (Connolly) joined us for a drink. He said he was very anxious to come and stay with us at Gstaad but I must impress on Hansi Lambert that his relation with Barbara* was completely at an end and that he was not going to bore any of us about it. It has certainly got to the stage when having to listen about it gives one the impression of taking part in some frightful kind of collusion.

The house at Le Zoute is somewhat like a pavilion, white inside and outside, very clean and light, hung with abstract paintings by Hartmann, Ney and Poliakov. It is at the edge of an abandoned golf course, with grass growing on sandy soil, and pine trees, and near the sand dunes which front the sea. The children adored this landscape in which they could run wild, where Matthew could set up his archery and shoot arrows, and they could fly kites. When they were bored with

* Barbara Skelton.

this they could go down to the beach and dig castles, or paddle. The weather was hardly fine enough to bathe more than once or twice.

I worked at the libretto for *Rasputin*. Nicky Nabokov came over for two days and we were able to discuss it. Nicky and I went to Bruges to see the collection of Flemish paintings from English collections. We also went to Rotterdam to see the great Rembrandt exhibition.

No other exhibition of an old master has ever seemed to me to throw such a critical light on modern painting. Just to go from this exhibition to the other rooms in the Boysmans museum, where there are Impressionist and more recent paintings, is to receive a shock. Suddenly these seem thin, light, empty. Even Courbet seems pale.

No exhibition of an Italian master would produce the same disconcerting effect. I can only think it is because Rembrandt has some of the problems which are peculiarly modern, and deals with them in a way which makes later attempts seem scattered and evasive – gestures, expressions, flights, virtuosities instead of penetrations to a centre.

Rembrandt's late self-portraits are like a chord driving through all the stages of his life. They portray a figure that might well be likened to the helmsman of a ship, *der fliegende Holländer*. In the earliest portraits a figure in full sail, pennons flying triumphantly, scudding through sunlit choppy waters, acclaiming the toast of the Voyage to Happiness. At the end, the ship is a hulk, with the noble battered look of awaiting the breakers.

If one could see an exhibition consisting entirely of Rembrandt's self-portraits, one would have, I think, a sense of superimposition, as though the increasing thickness of the paint in the later work was caused by the painting of the old painter over successive layers of ever younger and younger Rembrandts.

And of course, the density of the superimposed layers of paint in these pictures which are not self-portraits, shows the same preoccupation with his own identity. Every subject is really a self-portrait. In some works the painting of the subject itself is not nearly as moving as the painting of some part, not the face of the sitter (for this reason reproductions always do Rembrandt a disservice, since they inevitably concentrate on the subject and not on the actual paint). In the portrait of Titus seated at his desk, more impressive than the face of the boy (which in photographs looks a bit like Greuze) is the density, colour, and brush strokes of the wooden front of the desk. In the wonderful family group at Brunswick it is in the texture of the mother's and child's skirts that is as moving as the painting of the skin.

Why then, after the Rembrandt exhibition, if one wanders through the galleries of modern paintings, does so much of what one sees seem superficial? The reason I think is that Rembrandt's preoccupation in his painting was the search for his own image or identity towards which his religion was an aid. The impression made by the exhibition is that he solved his problems, which are those that are still with us, by this single-minded pursuit of his ultimate self. That is why this exhibition makes later painting seem specialized (the Impressionists) or centrifugal (Picasso). Cézanne seems the one great modern example of singleness of purpose. And remembering Rembrandt's self-portrait one sees Cézanne's images of himself looking through the transparency of his landscapes.

Of course, this only expresses a mood, and very soon the relations which catch in the nets of other art will re-establish themselves, and I shall be involved again in the inventions and discoveries of modern art.

I have always felt rather badly about Gstaad, because just after the war Hansi lent the chalet to us for a month. This was a great opportunity to work, but actually neither of us did anything, or rather both of us played patience, for almost a month without stopping. As I have never played patience before or since, this seemed a rather odd vice to develop just for a month. However, Gstaad had much the same effect on me this time. I spent most of the fortnight drawing exactly the same view - the only view there was to draw - from the veranda outside my room.

The sky shines down on a landscape which consists of great green fields, very dark pine trees, and rocks. Boxed in by the valley, the effect is that of being framed in by very tall, yellow-greenish stained-glass windows which give off coloured light and heat the whole time. The quality and quantity of this light changes according to the state of the sky. I feel both shut in and unable to rest.

One question which preoccupied us a good deal was whether Cyril should come or not. From Le Zoute, I wrote him a letter saying it would be delightful to have him, but I was not going to take my car. I thought this would put him off. Hansi added to my letter an indifferent postscript, saying she was sure that he would be bored by

Gstaad. However, his telegrams continued to be persistent, so we sent two or three of our own saying that unless he brought work he would be very bored. He took this to mean that he was in disgrace with Hansi, but he still wanted to come and finally did so. The moment he arrived he said that he had his work with him, and that all he wanted was kind faces and good food. He was put in a room of a hotel a few yards from the chalet, which, as he was soon to explain, he found unconducive to work. However, for the first three or four days he was an absolute model of good behaviour: amusing, lively, and not talking about Barbara. After a week, however, his boredom began to reassert itself, and brought back all the obsessions about Barbara. He had left Barbara on the verge of getting married to George.* Cyril pretended to be interested in a detached sort of way in whether the marriage took place. Then one day a telegram arrived saying that she was going to marry George on the following day, and sent Cyril all her love. After this we were all sunk into the awful maelstrom of Barbara's and Cyril's marriages, divorces, and remarriages. Cyril telephoned her but only got on to her mother, who said Barbara was up in London marrying George. Barbara then suggested she should come out and join Cyril. He said he thought that this would be an immoral course of conduct in view of her marriage. She said that her excuse would be that her visit to Cyril was on a mission similar to that of Mr Menzies to Colonel Nasser in Cairo: to explain matters. He said this would mean her spending at least a night in Geneva and they would be compromised. At this point we all became involved in discussing where Cyril should go to console himself. Finally he and we decided on Ischia. So he rang Barbara to announce to her that he was going to Ischia. She said she was delighted, because George and she were going to spend their honeymoon there. Cyril said that if she did this he would never speak to her again. She then consented to take the honeymoon in Capri. This is more or less where we left matters at Gstaad.

What was evident was that Cyril's chief motive in his behaviour is simply dread of boredom. He was drifting back to Barbara because he had not got anyone else, and not having anyone else meant that he might have to spend days and nights alone. A kind of inertia has become so powerful that it is like a driving force with him. Or rather his inability to be anything but inert sends him from place to place,

* George Weidenfeld.

from person to person. And back to Barbara. What causes him at any given time real suffering is the failure even for a short while to be amused. Thus after a week of Gstaad, he expected us to sympathize with him for being bored by it and by us. He and I went down to Geneva to see Natasha off, who was returning to London by air, and then to stay overnight with Denis de Rougemont. The moment the train got away from Gstaad, he gave a sigh of relief, said that anywhere was wonderful compared with Gstaad, that he hated being up in the mountains more than anything, that he could not work, that he could only play Scrabble, that there was something morbid and unhealthy about our life there, and that in Geneva he could again breathe the air of French civilization. When one is with him, one realizes that most people are to some extent kept going by a sense of minute obligations. For instance, if one is invited to stay with people, and conditions are not ideal, one may still be kept going and even enjoying oneself out of a sense of gratitude. With Cyril no such sense of day-to-day obligation exists. Therefore unless he is very positively enjoying himself, that is, surrounded by all the circumstances of a children's outing or treat, he is in a state of disappointment. We did have one such treat: when Hansi took us to Berne to see the Paul Klee exhibition. But the two or three private collections we saw the next day did not come up to any of our expectations, and Cyril immediately became an object of pity to all of us.

14 November / *New York*

Two days ago, at Princeton, I saw George Kennan. He entertained the Buttingers* and myself at his pleasant frame-built house. With his very bright blue eyes he looks like some tall, fair oriental philosopher who has played football in his youth. He spoke in that manner where bitterness seems to contradict a faith that shines through his expression. He was extremely disappointed, disgusted even, by the election of Eisenhower. He could hardly bring himself to believe that Nixon could have been elected Vice-President, meaning, he pointed out, that

---

* Muriel Gardiner (Buttinger) occurs as 'Elizabeth' in my *World Within World*, where I describe our first meeting in 1934 at Mlini near Dubrovnik, and subsequently our love affair in Vienna. In her memoir *Code Name Mary* she described this and her life in Vienna doing underground work for the Austrian socialists after the *Anschluss*. She married Joseph Buttinger, one of their leaders, in 1938. After the war she worked as a psychoanalyst, and became a friend of Anna Freud. She died in 1985.

Nixon was bound to become President. Kennan said that when he turned on television, and saw the American delegation being supported by all the riff-raff of the Middle East in its denunciation of British policy in Suez, he felt that this is where he got off. People like him no longer had anything to say in American affairs. He recalled how he had felt that if Asians regarded the West as to blame for everything then it would be best for us to have nothing to do with them. His own impression was that, during the past few years, the West had been more abused and ill-treated by the East, than the other way around. Jo Buttinger mentioned Africa, and Kennan said: 'There's only one solution in Africa. That is for all the White settlers to be removed. This would be a major operation involving shifting about two million people, but if we in this country had the will and good sense, we could do it.'

The day before this, with the Buttingers, I went to lunch with Robert Oppenheimer.* Oppenheimer lives in a beautiful house, the interior of which is painted almost entirely white. He has beautiful paintings. As soon as we came in, he said: 'Now is the time to look at the van Gogh.' We went into his sitting room and saw a very fine van Gogh of a sun above a field almost entirely enclosed in shadows.

Robert Oppenheimer is one of the most extraordinary-looking men I have ever seen. He has a head like that of a very small intelligent boy, with a long back to it, reminding one of those skulls which were specially elongated by the Egyptians. His skull gives an almost egg-shell impression of fragility, and is supported by a very thin neck. His expression is radiant and at the same time ascetic. Natasha said that he gave a great impression of moderation combined with steady, strong feelings. He told us his wife was ill upstairs, and added: 'Who could be well this week anyway?' Unlike Kennan, he did not approve of the English action† but regarded it as a mistake more than that it was reprehensible. He said: 'For someone who is writing an essay on "The Future of Force" my ideas have undergone a lot of alteration in the last week.' We talked about Nehru's reluctance to comment on the Hungarian situation. I remarked that Nehru was extremely vain, and that one had more confidence in his sister's and his daughter's judgement than in Nehru's. Oppenheimer agreed about the women sur-

* The physicist.
† This was the time of the English invasion of Suez. At the same time the Soviets had sent tanks into Hungary.

rounding Nehru, but not about the vanity. He said: 'Perhaps he is not so much vain as something deeper and worse. At the end, what he may be judged for is not vanity but pride, which is something much more serious.' I had the impression that Oppenheimer examined whatever was said to him, and condemned what was superficial.

December / *London*

I drove Eliot to the Savoy [to meet Stravinsky]. He was in a good humour. The conversation was carried on mostly in English, though some of it was in French, which Eliot talks slowly and meticulously. Stravinsky started talking about his health. He complained that all the doctors told him to do different, sometimes quite opposite things. He suffered from an excessive thickness of the blood. Moving his hands as though moulding an extremely rich substance, he said: 'They said my blood is so thick, so rich, so very rich, it might turn into crystals, like rubies, if I didn't drink beer, plenty of beer, and occasionally whisky, all the time.' Eliot observed that a pint of beer did him less harm in the middle of the day than two glasses of red wine. Stravinsky returned to the subject of the thickness of his blood.

Eliot said meditatively: 'I remember that in Heidelberg when I was young I went to a doctor and was examined, and the doctor said: "Mr Eliot, you have the thinnest blood I've ever tested."'

Stravinsky talked about Auden writing the libretto of *The Rake's Progress*. He said it went marvellously. Auden arrived at the Stravinskys' house in Hollywood, ate an enormous dinner and drank much wine, went to bed at exactly half-past ten, and then was up at eight the next morning ready to listen to Stravinsky's ideas. No sooner were these divulged than he started writing the libretto. He would think of something, write it, then ask himself where it could be fitted in, pulling out lines and phrases, and finding places in which to insert them, as though he were fitting the pieces into a puzzle. After consulting with Chester Kallman, within a few days Auden returned the libretto, neatly typed out. Only minor alterations had to be made, and Stravinsky only had to suggest that there was some difficulty somewhere and the solution to the problem would arrive by return of post.

Stravinsky started talking about the annoyance of publicity. A reporter had rung up and suggested coming to his hotel to take down notes of his reaction to the performance of one of his works on the BBC. Vera Stravinsky chipped in here and said: 'We explained that we never listen to the radio.' Stravinsky added a terse comment on the British conductor.

Eliot asked him what he did when people wrote asking for photographs.

Stravinsky said he did not send them, because the postage cost money. He said that when he was in Venice, where a choral work of his was performed in St Mark's, *Time* had created a link between him and T. S. Eliot by captioning their review of it: 'Murder in the Cathedral'. He said that after this performance he waited twenty-five minutes so that the crowds might disperse, and then, accompanied by his friends, walked out into the piazza. There were very few people by this time, but as he walked across the square a few people seated at tables saw him and started clapping. He said he was extremely touched. The performance had been broadcast through amplifiers into the square, and these people, most of them young, had waited in order to applaud.

I asked Eliot how it felt to address 14,000 people at a meeting in Minneapolis. He said: 'Not 14,000 - 13,523. As I walked to the platform, which was in the largest sports stadium there, I felt like a very small bull walking into an enormous arena. As soon as I had started talking, I found it much easier to address several thousand people than a very small audience. One has not the slightest idea what they are thinking, sees no features of any face, and one feels exactly as if one were speaking to an anonymous unseen audience through a broadcast system. They all seemed very quiet, but I could not tell how they reacted ...'

1958

16 April / *Louisville, Kentucky*

Left London Airport. Seen off by Natasha. After last crowded days of organizing the repainting and clearing out and cleaning up of 15 Loudoun Road, final work on *Encounter*, social life (lunch with Edith Sitwell, party for the Gaitskells), I feel as if a lot of things are coming to an end, a new phase of our lives starting. For the children also – Matthew going to Westminster, Lizzie to school in the country. Also a lot of very stringent action to clear up our finances.

The night flight to New York easy, arrived International Airport two hours early. Went direct to Idlewild and got a plane which reached

Louisville by two. In the dining room of Brown's Hotel found Nicolas (Nabokov) lunching with one of the directors of the Louisville Opera.* In front of the director he had to be fairly discreet. Afterwards he told me to expect nothing from the performance. Rasputin looked like a head waiter, the room in Yousoupov's palace like a German Bierkeller, etc. After lunch we went along to the opera house. This resembles a town hall and has almost none of the equipment of an opera house. Three young men in slacks, who looked like workers in an automobile factory, were rehearsing. Another youth was stage-managing. The energetic German conductor was carrying on the rehearsal. The scenery was drab, consisting of one built-in set and some crêpe curtains, and some furniture which looked as if it had come from a secondhand store.

On the afternoon of the following day I drove round Louisville and down to the Ohio river with the ex-Mayor, a tall heavy-looking man, extraordinarily sympathetic in all his attitudes. He showed me the parts of Louisville which are still Dickensian, the Ionic façade of an old boarding house, the very beautiful columns of the water works, dating from 1865, on the river. He was trying to preserve all these buildings. He seemed depressed at what is happening to Louisville. The centre of the town is becoming a slum, because the wealthy are moving into the suburbs. More rent can be gained from parking lots in the middle of the town than from a building. The industries from the North which have moved to the Louisville area contribute nothing to the city. I was told later that the ex-Mayor was trying to set up a cultural centre. He encourages such things as the Opera and Orchestra, libraries, and a vast collection of recorded music and poetry, which is broadcast to subscribers every day on a local wired-radio system.

The performance of *Rasputin* was better than we anticipated, despite the innumerable blunders of one done on a shoestring, and after only four rehearsals. The first half of the opera is powerful and carries the story forward without any break. The trouble is that the second act is far too episodic, in fact the action is simply a series of explosive scenes. If only Nicky can be made to see this something might still come of the opera, in fact I think it might be really effective. I wrote him a letter suggesting a new scenario for Act Two, from St Louis Airport, while waiting between flights.

Went to a party after the opera at which I sat next to a lady who

* The Louisville Opera put on the first performance of Nabokov's opera *Rasputin's End*, for which I wrote the libretto.

said, 'Now I like Mr Nabokov. He belongs to a nice generation of refugees who came out of their countries after the First World War. They knew their place and they took jobs as waiters and taxi drivers. Today refugees aren't like that. They come into your house and complain because they aren't waited on.' 'What refugees do you mean?' I asked. 'The whole lot of them. All refugees today are the same. They all behave like that. They're all bad, there aren't any exceptions.' There was a rather similar conversation in San Francisco a few days later, when the wife of the Head of the English Department said to me, in the course of a discussion about the state of France, 'The only hope for France would be if the whole French nation – every single French man and French woman – were psychoanalysed.'

Went to Santa Monica (18 and 19 April) and stayed in their extremely pleasant house with Christopher (Isherwood) and Don (Bachardy). They have achieved a relationship which seems wonderfully happy for them both. They were all sweetness and light these two days. They live quite a sequestered life, Christopher working on an idea for a movie about Mary Magdalene, and on two books; Don studying art. The relationship has really transformed Christopher. He explained to me his views about religion. He encouraged me in the most tactful way about my work, by returning frequently to things he liked in it. We met a manic television star and interviewer, a real Christopher character with public exhibitionist qualities tied up in a bundle with compulsive personal ones by strings of neuroses. Also saw Evelyn Hooker* who was full of plans for our Western stay next year, and the millionaire brother of George Gershwin, and his wife, sitting alone in an immense totally depersonalized Hollywood mansion, with Rouaults, Modiglianis, a Utrillo, a Soutine on the walls, fantastic gadgets in the kitchen, a bed upstairs which writhes like a cobra when you press a button, a bath of alabaster – all incredibly cold and bright and sad. Gershwin, a man in his sixties, showed me some very talented paintings he had done during six months of his life. He said he gave up because he could not paint for less than fourteen hours a day.

San Francisco

In my day at Berkeley I saw the campus, fixed up my schedule for

---

*Psychologist who was at that time making a study of homosexuality. Married to Edward Hooker, professor and editor of the works of Dryden.

teaching, arranged to take on a house, two Siamese cats, three lizards, and two cars, and recitals for Natasha. Everyone was extremely cordial. In the evening dined with Ruth Witt-Diamant* who had with her Ruthven Todd,† who was very drunk, chattered endlessly, revealing his interests and symptoms in one interminable stream, any segment of which contains the same strata of his character running along it. Interests: his poems, which he considers at least as good as everyone else's poems; his flower drawings, which are, in fact, better than those of others; his teeth, false and genuine; girls whom he has loved and who have loved him; the extraordinarily helpful and useful role he has played in others' lives. There is nothing bad about him. He has also recently developed a philosophy: undepressibility! Whenever Ruth, trying to relive the cheerfulness, mentioned a suicide, abortion, or case of insanity, Ruthven would give a guffaw and say: 'He got what's coming to him' or 'There's nothing in that to be so upset about', etc. Said quite kindly, and quite true, but morally monotonous. He did say one or two funny things. Describing how he had greatly aided Edith Sitwell during the time of Dylan's death, he said, 'I took her in a taxi and there she sat weeping on my shoulder. I never realized till then what it was like to have a crow cry down one's neck.' The only trouble about his stories is they give such an impression of coming from the repertoire. We pub-crawled a bit and I was more or less greeted by some angry young San Francisco poets.

20 April / *Tokyo*

Flew to Honolulu. Spent an hour there in a taxi looking at the completely Americanized harbour, etc. The largest hotel somehow manages to combine features of a native village with the utmost modern luxury. From Honolulu flew overnight to Tokyo, which I reached two hours ahead of schedule. Three representatives of the Cultural Forum were there, Hoki Ishihara, an Eurasian called Hillary, the other a very diminutive lady called Yoshie Nakajima. Within a few minutes they explained to me it had been fixed that Hillary will travel with me to Kyōto, Kōbe, etc., on 2 May, and Yoshie Nakajima on 17 May for my journey north.

---

*Teacher at San Francisco State College who ran a programme of poetry readings.

† Author of several volumes of verse and prose. He wrote as he talked, most volubly, but seemed incapable of revising works which were written in a few days. He did very beautiful drawings of flowers and minerals.

Went to International House, a glorified YMCA but without any young men. At ten Masao* rang me to say he had been at the airport but had missed me owing to the plane's early arrival. I arranged to spend the afternoon and evening with him. Rang Don† who came to lunch. Don told me that the worst thing yet had happened about Masao. He had tried to commit suicide. He had been found in a dying condition on the floor of the apartment of an American who had rushed him to hospital. If he had died, said Don, the American would have had to leave Tokyo within forty-eight hours. I said that Masao had telephoned and was going to spend the evening with me.

He came at five and was exactly as he had been before. I asked him about his life and he said that he had given up his job, had been dropped by his American friend, but now had another job, as a waiter. Finally I asked him about the suicide attempt. He said that he had been without a job and was quite alone and had become very nervous and could not sleep. So one day he took a great many sleeping pills and then felt quite content and thought: 'I am going to die.' Then he thought he would visit all the people he owed anything to and put things right with them. He had some gramophone records belonging to the American, so he took them to his apartment. When he got there the American was away. So he waited. When the American came in he shouted at Masao, 'What are you doing? Get out of here!' At this Masao fainted. He said, 'If he had not shouted, I would not have fainted and I would have made everything right.'

He was annoyed with Don and said, 'I like Don, but he tells everyone everything and talks too much in a way that is dangerous to me. I really do not want ever to see him again.' He said his present job was wretched and he would give anything to obtain work without having to use his connections with friends he knew. Then he suddenly asked me – 'Will you come and see my father?' Although I was tired after the journey I felt that I must accept this at once. So we set out. Then he said, 'Will you see the room where I live, too? I don't know why I ask this, but I want you to see it.'

His room was about 14 foot square. He shares it with his sister and his four cats. We sat in his room for a bit and were about to leave when his father, stepmother and sister appeared. Then we went in a taxi to their

* I had met Masao on a previous visit to Japan. See page 131.
† An American scholar living in Tokyo.

little house, where there was also his brother, a sub-editor, and his wife, and 2-year-old baby.

On our way back to International House, Masao asked to see my schedule. I was a bit apprehensive and thought: 'He is certainly going to be possessive with me.' He looked at my schedule and copied all my dates down. Then he said, 'Tomorrow week will be the first time we are both free.' I said we should try to meet before that, on Sunday.

On Wednesday morning Shozo* telephoned, and since then I have seen him every day. He is intelligent and sensitive with a very analytic mind, clear but capable of getting confused. Then he will say, 'I am very confused' about whatever it is.

Your Japanese friend never likes your other Japanese friends. If you are too sympathetic to them you are liable to become involved and then they are liable to become possessive and false situations arise, leading to the worst of evils – humiliation. I asked Shozo yesterday whether he could help Masao. He said he would like to, a problem being that it would be extremely difficult not to humiliate him in the process. A few minutes after this, I saw Shozo humiliated. Bill McAlpine,† Mishima‡ and Ivan Morris¶ arrived to take me out to dinner. Shozo was very anxious to join the party, and Mishima, out of politeness, I think, asked him to do so. Then I took McAlpine aside and asked if it was all right, and McAlpine said, no, it would be very awkward. So I tried to make this clear to Shozo, but said none the less we would take him in our taxi to his station. In the taxi he suddenly said to me, 'But I would like to stay and dine with you', all of which caused general embarrassment, and my having to explain things all over again.

The dinner party itself, at which we were joined by Kenichi Yoshida, was very amusing, with many dishes, and ending up with dancing girls singing songs to us. Mishima is quite small when standing, but with his lean face and elongated hands, one imagines him very tall when he is seated. He leads an extraordinary life, living with his parents, working all night, and sleeping all day. At the age of 32 he has written thirty-six novels. He is extremely frank about being homosexual, and started dinner by talking about a classic called *Great Homo-*

---

* My Japanese translator and interpreter sometimes while I was in Japan.
† An English member of the British Council.
‡ Yukio Mishima, the Japanese novelist.
¶ American scholar and translator from Japanese.

sexual Love Stories of the Samurai. After dinner we went to two or three bars, which had very much the atmosphere of Berlin of the 1930s.

28 April

Went to Noh plays with Shozo and Yoshie Nakajima. They were both very bored by the extreme slowness of them, as I was. I find I am bored seeing them but get a lot out of them retrospectively, remembering, for instance, the slow-motion walking on to the stage of a woman (really a man) wearing a brocade coat and with a mask superimposing on her features a gracious downward- or upward-gazing smile. Humans become puppets and they never make a movement which could not be the result of pulling a string. The chanting and the strange noises made by voices which have become indistinguishable from instruments are wonderful too. Everything goes to achieve the utmost impersonality, so that when the action becomes violent it seems a supernatural violence – the storm or the ghost.

But I think the Japanese, so far from being blamed for the falling off of the audience at Noh, are to be admired for going at all – especially the young. It is difficult to see how a form, divorced from the ritualistic attitudes and the mythology which could make it a focus of belief and aesthetics, can survive.

I got home, ate at International House, and waited for Masao. He telephoned at nine, said he would be with me at nine thirty or ten, arrived at about ten fifteen. I felt anxious while I was waiting, as I really am concerned about him. He was very nice when he came, but very tired I thought, as if he would sleep for about two days if I just allowed him to do so in my room. He left me feeling that more than anything else I would like to try and get him out of the rut of humiliation which he has got into on account of his suicide attempt.

On Monday evening I went with Mrs Matsuoka* to dinner with Kawabata† at his house in Kamakura, about an hour's train ride from Tokyo. At Kamakura, we went to see the famous fourteenth-century bronze Buddha. In the evening light this figure, with its rounded forms of the head, shoulders, crossed legs and robes, seemed to combine

---

* A writer, feminist and daughter of a former Prime Minister.
† Yasunari Kawabata, the Japanese Nobel prize-winning novelist.

great weight with the anchored lightness of a balloon longing to float away into the sky.

Kawabata lives in an old-style, rather elaborate, and very perfect Japanese house – all wood outside and mats and paper walls and screens and scrolls within. He provided a quite marvellous Japanese meal, of about sixteen to twenty courses, washed down, a bit oddly, with whisky. Besides Mrs Matsuoka and him, there was a poet, a professor and his wife, and Kawabata's wife and daughter. The professor, who was a statistician it seemed, told me that the feelings of the young in Japan are disquieting. Whereas in other parts of the world the suicide rate among the old (40–60) goes up, in Japan this decreases and it goes up with the young. He found it difficult to account for this. The poet (who also teaches, I think) said he thought this was the result of the educational system, which was quite unadapted to modern needs. The professor said that although the young live in a comparatively modern environment outside their homes, it is still the circumstances of the home which they are bound by and which condition them. The poet said that for a young Japanese to break with his home even at the age of 25 or 30 was a terrible moral blow to him and led to loss of prestige. Marriages were not a matter of a young couple going out into the world to find a home of their own but of whole families taking up residence with one another. Mrs Matsuoka (a feminist) said that the young wife would be considered a bad wife by her in-laws if she spent time reading the newspapers.

I asked them about suicide. They seemed to accept this as part of the course of events and not feel that it was especially tragic. No guilt was attaching either to the person who did it or those who may have been close to him and perhaps indirectly the cause of his doing it. 'It's just a person's own business if he kills himself,' as Kenichi Yoshida said at lunch, when with McAlpine I brought the subject up again.

At dinner with McAlpine, he talked about Dylan Thomas, whom he knew well. He said he thought there may have been a drying up of Dylan's talent towards the end. He found it more and more difficult to write. Sometimes he made a hundred or more versions of a poem. He used to write two or three lines on a piece of paper, then as soon as he made an alteration throw the paper away, as he could not bear to have a manuscript with alterations. He found it easier to do all the money-making things than write poetry. He really made a lot of money and it is difficult to say how he spent it. McAlpine said that in the country Dylan was a warm and simple person, but he could also be extremely unscrupulous and it was difficult to explain – far less justify – his behaviour sometimes. For instance, when he went on his first trip to the US there was a girl he was seriously in love with. She followed him to England and they started having an affair in London. Somebody, out of spite, told this to Caitlin, who immediately attacked Dylan about it. Dylan promptly repudiated the girl and said he had no feelings about her, while continuing to carry on. He was also singularly unscrupulous about money. He had once told McAlpine, who was staying with him, that he was just about to get a cheque for £50. On the strength of this McAlpine lent him £50. Dylan then got the letter with the cheque for £50 from the postman before it arrived at his house and cashed the cheque, in this way getting £100.

He said that at the end of their married life Dylan and Caitlin were not so much a marriage as a war. Earlier, some very deep sympathy had kept them together. It was Caitlin who had struggled to keep Dylan at work – get him to the country, keep him from distractions, make him fulfil obligations.

Under Milk Wood took Dylan on and off about eight years to write and even so the version that was published was not final, the ending being improvised.

4 May

We went yesterday to Nagoya. In the morning visited the museum where there was an exhibition of Chinese art. In the afternoon, to Seto, a pottery town. At the pottery we saw the studio of two masters. The second of these were a father and son, Kaito by name. The son, Takikawa Kaito, had a wonderful artisan's face with smiling eyes, and a mouth enclosed in lines curved like brackets, creasing frequently to a smile. He took us to his studio and gave us plates to draw on. I made a great mess of mine and then he drew loosely and freely the carp-flags and kites on plates which will be given us. He also gave me a very beautiful black vase, apologizing because there was a minute flaw in the colour.

We came this morning to Ise. A most beautiful coast with little torn-off rugged islands in the sea, hedgehog-shaped, steep yet all in scale, not unlike Devon translated into Japanese fishermen, boats, conifers.

12 May

A week of travelling and giving lectures. Routine the same everywhere. Met at station by a team of two or three professors with their grey, solemn faces. Such gleam of life as they usually have seems to have sunk deep inside them, like a shell into mud flats. In Japan, sake is the best way of retrieving it.

Then to the Japanese-style hotel. The doorway like the step before the platform of a temple. Sitting on this platform, you struggle out of your shoes, select a pair of slippers from those ranged in the entrance of the interior, allow yourself to be taken to your room by one or two of the vestals of the hotel, and then put on your kimono. You can now complete your initiation by taking a bath. When I had Masao with me, he acted as a kind of protector, warding off the vestals, and seeing that we could undress alone. It was he who ordered the bath and took me down to it. Our happiest moments were when we cooled the water till it was of bearable temperature.

We are taken to the university and received by more professors seated in two lines of armchairs exactly facing one another. The professors sit there very stiff and upright like Egyptian pharaohs. Some very formal conversation follows about Mr Edmund Blunden, Mr D. J. Enright, Mr G. S. Fraser. English poets have become almost legendary figures, and Edmund Blunden is a kind of demigod. Occasionally a remark falls with the faint suggestion of a spark which goes out almost instantly. 'Mr Ralph Hodgson, he was eccentric.' 'Mr William Empson – strange behaviour.' Tea is drunk. Then I am ushered in to my lecture before anything up to 2,000 students. The most impressive occasion for me was Kyōto, where I spoke and answered questions and was translated for over two hours, in a packed room of students who seemed completely attentive.

At Osaka I was received in the largest hotel by the Osaka Writers' Association. The qualification for entertaining me – or belonging to the Association, I suppose – was to have received a prize – and everyone looked as if he had received first prize for stuffiness. The bright spot at Osaka was the librarian, Nakamura, who had translated J. A. Spender's *Great Britain 1886-1935*. He had done this in the middle of the war, corresponded with my uncle, but of course never met him. The book had been given to his officers by an admiral to acquaint them with the history of the enemy. This would have amused my uncle – also that the admiral was fired for his liberal sympathies.

Nakamura said, 'This is a big day in my life. It is my opportunity to repay my debt of gratitude to your uncle!' He did this by giving me a copy of my uncle's book in Japanese, and by arranging a geisha party, after the Writers' Association meeting that evening. A lot of sake was consumed as the geishas and the professors unfroze a bit.

At Kyōto we did some sightseeing in the morning. We saw the royal garden of Katsura Rikyu, which I had already seen before with the PEN Club. I remember it in September chiefly as a chase by Angus Wilson, Moravia and myself to get away from the rest of the PEN, led by the Duchess of Rochefoucauld. This time there were not so many people and it seemed to me incredibly beautifully laid out to be a whole and yet gardens within garden, divided from one another by verticals of trees, bridges, reflecting water, like screens, We went into the Summer Palace, an airy wooden structure, like the garden itself, a unity divided into intimate detailed spaces by screens (sliding paper walls painted with the most delicious pen drawings, a different common theme in each compartment).

There was a rather strange young English teacher who went round with us. He seemed never to look at anyone or anything at all, keeping his eyes fixed on the ground. When I made some observation about everything in a garden being perfectly arranged, he said, 'Yes, sometimes one longs to kick a stone out of place in a pathway and upset the proportions of the whole garden.' Standing on a bridge, and looking down on three trees which carried in them, like heavy fruit, gardeners who were tending their branches, I said to him, 'I can understand why one wants to commit suicide in Japan at moments.' 'You mean because everything seems so perfect?' He seemed to understand surprisingly well. Afterwards, in the car going back to the hotel, he warmed up, talking about Cambridge, Dr Leavis, etc. I realized I had felt reserved with him because I imagined he felt hostile to me. I imagine the young reading nothing of me but the bad notices other young critics write.

Hiroshima

The city has been completely rebuilt. What is more surprising than the Midwestern-like streets in the centre is the wooden houses along the sides of the river, delapidated, centennial-looking as though they belonged to the beginnings of that Asia which clusters along the sides of rivers in shacks on stilts all over the continent; and the proliferation of bars, night clubs, etc., which light up after dark like a funfair revealing 'the other side' of Japanese cities, off the main streets. One ruined building, near where the bomb is supposed to have struck the town, is left in the centre of Hiroshima. Near it there is a bridge designed by Noguchi called the Pearl Bridge, a memorial to a 12-year-old girl, and another memorial, saddle-shaped concrete structure that encloses a coffin-shaped stone block as memorial to the Unknown Citizen killed by the A-bomb. This has an inscription which reads something like, 'May these errors not be repeated.' A lamp burns just in front of this stone and everyone who passes pauses and bows to the monument. This is the first time in Japan that I have really seen a shrine treated with a reverence that seems entirely convincing.

I gave my lecture in the new buildings of the University – the nicest university I have seen. Later there was the usual dinner with professors – rather dominated by Americans. On my left was the local American Information Service officer, a tall earnest-looking man, whom I learned was a teetotaller. During dinner, he said from time to time, 'If the conversation turned to comics, I'd feel more at home.' Then he started racking his brains to remember the name of any book he'd read. Unfortunately those he did remember I hadn't heard of.

After dinner, I had a few drinks in the different bars with a strange young New Zealander, who had the reputation of being a 'kind of Boswell'. He did tell me the first two chapters of his Japanese life. He arrived in Tokyo on a ship two years ago, an innocent from a puritan background. He got off the ship, wandered around and found himself at some bar where there was a girl who offered to take him to see a 'typical Japanese home'. She took him to an apartment which was quite dark, explaining that her parents were away. Of course, he quickly learned that she did not live with her parents. After a little conversation, she proposed they go to bed. He was rather shocked, being such a puritan, but he never looked back from his first adventure. After he'd been in Japan a year, he was interviewed by the *Mainichi* newspaper. He got a lot of correspondence as a result of this article. One letter from a young farmer suggested he go north and stay with him and see a 'typical Japanese farmhouse'. He went, and as the farmhouse was rather small, shared a bed with the young farmer, who turned out to be the son of the family. During the night, the young farmer started playing about with him, much to his surprise. Next morning, he explained that he came from a puritan background and did not know of these things. The young farmer said, 'We young farmers are not rich. We can't afford to go often to brothels, so surely you will appreciate the economics of our situation which obliges us to do this.' The New Zealander said that such practices were very widespread among Buddhist monks (in particular) and all young people who could not afford to go to brothels. He came back to the hotel with me at midnight and was suddenly very helpful in suggesting how I should amalgamate two versions of my poem for the Japanese translator.

Kyūshū is an ugly place filled with people of almost unrelieved ugliness. The hotel where we stayed was womanned by a staff of frightful sluts who would not leave me alone for a moment. After tea two professors called to take us to an exhibition of pottery in a department store. One of the professors was fat and coarse-looking, the other thin and tormented. We had lunch at a Western-style restaurant. The fat professor ate macaroni by the vacuumatic method, forcing his mouth into an O and drawing in his breath with a loud hissing noise. At the lecture I was rather surprised that the thin professor introduced me in quite good English, as he had scarcely uttered a word of English until then. After the lecture an extraordinary creature called Sivo, wearing a sky-blue beret, and sweating in large clear drops from every pore of his nose, came up to me and said excitedly, 'You remember me from the PEN Club Conference, Mr Spender. I translate your poems and want to publish them in my magazine *Apollon*. I admire you greatly. I want to be your introducer to Japanese people. Here is a girl who would also admire you if she knew English' – and he suddenly dragged forward a girl who was by his side. 'I want to see you tonight – tomorrow – every time', etc. He pushed himself into the car and sat beside me, talking absurdly. We managed to get away from him but he appeared half an hour later at the dinner the professors gave me. This time he was with another maiden – a very attractive one – and said, 'Beautiful art-student admirer of your poems brought this big bunch of flowers.' With a kneeling bow she gave me a huge bunch of enormous flowers. Someone whipped out a camera and started photographing us furiously. I had managed to whisper to one of the professors that I did not want Sivo next to me, so he was about three places away. However, he was not easily repressed. As soon as the meal was finished he got up and recited 'The Funeral' in Japanese. I protested that this was my worst poem and mentioned that I had written as much in the Introduction to my *Collected Poems*. The professors now fired questions at me. Then they gave me a memento consisting of their names with various messages on a bit of cardboard. '*Usus est tyrannus* – S. Ban.' 'Life is but an empty dream – K. Yanaga.' 'The most important thing is the most unnecessary – Massara Monsi.' 'You came up a giant while I had expected somehow a rather short gentleman – Sakae Morioka.' 'Life is what you make of it – Y. Mori.' 'Kinichi Fokima Admirer of Keats and Spender.' Mr Sivo, rather surprisingly, confined himself to 'Bon Voyage' in very black ink.

An English teacher was at this dinner and after it he asked me to meet four of his friends who, he said, were schoolteachers. We met them in a coffee bar where they did not let us linger but jumped out into the street and started welcoming me effusively: 'We are the gentle angry young men,' the first said. 'We are Bohemians,' the second. 'We are relaxed,' the third. 'We are afraid you have had a very institutionalized evening,' the fourth. The first began again with, 'We take you to a bar where there are beautiful waitresses.'

All this sounded quite promising. We went to a bar which had one waiter and one waitress and no one else in it, and proceeded to drink whiskies. Suddenly the young teachers became very serious and started asking questions, just as the professors had done. 'I read your Japanese observations in Tokyo, and I noticed you said that Japan reminded you of the Weimar Republic. I am discontented with that. Can you explain further?' I said the resemblance with the Weimar Republic was the rather relaxed standards, pacifism, unemployment, good will, all leading to no very satisfactory fulfilment for the young. They thought that there was more likelihood of Rightist authoritarianism than of communism in Japan. They took no interest in Noh plays, which did not represent their interests or attitudes. I asked whether they liked Kabuki better. They discussed this a bit, then one of them said, 'What we want you to understand is that novels from Europe interest us much more than Kabuki.'

17 May / *Beppu*

We stayed at a luxurious hotel where the Emperor and Empress once stayed. In the afternoon we made a brave attempt to see some extremely sexual sculpture, which is part of an amazing miscellaneous collection of antiques, which is somehow part of the hotel. We were told that since the anti-prostitution laws, the obscene sculptures are no longer on public view. The logic of this seems extremely complicated, and somehow it is consistent with a further rule that if you stay a night at the hotel you are admitted (perhaps in the middle of the night?) to the closed-off galleries. Perhaps the idea is that the sculpture is so provocative that it results in almost instantaneous sexual intercourse.

18 May / *Kansai*

In my dream, I was deeply troubled by the thought that I should suffer some kind of punishment such as standing for a year up to my neck in mud – and my realization that to have this thought was utterly different from the reality, which I did not wish at all – that actually whatever my mental discomfort I live in a kind of complacent state of being. Then my dream shifted, and I dreamed I was lying with two people – perhaps Thomas Carlyle and (certainly this was the other) Lytton Strachey, and I was filled with the consoling thought that these were people who felt suffering and yet loved the sounds and sights of the earth (it was my love of these that had really made me question whether I felt anything except enjoying myself). They were watching a bank of beautiful flowers like honeysuckle, which kept on filling, flower by flower, with bees. And as he watched, Strachey's eyes kept filling with tears, which overflowed through his eyelashes and trickled down on to his beard.

Three days in Tokyo passed in giving four lectures at Tsuda University, the University of Tokyo, Cultural Forum and something called the East–West group.

Masao went to see Shozo to tell him how to behave to me on the week when he acts as my interpreter.

We came after a frightful long and tiring journey to Sendai.

19 May / *Sendai*

We went with two professors to Matsushima islands. Very beautiful, and fantastically shaped. One looks like Jove as a bull rising from the sea, another is 'backed like a whale'.

Such scenery in Japan looks as if it were a large-scale version of a miniature-scale model of itself, in which the sense of the miniature was retained in the enlargement.

Very old sculpture on rocks at the Zuiganji Temple. We also went to a temple – Kanran-tei – by the sea where there was a wonderful screen of large birds. Lunch at the hotel by the sea. Then a very short trip among islands in a motorboat. Then went to the University. Met the President, a doctor of medicine, who knew Freud in Vienna. My lecture was rather short, followed by Shozo's translation, which was much shorter, as the Dean had told him to make a summary. We dined with a lot of professors at a Western-style hotel. They scarcely spoke a word. There was a great gangling theological American who said things about Kyōto such as: 'The muse seems to have come to us there more readily than elsewhere' and of Auden: 'His work seems more than most to show the reflections of all the waves of his time.'

In the morning, went with the two professors in the rain to see the castle. After that we spent an hour in UNESCO House, with a doctor who is called 'the Japanese Schweitzer'. Then, next door to UNESCO House, went to visit the house and the sister of the poet Bansui Doi. His deathbed, his bust, his Order of Merit medal. His 80-year-old sister showed us around. An odour of death and piety everywhere that made me feel quite ill.

21 May / *Hokkaidō*

We travelled eight hours from Sendai to Aomori where we took the ferry and arrived at Hakodate at 5 a.m., when we took another train, which got us to Sapporo at midday. There we were met by a lot of photographers and pressmen. One of the interviewers asked, 'Evidently you are deeply in love with Japan, please will you tell us why?'

Some professors then took us away to lunch at the hotel. There was little conversation as none of them could speak English, but one of them was Nakaya, a great expert on snow. He goes to Greenland and takes segments of snow at a depth of 1,500 metres and 10,000 years old. He said that the temperature of the world has risen by 1 degree in the present century, and if this continues, within 150 years the North and South Poles will have melted. By analysing a bubble of air enclosed in snow 10,000 years ago they can compare the atmosphere then with that of today.

Another professor then took us to Jozankei Hotspring. He is by far the most boring professor I have met so far, and in the car his conversation literally sent me to sleep, while Shozo tried to explain to him that I was tired after the journey. When we got to the hotel, I hoped he would say goodbye and take advantage of having the car to go back to the university with it. But no. He said, 'It is my duty to look after you. Let us go to your room.' We went upstairs and then he said, 'We shall now take a multitudinous bath, after which you will feel greatly refreshed.' The idea of having a bath with this professor really infuriated me. But there was nothing to do except have a bath as quickly as possible. The bath consisted of two storeys of several baths, not very full at this time of day, as they were rather cool. After bathing, we went back to our room. The professor said, 'And now we shall have some beer. Let us order three bottles.' So we each drank an interminable bottle of beer while he said, 'I am not a great lover of poetry. In fact, I do not like literature at all. Literature I consider to be specialization. I let the other professors specialize. What I am interested in is just ordinary English. I am exactly your age, Mr Spender, and I'm getting very old. At my age I can no longer interest myself in what is new. Now when I was young I could read the Oxford Classics, *Selected Short Stories*, Volume 1, Bennett and Wells. But I was never able to get to Volume 2, and now I shall never interest myself in it. Now I am very glad you have brought your translator with you, because if you had not done so, I would have had to stay here the whole night and spend all the evening studying your speech with you, in order that I could make a good account of myself the following afternoon.' He spoke in a way that seemed to me slightly malicious, as bores do sometimes when they find out they are boring you and decide to take pleasure in it. He told us he was giving a course of radio programmes in English on Tennyson's 'The Brook'. 'Now it is very difficult for me to do this. I do not understand what the brook symbolizes and I do not even know how it should sound when I come to read it aloud.' 'It is about a brook and sounds like a brook,' I said. He retorted by saying he did not expect any more than a hundred students would attend my lecture. 'We also have an American English teacher here: he probably won't come to your lecture, and if he does he certainly won't understand any more of it than anyone else does – which will be not at all.'

There were two watches lying with faces down on the table. They seemed to be carrying away the only evening Shozo and I would have alone together. However Professor T. suddenly turned one of the watches over. It was six twenty. 'I'll have to be going very soon now,' he said, and settled back comfortably again. However, at about six forty he suddenly jumped to his feet, was changed from his kimono to his clothes in a moment, and rang for the bill. We had quite a job preventing him from paying. He did not want to impose on us by letting us pay, and I did not want to impose on him. We won.

Next morning we took a car and drove along the dusty road through the winding valley to Sapporo. The hills were covered with trees through which the light shone, showing up their pale green and yellow blossoms. The branches seemed to curl down the hillsides like silken hair, every tress gleaming, each single hair golden. It seemed more beautiful even than Japanese painting, with the loving detail of Leonardo's studies of forms in water.

I suddenly thought of two or three poems all at once as we drove along.

As soon as we got to Sapporo we were absorbed into the machinery of the university. The lecture was shifted from one room to another as the professor had arranged for it to be in too small a room. I hoped he had lost a lot of face over this, and still more when there were nearly 300 people at the lecture, when he had said there would be only 100.

After the lecture there was another meeting with about twenty teachers who asked questions. One of them said that the Japanese had no faith or philosophy to fall back on, and that this made a great difficulty for poets in their writing, and resulted in complete scepticism among the students. Another added that the idea of belief in humanity had been put into the new Constitution, but it was like something imported from abroad and corresponded to no deep feeling or tradition among the Japanese people.

Next morning we went to see a sheep farm, in beautiful upland country, with the professor. 'We hope he will lie down in the fields and be content like a sheep or cow,' said the professor to Shozo, pointing to me. We passed some boardings with election results. 'How is the election going?' I asked him. 'I have had no time to think about the election,' he said. 'I am not permitted to think about anything but you.' At the sheep farm all the sheep were being sheared in a shed, lit up by lamps while a movie man filmed. The sheep looked very passive. Shozo could not bear the sight and felt sick.

On our way back, the professor started talking about his motorcycle. 'I care for that much more than English literature.' He explained that he now had a licence to get a more powerful machine than his present one, but could not yet afford to do so. I asked him whether he would like a car and he said he could not get a licence for one (even if he could have afforded it) because of defective eyesight. 'All the English

books I have to read have ruined my eyes. By the way, will you read
Longfellow's 'I shot an arrow into the air' on my radio programme?'
I said I would prefer to read 'The Brook', and he said he thought the
broadcasting of election results would leave no time for 'The Brook'
now.

We invited him to lunch with us at the Chinese restaurant. He
cheered up quite a lot and became much more expansive. 'I have been
reading your autobiography and am half-way through. Of course, what
really interests me about it is the use of prepositions and articles.' It
turned out that he had an ambition to write a dictionary. There was
no simple up-to-date idiomatic translator's dictionary which gave the
most common current usages. He would limit his dictionary to 1,000
words. He suddenly waxed eloquent about this. I put it to him that if
the dictionary was to be idiomatic it would have to be rather more
complete – there was not just one exact current idiomatic usage for
each word, as he appeared to think. I said I thought his dictionary
would turn out much larger than he envisaged. Then in a renewed
burst of confidence he said, 'Excuse me, I have a cold and two boils
as a result of anxiety concerning your coming to Hokkaidō.'

23 May / *Tokyo*

We returned by air to Tokyo. Shozo had been rather persistent about
translating my Japanese lectures and publishing them in a small volume, and I felt, and said, that he was pushing me. But I also said –
which is true – that perhaps the fact that he wants to get on and do
things is less of a weight than Masao's real lack of concern about
anything but personal relations. I am really puzzled and lost when
people behave in ways that seem in the least self-interested. The
slightest degree of self-interest seems monstrous and introduces an
element of the incalculable into a relationship. Yet this is prudish.
Shozo may well feel I ought to think that it is in my interest to have
a good translator in Japanese, and feels qualified to fill this job. If I
had confidence in myself, himself and my work, I would not feel this
was a wrong ambition. However, I did give him a bit of a lecture
about mixing up business with personal relations. His reaction simply
was that he seemed to understand very well, and at the end he said he
would keep his personal feelings for me separate from everything else.

24 May

Arrived at the International Christian University, which is 17 miles outside Tokyo. Agreed to give a talk there next Thursday. After a little conversation, the President raised the question of my giving a scholarship to Masao. In this institution Masao and his 'case' seemed strangely improbable. I remembered how Polynesian Masao looks, how unacademic, and thought there is really something about him that anyone in authority would immediately distrust. He is really designed to be Man Friday, I thought, and as Don remarked when I told him this afterwards, I was the Robinson Crusoe who saw his footprint in the sand.

Went to dinner with the Snow Professor; also there, Professor Mizushima, a chemist, a Miss S. from Pittsburgh and others. Professor Mizushima writes haiku, and asked me to translate one of his efforts from his French into English. He was interesting about haiku and amusing to talk to in his polymath way. For some reason we got on to the subject of Beethoven and I told him about the recently published biography which portrays Beethoven as the brutal persecutor of his sister-in-law from whom after the death of his brother he successfully stole his nephew Karl, in whose life he tried to enact the role of a mother. Miss S. was quite dismayed: 'You do disappoint me, Mr Spender. Until now I had always thought his music so beautiful. In fact one of the things I used to look forward to after I was dead was meeting Beethoven to tell him how very much I had appreciated his music on earth.'

26 May

Went to an exhibition called *Masterpieces of Modern Japanese Art*, at the National Museum of Modern Art. Like everything else, sharply divided between the traditional and the modern. Some of the purely traditional water colours by Taikan are very good and seem to stand up to the present with a quiet strength that resists the accusation that they are demoded or archaic. The oil paintings are disappointing. Whereas the Japanese are clean and fresh in watercolour, they are nearly always muddy and fussed in oils. Very few paintings seem to combine the tradition with a vision that is of this century. In this respect Kondo Ko *Fishing with Cormorants* is refreshing because, while obviously traditional, it gives a feeling to the boats of a mysteriousness, which includes travelling at high speeds among the stars. One goes from painting to painting at this exhibition naming the European influence – Cézanne, Renoir, Bonnard, even Corinth and Soutine. What is so discouraging when Asian artists fall under Western influence is that they do so superficially, without a sense of the difficulty, the problem often stated rather than solved (left, that is, to the spectator to solve in the moment of looking at the work), which is the characteristic of so much that is best in modern painting.

Dined with Shozo and friends. It was much better than I expected, and a good mark for Shozo in the debate about his character which goes on in my mind. After that I spent two hours with Masao discussing his future. He has a simplicity which I always find touching. I asked him, 'What do you want to do in the long run?' and he said, 'Go to another country.' I asked him what he would do if he went to America, and he answered, 'I know that in America I would have to start down here,' and he put his hand on the floor.

27 May

Signed a lot of copies of my books at the bookshop, then was taken to a teashop where students were assembled to asked me questions. One of them asked – or remarked rather – 'Mr Spender, it may interest you for me to contrast my impression of you before and after you came into the room. I imagined the young man who went to Spain and wrote poems about the Civil War, which expressed very much the point of view of students in Japan after the recent war. Can you explain the change?' I was too baffled to do more than murmur something about time flying. My host came a bit ineffectively to my rescue with, 'I'm sure you don't have to worry yourself thinking Mr Spender might be offended by that question. He is flattered because there's nothing which we English like more than hearing other people's opinions of our characters.' 'I did not mean to compliment Mr Spender,' the student went on imperturbably and added that he had forgotten to mention that he found my poems immature. After this he smiled at me from time to time in a friendly way.

I just managed to get away in time from this snub to appear at four thirty at the Kabuki where I was given by the management a consolation prize in the shape of two very fine posters. I enjoyed the Kabuki very much. There is something extremely clear and clean about its lines of development, little though they resemble our idea of the dramatic. The long narrow stage and the pathway leading through the audience to it emphasize this feeling of a procession moving along the flat edge of a horizon. Rhythmically, the speech of the actors sounds like *Hiawatha* without the least attempt to disguise that it is *Hiawatha*. There is no speaking across lines, no bashful saying of them as if they were prose. The effects with drums, strings, wind instruments and hammering on the stage are always dramatic and pure. I love the melancholy effect with which singers sometimes take up the story from the stage and recite it as a ballad. Then the apparitions, dragons, warriors, bandits, etc., are darkly ominous. And the actors can assume a poised pose which seems sculptured. Throughout most of the action there is a feeling of ferocity controlled and therefore heroic. The audience can partake of that ferocity, even in their way of approving.

28 May

Worked in the morning. Masao and Shozo both appeared and helped a lot with organizing my departure. In the afternoon Masao, Miss Nakajima (who turns out to be very amusing and kind) went with me to buy presents for London. They laughed a great deal, were very helpful, and we were extremely happy.

I had a talk with Shozo. I said it was a great effort to rewrite transcripts of lectures: also that I had no idea of his qualifications as a translator, so that if someone wrote to me and said my translator was inadequate, this would be upsetting. Altogether, I said, I feared we risked the results of mixing up business with friendship. Shozo took this very well and said he was quite determined to keep business and personal relationships separate. He said he was confident that he could translate my poems better than anyone else. He seems to have a mission to translate me into Japanese so perhaps I should let him do so.

Commentary
1960

In 1960 my old friend Muriel Buttinger (Gardiner), who is called 'Elizabeth' in World Within World, *invited me to go with her and another friend of hers to Moscow for two weeks in February, to visit the sculptor Konienkov whom she had known in Vienna in the thirties when he was an exile there. He was a man of extreme eccentricity belonging to a religious sect that inspired him to make extraordinary prophecies. One of these made, I think, as early as 1940 (when Konienkov, aided by Muriel, was living in New York), was that Germany and Russia would go to war on 21 June 1941, and that he would then be summoned by Stalin to return to Russia as a sculptor of the Soviet Union. All this did happen, and in 1960 Konienkov, who had an American wife, was a much honoured Soviet citizen: but he was in his late eighties, and Muriel was quite right to think that this was the last time she would see him.*

5

Moscow Journal
1960

February 2-10

Our Intourist guide is called Lydia and she wears exactly the same fur coat and green beret every day. She bears a striking resemblance to the Queen of England in her youth.

I told Lydia that I had been a communist for a short time. 'Why aren't you one now?' 'Because, much as I admire the achievement of the Soviet Union, I still think that the most important thing – from my point of view – is the freedom to say and write what I think.' 'Oh, but there is more freedom in Russia than in any country in the world.' 'In that case, why is there no press which represents a point of view critical of the government?' 'There could be.' She smiled. 'But, you see, no one would read it. In the communist world there are no contradictions. Everyone agrees about everything.'

Muriel [Gardiner], who is a doctor and psychoanalyst, wanted to see a hospital or at least a school. Lydia said that she had to enquire about this. One morning she rang M. at 8.30 a.m. and said if she came down within ten minutes she could see a school. Otherwise nothing could be arranged. M. said she was not up yet, and could it be some other time? Lydia said she was sorry. Unless she came at once, it could not be arranged. After this when M. asked about the hospital or clinic, Lydia parried by pointing out that we should each of us, strictly, have separate guides and separate cars, and that she could not help M, as she was not our 'real' guide.

I rang Mr Gromeka of the Writers' Union, and he invited me to meet him at four in the afternoon; I would also meet the Secretary of the Commission dealing with foreign writers. I was received by two ladies who took me into a room where we sat and talked at one end of a long table. They told me that the house was the one that had belonged to the Rostovs in *War and Peace*. They asked me who I would like to see and I gave them five or six names. They went through them one by one and said, it was most unfortunate, everyone was away, or ill, or terribly occupied. They explained, with some frankness, that they thought it would be extremely difficult for them to arrange for anyone to see me, as he would have to be a great expert ('a real specialist, one might say') to have heard of my writing!

Guy Burgess telephoned me at 1.15 a.m. one night at the National Hotel where we were staying. He called on me at ten the next morning. As soon as he arrived, and I had asked him how he was, he said: 'I love living in this country. It's solid and expanding like England in 1860, my favourite time in history, and no one feels frightened.' But a few minutes later, while we were talking, he waved in the direction of a corner of the ceiling and said: 'I suppose they're listening to everything we're saying.'

He seemed oddly changed: looked at full-face he was quite like he was before – somewhat florid, the same bright eyes and full mouth. Side-face, he seemed very altered indeed – almost unrecognizable: thickset, chin receding, eyebrows with tufts that shoot out and overhang. Some-times, looking at him, I got the full-face and side-face impressions disconcertingly together – a person I knew, who had added an unrecognizable mask to his familiar features. I was puzzled as to whether this was just the effect of jumping the span of years (as he might find, looking at me) or due to all that had happened to him. He had a seedy, slightly shame-faced air and a shambling walk, like some ex-consular official you meet in a bar at Singapore and who puzzles you by his references to the days when he knew the great, and helped determine policy.

He said, 'I have a black mark against you' and cited a letter I had written to the *Observer* about him. I said that I didn't remember very distinctly what it was and he said, 'Never mind, only a tease', quite affectionately. Later, I did remember and said, 'When I wrote in that letter that Auden (who you failed to contact at my house, just before you left) might have refused to see you anyway, I was not attacking you, I was trying to protect Auden.' 'In that case, it's perfectly all right. I understand completely.' He added, rather wistfully, 'There's probably some quite reasonable explanation for Goronwy's articles about me – in which case I would forget everything.'*

He told me he was advising for a publishing house. We discussed

* See p. 214.

books they might translate. They have never done Jane Austen. He was trying to persuade them to do Trollope. He was also, he said, working with a branch of the government which spread peace. 'Although he won't be aware of it, I was able to be a good deal of help to Macmillan during his visit.* I wrote a report that he was in favour of friendship and should be trusted, whereas all the others wrote that he was a dangerous reactionary. I got a note thanking me afterwards. So at present I am in good odour.'

He wanted chiefly to hear gossip from me about the old days and about our friends. The person he spoke of most affectionately was Rosamond Lehmann. I was astonished at the extent to which he had woven most detailed legends around every day belonging to the past. For instance, although he and I were never at all close, he remembered, it seemed, every occasion on which we had met: how, in Paris, at lunch, I had told him about being psychoanalysed; how I had once lent him my flat in London – things I had completely forgotten. He talked about all his friends in the same way. I asked him whether he had friends in Moscow. He said yes. 'Are they like your friends in England?' 'No one has friends anywhere like they have in England. That's the thing about England.'

I asked him whether he'd like to go back. He said, only if he were sure that he would be able to return to Moscow. He thought the authorities might make this impossible. He said he would like to see his mother but that she was getting too old to travel to him. I suggested perhaps they might meet in some place equidistant from Moscow and London. He said the Russians wouldn't give him leave to go anywhere but England. They were, he said, pressing him to become a Soviet citizen.

He seemed quite nervous and never stopped walking up and down the room. I ordered a bottle of champagne, which we drank between us. He started talking about his disappearance from England with Maclean. The background to this was his time at the British Embassy in Washington when he had become horrified by the 'police methods' of the State Department. 'So when Maclean came along and told me that he could not go anywhere in England without being followed, and would I help him, I thought: if they're going to start doing that kind of thing in England, well, I *will* help.' He said that the reason why, just before their

---

* When Harold Macmillan visited Russia.

escape, he telephoned me to get on to Auden, was that he thought that he would accompany Maclean as far as Prague and then himself go south to Ischia and perhaps stay with Auden or borrow his house there. But when they got to Prague, the British press exploded with the news of the 'missing diplomats' and Maclean persuaded him to go on to Moscow. In Prague they spent two weeks trying to obtain visas to enter Russia – and they were admitted, in the end, because of the public scandal at home. When they got to Russia, they were completely isolated for the first six months – given a dacha, servants, a car. 'There was an awful time', Guy said, 'when we were sent to Kuybyshev. We were given a flat and servants and cars and were well looked after, but it was a horrible place and things were made worse by the fact that just then Beria,* in an effort to gain popularity after the death of Stalin, released 80 per cent of the criminals in Russia. Kuybyshev was invaded by gangsters and scoundrels. That's how I lost all my teeth on this side of my face – as you must have noticed.' ('I hadn't noticed.' 'Oh, but you must have.') 'I was walking along a street when a thug saw the watch on my wrist and knocked me down.'

I recalled Cyril telling me of a conversation he had with Maclean in which Maclean had said we were wrong about the Korean War in taking the side of Syngman Rhee.† I repeated this to Guy but he said, no, the turning point for him wasn't the Korean War but Greece – the surrender of Greece 'to the fascists'. He added, 'Of course, you won't agree about this' and indicated that he recognized – in a perfectly friendly fashion – my 'true position as an American agent'. (Whenever I took the trouble to repudiate this idea of me, he laughed. 'Only a tease!') I told him that I wasn't at all enthusiastic about the Greek regime. I remembered once dining at a restaurant on the top of a hill overlooking Corfu. As it became dark, the whole landscape became filled with shouting and clanking noises. I asked an elegant Greek lady – daughter of an ex-premier – what the noise was. She replied, 'Oh, it's the political prisoners. They always make this noise on a Saturday night because it's the only night they get enough food to be strong enough to protest against not having more.'

However, I added, having recounted this story to Guy, if *his* side

* Former head of the OGPU.

† Cyril described to me having had this conversation with Maclean in the Gargoyle Club in London.

had won, precisely the same scene would have taken place, if indeed the prisoners would have been in a position to protest at all. He did not reply to this.

He invited me to lunch at his apartment and telephoned through to his cook to say we would be coming. 'We shall lunch off grouse!'

We waited for a taxi and he asked a policeman how to get one that was not pre-empted by Intourist. ('Moscow policemen are sweeties,' he said.)

The apartment house where he lives – one of the ugliest – is near a beautiful monastery. 'I chose it so as to be near here.' He seemed nervous about the impression his apartment would make on me. 'I was offered something very grand but insisted on living in this place for very Spenderish reasons. I thought I couldn't live in five or six rooms when whole families are living in one room.'

His attitude to me – which was rather flattering – surprised me because in the old days he had always seemed somewhat contemptuous, as of an ideological superior to an intellectual inferior. But perhaps his changed manner was not just flattery but partly the effect of his minute examination of the old days, partly of pleasure at seeing someone from England. One thing in my favour that he remembered was that when John Cornford was a schoolboy he had sent me his poems and I had written him – without our having met – five pages of careful criticism. I had quite forgotten this episode.*

Before lunch we walked into the monastery, talking of our common friend Derek Kahn (Blaikie). I said that Derek had been unfortunate but rather stupid. 'Yes,' said Guy, 'he was very mixed up about his Jewish and Gentile blood. And Maurice Bowra was very cruel to him. But he wrote the best essay on Social Realism in the literature of our time. It appeared in the *Left Review*.' I did not remember – and could not really believe – this, and mentioned that at the end of his life Derek K. had become some sort of seminarist. 'That is deeply shocking,' said Guy. After we had gone into the church and watched Czarist-looking peasants praying, he asked me whether I was a believer. I said, no, but that I could not understand friends of mine who objected to other friends becoming (say) Catholic because they

* I think Burgess may have been getting this wrong and that it was Auden to whom Cornford sent his poems. A poem was sent to Auden by one of John Cornford's teachers at Stowe. Auden wrote a reply. See *Journey to the Frontier* (pp. 173-4) by William Abrahams and Peter Stansky.

regarded the Pope as a political reactionary. 'That isn't my objection at all,' said Guy. 'It's the intellectual betrayal involved. Last time I met Christopher (Isherwood) I made him cry by attacking him for his religion.'

I said that a mutual friend – R. – had become religious. 'In her case,' said Guy, 'I feel sorry for her. But if it was you, I would feel indignant. That anyone like you, in the world of 1960, should believe, would seem to me to be intellectual betrayal.'

He apologized incessantly for his flat. It seemed to me small but very nice, neatly and sympathetically arranged: lots of books, a small upright piano with volumes of Bach and Mozart sonatas open upon it, a Chagall reproduction, one or two paintings by gifted amateurs, modest furniture. The elaborately carved headboard of a bed – Guy explained – had belonged to Stendhal. I had said earlier that I would not publish an account of our meeting in the press. He pulled a volume of Winston Churchill's memoirs from the bookshelf and opened it at the flyleaf, which was inscribed: 'To Guy Burgess, in agreement with his views, Winston S. Churchill.' Under this was written in pencil: 'And we *were* right, Anthony Eden.' (He explained that Eden had said this at the time – at Yalta? – but not written it, feeling that he should not add to Churchill's inscription, so Guy had pencilled it in himself.)

'If you like,' Guy said, 'you can reproduce that in *Encounter*.'*

The conversation turned to what people had written about the 'missing diplomats'. Guy asked again why Goronwy had written his pieces in the *Sunday Express*. Was it just for the £5,000? I said I thought that this figure was exaggerated. A view was that, after Guy's reappearance in Moscow and the publication of his own article, Goronwy panicked for some reason or other: perhaps he thought that Guy would start disseminating articles from Moscow about his past and friends.

'Well, in that case, the most likely thing to make me do so would be for him to write an article "provoking" me.'

'I dare say that is so, but all the same he might have wished to tell his side of the story first.'

'Why?'

'Well, supposing he thought you had given away secrets. Then he might have wanted to dissociate himself from that.'

Guy said that he particularly resented certain attacks coming from

* As I had promised not to publish an article of course I did not publish a reproduction of the flyleaf.

people whom he knew to have been in MI5 or MI6. One of our mutual friends, who had attacked him, had, moreover, been a paid communist agent in Vienna. I said that it wasn't quite clear to me what was the borderline between giving away information and giving away real secrets. I supposed that Spring-Hall,* who gave away plans for aircraft to the Russians when they were our allies, was one kind of offender; but that giving away information about personalities and policy was a different matter.

'Everyone gives away information,' said Guy. 'When Churchill was in opposition he used to give away confidential information about what the government was thinking to Maisky, then Russian Ambassador.' He seemed to think that Maclean and he were in much the same position as Churchill. He said that, during the war, there were frequent exchanges of information between the British and the Russians, in which the rules of secrecy were more or less ignored, or considered to be suspended.

He was particularly annoyed, he said, that Goronwy had written in his article about 'orgies' that he claimed had taken place in Guy's flat. The flat, said Guy, had belonged to mutual friends, and he had been most careful that nothing scandalous should happen there.

My own feeling about Guy, which is, I think, shared by several of the British in Moscow, is to be sorry for him: and, as someone said, to wish that he could go back to England, that the whole thing could be forgotten, and that he could have some kind of a new start.

There is a postscript to my visit to Moscow. Shortly after my return I happened to go to a party where the then Home Secretary, R. A. Butler, was a guest. He came up to me and said in his urbane manner: 'I hear you've seen Guy Burgess in Moscow. Now tell me – do you think that he would like to come home?' I said I thought he would like to see his mother. RAB said: 'Well, if you write to him, please tell him that, as far as I'm concerned, he's perfectly free to come and go as he chooses. I know of absolutely nothing to prevent that.' He went on: 'Of course, if he does come back and the Home Secretary takes no action, I'll be criticized, the press will be after me, but I'm prepared to face that. As far as I'm concerned, there's nothing against him.' Then he added: 'Of course, the fellows at MI5 may take a different

---

*D.F. Spring-Hall, a political commissar in the International Brigade, later imprisoned for espionage.

view of the matter. I know nothing about that. As far as I'm concerned, tell him I'll stand by what I say.'

Shortly after this conversation Tom Driberg* rang and said he wished to see me urgently. I invited him to lunch at the Garrick Club, and as soon as we sat down at table, he made it clear that he had heard about my conversation with the Home Secretary, and that he was in a state of great alarm at the prospect of Guy's return to England. He said it would be an absolute disaster for many people if Guy came back. I should do everything I could to prevent his returning.

I did not write to Burgess since it was clear to me that what Butler had said did not provide the slightest guarantee for his safety. MI5 would be sure to have the last word. Besides, Guy had not expressed any wish to come to London: only a faint regret, really, that he would not be able to see his mother.

Another sequel to my Russian visit was that six months later I was rung by someone from the British Council who said that Fedin† and Tvardovsky,‡ the editor of the literary magazine Novy Mir, had arrived as guests of the British Council in London, and that, much to their surprise, the first person they had said they wished to meet in England was myself. I invited them to lunch the same day, and we had the conversation reported here (this is not a passage from my journal but a note I wrote for my colleagues at Encounter). The meeting was cordial. At the end of their visit, Natasha and I gave a dinner at Loudoun Road for them. I showed Tvardovsky the guest list, and he said there was one name he would like to be crossed out. It was that of Hugh Gaitskell. I asked him why, and he said it was because Gaitskell was an official, a politician. He seemed convinced that anyone in politics was a government lackey. I managed to persuade him that Gaitskell was a gifted and interesting man of independent views and leader of a real opposition.

31 March 1960

I took Fedin and Tvardovsky to luncheon at the Garrick yesterday. They were accompanied by a young British Council interpreter, Mr

---

* Tom Driberg (1905–76). Originator of the 'William Hickey' gossip column in the *Daily Express*. Churchman. Member of Parliament. Chairman of the Labour Party. He wrote a book about Burgess in 1956.

† Alexander Fedin. One-time President of the Writers' Union, whom I had met at the conference in Venice described in *Engaged in Writing*.

‡ Tvardovsky. The courageous editor of *Novy Mir*, who published, amongst writings of other dissidents, works by Solzhenitsyn.

Peter Norman, who was excellent, and whom they obviously liked, and who contributed a lot to the party. Fedin talked pleasantly about our meeting in Venice. I asked Mr Tvardovsky whether, with the help of Max Hayward or Madame Harari, I could translate one of his poems and publish it in *Encounter*. He seemed pleased at this suggestion, and said that he would like to translate one of my poems and publish it in *Novy Mir*! He also said that he was very willing to enter into an exchange of articles between *Encounter* and *Novy Mir*. I mentioned that I would be glad to have non-political articles on Soviet literature. I suggested that such an article might be an attempt to answer the question in the minds of some English readers: 'How does Soviet literature compare with nineteenth-century Russian literature? Are there Soviet writers who should have the same impact on the writers of Europe as Tolstoy, Dostoevsky, etc.?' I said I thought that this question is buried in the minds of most readers here, and it would be a good idea to try to bring it out into the open. They thought this was a real question and discussed it at some length, saying that although today no one would dare to assert the greatness of twentieth-century Russian literature, also in the nineteenth century it had not been realized how great it was. Mr Tvardovsky brought up the question of my asking for a non-political article, and smilingly asked why we always seemed to assume that they were concerned with politics.

(While I was talking with them, I had an impression rather different from the one I got from meeting Fedin in Venice. In Venice, I thought the Russians were being rather cunningly political, in avoiding politics. But yesterday, I had the impression that F. and T. really wanted to be considered as writers, and they did not want to be implicated in our political thinking about them, nor did they want to implicate us in their political thinking about us. If we insist on talking about politics, they are embarrassed because it is not an area in which they express themselves very freely. So they really have a quite sincere reason for wishing to avoid the topic.)

Then I told them I had been to Moscow four weeks ago. They explained that they had not been there at the time. I said I thought there had been some coldness towards me by the Writers' Union, and I said I quite understood this, and had no grievance on that account, but I wanted them to understand that basically we were very well disposed to them, and that we thought that relations between Russian and English writers were of the greatest importance.

They said that perhaps it was a mistake of mine to have gone Intourist. I mentioned that Ehrenbourg had said in an interview in Rome that Silone and Spender would not be at all welcome in Russia. They pooh-poohed Ehrenbourg's remark, and Fedin added, rather oddly, 'In any case, we do not consider you at all like Silone.' I said that Silone was a friend of mine, and that I agreed with him about a good many things.

None of this conversation was at all sharp or disagreeable. Although we mentioned these things, we did so in a friendly way. I then developed a bit my own ideas about cultural exchange. I said that I thought that if one could arrange an exchange between writers, which had very little publicity and which was as little official as possible, and which would involve their studying together in some quiet place for some little time, this might be a very good idea. I added that I thought that a meeting of eight Russian and English writers for about a month of this kind might be very useful. Mr Tvardovsky said, 'Not eight, sixteen.' He took the idea up enthusiastically, and said that he knew exactly where it should be in Russia.

We then left this subject for a bit and talked about literature. They seemed to know almost nothing about T. S. Eliot and asked me to explain what kind of a poem *The Waste Land* was. I said that it was essentially a poem about the decline of Western civilization, with an idea that Christianity still offered a hope of salvation. I compared it with Alexander Blok's *The Twelve* (which I had read in a German translation) and which also contains the idea of the complete breakdown of everything, and the idea that salvation might be achieved by the Red Army soldier, who is identified with Christ. They indicated that perhaps the difference between Eliot and Blok is that Eliot is an extremely intellectual writer, writing for an intellectually privileged public, whilst Blok was a popular writer whose poetry was taken to the hearts of the whole Soviet people. This interested me because it seems that in their thinking they have come to attach much more importance to the idea of the popular bases of Soviet writing than they do to its ideology. They asked me whether Eliot's style was based on popular ballads, and I explained that it was based on Shakespearian blank verse. (It was explained to me that 'blank verse' means 'free verse' in Russia, but Fedin then recited to me some pentameters of Pushkin. I asked him how much he thought Pushkin was influenced by Byron.)

All this went very amicably, and made me realize how many things there would be to discuss if we had such a seminar, and if it was not conducted in setting one side against the other, and with interested parties looking over shoulders.

By the time we had finished talking, we suddenly realized it was nearly four o'clock. Mr Tvardovsky then made a little speech to me, in which he said that we should complete our meeting by deciding to carry out the idea which I had thrown forward of the seminar. He said he would like me to be responsible for this. I was slightly embarrassed at this suggestion, because I thought it might prove embarrassing to them.* I tried to explain that I was very willing to help and that I very much hoped that I would be present at such a meeting, but that perhaps in the course of studying the possibilities we might find that I was not the right person to be at the head of it, and I tried to make it clear that I did not wish them to feel that they were committed to having me.

They said they very much wanted to meet again before they left. So I am trying to arrange to give them a dinner at home in the middle of April, and I shall also see them through the British Council next week in order further to discuss the idea about the seminar.

* I was concerned for his position as a Soviet writer, on account of the known anti-communism of *Encounter*.

Commentary
1960-3

Our great friend Hansi Lambert died in the early summer of 1960.

In the late summer of 1960 we went for a tour of the south-west corner of France, and found ourselves greatly drawn to Provence, the Alpilles – Avignon, Arles and St Rémy – the country of van Gogh. Four years later we returned there and bought, for £500, a ruin consisting of about seven walls with trees growing between them, of a farmhouse and bergeries (the adjoining space in which sheep and goats sheltered) and about an acre of land. The local builders were skilled at rebuilding the many ruins in that neighbourhood and after two years we could move into the Mas St Jérôme as Natasha had named the house. We have spent about four months of every year there ever since.

In September 1961 the Old Vic Company staged the first performance of my version of Schiller's play Maria Stuart *at the Edinburgh Festival, to be opened a month later at the Old Vic. With Irene Worth as the imprisoned Scottish Queen, and Catharine Lacey as Queen Elizabeth, it had a considerable run.*

In 1963 I went for a semester to Northwestern, at Evanston, near Chicago, a university to which I was greatly drawn because friends of mine, Erich Heller and Richard Ellmann, were professors there. I returned to Northwestern for one semester in each of the following two years. At that time I was particularly interested in modernism, and wrote The Struggle of the Modern.

6

Journal
1960-2

1960

[undated]

We went to see Henry Moore. He showed us the new large room which he has built on to his house, where they have been living for only the past two or three days. I explained to him my plan for *Encounter*, namely that we should ask artists for illustrations, pen-and-ink drawings, demonstrating different aspects of their work. I told him that I would like very much to know what were the differences of his aims when he did an abstract drawing, or a representational one, or a portrait. He told me that there were at least five or six different kinds of drawing:

(1) The kind of drawing he made when he was trying to study the organic form or nature of an object. This was the kind of drawing which consisted of trying to find something out. He said in this connection that it was impossible for anyone to do drawings without making discovery about the structure of objects.

(2) Trying to describe the objects, for example, when he did a drawing of his daughter or some other life figure, or perhaps even of a bone.

(3) The kind of drawing he did when he was trying to clear his mind of an idea for a piece of sculpture: to plan it out, to see it from different angles and so on, to get an idea of what it would look like.

(4) Drawings which he would call exploratory. He would start simply perhaps by scribbling a few lines and then discovering from them a shape which led on to something else. These are the kind of drawings which arise from doodling.

(5) Drawings in which he attempted to explore the metamorphosis of objects. He would draw something realistically and then try to discover how it could take some other shape. He would turn realistic subjects into an abstraction through drawing it first realistically and then abstracting from it.

(6) What he called 'imaginative' drawings in order to create an atmosphere of dream. In this category, he would draw figures standing against a background.

I asked him about using colour in drawings. He said that he often used colour for amusement or in order to get better definition, or to distinguish one part of the drawing from another, but that he did not consider himself a colourist in the sense that a good many painters were colourists. I asked him whether he ever thought of using colour in sculpture. He said that he was very conscious of the colour of material in sculpture: of the colour, that is to say, of the kind of stone that he was using, or of the patina that a work might acquire, or of wood. In what he called his string sculptures he had sometimes used a different colour in the strings in order to suggest atmosphere. He showed us, for example, a piece of sculpture with strings of blue which were meant to suggest the air in the spaces. But he was not keen on using colour on the material of the sculpture itself, because he thought that colour tended to destroy the form. We went into the fields around his house where he has placed various pieces of sculpture. He showed us things he was working on, particularly a very large wooden figure seeming to be climbing up a wall or a tree. This was lying on its side in order that he might work at it. He explained that he now found this work very tiring and that to hollow out a little space between the thigh and the side of the tree might take him up to two days. This piece was meant for a museum in New York but he was months behind with the work. He kept on finding other work that he wanted to go on with that interrupted the work on this wooden figure. He showed us a very large figure now cast in metal, which consisted of two completely separate pieces. He said that he was very pleased with this, because when one looked at it from different angles it appeared surprisingly different. He said that his aim in these figures was always to try to show the affinity between the human figure and landscape, and that by doing the work in this way it was much more effective.

In a figure consisting of one piece there was always a continuity which gave it a certain sameness from whatever angle it was seen. But here from some angles the figure looked like mountains or rocks laid side by side. He was very pleased because one part of it looked rather like a cliff side in a painting of Seurat which Kenneth Clark used to have in his house.

We went back to the house, and he showed me various drawings which I might choose from for *Encounter*. I selected eight of these. I also chose three drawings which I might choose for Jim Hart* and for myself.

I forgot to say that when we were in the studio we saw a study for a head, and I asked him how he arrived at these heads with great clefts down the whole of the centre. He explained that when he was a boy in his Yorkshire mining village he used to go with two or three other boys to a slaughter house and see animals being killed. The men who killed them used to do this by hitting them with a mallet in the centre of the forehead. If they hit in exactly the right spot the animal died at once, but if they didn't succeed in doing this they had to hit two or three times more. There was one man of whom the others said that he was a wonderful slaughterer because he never had to hit an animal twice. Henry said that he had only been two or three times to the slaughter house, that it was a terrible experience that had haunted him all his life.

When he did his statue of the warrior he wanted to suggest a stricken dehumanized head, and he found himself, without first realizing that he was doing so, influenced by his memories of the axed animals in the slaughter house. Of a piece of sculpture of a pregnant woman, he said that he had tried to alter it because it seemed too descriptive. When we got back to the house I asked him what he meant by 'descriptive'. He explained that sometimes when he was working he found that he was becoming too influenced by his feelings or memories about real things. For instance, when he was doing the pregnant woman he found himself thinking of his mother and her pregnancies and somehow he was describing his feelings about them. So he tried to alter the work.

5 April

We had dinner with T. S. Eliot and his wife Valerie. We arrived a little late and found that the other guests were already there. They were the poet Ted Hughes, and his wife Sylvia Plath, who is also a poet and short-story writer. They were a good-looking pair, Ted Hughes having a craggy Yorkshire handsomeness combined with a certain elongated

* Professor James Hart, Director of the Bancroft Library, University of California at Berkeley. I had promised him that I would ask Henry whether he might buy a drawing.

refinement, very sensitive drooping hands in contrast to his ruggedness, rather soft-toned voice and not saying very much.

His wife, who talked more, was a very pretty, intelligent girl from Boston.

Cyril Connolly had given me an early edition of a book by Eliot called *Ara Vus Prec*, which he asked me to get Eliot to inscribe. So I quickly asked him to do this, in order to get that business over, and at the same time he signed my edition of *The Waste Land* printed by the *Dial* magazine. He said that the title of the book was misprinted as it had '*Vus*' for '*Vos*', and he corrected this. He said that Ezra Pound had been very shocked by the misprint and given him a wigging for it. He asked me whether I had recorded poems for a poet called Anderson who is making a lot of records for Yale University. He said he had not done so himself but that Mr Anderson had called. Mr Anderson, he said, apparently wrote poetry and had explained to Eliot that his poems were, like those of Eliot, 'fragmented'.

We went into the dining room and ate roast chicken served by Mrs Eliot. Eliot seemed relaxed, talked about Virginia Woolf and Wyndham Lewis. Mr and Mrs Hughes said very little. Whenever there was a pause in the conversation Mrs Eliot gave her husband an encouraging look across the table which positively radiated help. This made me nervous and I talked too much to keep the conversation going.

1962

11 May

Returned from Rome. Found Natasha practising the Stravinsky *Capriccio* for tomorrow's BBC concert. Tremendously complicated plans for going to Bruern and taking with us Yevtushenko and his wife, perhaps. Felt that all this return to things as usual was as if I were plunged in a tunnel fifty miles underground. Could not sleep. Read Volume I *Early Italian Literature*. Started a canzone-like poem. Won't be able to work till this weekend is over.

12 May

Dinner at William Sansom's for Yevtushenko. Some conversation about poetry with Y, who wanted to know why English poets never seemed to know their poems by heart. His concept of poetry very public. N,* who

* Translator of Russian poetry.

has spent several days with him, describes him as insincere – an actor playing a role – but whilst being profoundly political, he looks and is charming. When he danced one saw the jitterbug night-club side of him.

13 May

Still felt tired after journey and could not work. Read Italian poems. Later went to Mayfair Hotel, and picked up Y. for his reading at the Royal Court Theatre, at which I took the chair. I liked one or two of the poems better than (reading them in translation) I had done before. But they seemed Victorian in spirit – rather like Longfellow's 'Barbara Frechie'. There was a mixed audience, some enthusiastic, a few asked loaded questions afterwards about Pasternak, etc. The manner of the reading was theatrical.

14 May

Matthew said last night: 'Dad, if I get a scholarship to Oxford will you promise to leave *Encounter*, and do nothing but write poetry?'

This morning Peter Levi and his fellow translator came to see me. They talked enthusiastically about Y. I said: 'Do you think he *likes* anyone?' The translator said: 'He is his own best friend.'

16 May

Paris, for Stravinsky 80th birthday celebrations. Called on Jean Cocteau to give him back his *Encounter* drawing, but he was away and I was told he returns tomorrow. At six went to Stravinsky's hotel and found Pierre Boulez and Bob Craft and others surrounding him. Stravinsky very cordial. Dinner at Chez Laurent. About a dozen people there including Simone Signoret and husband. I sat far away from Stravinsky. When the party broke up Stravinsky was still very lively, violently denouncing to the Head of French Radio the attitudes of French writers to him in 1922.

17 May / *London*

Called at Berkeley Hotel to say goodbye to Stravinsky and Bob Craft. Stravinsky was sitting up in his chair with bright eyes like some creature in a Beatrix Potter drawing. He was excited about going to Africa, and showed me Alan Moorhead's books, especially a photo of a rhino. 'I want to see that animal,' he said. 'It's like this ...' suddenly he was on all fours, his stick with hook turned up like a horn, his eyes glazed – a rhinoceros.

18 May

Went to office. Dispatched review to *Sunday Times*. Lunched with Reynolds Price* who goes to the US this evening. Both of us a bit distraught, he through packing and getting ready to leave, I through just coming back. We went to the Marlborough Gallery and looked at van Gogh exhibition, then to ICA to look at the Nolans. R. thought only two or three of the Nolans were good. We both felt oppressed by its being a farewell. He is also nervous about having a film made of his novel.

Drove to Bruern. Dined with Michael and Pandora†. Michael very interested about Yevtushenko and rather inclined to the view that I was antipathetic to him and him to me – so I misjudged him because he did not like me.

19 May

I drove to Oxford and lunched at All Souls, a lunch for twenty people given by the Berlins for the American Ambassador. Afterwards went back with Isaiah for a few minutes. He said I should write to Evelyn Waugh breaking off relations with him.‡ At dinner I asked Michael (Astor) whether I should do so, and he said I should do nothing about it.

20 May

Lunch at the BBC to arrange three broadcasts. At three went to British Council to report on my South American and Caribbean tour. There was really nothing to say. They want me to go to Ceylon and Nepal, which throws me in turmoil. I think I will refuse.

Natasha and I went to the Wesker play *Chips with Everything*. The first act had characteristics of a very good charade, amusing and inventive, lively dialogue. Second act gets serious and collapses. The idea is that the airman in the training squad who first resists the order to bayonet a sack representing the enemy and later consents to do so,

---

* American novelist and poet, former Rhodes scholar. Lives in North Carolina.
† Michael Astor and his wife.
‡ Evelyn Waugh must have written something attacking me.

becomes identical with the bloody flight officer who orders the exercise. Wesker is too good a writer for this to seem anything but flimsy. The characters he creates are too lively to fit into the black/white which, as ideologist, he prepares for them.

Coldstream arranged that his portrait of me returns to me after his exhibition.

22 May

In the afternoon Sydney Nolan called at *Encounter*. We went to Larry Rivers's exhibition. He paints like an uninhibited, more whimsical Coldstream. Very good portraits with great economy of means. Can get a likeness by the drawing of an eye.

23 May

Lunch with Dom Moraes. Went to see Harry Fischer* about lithograph of Kokoschka as a projected *Encounter* cover. It is of a man sitting back to front on a donkey. Somebody said: 'People will say K's cover describes *Encounter*.' Saw Francis Bacon exhibition at the Tate. The paintings make horrifying statements with very great force. They are by an observer so profoundly affected by the kind of life he observes that, although protesting, they seem corrupted by the corruption. After Bacon most other contemporary painting seems decoration, doodling, aestheticism or stupidity. His work extremely devoid of pleasure, perhaps this is partly due to the life of disillusionment he leads, which he faces in its implications; perhaps it is the old English puritanism and dislike of pleasure cropping up again. Wrote, played *Rheingold* with libretto. Decided not to go to Ceylon and Nepal.

24 May

Finished final version of *A Voice from a Tomb*.

25 May

Fetched Stuart Hampshire and drove to see Coldstream exhibition in South London. We were kept waiting outside the gallery because the BBC was filming. When we went in, Tom Driberg was there. While I stood transfixed in front of Bill's portrait of Inez,† Tom Driberg

---

* Harry Fischer (1903–77). Co-founder and chairman of Marlborough Fine Art, then of Fischer Fine Art.

† My first wife.

made a speech to the camera about the Arts Council. Then he came over and said urbanely that this was a party political broadcast because support for the Arts Council was one of the few things the Labour Party agreed about. He asked us if we would be interviewed and we said no.

Interesting pictures I had not seen. Bill said his portrait of Lord Avon in his Garter robes looked like 'a dressed-up dog'.

26 May

Bruern. Worked in the morning. Larry Rivers and his wife came in a kind of bus, on their way to Wales. We had lunch late. Larry did two drawings of me. We dined at the Astors'. Lady A. talked about Charlottesville and her childhood in Virginia. Told about going to Russia and telling off Stalin. The Rivers greatly enlivened the party, doing the Twist to show Lady A. how it went. We stayed much longer than usual.

27 May

The Rivers left early. I worked at essay for *Encounter* on Penguin Modern Poetry Anthologies, attacking Alvarez.* The Astors and Patrick Kinross† called and were very nice. We left for home soon after lunch. Called at Berlin's *en route*, and played him recording of Stravinsky's *The Flood* which he liked. At home found postcard from Bob Craft saying that when Stravinsky and he called on Cocteau: 'Seeing Mr S. he fell all over himself, gave him a drawing and would have given him the whole house.' Letter from Christopher (Isherwood), protesting because *Encounter* had set up one of his lectures in proof. Tried to work at poems this morning, but without success.

28 May

We gave dinner party for Jimmy‡ and Tania Stern, Angus Wilson, Sydney Nolan, Sonia Orwell. It went on a long time, everyone talking at once.

This afternoon heard Isaiah giving lecture on Russian attitude to painting, at Slade. Coldstream said that when he gave a lecture or a

---

* Al Alvarez's introduction to the Penguin anthology, *The New Poetry*.

† Patrick Kinross (3rd Baron Kinross) 1904-76. Author of many travel books on the Middle East.

‡ James Stern, writer of stories and reminiscences.

speech, he was unutterably bored listening to the sound of his own voice coming out of his head as though out of a wooden box. Isaiah said he was nervous before a lecture: during the lecture he fixed an eye on the right-hand corner of the ceiling and heard a torrent of meaningless words coming out. After the lecture he felt shame. No one could ever persuade him that the lecture was good after he had made it, he simply was incapable of believing it could be good.

When I speak in public I have the experience of boredom with what I am saying. As Angus Wilson also said that evening, when one states ideas one is bored because one knows what they are and one is preoccupied with the effort of stating for others what one has thought out already. When one is writing a story or a poem one really does not know how it is going to develop, whether one can do it – so one is fascinated to see *what will happen*.

Experimental way of writing poetry. Simply write out anyhow without bothering about form or language or imagery – the idea from beginning to end. Write it out almost without thinking, in a kind of trance, simply the outline which is in one's head.

Maybe this is what people mean when they say Goethe first wrote his poems in prose. Yeats's drafts look like Ezra Pound's or William Carlos Williams's finished poems.

29 May

Tired after last night's party. Wrote a lot of letters at office. Welfare Officer came and told me story of Stuart Rodd. Twenty-year-old boy now in hospital, with stomach wounds from stabbing, whose poems I think good. Lunch at Savile Club. Table talk about purchase of Royal Academy Leonardo. Bought Lizzie's birthday present.

Dined with Magouche Phillips.* Francis Bacon was there. Francis told me his oldest friend had died suddenly in Tangiers two weeks ago. He seemed interested in reaction of Nolan, etc., to his exhibition, which was one of feeling challenged and horrified. Francis said that all the critics said his pictures were full of hatred and expressed no love. He had spoken very movingly about his dead friend and I said it did strike me that he did not express in his paintings what he must have felt about him. He said he was not able to do this at present; that certain friends were far too beautiful for him to distort – and he had

* Former wife of Arshile Gorky. Matthew Spender married their daughter Maro in 1967.

always distorted. I said Picasso had painted pictures of Dora Maar*
and that there seemed no Dora Maar side of Francis's painting. He
said: 'The paintings of Dora Maar are distorted.' I said: 'That's what
I mean. You can also distort to do a beautiful painting.'

30 May

Office. Lunch with Peters† who told me *World Within World* will
appear in a paperback between H. Hamilton and Faber. Agreed to do
book on modern poetry as this connects with Evanston lectures next
year. Not to undertake any other contracts as most of my commitments
are now fulfilled. He advises me to stick to *Encounter* for the time
being.

Francis Bacon and others come for drinks. After they had gone I
wrote until 1 a.m., mostly at the canzone-like poem.

Lizzie's birthday. N. gave her jewel case and I a desk fountain pen.
Granny gave her £1 and Francis did. She seems very happy.

31 May

I write poetry for some time each day, getting nowhere. The trouble
is I'm not sure I *want* to get anywhere, to finish anything. The pleasure
of not having to write for publication, before critics, and so on is so
great. Also my aims are so unattainable. It's more the fascination of
the impossible than the difficult. Still the poems themselves nag; they
want to get finished. But when they are at the stage where I see what
they're going to be, I'm disappointed. Also I suffer always from an
excess of ideas for things and at the same time a lack of vitally experienced observation.

The accountant came to *Encounter* and we discussed our finances.
For the first time in ten years they seem to be getting into order.

1 June

At the office wrote to Wystan confessing loss of his Brecht manuscript.‡
Corrected proofs of anti-Alvarez piece. In the afternoon we drove to
Bruern. I wrote poetry after dinner. The canzone-like poem is very
much changed and will be in quatrains I think. At midnight wrote some
lines which seemed in the right mood and form.

* Painter and at one time mistress of Picasso.
† A. D. Peters, literary agent.
‡ This was a typescript of a translation of Brecht's *The Seven Deadly Sins*.

On reflection I think that Edward Upward* is the best of all the generation of the thirties and that his novel will be in more ways than one the justification of that time.

2 June

Bruern. I wrote a poem most of the morning. Started Shelley piece for BBC. Went to Oxford and dined with Berlins.

Vita Sackville-West died. She was very kind to me when I was 20 and when my left-wing politics greatly alarmed her.

3 June

Completed Shelley piece for BBC. Wrote yet another version of *A Voice from a Tomb*. Still not happy about last few lines. Was too exhausted after returning from Oxford at 2 p.m. to be able to work effectively today. Half in sleep last night thinking again about Edward Upward's career of schoolmastering. How decent, how entirely honourable. Thirty years seemed to me finished almost before begun. Then thinking about the children and how although I realize they are older they nevertheless do seem to me at the same time 12 and 17 and as they were at 4 and 9. And I realize that I am both still 30 and 70 writing this at the age of 53. Time really is the greatest illusion. One believes in a future when one is young, and then when one is older and achieves what one believed in one no longer believes in it, and that is the great disillusionment.

I thought that writing poetry every day is like holding a magnifying glass over my interior life and realizing that it has become very sluggish. I do not think that I have a very energetic imagination – if I had I would have used it, ruthlessly, allowing no one to stand in my way. At the same time I have confidence that by endless working and reworking I can arrive at good results.

4 June

Letters and telegrams re my CBE. The nicest was from John Hayward† who almost justified the existence of honours.

---

* Author of a novel, a trilogy called *The Spiral Ascent* about English communists in the thirties. All his working life a schoolteacher.

† John Hayward (1905-65). Scholar, anthologist and bibliophile. Edited Rochester, Donne and Swift. Shared a flat with T. S. Eliot 1946-57.

5 June

Visited – for five minutes – Oskar Kokoschka who was determined we should use his design for cover of September number. Then joined Natasha and Michael Astor at Edith Sitwell's flat in Hampstead. She seemed better than we had seen her for several years. Her secretary told us that a previous nurse had put her on tranquillizers and this had been bad. She now has a much better nurse. Talked maliciously about Eliot who is in disgrace because he wrote to the *Observer* protesting against the memoir she had written about Wyndham Lewis. Told us that when she was 4 she fell madly in love with a peacock which was slightly larger than her – then it fell in love with a peahen. She was nasty about DHL. Said: 'Lady Chatterley is about the Sitwell family.' When DHL visited them he spent the whole afternoon explaining to them their relationship with their parents and their parents' with one another!

6 June

Lunched with Cyril (Connolly) at White's. He said M. suffered from 'a fundamental need to talk without stopping for three or four hours a day'. Did very funny imitations of their rows. Worked in the afternoon. Evening, Lord Mayor's Summer Banquet. Sat next to Jill and Cecil Day Lewis who were agreeable. Jill 'reacted' extravagantly to all the speeches. I wore a black tie, and Victor Pasmore* said: 'This isn't a kitchen-sink gathering.'

Went on with the poem suggested by the Sistine Chapel ceiling. But this isn't the poetic life.

7 June

Went to Sutherland exhibition and bought a small painting on the theme of a pair of scales. The exhibition rather uneven but much better than the previous one with pictures of Venice. Some of the most recent pictures painted freely and loosely are extremely impressive. There are various themes: machinery, animals, gardens, fruit, etc. Perhaps true what one critic says, that S. is a miniaturist. Sometimes illustrations in the catalogue give a better idea than the paintings, which seem blown up!

* Victor Pasmore, the painter, founder member of the Euston Road School 1937-9.

Dined with Francis Bacon. Francis looked sad and talked about his friend who had died.

Showed us two sections of a triptych he is painting. We dined at Etoile. Francis talked a bit about his life in Berlin in 1930. Cheered up a lot during dinner. Talk about Raphael and Michelangelo. Francis said: 'My ambition would be to do something really beautiful and not ugly as all my paintings are, before I die.' Went back to the studio after dinner. Talk about Graham Sutherland: Francis on Graham's liking for publicity, the company of Somerset Maugham, Douglas Cooper and Picasso, etc. Francis refused an honour. 'Didn't fill in the papers. All this has nothing to do with being an artist' and so on. 'Still it may help you to get a better room in a hotel.'

8 June

Office in the morning. Then drove down to Bruern. Marvellous day, light and very deep shadows. It is the trees, coal-black against the bright sky, the starkness of walls and buildings in shadow against the white – these contrasts which give a brilliant day its eeriness.

9 June

Bruern. Drove in to Burford for shopping. Worked at the Sistine Chapel ceiling poem. Did a drawing of Bruern. Read German modern poetry anthology. Thought about whether I will use a chorus in *Samson Agonistes* as model for poem about the human tree.

Heard that my uncle Parkes Weber has died.

In the evening till midnight worked on the canzone poem. Also worked on a book of essays. Desultory.

10 June

Bruern. Whit Sunday. Drove over to Fawley Bottom lunch with John Pipers. Saw his new studio with model of the window in Coventry Cathedral which, he said, he had made there, over two years. Said how fond he was of Bacon as a man, and that he was almost a saint, unlike Graham S.

After lunch we went into the wood near the farm where the Pipers have put up a slender monument made of broken flints and surmounted by a bull: also an arch made from two classical seventeenth-century figures, which they bought from an antique dealer. I asked John during our walk whether when he went to Venice or Rome, he had some idea in his head of what the relationship of a painter today was to the work of previous artists who have worked in those places. John said that he had given a great deal of thought to this and that what interested him when painting Rome or Venice was to maintain the tension between modern abstraction and topographical art. He thought that English artists had a topographical tradition and that they still had a contribution to make in relating the past to the modern.

11 June

Returned by train to London. Took Matthew to *King Priam*, Tippett's opera at Covent Garden. Very serious, sometimes beautiful music, not sufficiently varied – or rather apt to get stuck down in some 'beautiful' mood which appeals to the composer who is also librettist. This especially so in Act III. Music and libretto much too philosophic. The story is not simplified enough and the characters illustrate the moralizing too much to attract as people. All the same there is original and intense writing and one felt fascinated. The production marvellously good and Richard Lewis as Paris looked staggering. The climax of Act II strange and effective. In fact the music had sincerity and integrity throughout. It is a very original and personal work. The libretto is prosey, awkward and frequently absurd – the second act overlong, and particularly badly handled and exemplifying in every way Tippett the librettist indulging Tippett the composer.

Suddenly had a feeling of the twenty or so poems I am writing and that I know my way about them and they are part of a single work.

12 June

Office. Fetched two Nolans, one Picasso etching from Zwemmers. Met John Wain and Robert Conquest at pub. John Wain was wearing a cap made, apparently, from plaited straw. He is going to Canada for four months.

Gave the first of my four lectures to Gresham College. The usual audience of a few lecture addicts, a couple of crazy people, and, I suppose, a half-dozen people who are really interested.

I read through my 25-page lecture, which seemed to me interminable, full of material, in places interesting, and then ending abruptly. People seemed a bit surprised. When I got outside the hall, I realized I had been speaking for only thirty minutes.

13 June

Went to BBC and did *Desert Island Discs* programme. It took about four hours and by the time it came to the 'talk' I was quite bored and not really concentrating. Lunched with Roy Plomley the interviewer. Went to office. Gave my second lecture at Gresham College. The audience seemed attentive but I had only a strained relationship with them. It would be impossible to get them to ask questions because there are so many crazy people there.

14 June

At six gave my dreadful lecture to the dreadful Gresham College. Went to a party full of people who hadn't met for thirty-five years and were trying to be cheerful about it.

15 June

Pauline de Rothschild rang and I lunched with her and Philippe at Prunier. After lunch took them to the Francis Bacon exhibition. Wonderful light and I noticed a lot in the quality of the painting I had not realized. N. took the children to the country. Got out of giving my lecture by having a questions hour instead. The questions proved that several members of the audience were crazy, as I had been told.

To the ballet – *Giselle* with Margot Fonteyn and Nureyev. We had good seats but were too far away for me to feel involved. It seems that I can get involved now only from something nearer the stage than the twentieth row. MF is a very individual dancer, almost the opposite of other dancers. She has a thistledown movement, seeming to float rather than leap, and her real personality is felt all the time and has great appeal. Nureyev has a blue-period Picasso quality. He danced well, but his most moving moment was when he took the curtain call. She handed him her rose, which he held up with right arm extended. He is best in repose, which seems odd for a dancer.

Went to dinner at Margot F's. She appeared and was just the same as on stage. Nureyev appeared a gaunt, haggard beatnik with untidy hair and considerable charm.

16 June / *Hamburg*

Had great difficulty finding taxi to airport. Met Natasha, flew to Hamburg. Arrived at hotel to find Stravinsky doesn't arrive until tomorrow. I went for a walk along the Alster, which was beautiful, reminiscent of when I was 20 and first came here. Conscious of being old. Young lovers walking along bank hand in hand. Possible to think of them on a spring day near the wistaria and being inwardly as sunlit, responsive to one another, as oblivious of everything but themselves, as sincere, as the light shining on surfaces makes them look. But inside he is already adding up sums; there is a question mark inside her. Can she work, make both ends meet? Baited traps. When you are young your beauty is quite sufficient to ornament the barest bedsitter, your laughter almost warm enough to keep it heated. The only compensation for being old is to be spiritually and intellectually very alive, to be several astonishing stages beyond the young, to make them seem geese. The old need a certain public life even to keep alive privately, perhaps.

17 June

Went with Rolf Lieberman and his wife to meet Stravinsky at the airport. Many photographers. Stravinsky very charming with them, smiled, held out his arms, kissed us all, etc. What is nice is that he does this not out of vanity but genuine liking for these people, including the photographers, who came to meet him. I asked him whether he was tired. He said: 'Not tired, just drunk.' Bob Craft said later, *en passant*, 'The last time he was sober was in Paris on March 17th.' Went to hotel ... Had drinks with Stravinsky and Liebermans, Bob Craft and Balanchine* till nearly midnight. We gave S. for his birthday *A Latin Portrait*† with an inscription:

> Spenders, simple Spenders, offer their Latin gift to
> Strávǐnský, making a dactyl to honour his eightieth birthday.

Stravinsky explained to Balanchine about tempi of his ballet *Agon*. Balanchine said later to me: 'It's a matter of his arm. He begins quite right. The mind knows. But the muscles do not quite function. So he begins to get slow. It is a question of sickness, the muscles of the right side. But if one understands one can adjust oneself.'

18 June

Sketched, fairly completely, three poems. In the morning went to

* George Balanchine, the dancer, director of New York City Ballet.
† An anthology of Latin poetry edited by John Sparrow, published by the Nonesuch Press.

rehearsal by Balanchine but this failed to materialize. After dinner returned to hotel and joined Stravinskys. S. seems tired and suffering from the heat. He perked up and talked from time to time. 'Alban Berg was not just a composer of operas but also of *Lieder* as beautiful as Schumann's; the *Lyric Suite* is beautiful as Shakespeare.' He drew me, and gave me the sketch. Bob had asked him to do this and said something to the effect: 'It will pay your hotel bill.' Bob's awareness of ALL values rather touching.

19 June

Stravinsky said last night and again this morning so I feel he must have meant it: 'I can see you are a composer. I don't mean by that music – but as a poet: you like syllables. I like them too.'

Went to rehearsal of *Agon*. Bob conducting. It was very good. Stravinsky whispered to me, about the orchestra: 'It is a Wagner orchestra, a Strauss orchestra . . . *emmerdant*.' Stravinsky invited N. to stay on two days in Hamburg as their guest.

20 June / *Berlin*

I realize this morning, reading Michaelangelo's and Gaspara Stampa's sonnets, how old-fashioned my idea of poetry is. It's that poetry is, first of all, an existence which simply is what it is, and seeks to be nothing else; secondly, the expression of a faith, a feeling, an experience, or observed truth of life or nature; thirdly, the invention of a form which is an 'echo' (imitation), and has the movement, of the living impulse; and it is hoped, from this that a triple correspondence between (1) being, (2) experience, (3) form will run so that the achieved poem will complete the circle of the life from which it sprang and became a form of existence.

Evening, went to *Andorra* by Max Frisch at J. Theatre. The reaction of the audience seemed part *of* the play, because even more than in films, like those about Nuremberg Trials, the Germans were on trial in this play for anti-Semitism and for their refusal to accept guilt for what had happened, and their behaviour during the Occupation.

21 June / *Berlin*

Morning, worked at poems. Visited Wall with Hoffner (my guide). Lunched at restaurant in Wannsee.

Evening, went to a poor performance of *Così fan tútte*. I was struck by how provincial the standards were. A test of a provincial performance, I should say, is how the producer presents the character of the chambermaid, recurrent in Mozart operas, in *Così*, Despina. The buxom Lisa Otto, obviously much loved by the public, was allowed whenever she appeared to steal the show by fluttering her fingers and her eyes in a very repulsive way.

22 June

Continued sonnet on Berlin Wall. Thought of doing a second one, sealed at both ends AA BA BA BA BA BB and tried a few lines - very bad. Usual torments of writing poetry (a) neglecting my prose book, (b) my utter incompetence technically and lack of certainty about form I want, (c) lack of ability to invent anything of pure imagination - dependence on event, (d) divorce between the life I live and the poetic life which I conceive of, a life identical with the subjects of my poems, (e) have I the right to write a sonnet about Berlin - do I really care? Answer: this is my existence even if I am bad at it, I am committed to finding out how bad I am in performance and sensibility. Also I do believe I do have an existence and it is poetry.

Went to Berlin Art School to see Professor Heiliger, the sculptor. Charming atmosphere and studio. A young sculptress, very simple, very straight, very honest-looking, passed me some apples to draw while I was waiting (she saw I was getting nowhere near drawing a cat!); put me in mind of Clara Rilke.

Heiliger was very nice and showed me two projects for a memorial to Ernst Reuter. After this I went to see exhibition by the students of 'applied art'. Marvellous German technical work in printing, lettering, advertising, every kind of design, which gives me a very deep nostalgia. After two wars, this still goes back to art nouveau, Expressionism, the serious simplicity of the early century, artists living a kibbutz-like existence, inventing a language of massive sincerity expressed with a taste which is very close to a faith, and with a very thorough and unerring technique. It also has a lot of atmosphere. In a way teutonic but also aesthetic, which is a reaction from the teutonic.

One student was stripped to the waist; rather tall, Slavonic features, his colouring like a pastry cook, chalky and the skin in fact plastered over by the white plaster in which he was working. The moulded musculature of the stomach and chest and the lithe arms. He stood there smiling, more like a model of Michelangelo than a sculptor, I thought. Oh, that life of visual and kinetic artists for ever living in the centre of the materials they use, where in studios they are colleagues and friends, and from wrestling with paint and clay, then can suddenly turn to each other's bodies, as artists, as models, as lovers.

What I most care for in writing has nothing to do now with being published. It is for a friend, not all that racket.

In the evening I walked down Kurfürstendamm ... which was crowded as in pre-war, pre-Nazi times, the Film Festival more than the warm fine evening bringing out the crowds. There is more feeling of community, of belonging to each other in Berlin than in other cities, because, I think, there are shared points of view here, beginning with a general tolerance of nightlife, vulgarity and entertainment, and rising to respect for individuality and culture.

Went to a bar just off the Kurfürstendamm which was almost empty because all the habitual visitors were walking up and down looking for film stars. The waiter had nothing to do and sat next to me at the bar grumbling cheerfully. He told me about ships he'd been a sailor on until he had found this bar where everyone was like one family. Started doing his sums and said on all the money he had taken he had earned nothing, so I said I would give him 20 per cent on my bill, so he said: 'Ich sage nie Nein.' Quite felt I belonged in Berlin again.

23 June

Morning, went to twentieth-century art gallery near the Bahnof-am-Zoo. Very good Beckmanns, then to the palace of Charlottenburg where I can't remember having been before – lions, medieval carvings specially good. Aeroplane to München.

25 June / *Munich*

I go on with the Berlin poem, quite unsure about it. Morning, went to Alter Pinakothek and various churches. Evening to *Salome*. The performance very good and the sets beautiful, but I was ferociously bored by a work which is too good and original to ignore, too violent, unpleasant, and basically inhuman, to forgive.

The fascination of Salome as a subject is difficult to understand. Salome is a tiresome bore, St John is a monotonous preacher, Herod is the only character faintly alive. The whole point of the work is that Salome kisses the lips of the severed head of John the Baptist and if one does not think this is in some sense an interesting thing to do, the work is bound to fail. One can see that Wilde may have thought that kissing the lips of the executed John was a pure aesthetic act, rather like the existentialists' *acte gratuit*. But the utmost extent of perversity of which Strauss would have been capable would have been to kiss the lips of a dead Alpine cow and therefore his imagination doesn't enter into the perversity of his theme.

27 June / *London*

Drive to Oxford for the All Souls Encaenia as the guest of Stuart Hampshire. Met in his rooms. Watched from the window the gathering of dons and guests in the quad, many chairs and tables with drinks, waiting for the procession. Then we went down to the quad. The gowned procession arrived with Dean Rusk, Charlie Chaplin, Graham Sutherland, Yehudi Menuhin, etc., who had been made doctors. Talked a bit with Graham about his exhibition. He has a very Kenneth Clark manner and his wife has a very Jane Clark manner. Moved in to lunch. Sat between Tess Rothschild* and Mrs Beloff† who talked about how marvellous Yevtushenko was; and opposite Robert Graves, who was a bit remote. He is a very 50–50 man. As Osbert Sitwell once said: 'A unique case of a man who is 50 per cent schoolmaster and 50 per cent schoolboy.' Fifty per cent nice, 50 per cent nasty, 50 per cent a good poet, 50 per cent a bad one.

30 June

I worked most of today putting together about 200 pages of my book. Relieved to find it really looks like a book, if not with one subject, at least of interconnected essays! When I've done with this will feel free for poetry.

6 July

Got home to find Wystan there. He gives the impression of being somehow sated; fairly contented but self-sufficient and not wanting to see anyone. Only interested in what has long interested him. He has an odd way of hardly looking at one while he makes himself comfortable, putting on his carpet slippers, and settling down to his own thoughts, or a book. I don't think there is anyone from whom he gets

* Teresa Rothschild (*née* Mayor), wife of the 3rd Lord Rothschild.
† Nora Beloff, *Observer* correspondent on Soviet affairs.

anything new, unless perhaps a theologian. However when he gets into his subjects he is more interesting than any other writer I know. We listened to the new recording of *Rheingold*, which warmed him up a lot. After dinner he talked about form and surprised me greatly by saying he thinks endlessly about what form would best suit his subjects. Explained he wants now in his poetry to write something which seems to the reader almost like prose but in which he is playing an elaborate formal game, e.g. Encomium Balnei, is written in lines each of which has either thirteen feet or eight feet and that then are broken up into what looks like separate lines.

it is odd that the English

a rather dirty people   [13]

should have invented the slogan   [8]
Cleanliness is next to Godliness

meaning by that   [13]

etc.

In 'the English', 'the' and 'Eng' elide and in one foot ('th'English').

He said that for him poetry now meant (1) having something truthful to say, (2) exploring the possibilities of the English language.

Discussed how what he hated about writing was the whole business of the literary life.

William Faulkner died.

8 July

Woke up with usual thoughts: 'Getting and spending we lay waste our powers.' Thought too how wrong is the fairly prevalent idea that poets need to be quizzed or corrected by critics. All that is true in this is that perhaps occasionally a whole generation needs a big push, a trumpet blast, a revolution, a manifesto, a preface to *Lyrical Ballads*. After that what they most need is to reread past poetry, to make comparisons.

9 July

Went to dine with Elizabeth Bowen. Natasha talked about Mary McCarthy. The Berlins arrived, there was more talk about Mary and others. Just as we were about to go Isaiah started to talk about the Romantics. He said Romanticism was not a French movement.

Essentially it was the expression of German resentment for France, an assertion of German characteristics. Romanticism basically existentialist: the feeling there was no order or significance given in nature or metaphysics outside human individuality and therefore they had to create their values for themselves. Idea of shaking fist at universe, making one's own world, standing up to defend it and die for it.

11 July

After breakfast Wystan questioned me about biographical facts for my obituary, which he is writing for *The Times*.

Later I thought I would like him to say somewhere that my life was in some way ambiguous, like one of those arranged photographs, which if you look at it from one direction has a different face from that which you see from another.

12 July

Office. Lunch with Dom Moraes. He took me to a Chinese club near South Kensington. He was nice, showed me a longer poem, very gifted but too facile; his inability to work into the detail. He gossiped amusingly about various figures in literary life. An impression of people entirely concerned with one another's affairs, getting money by any means, smilers with knives, verbal in a personal or perhaps a critical-scholarly way, but with no test for anything but their own words, each other's personalities, sex, money, drink, living in stuffy rooms, drinking rather than eating – no pictures, no music.

13 July

Attended the meeting of Gresham's professors at Morris Hall, followed by their luncheon. The chairman said that the Master had communicated to him an eight-page letter suggesting various improvements, the contents of which he did not think he should divulge to us. Someone said that according to his testament none of us should be married, but in fact the document expressly said that professors might be married. The chairman said a committee would be formed which would have perhaps twelve meetings in the course of the next two years. He did not think that any alteration in our arrangements was contemplated for at least three years. Everyone seemed to deplore the present state of lecturing in an abyss to a few eccentrics but none seemed to want to do anything about it.

We were then given a wonderful City lunch, with excellent wine. I sat next to H. V. Hodson who talked about Ditchling. The new Master seemed quite annoyed when he learned that none of us had been told about his proposed reforms.

14 July

After the office collected Matthew Smith and Bomberg paintings, which have been reframed. Also got the small Sutherland from Marlborough Fine Arts. Then rearranged paintings at home. Was too tired to do anything else. All the same I think I spend far too much time doing this sort of thing. Surround myself with art instead of writing my own art.

Met Francis Bacon in the street and had a drink with him. He said he liked the two little poems I sent him and wondered why I did not think they were good. I said maybe I was predisposed towards the poems I had been working at a great deal. He said he thought sometimes it was a good thing to take a very long time over things and he was thinking he should do just this.

18 July

Spent much of the day recording three BBC talk programmes to be done in October, for Anna Kallin.

Took Matthew to Patrick Woodcock who wrote a letter saying he was run down and needed a holiday, but otherwise OK.

Party for Hillary Trust at Michael Astor's.

Dinner at St James's Club given by Osbert Lancaster for Seferiadis.

19 July

Lunch with Alasdair Clayre* at the Garrick. He is a young Fellow of All Souls, vague, talented, gently rebellious, who has written a novel, and is now working at poems. He said he hardly goes to AS because it's not conducive to work. Talked about the anti-creativeness of Oxford Senior Common Rooms where every impulse that provokes the unreasonable compulsive fantasizing effort which is creative dissolves in talk. Oxford is too sceptical, asks too many questions, is too superior. The attitude of Oxford when I was there – an 'Oxford aesthete', an 'Oxford poet', an 'Oxford undergraduate in love' – in every case the label 'Oxford' implied

* Poet who recited his poems accompanying himself with guitar. A brilliant eccentric who later committed suicide.

consciousness that this situation had arisen before, that Oxford had been through it, ignored it, survived it, tolerated it, laughed at it, known better than it. When I was at University College the thing that really brought the Master, Sir Michael Sadler, into contempt with his SCR was not that he was an old fuddy-duddy who waffled on about education, but that he had the most wonderful eye for modern painting, and had Gauguins and van Goghs, etc., at the Master's Lodgings. As the son of the tutor who was professor of aesthetics said to me once: 'The other dons simply pee on Sadler because he has those crazy paintings.'

To write a poem or novel is to the Senior Common Room a way of giving yourself away, showing that you are unhappy, or obsessed, or in love, that there is something in you which has been held back and is not resolvable into the Oxford of shared conversation. If you write a poem or novel, or paint a picture, it is about something, and this means that it is about a situation which has already arisen and been made a subject of knowledgeable discussion – moreover, it has probably already been written and painted better than you are likely to do it. Therefore to create anything reveals your ignorance of what has been done already. Moreover, if you do it, you do it in one way rather than another, which indicates ignorance of the many alternative ways in which it might have been done, probably better.

25 July / *Ireland*

Glenveagh, staying with Henry McIlhenny*

We went to an island off the coast and picnicked there. Wonderful shapes of druidical-seeming stones. This was the first time I thought of the country not just as scenery, but as presence, something still and locked which you do not look at so much as it looks at you, stares its way into your head.

29 July

I skip several pleasantly uneventful days. Lizzie fished, providing trout for breakfast every day. I drew, and worked at the last section of my book. N. rested and practised. We went for another picnic on the coast. Not as wonderful as the first one but very nice. Marvellous rocks. For the first time I really enter into Wystan's geological passion for limestone and rocks.

* The Chairman and benefactor of the Philadelphia Museum of Art, who presented Glenveagh Castle, County Donegal, to the Irish nation, in 1983.

1 August

When I was in Ireland I read Wilde's *Letters*. The extraordinary thing about Wilde is his complete confidence not just in his genius but in his seriousness as an artist. He doubted everything else about himself except that he was a marvellous poet and genius who turned philosophy into myth, etc. Yet I feel that the significance of his imprisonment and *De Profundis* is that it made him get beyond his superficiality as a person: he accuses Douglas again and again: the greatest crime is to be superficial, and yet though he could see through his own behaviour he couldn't see through himself as an artist. He couldn't even see that it is serious to be a comedian. He regarded his epigrams, etc., as sugaring the pill of a profound philosophy, and when, as in *The Importance of Being Earnest*, he was free of this pretence and therefore his realest self, as an artist he regarded this, his masterpiece, as mere *jeu d'esprit*.

Part of his fatal lack of seriousness was his inability to have a relationship with anyone else which was of an unquestioning mutually respecting kind as between equals. Friendship should be based on two people being able to meet, seeing in each other the fundamental situation of being alive and having to die, and disregarding who is more successful or more beautiful or more gifted than the other since as regards each other they are *dans le vrai*. Intelligence and sensibility and imagination are necessary only to the extent that without them there cannot be understanding. But given such understanding when two people are friends, then the qualities in which one may excel the other are evident to the world, but do not come within their friendship. The greatest defect of Wilde's letters is that one feels that he scarcely ever ceased to be in competition with his friends. In the crucial letter to Douglas just before he went to prison, he seems to have tried to get beyond this, to see that his feeling for Douglas must rest in mutuality, but the attempt was no sooner made than he abandoned it, and this letter was the turning point of his relationship with Douglas, which then became embittered as never before, though resumed as macabre caricature.

There is also something of an exercise in Shakespearian criticism in Wilde's relationship with Douglas, as though he were acting out the role of the poet in the Sonnets, and forcing Douglas to be the young man. Or perhaps there is a real parallel between Douglas and Shakespeare's young man. (Shaw hints at this.)

Wilde had the forgivable weakness of the addict, forgivable at any rate by posterity, which always forgives addicts because it does not have to pay their bad debts or smell the whisky on their breath. Apart from this addiction he had the virtues of generosity, an affectionate nature, infectious gaiety and great courage.

4 August

Whenever I try to write down my views about art, literature, etc., I find I am quickly bored, or suddenly I feel unserious. Today I was typing out my book and I discovered that my damned typewriter – the instrument of my working subconscious – had typed out as one word: 'visualfart', instead of 'visual art'. How can one go on after that?

Modern Christian writers like Eliot, Tate, etc., are ironic in their poetry and evidently consider irony a necessary 'modern' virtue. But Christianity is entirely without irony and does not even contain the potentiality of such an attitude.

5 August / *London*

N. and I alone at Loudoun Road. Everything extremely quiet without the children.

Worked all the morning. At six we went for drinks to Edith Sitwell whom we found in bed. I did not realize for quite some time that she had had a kind of relapse – a return of symptoms she got from a fall a year ago, when, as she explained to me, she 'dislocated several vertebrae'. She described the original fall vividly, how she got up in the night to open a window, could not find it and then missed her way back to bed, fell over a chair and was not found until the next morning. She said she was accident-prone as a result of having been kept in iron braces by her parents when she was a child: 'They finally even tried to put my nose in irons.'

The present accident, causing the dislocation to recur so that she had been 'screaming with pain', was the result of the chauffeur braking too suddenly. Edith, who was standing up to get out of the motor, was flung down. It is quite difficult to believe that Edith is in great pain and ill a lot of the time, though it is equally obvious that she really is. But everything she says seems to be on the same plane of unreality and almost all of it is said in exactly the same tone of voice. She said she had had one of the most terrible weeks of her life because the *Sunday Times* had sent round an interviewer who asked her whether she liked being 75, was afraid of dying, etc. Another thing – the papers had announced that the sale at Christie's of her manuscripts had brought in £3,000 when it was really £15,000. This she considered libellous. Finally, Marilyn Monroe has died today and the papers keep ringing Edith about this.

Another reason it is extremely difficult to take a Sitwell illness seriously is that the whole ménage is given to falling down on a scale that seems grotesque. With her, one never knows who is in favour, or out. It is safe to assume that all catty remarks about women writers will be well received. But knowing she greatly liked L. who, I read, has been imprisoned in Portugal, I asked tenderly after him. She replied that he had a terribly swollen head before he went and that she hoped that prison would deflate it a bit. There were a lot of grim truths about L, she indicated, that she would not tell me. Arthur Waley had sent her a postcard saying that L. was released so she assumed he was all right.

She was genuinely upset by a paragraph in the *Sunday Express* about two boys who tortured a cat and gouged out its eyes. All that had happened was that they were fined £5. She said she wanted to write to the *Sunday Express* suggesting that people who were cruel to animals should be pilloried, the police standing by to make sure that onlookers did not attack them. It was Osbert's idea – Osbert is a magistrate – that this would be a suitable punishment. N. said she thought the onlookers would take no notice of those put in the stocks. I tried to discourage her from writing such a letter.

11 August

I went to Francis Bacon's studio this morning and he talked about painting. F. doesn't think painting should be a record. It should be an exploration of reality which gives it a new twist. 'What I am thinking all the time is how in painting I can slightly complicate the game. I can do very little but I think when I am optimistic that I might still live to make the game a bit more complicated.' We talked about the weight of the tradition, and how with the whole of past painting behind him, there was so little one could do to give it a new twist. He thinks the New York school are wrong because they simply ignore the past, treat painting as though it had never happened before and thus simply arrive at decoration. Picasso, he thought, often went too far and simply produced caricature.

F. also went some way towards expanding what he meant by the twist. He said he wanted to do some little thing which gave the image added depth and poignancy.

16 August

Last Sunday we called on Henry Moore. He was in very good form. He likes to receive on Sunday afternoons, he says, because when he was a boy he was so miserable on Sundays that now he wants to be distracted and cannot work.

He is experimenting with breaking up the reclining figure, into two or three portions. In the most recent, the two separate pieces are almost at right-angles.

19 August / *Edinburgh*

We did not set out till midday for York.

Drove across the Yorkshire moors along the beautiful route which leads through Muker, where I went with Matthew three years ago. It is a road along a very long valley, with villages all built of the same stone. The moors with their gold-green grass, polished, mirror-like, reflecting the sky. Seems like nowhere else. It is a bit of England outside the rest of the world.

Matthew, then 14, discovered this road and insisted on my taking it. I was rather annoyed at first because the car, which we had just bought, was going badly and I did not like to drive thirty miles away from a garage. Also this was a very disturbing time for me. But Matthew was so enraptured that I forgot everything else. We came to a bare part of the moor where I stopped because the engine was overheating. M. got out and rushed to the top of a ridge. During the journey, what I remember best was that when I was looking preoccupied, he said: 'Don't look like that, Dad, I simply can't bear it' and I felt grieved for the burden one inadvertently puts on children. It was also before the Edinburgh Festival *Mary Stuart*. Just before the play began Matthew said encouragingly: 'Remember, Dad, whatever happens it can't be as boring as *Hamlet*.'

He was as involved with the success or failure of *MS*, as I had been at the age of 11 in the General Election when my father stood as Liberal candidate for Bath. Matthew was enthusiastic about it, but a bit exhausted I think by the strain. After telling me not to worry, he said: 'As a matter of fact I know nothing about the theatre and things like that, but it seems to me very good.'

21 August

We drove into Edinburgh. Lunched with the writers. At 2.30 there was the first meeting of the conference about the novel. The hall was packed. Angus Wilson and Mary McCarthy spoke first.

These two introductions seemed immensely promising – but after this there was the usual collapse into back-scratching, sly self-felicitation, over-modest disclaimers, special pleading of special groups, which is inevitable in writers' conferences.

Lawrence Durrell was grand and simple and unhelpful. 'The only yardstick is to ask yourself three questions of a novel: "Has it made me care? Has it brought me joy? Has it changed your life at all?"'

Later, Muriel Spark got up and waxed indignant about the question: 'Has it changed your life?' She said the last thing a novelist should do was to attempt to change anyone's life. 'Don't let us forget the dignity of our profession, which is not to change the public but to serve it.' She also claimed to know nothing about novels because she wrote them. 'I couldn't write them if I knew anything about them.'

The novelists seemed much less knowing of criticism than the poets were. But then poets today are simply critics' guinea-pigs – at any rate their poems are. The so-called 'science' of modern criticism has been invented specifically for performing vivisection on poets. The novelist is too large, too untidy, too untamed an animal to receive the attention of critics. Lawrence Durrell's remark about the novel changing the reader's life is one of the hoariest clichés of modern criticism (I. A. Richards, Leavis, etc.). Durrell presumably had picked it up because he is a poet. Perhaps because she is a novelist, Muriel Spark seemed never to have heard of it.

Rebecca West said it would have been no loss to the world if most of the writers now writing had been strangled at birth. She seemed to attribute to T. S. Eliot the view that the novel should not be about character. Her general grudge was that if you wrote novels with characters in them they got bad reviews, whereas if you wrote the novel of sensibility or about the state of consciousness below the level of conscious character, you got praised. Perhaps the person who should really have been strangled at birth – to satisfy Dame Rebecca – is Freud. Anyway it is not Eliot, but a novelist, D. H. Lawrence, who wrote to

Edward Garnett that he was sick of the novel of character and interested in the forces of moving through life which were below the 'level
of character'. And another novelist, Virginia Woolf, attacked 'the
characters' in Arnold Bennett's novels and suggested they disguised
the real nature of people.

Colin MacInnes praised Henry Miller; and Henry Miller got up and
said he didn't see why we were discussing the novel, which had been
dead a hundred years anyway. He had made the journey to see Edinburgh. He hoped we'd get around to discussing something interesting,
like painting.

20 September

The gap of a month in keeping this journal has been filled almost
entirely with proof correcting. We came home at the end of August by
way of Derby.

26 September

If you put all the factors of political conflict into action you arrive at
the lowest possible common denominator revealed in all too human
behaviour.

3 December

Bruern. A big gap partly filled by a separate volume with something
about South America and Malta in it. But very scrappy. I have either
had more than I feel able to write about when I have been doing the
proofs of my book – and am now frantically trying to do articles – or
things so trivial I am ashamed to record them.

Suddenly realized that I want very much that Matthew should go
up to Oxford. That it is an élite, that his friends are going there, and
that if he doesn't he will be left behind by the best members of his
generation. I felt this especially when driving into Chipping Norton to
get the Sunday papers. It is a thought that runs contrary to my
principles and even my sympathies, but I realized that I thought my
Oxford contemporaries as in some way superior beings. Going there
makes me enjoy such conversation and exchange of ideas in circumstances of easy companionship and comparative leisure with the best
contemporaries of one's generation during their most formative years.
For M. not to continue there with the very nice friends he has at

Westminster is like a relationship being cut off just when it's maturing and may be most valuable.

Then I thought how little Oxford had done for a good many of my friends, and how it made people in some way unreal, how as a community it isolated us for the rest of our lives, how the most energetic tough and creative people will probably now not come from Oxford and Cambridge. But I still wanted him to go. The alternatives of the Slade, travel, London, etc., all seemed scruffy.

6 December

Went to *Observer* Club lunch at Bertorelli's. Only about six of us there, but much nicer than usual as among them were Stuart Hampshire and Bernard Williams. Discussion after a time settled down to the usual Common Market debate. The fog continues. At the office this morning I noticed my hair had gone quite black, and at luncheon, that Stuart's was also darker than usual. In fog I feel like a frozen gas main. I really can't bear lacking light.

8 December

Yesterday morning much agitation about Matthew's birth certificate for entrance to Merton and New College.

I wrote a very short story (1,000 words plus) called 'The Best Christmas', commissioned by the *Sunday Telegraph*. At this stage I think it is good, better than I feared it might be. It is difficult to say as it was very painful to write, being (a) about Christmas, which I find a painful topic, (b) about my father. It is not only painful to think about that period in which all that has been from the start is rooted, but there is something about my father's and mother's families which makes me feel cheated of life. At the same time I am much more sympathetic to my father than previously, and this makes the unhappiness we caused him seem unjustified, whereas in the old days I used to feel that we were in the right.

18 December

Dined with Edith Sitwell. There were about five people there. Edith sat in her wheelchair looking very pale and tired and ill and really doing all the talking because when she is with a group of people she can listen and talk only on her own wavelength. There was a humiliating atmosphere of everyone being sycophantic, courtiers, feeding her with titbits of gossip and malice which would amuse her and draw her out. Whenever there was a silence it was appalling, as though boredom and sterility might seep like the fog outside through a chink in a door or a window. Anecdotes were dragged out of the past and held up for inspection. No one was quite successful in living up to Edith's tone. As a matter of fact she was rather brilliant, although this gave one the feeling that she had to make all the effort and added to the sense of humiliation. She gave one or two amusing examples of her replies to foolish letters. She had a letter from some silly woman saying, 'Dear Dame Edith, As an admirer of your poems I am nevertheless greatly disturbed by a poem containing a line about the mating of tigers. I have a daughter of 19 – at that age – where the brook runs into the river – and a son aged 10 who is very restless. I wish to entreat you dear Dame Edith when you write your poetry, to consider the disturbing effect that lines like those about the mating of tigers may have on the young.' Edith wrote back: 'Tell your dirty little brats to read *King Lear*.'

25 December

Came to Bruern for Christmas with Lizzie, Matthew, Granny and Philip* Spender.

Have been working intermittently – without much success – at the difficult second section of my poem.† The more I think about it the more absorbing I find the whole subject of pronouns ... The first section explores the discovery that one is 'I' and that others must also realize that he or she is 'I'.

Christianity is about the fact that every individual is to himself or herself 'I'. The figure of Christ crucified is that of the 'I' of each individual. The 'I' of Christ is the common denominator of all humanity entering into everyone and which everyone can enter into. In the example of Christ this common denominator is reduced to the lowest level of suffering and deprivation with nothing but the requirements of 'bare necessity' added to it. There is the contradiction though of the last being first – that by making himself last Christ makes himself

---

* Philip Spender (born 1941), my nephew. Son of my elder brother Michael and his second wife Nancy. Godson of W. H. Auden (see *Epistle to a Godson*). On the staff of *Index on Censorship*.

† A long poem about pronouns.

the most famous. One wonders whether people would admire Christ so much if he had not discovered this very subtle way of being super-star.

So Christianity is the religion which recognizes everyone is 'I'. Marxism is the religion of 'he'. Each individual is required to regard himself not as the 'I' separate and subtracted from all others, but as 'he' the objective result of his conditioning by the social class to which he belongs. That he regards himself at all as 'I' either for the purposes of believing himself to be guilty or innocent is an illusion produced by the old religion. He can change himself only by transforming his circumstances, making himself the objective result of a different class – for example by the bourgeois going over to the proletariat.

'We' are the people who make revolutions in the belief that when we have done so the new society while incorporating 'our' interests will also be the realization of the generous impulses and ideals of 'us'. Actually 'we' represent only a transitional phase of changing one kind of society for another, for the reason that 'we' care only for the realization of our own humanity, 'we' are not interested in power.

'They' are the ruling class, the directors, organizers, police who embody power – the new power consolidated after the dissolution and overthrow of the old power by 'we'.

'He' is the spearhead and subsequent dictator of the new ruling class, supreme representative of their interests, maintaining his position because he has convinced them that he is theirs, and that he thinks of nothing day or night except power – for the ruling class 'they' for the most part are rather sleepy. Secure in their power, vested in his, they like to think of his lights turned on long after midnight in the citadel.

26 December

Quite a subdued Boxing Day. I have gone on with my long poem.

Commentary
1965–70

In October 1965 I became Poetry Consultant at the Library of Congress, the appointment lasting for an academic year. After my return to London in 1966 I gave the Clark Lectures at Cambridge on the relationship between English and American writers, which were later published, much expanded, under the title Love–Hate Relations.

In January 1966 Frank Kermode succeeded me as co-editor of Encounter, *for which I continued to be a contributing editor. In the following year, from January to May 1967, I was a Visiting Fellow at the Center of Advanced Studies at Wesleyan University, Middletown, Connecticut. In April of that year, an editor of* Ramparts, *the muckraking magazine, telephoned me from California to tell me that they were about to print an article to show that the Congress for Cultural Freedom was financed by the CIA, and that the many Foundations that were listed in its literature as its sponsors, were in fact themselves receiving money from the CIA, which they channelled into the CCF. I immediately got into touch with Michael Josselson, then head of the CCF. Instead of assuring me, as he had done a few weeks previously when a similar charge had been made and I had asked him about it, that the Foundations did indeed independently pay for the CCF, he now replied that the charge was true. I went to London, and after a meeting of the board of* Encounter *and subsequent ones with Cecil King (the British sponsor), Frank Kermode and I resigned as editors. We objected to having been misled, I for fourteen years and he for two, by our CCF American colleagues, and to having consequently in good faith defended* Encounter *upon information now shown to be untrue.*

Many people then and subsequently took the line that since the CCF promoted some outstandingly good cultural enterprises (such as the Festival of Twentieth-century Masterpieces in Paris in 1952, and a conference of economists and political thinkers in Milan in 1958, which Hugh Gaitskell told me was the most interesting meeting of its kind he had ever attended), it was immaterial where the money came from. This might have been true, provided there had been no concealment, that no false source was named, and that the interest of the sponsors was declared. On the information I had hitherto consistently been given, I had believed that, in having it printed in the pages of Encounter that it was sponsored by the CCF, its American interest was declared. But the interest of the CIA was not declared either to the general public or to the English literary co-editors.

In 1968 I gave the Mellon Lectures at the National Gallery in Washington on the relations between painting and literature. It was interesting to be in Washington at this time. There were riots and student unrest in the US as in other countries. I happened to be in New York in April of that year when English friends asked me to look for their daughter who was at Columbia University. Climbing through a window, I caught up with her in the President's office, which, together with other students, she was occupying. I became very interested in the students' revolt, which reminded me of ideological debates in my own youth, and I decided to write about it. So in May I went to Paris where I was stuck for a month by a general strike coincident with the very stylized student re-enactment of past revolutions in Paris, with barricades built of paving stones blocking the boulevards. When I was able to leave Paris, I went to Berlin, and then to Prague. I wrote a book called The Year of the Young Rebels. The Czech students of Karl University in Prague were the ones with whom I sympathized because, essentially, they were fighting for their university, its traditions and freedoms, and not against it. Later in the summer, at Mas St Jérôme in France, I listened to the news on the radio, hour by hour, as the occupation of Prague by the Red Army was reported.

In the previous year (1967) The Times published an open letter by the Russian dissident Pavel Litvinov, with Larisa Daniel, protesting about the conduct of the Galanskov-Ginsberg trial in Moscow, and appealing to the world for those who sympathized with the dissidents and their cause to write to him at an address given at the end of the letter. In order to make an immediate response, Natasha and I had spent two days telephoning to friends all over the world. After this we sent a telegram to Litvinov declaring that the signatories had read his appeal, admired his courage, sympathized with his cause, and would do what they could to help. They were W. H. Auden, A. J. Ayer, C. M. Bowra, C. Day Lewis, Stuart Hampshire, Jacquetta Hawkes, Julian Huxley, Mary McCarthy, Yehudi Menuhin, Henry Moore, Sonia Orwell, J. B. Priestley, Bertrand Russell, Paul Scofield, Stephen Spender and Igor Stravinsky.

At the time of the invasion of Czechoslovakia, I received a reply to our telegram from Litvinov, a long letter taking our offer of help seriously, and asking me to form an organization in England that would concern itself with making known the fate of victims of persecution and censorship (writers, scholars, artists, musicians). He emphasized that it should concern itself with cases not only in Russia but wherever they occurred in any part of the world. This was the origin of the founding of Index on Censorship. *David Astor, Stuart Hampshire, Edward Crankshaw and I, with advice and encouragement from Amnesty International, formed a charitable trust, under the chairmanship of Lord Gardiner, called Writers and Scholars International Trust, which publishes* Index.

For my sixtieth birthday, on 28 February 1969, Natasha joined me at Storrs, Connecticut, where I was teaching at the University of Connecticut. I was at Storrs again for a semester in the following year, in early 1970. In the Classics Department, the star of the University was Rex Warner, around whom the social life of the English Faculty seemed also to revolve. This was the most congenial English Faculty I was to know in all my years of teaching in America.

At the end of 1970 I was appointed Professor of English Literature at University College, London, where I remained for the next six years.

7

Washington Diary
1965

16 October

I telephoned Robert Lowell in New York. He was very upset at the death of Randall Jarrell. RJ had been ill – nervously ill – for several months, seemed to be better, went home, started teaching again, had returned to the hospital for further treatment. He walked out of the hospital and threw himself against a passing car.*

Randall had been Poetry Consultant at the Library of Congress, and everyone from the Reference Division (to which the Poetry Consultant is attached) seemed upset. They asked me downstairs into an office where we stood round listening to the Chief Librarian's remarks about Randall, which were broadcast.

The thought that Jarrell had perhaps become disillusioned with poetry occurred to me. It was reinforced by the accident that a marine brought me his poems to read at the L. of C. They are interesting. He said he had stopped writing six months ago because he had become disillusioned with poetry. I asked why, and he said because he had decided that poetry was rhetoric and he didn't see how poetic rhetoric could affect the world today. He is being sent to Vietnam and he has decided to cultivate a detachment towards life and to regard fighting in the jungle simply as 'experience'.

All this relates to what appears to me to be a fatality of American

---

*Elizabeth Hardwick (then Mrs Robert Lowell), to whom I sent this passage from my journal (in 1966) commented:

(1) Jarrell was not in a mental hospital at the time of his death but being treated for a physical ailment. At the time my husband saw you he thought Jarrell 'had thrown himself against a passing car'. Mrs Jarrell now says it isn't true, and has gotten an official verdict of 'accident' to replace the one of suicide.

(2) My husband actually feels he has been able to write 'in spite of the breakdowns'. He does not consider them an aid to writing poetry in any sense! Of course, everything is a part of one's persona, as he said, like a broken leg.

Randall Jarrell's Letters (1985), edited by Mary Jarrell, gives a full account of the circumstances of the accident.

poets, which is different from any English attitude that I can think of. Theodore Roethke died a few months ago, after several mental break-downs. Lowell makes his own breakdowns the subject of some of his poetry, so that he evidently regards them as an inseparable part of his poetic persona. Berryman has breakdowns, and so on and so on. One of the things that puzzled me about Jarrell was his bitter complaint that the modern poet has no audience. I once heard him give a lecture, at Harvard, to 2,000 people, going on about this, which struck me as rather absurd, but in the light of what has happened it now seems tragic. I think that American poets, far more than English ones, cling to the idea that the poet is 'unacknowledged legislator'. (I was surprised to find in Pound's letters a remark that Shelley was right about this.) They have a public concept of the efficacy of poetry: and usually they accept bitterly that the poet is quite inefficacious. The fact that they have readers, and audiences who listen to them reading their poems, does not at all console them. Indeed the more readers and listeners they have, the more it is demonstrable that the values of American life are not affected by poetic values.

One great difference between English and American poets, ever since the early part of the century when Pound and Eliot came to England, is that the American poet feels himself to be conducting a war, through the values which he creates in his poetry, against the debased values of modern society. And this, of course, is a tragic conflict. English poets do not, like their American colleagues, reflect bitterly that all they are doing is writing poetry for other poets. It is exactly this which they want to do.

19 October / *Washington*

Last night a 61-year-old Negro poet, M.R. Tolson, read his poems at the Library of Congress. A tall, bald, distinguished man with a classroom manner (he teaches). He began by reading early poems, which were of the Uncle Tom variety. One was about how Uncle Sam goes to sleep for a long period, then wakes up, if conked over the head at Pearl Harbor or the likes. But half-way through the reading, he switched from being a tame progressive good-boy Negro to being a licensed rebel. He now read a poem about a White man ordering drinks at a bar, 'One for you and one for me and one for the nigger.' As he went on he became more and more colour-conscious, more rhythmic and Spiritual (Negro Spiritual) in manner. He chanted a song of Liberian Independence in celebration of which he was wearing a medal. He read African proverbs, several of them obscene and directed at White men. He ended by reading what seemed a subversive poem about a shark swallowing a turtle which eats its way through the black interior of the shark and, finally, through the wall of the shark's stomach.

The audience consisted of some Whites (mostly women) and some respectable-looking dressy Coloured people. The whole occasion had the air of a hypocritical conspiracy of forces which had to accept each other's existence – a progressive cause which had to be swallowed by both sides like the shark swallowing the turtle which ate the shark.

10 November / *Princeton*

Conversation with Isaiah Berlin about the Romantics. He said they were all haunted by the fear that the universe might be a perfectly regulated totally unalterable machine which man stood outside and could not influence in any way nor enter into at any point. They wanted, in their works, not to stand outside nature but to enter into it with their own feelings, so that tree or landscape became a vital animistic object felt as a form of life and energy responding to the feelings of the poet.

Read Louis MacNeice's *The Strings are False* – memories of Ireland, school, Oxford, etc. Clear and lively, sharply remembered, written with the speaking voice. Very decent and warm and courageous his attitude to politics in the thirties: his going at the last moment, the moment of defeat, after the honeymoon of the Left, to Barcelona in the autumn of 1938. His limitation (also his virtue) is the result of his excessively well-trained mind, which makes him rarely write the unexpected. There are no weeds, no ragged borders: flower beds planted from bright, gay, intelligent seeds out of known packets. If by free associating words from time to time he allows himself some freedoms, the effect is of someone who has gone into the woods, uprooted some primroses and ferns and planted them in his own back yard. It is really like a book by a superbly trained human animal, whose whims still display his high breeding, not moving an inch beyond the curve described by the light lash of the whip. He is more mannerist than surrealist. To judge from his recollections he always seems to have been fully conscious at the time of any one relationship he had of his attitude towards it, e.g. in the account of his first marriage, it seems that he had from the moment of falling in love with Mary Beasley the same detached awareness of her character. He certainly did seem to 'cast a cold eye' on the world around him. One thought of him leaning back, regarding one with amused detachment through half-closed eyes. In fact his memoir shows he did regard me in this way. But I can't believe – from remembering them together at Oxford – that he judged Mary quite as objectively, at the time of their engagement even, as here appears.

Louis's almost cold-blooded air of superiority made a great impression sometimes. During the war, at the time when he was Ambassador to Moscow, Archibald Clerk-Kerr (later Lord Inverchapel) on a visit to London gave a party for those English intellectuals who might be considered sympathetic to Russian writers. One of the poets was Louis MacNeice who, leaning back against the chimneypiece, and holding a glass in one hand, surveyed the party through half-closed eyes, without addressing a word to anyone. As he was leaving the party, Clerk-Kerr went up to him, and asked: 'Are you Irish?' 'You might call it that,' said MacNeice. 'From the North?' 'Yes.' 'From the east coast?' 'Yes.' 'Well,' said Clerk-Kerr, 'that confirms the story I have heard that a school of seals went on shore and interbred with the people living on that part of the coast of Ireland.' He then made his ambassadorial exit from the party.

11 November

At my Poetry Consultant's office this morning, I had a call from a man who wanted me, straightaway by telephone, to provide a metaphor for – I've forgotten what. He gave me examples of metaphors he had thought up. One was for a bank, which he likened to 'a dam that collects the driblets which might otherwise flow away and banks them up, thus fitting them into the whole social spectrum'.

14 November

Dinner at Henry Brandon's (American correspondent of the *Sunday Times*). The James Restons, the Joseph Krafts, and the New Zealand Ambassador and his wife were there.

Reston talked about President Johnson and the United States in a somewhat idealistic way. He said that the great aim of America after 1945 was not to repeat the mistake with which she was reproached after the first war, of dissociating herself from the rest of the world. At Yalta Churchill and Stalin had asked Roosevelt how long now he intended to stay in Europe and he had answered, 'Two years'. Already now they had stayed twenty. Reston said that even in Vietnam America was observing the principle that wherever there was aggression she would step in and stop it. The rest of us demurred at this point and said that America's aim in Vietnam was simply to stop China. We discussed imperialism and I argued that America was filling the vacuum left by the European empires in Asia. Also America was becoming obsessed by the Balance of Power (on a world scale rather than a continental one), just as Britain had been. Reston said there might be truth in this, but none the less America had aims more far-reaching than those of Wilson, Heath, Shastri, and others; and if she was not supported in these aims she would probably withdraw into some new form of isolation. He said that what Johnson now wanted from India was some sign of readiness to carry out in her own country action corresponding to Johnson's promotion in America of the idea of the Great Society. He thought the time had come when America expected some greater conception of the future from her allies than any of them had shown to date. He insisted on the idea of 'greatness', and he quoted Walt Whitman's 'O pioneers!' Whereas in the past Americans had thought that perhaps Europeans were tired and that America must turn away and discover her own goals, since the war she had been turning to the rest of the world for an affirmation of the 'American dream' of fulfilling aims which lay beyond empire and the use of power. 'When we expected some response from the English,' one of the others said, 'all that happened was that Macmillan came to Washington to beg for some Polaris submarines.'

The conversation – as always at Washington parties – turned to the President, and all three said from their experience how different he was when he talked in private from when he used his public voice. In private he was full of ideas, pithy. He employed brilliant metaphors and many anecdotes. In public he failed to communicate. 'Compared with Kennedy, he is like a man who has the words but can supply no melody,' said Reston. Reston recalled how at the White House once when he had seen Johnson being followed round by his photographer who was trying to record an image which would supersede other inferior ones, he had said to the President, 'You are using the wrong instruments. What you should have is a tape recorded to take down the things you say when you are grappling with your ideas among a few friends.'

21 November / *Washington*

Dined with Professor Y, who is a philosopher with tenure at a great American university but who has been granted leave of absence to work for the Administration. There were two other professors in the same position, as advisers – Professor T. and Professor K. What struck me was the mental or spiritual self-intoxication of the professors when they are transferred from the academy to the centre of power, as though they had been promoted from dream into reality. Y. told me that he regarded President Johnson as 'a natural force which drives ever onwards and cannot be stopped'. He recounted the delights of getting a few things done when he is able (as occasionally happens) to put forward a proposal (he has just scored one about visas) which is adopted by this human force instead of being rejected by it. He told me one or two anecdotes to illustrate 'the appalling mix-ups' which occur at this power-centre and which, he said, 'one can't imagine happening anywhere else'. E.g. (1) the National Opera and the Philadelphia Orchestra are both booked to go to Mexico City, the same fortnight, at the same hall; (2) the chess champion Bobby Fischer was not allowed to go to play an international match in Cuba, and then after his having played the match by thirty hours' telephoning, got into great difficulties trying to cash payments from Cuba consisting of his fee and his prize. Finally, after rebuffs all the way along the line, the Secretary of the Treasury allowed him to take the prize money but not the fee because the fee was a Cuban government payment. The prize, however, could be regarded as exceptional. I record these anecdotes not because they are particularly amusing, or even very much to any kind of point – for surely they are examples of the kind of thing that happens with government departments all the time – but because they give a sense of the self-importance which the professor attaches to himself when he feels that he is close to the machinations of real power. The examples themselves seem as slight as froth blown off tankards of beer into the audience during some old-style performance of a Restoration comedy. (Note 1985: during the Johnson Administration, one had the impression, from endless discussion about the President, that Washingtonians regarded the American President as some superhuman power-obsessed monster installed in his shrine of the

White House, pawing the ground and breathing fire, like the Minotaur. Stories of his amazing language and uncouth manners seeped like smoke through crannies of doors and windows. The representative of a small but powerful state told me that when he visited the President on a mission for his country, Johnson greeted him with the words, 'Ah was just scratchin' mah ass this mornin' when ah started thinkin' of your little country.')

8 December

Pennington, New Jersey: staying with Jo and Muriel Buttinger

A week ago I took the Conrad Aikens out to lunch in Washington, before doing so calling for them at their rooms for a drink. They each had two Martinis before lunch (and were drinking already when I arrived), and they continued to drink Martinis throughout lunch. Aiken has an exposed look from wide blue eyes staring out of his enflamed-looking face. *Enflamed* really is the word that characterizes him, I think. Mary Aiken: cosy, intelligent, a bit dishevelled, but friendly and reassuring – as indeed they both are. I took them to lunch at a restaurant on Pennsylvania Avenue, which he said he had frequented when he was Poetry Consultant.

He talked about the early days when he had been a fellow student of Eliot at Harvard. He remarked that a young man had recently written a thesis on the influence of Santayana on Eliot, on Aiken himself, and on someone else, whose name I did not catch. The young man had sent this to Eliot and received a very categorical letter written in his own hand, from Eliot, telling the author that Santayana had never had the slightest influence on him at Harvard; indeed Eliot had considered Santayana rather a charlatan. Aiken thought this an example of Eliot covering up his tracks, because nothing could be less true, Aiken said.

Aiken said that he remembered very well Eliot writing to him when he first met Ezra Pound that EP's poetry was 'pathetically incompetent'. That was a great difference from his attitude three years later when he wrote the essay on Pound's metrics.

We talked about Robert Frost. I said that everyone seemed agreed that Frost was very designing, but I did not suppose that to have been the case when he was a young man. 'Oh no,' said Aiken, 'he was always the same.' When he returned from England to America, he gave Aiken advice about whom to meet there. The name of J. C. Squire came up and he said, 'Greet him from me, but in an off-hand way.'

Aiken's conversation is full of such anecdotes – pellets hurled very effectively at reputations. He said that Eliot was extremely adroit at handling his literary career. His real ambition was the drama, and in fact his poetry was always dramatic. When Aiken went to visit him a few years ago at Faber's, he found Eliot holding in his hand a book which had just come out. As soon as Aiken came into the room, Eliot got up from his chair, pressed the volume into his hand and said, 'I've done it again.' It was *The Cocktail Party*.

Something of Aiken's own sad character comes out in this. His role as Greek Chorus to Eliot's success. The Greek Chorus is capable, of course, of acid comment.

8

Diary Poems
1970

During the first months of 1970 I was in Storrs, teaching at the University of Connecticut. I did not keep journals but I wrote what I called to myself *Diary Poems*. These were accounts of day-to-day events that struck me as suitable for such treatment, written in free verse: worked on a bit afterwards, always with a view to getting closer to the events described. Two of these, 'Art Student' and 'Central Heating' were subsequently published in *The Generous Days*; and a third, 'Auden at Milwaukee' in the collection *W. H. Auden: A Tribute*, which I edited. Of these three, I print here only the last. The other poems have not been previously published.

The first of these poems written in Storrs is the recollection of a reading that Auden gave in London a month previously at some Bloomsbury church; after which Tom Driberg who had, in his Church of England capacity, arranged the reading, took Natasha, Lizzie and myself, together with Marianne Faithfull and Chris Jagger (brother of Mick Jagger), to dinner in a private room at a nearby hotel.

26 January 1970

> November, Auden came to stay in London.
> Famous, much-photographed creased face
> Netted in the past, his eyes can only tell
> Their solitude. His talk
> Is concentrated 'I', 'I get up at eight,
> Then I have cawfee and rolls, then I do
> *The Times* Crossword, if I can get *The Times*.
> Then I go to the john, and then I work
> Until elevenses, when I have tea.
> I have to have lunch at one precisely.

At six precisely I fix up Martinis
90 per cent vodka 70 proof.
Dinner at 7.30 not one moment later
Or I tend to become repetitive.
Then at nine byebyes like mother taught me.
Oh! the relief of getting between the sheets!'

'How should I educate my 4-year-old son?'
Marianne asks. He hoists his face towards her
Then blandly says: 'Send him to boarding school
As soon as he's 7. That's what happened with me.
Teach him Latin. If he makes a false quantity
Beat him like I was beaten if I did.' She tells him
Of her suicide attempt. 'I took a hundred tablets
In Sydney.' 'Now that's naughty.
I take one every night
For sleeping and a Benzedrine each morning
For working.' He clicks his mouth shut.
I say: 'You talk of nothing but yourself.'
He looks full at me with a kind of sweetness
And says: 'What else should I talk about then?
What else do I know about?' Now Chris produces
A magazine called *Suck*. 'Will you autograph this, please,
        sir?
Your wonderful poem called "The Platonic Blow Job".'
'I wrote that as an exercise in scazons.'
They smile. He can say what he likes, they know
He has written the sexiest beautifullest openest
Poem about a pick-up in Greenwich Village
The knock-out that makes all their sex soap-opera.
Back home, he says to me: 'Promise me one thing,
Promise me this one thing, you'll never
However she may ask you, show to Lizzie
That poem.' Under the net of lines, he smiles
Under the lines the heart ever the same.

27 January / *Storrs*

I went to New York to Robert Lowell's studio where he had suggested
we show each other poems, each criticizing the other's.

> Went to Lowell's studio room: the window
> A great tall frame that plucks out of the sky
> Hunks of cylinders of water towers,
> Biscuit-coloured among pent-houses
> Of skyscrapers like antique furniture.
> Both serious and wryly funny,
> He says the Trillings so love Oxford
> They talk of it like ducks about water.
> Then bows his head like a conductor
> Over a score spread out, his poem,
> His face and hands shape thoughts from air.
> Next, putting his typed text between us,
> He reads three sonnets: 'Richard II', 'Richard III',
> 'Napoleon': enislanded
> Images round which there flow
> Anecdotes like gleaming water
> From which words jump like frogs into our time.
> I show him three of mine. He likes
> One, but with great hands lays bare
> My sonnet rhymed that unlike his
> Unrhymed, has clichés in it: 'Heart'
> Rhyming with 'part': and that Shakespearian
> Bogged-down-in-its-own-time word, '*Semblance*'.
> All this is true. And can be dealt with. Can *I*, though?
> I leave with brain that runs like a computer
> Sifting alternatives, reprogramming
> The word game with a question that it bungled – *semblance*
> Thrown out upon the New York air.

28 January / *Storrs*

I had been in Florence on 2 January when our granddaughter Saskia
was born in a hospital there.

> We looked at Matthew's child, our granddaughter,
> Through the glass screen, where eight babies
> Blazed like red candles on a table.

Her crumpled face and hands were like
Chrysalis and ferns uncurling.
'Is our baby a genius?' he asked a nun.
We went to the Uffizi and he looked at
Italian Primitives, and found
All of their Christ-childs ugly.
He started drawing Maro and her daughter
Nine hours after Saskia had been born.

14 February / *Storrs*

Driving through snow from Storrs to Princeton to visit Stuart and
Renée Hampshire.

Driving along the road and looking
Through clear glass where screen-wipers weave
Twin circumferences, I see
Shadows and lights among which wheels
Make time in space. My brain
Is drugged by the inpouring emptiness
Through which I stare between the trees
That line the road each side, with branches
Like brooms shaking white dust. To keep awake
I must persuade myself this fairy stage
Is solid, and not swansdown. If
I crossed those margins or met head-on
Those white-owl headlights flying towards me
I'd be the killer or the killed. I have to
Fix my mind on friends, the firelit
End to this journey: or else on
The work that must not end before begun.

28 February / *Storrs*

I drove to New York and dined with Auden. My sixty-first birthday:
his sixty-third was two days ago, 26 February.

Dined with Auden. He'd been at Milwaukee
Three days, talking to the students.
'They loved me. They were entranced.' His face lit up the scene.
I saw there the picture of him, crammed into
Carpet-bag clothes and carpet slippers,

His face alone alive alone above them.
He must have negotiated himself into the room
Like an object, a prize, a gift that knows its worth,
Measuring his value out to them on scales
Word weighed by word, absorbed in his own voice.
He knows they're young, and, better, that he's old.
He shares his distance from them like a joke.
They love him for it. This, because they feel
That he belongs to none yet gives to all.
They see him as an object, artefact, that time
Has ploughed criss-cross with all these lines
Yet has a core within that purely burns.

6 May / *Washington*

When I was at the Library of Congress I had got to know Mrs Alice
Longworth, the legendary daughter of President Theodore Roosevelt.
Extremely witty and amusing, very political and of this world, she had
some quality of unvulgar Roman detachment which reminded me of
Virginia Woolf whom at times – perhaps by identity of opposites – to
me, she seemed to resemble physically. When, returning to Washington
in early May 1970, I had tea with her there was an American offensive
going on in Vietnam. I forget who the senator was at her tea party.

Famous old lady with the wicked gaze,
Sparse hair drawn back to clear the deck, her forehead,
Presiding at her tea-table, speaks of
Her girlhood: – daddy, then Vice-President,
Yearned for the White House. 'How I prayed
And prayed and prayed, and buried totems
Of dead frogs and tin soldiers in the garden
Of the White House, so daddy's wish be granted.
Then BANG! McKinley gone! For me, that day
Was rapture, purest bliss, when daddy got
Just what he wanted, in a trice, you see.'
Then both went on the presidential yacht,
Visiting royalties, the nicest was
Kaiser Wilhelm the Second, after him
The Empress of Japan. But now the door
Opens, a servant enters, says: 'The White House, madam.'

[273]

Mrs Longworth leaves the room, returning
Ten minutes later, rubbing her hands gleefully.
'What did he say?' the senator asks quietly.
'Oh, that I can't tell,' wagging a finger at him.
'All I can say is that the new offensive
Is going very well, yes excellently.
They're rooting out the enemy from his hide-outs
And capturing his weapons. It will all be over
Within eight weeks. Then, total victory!'
'They're killing them?' 'Deaths? Don't let's speak of deaths!'
She looks all round the room, a little wildly.
'What is this silence? Under your conversation
I hear a silence – a terrible silence.'

25 January / *New York*

This entry is printed out of context because it does not fit in quite with
the diary poems, though the anecdotes as told approach free verse form.

An elevator man at the Blackstone Hotel asked: 'Did you read Sir
Eesiah Berlin's article in the *New York Times* about the Historic Past?'
'I'm afraid not.'

'Well, Sir Eesiah's right. You can't know nothing about the past until
you're dead.'

I asked the students:

> ' "I should have been a pair of ragged claws
> Scuttling across the floors of silent seas."

Does it strike you about these two lines from Eliot's 'Prufrock' that
they are a shade too literary, too Jacobean?'

A girl puts up her hand: 'Don't they mean that he'd like-ter-have-
been a lobster and just grab her'?

I tell an assistant at the Museum of Modern Art that I've lost my
membership card.

He asks me my name, and then writes out on a pink ticket: 'Mr Spent.'

I say: 'That's not my name.'

He says: 'That may seem important to you but I assure you with
what's written on this ticket, they'll let you in.'

Part II

1974-1983

Commentary
1973-6

I continued being Professor at University College, London, until 1975, when I retired, a year before the compulsory retirement age of 67. We went to St Jérôme all these summers. For many of them Iris Murdoch and John Bayley stayed with us a week or two and there were other friends who stayed from time to time.

Late in September of 1973 we drove back from France by way of Normandy. As soon as we entered our house in London, a friend who had been looking after it told us that he had just heard on the News that Auden had died. We cancelled a dinner party that we were to have given with food we had bought in Normandy.

The following November, our friends Christopher and Elizabeth Glenconner gave a dinner at the Savoy Hotel to celebrate the seventieth birthday of Cyril Connolly. Cyril, who had interested himself tremendously in the menu, often visiting the chef to consult with him about it, was already ill. He ate very little of this feast. Neither – as he told me later – could he see the guests, who were as carefully chosen as the menu, for he was almost blind with cataract. Cyril's exorbitant standards of hospitality outlived his own gourmandise.

Cyril's death marked the end of the Horizon era, identified with his pleasure-loving personality, overflowing witticisms, aesthetic perceptions expressed in a prose like silver Latin: an era, overlapping with, and in many respects the opposite of that of the thirties' political conscience, transformed into theology in later Auden. There was so wide a gulf between the two – reflecting that between two Oxford generations of the aesthetic twenties and the political thirties – as to make it seem strange that Auden and Connolly died within a year of each other.

After retirement from UC I resumed my American life of freelance teaching, first at the University of Connecticut, then, in May 1976, I went for a semester to the University of Florida, at Gainesville.

9

Journal
1974-6

1974

15 November / *London*

I first saw David Jones* in the 1930s. The drawing which forms the frontispiece of *In Parenthesis* gives the best view of him – a soldier, younger, smaller, odder, more entangled in crucifying barbed wire, than any other soldier, yet taking upon himself the courage and companionship of his fellow soldiers and translating it into some image of a universal timeless soldier which reaches back to the Roman legions in Britain, the Roman soldiers who spat at Christ.

He remained, I should say, faithful all his life to the memory of the trenches – it was this that enclosed him in a neurasthenic envelope, taking the form of frightful migraines. He was isolated from everyone else yet not alienated nor an outsider. He was a very healthy glowing friendly invalid.

I was not a close friend of his but I think I may have been partly instrumental in getting him perhaps the only American prize money he received. An American publisher asked me whether I could recommend an English work, which he would produce as a 'rare book' in a beautiful edition. I recommended *In Parenthesis*, which accordingly was published and, I suppose, sold well. After this, through the advice, I think, of Kathleen Raine, David received the Bollingen Award.

This was given under terms carefully designed by the American donors to avoid income tax (as it would have done in America) on an award which was given as charity to sustain a writer working on a project from which he could anticipate only a minimal financial return. David Jones's *Anathemata* on which he was working exactly filled this description. So David received the first considerable money in his life, about £500. The English income-tax authorities took the view, however, that this award did not come under the terms of being an untaxed

* David Jones (1885-1974). Painter and poet. Author of *In Parenthesis* and *The Anathemata*.

'prize' (like winning on the pools) as it was specifically connected with David Jones's 'profession' of being a poet.

Three income-tax commissioners set aside a day in court to prove that DJ must pay tax on the Bollingen Award. David appeared, wrapped in a heavy greatcoat and muffler. Kathleen Raine and I as 'witnesses' spent a whole day trying to argue that being a poet is not a profession in the sense of meaning that receiving an award for writing a poem was payment for professional work. The answer to all our arguments was that the very term 'for work in progress', which relieved the recipient from tax in America, defined him as professional in England. The tax commissioners were tremendously patient and understanding – and absolutely relentless – in taking their pound of flesh – or spirit, rather – from the only serious money – if £500 is serious – that David had ever received for his writing.

24 November

Writing for the sixth time my memoir of Cyril Connolly. Rang his home and learned from his step-daughter that there is some hope. Heart and liver improved. He has rallied.

Evening. Robert Lowell, Roy Fuller, I.A. Richards and I read in honour of Allen Tate's seventy-fifth birthday at the Mermaid Theatre.

During the reading of a poem by Allen Tate, a poem came complete into my head. I thought it would be rude to make a note: I would remember it. I have forgotten it utterly – only have a vague, superficial idea of what it was about.

29 November

Cyril died on Tuesday. Deirdre* had been to see him on Monday and he was conscious and lucid. Deirdre seemed happy about the visit. The whole week is vague to me, dominated by thinking of Cyril and writing the memoir for the *TLS*.

Rang John Gross† who said he liked the piece. I keep on remembering things I'd intended to put in, but haven't, e.g., I mention Cyril's love, semi-identification with, animals (the lemurs in *The Unquiet Grave*, for instance). I meant to go on to say that, though not a visionary, he had a vision of the world of fauna and flora, which made them for him the earthly paradise.

---

* His wife.

† At that time editor of the *Times Literary Supplement*.

I was also hurried in what I said about *Horizon*. What I meant to say was that editing at the outbreak of war provided Cyril with a situation, partly passive and receptive (reading manuscripts) which also released an almost effortless flow of positive energy in the *Comments*, which are his most vital writing. *Horizon* in the early part of the war, when England suddenly became one beleaguered family, put him into a harmonious relationship with a significant, though limited, public which he could address as individuals, some of whom appreciated, others of whom scoffed at him and his hedonism (but he took the scoffing with great humour). The result was that he wrote *Comments* in which he was really able to relate his awareness of the sensuous particularities of living to politics.

A joke about Cyril was his love of eating lobsters expressed by Rose Macaulay's quip (*pace* Landor), 'Lobsters he loved, and next to lobsters, sex.' But since he was so much a person with a romantic idea of the things he loved, I wonder whether he did not love lobsters because of some deep affinity he felt with them, so that eating them gave him a sacramental sense of unity with the animal world in the depths of the sea. His imagination was a diving bell.

2 December

Cyril's funeral. We went from Victoria to Eastbourne by train with Sonia Orwell, Jack Lambert,* Noel Blakiston† and Diana Witherby.‡ Met by a cortège of Daimlers, which took us to Berwick Church. Very pretty interior, but over-prettified by murals of Duncan Grant and Vanessa Bell. Duncan was seated there at the back of the church, with his daughter.

Lesson and psalm all about the resurrection of the body – seemed unsuitable for Cyril. The vicar, who has a stick without which he can't stand up, talked very briefly and understandingly about Cyril and his work. We all stood round the flower-covered grave in the wet and cold, just a tarpaulin of some kind over the coffin. We drove with Alan and Jennifer Ross to a party at Deirdre's afterwards. Lots of champagne. Matthew Connolly¶ was brought in and sat docilely on people's knees – the party acquired the normality of any champagne party.

---

* J.W. Lambert. Literary and Arts Editor, the *Sunday Times* 1960-76.

† Noel Blakiston (1905-85), friend of Cyril Connolly's from Eton. Author-editor of *A Romantic Friendship*.

‡ Diana Witherby. A friend who helped in the founding and early days of *Horizon*.

¶ Son of Cyril and Deirdre Connolly.

12 December / *San Sano, Lecchi in Chianti*

Matthew met us at Pisa Airport. A bright cold day. The duomo sparkled in the sunshine like quartz. Shadows were transparent, geometrical, mysterious, as in early de Chirico. People grouped around the cathedral looked like figures on a stage set.

14 December / *San Sano*

Wonderful weather: cold and clear. We drove to San Gimignano for lunch, through dark brown fields, glossy and shining in lines like strands of combed hair, where they have been ploughed; bare-bone tree trunks and boughs, grey-stone farmhouses, bat-shaped, clinging to the sides of hills. Woods of holm oaks, which retain through winter their yellow-ochre leaves, and which sometimes, in the light and against the surrounding brownness and boniness, seem a flaming orange. San Gimignano, a cubistic dream with its towers – cubes on cubes – and its square piazza. We lunched at the hotel which looks out between two towers on a huge landscape with cypresses like cenotaphs against the amber plain, and in the distance the hills – the lapis-lazuli blue of primitive painting. I took what I hope are quite inspired photographs.

15 December / *San Sano*

Natasha is hooked on the idea of us buying a house here – which excites me too. But we never will. Maro* said: 'Matthew says that when you go out together you don't talk to him. You haven't had a conversation for ages. Why can't you and M. go away alone for a week together somewhere? Then you could really talk.'

Later I suggested to M. that we should do just this and he was delighted. So we'll arrange it somehow.

18 December

Drove to Florence. Matthew very gay, the visit was felt by all to have been a wonderful success. M. gave us etchings, and to take to Lizzie, Granny, etc.

20 December / *London*

Cyril's memorial service. I got up early and typed – entirely rewriting – my address. Cyril's friends seemed to like it.

* Maro Spender, Matthew's wife.

21 December / *Mishkenot, Jerusalem*

Flight to Jerusalem, with Natasha, and the Annans – Noel and Gabriele – Aline and Isaiah Berlin, and Stuart Hampshire.

23 December / *Jerusalem*

Whole day trip with Aline Berlin and Peter Halban, her son, and the Annans along the Dead Sea coastal road from Qumrān to Eilat and then inland to Dimona and thence to Kibbutz Revivim. The desert is a single land-and-sky-scape of clouds above, and rock and sand and dunes sculpted by wind and rain and erosion, below. The earth, an embossed reflector of the changes in the sky. Vehicles – such as our two cars – drive through it, passing, from time to time, those triremes – camels. With the evening, the land seems drunk with the sky. At sunset, when we drove back along the road from Beersheba, impossible to tell whether the plain, which had become one rose colour, was sky or land. At midday, seen against the then blue sky with its few white clouds, the great rock of Masada and the mountain ridge beyond, rust-red. To the north, the Dead Sea – black lacquer: to the south – green-black. When we had driven some miles further south, the sea – beyond the line of a long jetty which stretches several miles into it – became a very pale green. Here, where there are desalination plants and factories, the sea fades into shallows with the salt white as snow near the coast. Little floating islands of salt like gleaming ice-floes, in creeks.

We drove past Sodom (difficult to think of anyone ever getting anything as enjoyable as sin out of what is geographically, as well as its having been once morally, the lowest spot of the world) and then up to Dimona, where we had lunch.

Christmas Eve / *Jerusalem*

After dinner, to the Church of the Nativity, for Midnight Mass. The Church is large and bare. The Mass was intoned in Latin, with some dignity. The huge crowd consisted partly of devout pilgrims, partly of functionaries (the Governor of Jordan was there as well as, of course, the Mayor of Jerusalem, Teddy Kollek), military police and tourists, among them more than a sprinkling of American hippies. These had a dazed air of finding themselves at the greatest freak ceremony of all time. I saw two of them staring at the Stations of the Cross with a look of 'Wow!', contemplating perhaps their own crucifixion as a fabulous Last Exit. Two others, who found themselves separated by the vast crowd from their companion, a dwarflike woman with bright blue eyes staring through a shock of flame-coloured hair, could not bear to be parted from her and tried with stretched arms to make a path for her between some nuns, whose leader made disapproving noises, and signed them to desist. They meekly but sadly gave in, but I noted, a few minutes later, that the dwarf was reunited to them and the three wore what was probably the most blissfully religious expression of all the congregation except, perhaps, the Archbishop. The Bethlehem Boy Scouts who seem to have been brought in as police auxiliaries, behaved as though they were characters in a Firbank novel, much to the indignation of an Irish priest who said, in his brogue, that they could probably not understand, that he would *repart* them.

The most beautiful part of the evening was after we left the service and walked back along the road the two miles to Rebecca's Well, where our car was parked. We heard, from that distance across the valley dividing us from Bethlehem, the voices from the church still singing, which the cold night air seemed to purify of raggedness and wrong notes, so that coming from the hill above us, they seemed those of a heavenly choir.

Christmas Day

We drove with Aline to the Herodium, the fortress of Herod on a hill south-east of Bethlehem where Herod is supposed (according to Josephus) to be buried. From a distance, the top of the hill looks as if it had been cut off and flattened out, as by an egg slicer.

A wonderful drive from Jerusalem through a countryside of stony hills, fawn-coloured, under a sky in which clouds, looking like stony fragments of the hills below them, moved. Hillsides here are sometimes terraced and there are what seem pocket-handkerchief-size fields cultivated by Arabs. Stony surfaces, scraped and lined, engraved and combed, by ploughshares and heaven knows what weather through the centuries. From here Jerusalem seems the summit of the world, a jewelled crown uplifted to the heavens.

From the top of the mound of Herod's Fortress, vistas of Nazareth and Jerusalem on the one side, the Dead Sea on the other. The country is glossy like a deer's flanks dappled by cloud shadows.

The Annans, the Berlins, Stuart Hampshire, the Spenders – we all went to Cohen's Restaurant where dinner consisted of six varieties of meat balls stuffed into six varieties of vegetables. Teddy Kollek drove us there. On the way he suddenly asked for the cars to be halted. 'Get out', he said, 'and walk to the edge of the gully.' We did so, and saw, almost immediately below us, the old first-century Jewish cemetery with the tomb called after Absalom – a dazzling white pyramid.

26 December

Saw the Islamic Museum (or the Mayer Museum), which has recently been opened. Marvellous ceramics and miniatures, scenes from an *Arabian Nights* world. One miniature showed twenty-two Egyptian ladies of the utmost beauty scattering like just-shed flower petals from a centre, fainting with emotion on the arrival of two beautiful princes at the court. Strange to see these exquisite works from a civilization of luxuriantly developed sensuality casketed and cosseted as it were in beleaguered democratic modern socialist Israel surrounded by terri-tories of Arabian sheikhs who have spent their billions got from oil not on gold-embroidered silks, miniatures, ivories and bejewelled daggers but on aeroplanes, tanks, guns, Cadillacs, and who dress themselves up like the European and American tycoons one sees in the shop windows of Paris, London, New York.

27 December

Taken there by Teddy Kollek, we all lunched at the residence of the Armenian Archbishop in Jerusalem. I told him that our daughter-in-law, Maro, was an Armenian. At this he showed a lively interest. I said she was the daughter of Arshile Gorky and he said: 'Ah, that Gorky is a great painter.' The Archbishop then mentioned having met Archbishop Fisher, and Stuart said he had been the Headmaster of Repton, the public school to which he went. Stuart added that the Headmaster began every morning with studying his stocks and shares, which were of more interest to him than his prayers. Teddy Kollek said: 'Archbishops who are much interested in business are not un-known to us here either': at which the Archbishop as near as anything winked.

1975

3 January / *Jerusalem*

The Yad Vashem Memorial Museum.

Here we see exhibited the unspeakable results of the Final Solution. In our enlightened age of science and progress, the means provided by science were used by Hitler to commit what evil and superstitious tyrannies in the past had never been able to achieve on such a vast scale; and which in our time, only one other modern tyrant – Stalin – achieved – the murder of millions of their fellow human beings. What is incredible to people like ourselves, visitors to this museum, is that our world of enlightenment and reason (as we think) could exist side by side with this world of horror and appalling evil – that second world using the means of the first to bring forward and to multiply the most terrible crimes of an atavistic past. That this happened was indeed in part made possible by the sheer incredulity of all but a very few exceptionally aware people.

Ideology, that bridge between the old religion of superstition and the new religions of pseudo-science – whether Marxist or fascist – is what connected this atavistic hatred of nation for nation, class for class, to the scientific means of murder and torture.

One walks through rooms lined with the passport-style photographs made by the murderers of their victims, each photograph seeming to reduce the identity of the subject to the anonymity of a bureaucratic stamp. In the hard white light of the camera these faces have a curious dazed look, as though the flesh were a white halo through which the black eyes stare.

Attended a ceremony at the museum, which was preceded and followed by a rabbi chanting a traditional song of commemoration of the dead. This intense rapt lament had a poignancy which seems to come out of the earliest days of his race. Yet it also mixes with the modern and might have been composed yesterday by Webern or by Berg. Here, not in politics but in art, the atavistic and the modern merge prophetically. One may well think in Yad Vashem that our modern world, with all its sophistication, at the edges falls precipitately back into the primitive.

But are the Israelis right to insist so much on the horror of the Holocaust? There is, one may think, too much of the Wailing Wall about Israel. Yet this nation was brought to birth out of the ashes of

6 million victims. The Holocaust is the negative pole of the positive which is Israel.

The poet Abbay Kovner embodies in his life and expresses in his work the history out of which Israel arose and the spirit in which the kibbutzim exist. Kovner became the leader of the Warsaw ghetto after the Germans had occupied the city. He helped organize the smuggling of Jews through tunnels and sewers out of the city into the forests. He is, I suppose, a man for whom the Holocaust is the central reality of his life, though he knew also Russian purges as well as the struggles of the Jews in Palestine at the time of the Mandate, and the war which followed the founding of the Jewish state.

Kovner writes poetry which is not in the least what one would expect from a man of action, a mysterious poetry in which crude and violent events are related to traditions and rituals.

I think of Kovner as having been one of those pale almost transparent-looking youths, with a look of haunting devotion that illuminates his face, an exception among those photographs of the inhabitants of the ghetto where most expressions are reduced to the common denominator of the about-to-be-killed.

5 January

Afternoon, we called on President Katzir, whom we had already met at the Weizman Institute three years ago. He has a face that seems like granite cleft with lines on the forehead and between the eyebrows. He welcomed us and reminisced about the days of the Weizman Institute (he still goes there two days a week, he told us).

He joked about the duties of the president saying that they were like those of a British constitutional monarch. He touched a deeper note when he spoke of the problems and difficulties of having to deal with politicians. 'But doing so has taught me a lot about human nature, so perhaps it is a good thing.' Then, with more intensity, he said: 'Sometimes I wish that politics could be settled according to the requirements of a given situation, and not according to the interests of power and money and nationality and intrigue which the politicians represent . . .' He went still further – said that the disputes of politicians could make him despair of the human race. 'But I am a biologist and have to believe that human life will survive.'

After a bit I said we should go, as he must have things to do. But he pressed us to stay, saying it was a relief to talk among friends.

Mrs Katzir gave a tragic impression – which reflected on him as well. They both seemed sad. She asked me what I thought of the mood of people I had met and when I said they seemed serious but determined and confident, she said: 'Underneath they are very unhappy. The whole world seems to have turned against us. When I saw that the United Nations gave a standing ovation to our worst enemy – Arafat – I realized this was true. You know, sometimes in a family there is a very ill person and all the rest of the family and his friends suddenly feel disgusted by his illness, and don't want to see him. That is how we are.'

I tried to point out that the United Nations reflected a false picture of world opinion, but it was obviously impossible to comfort her. One had the impression that she was crying. Tears were infectious. Natasha and I felt, I suppose, that we might easily cry too . . .

7 January

Flew back in a jumbo jet, El Al having stopped their strike. There was a high proportion of rabbis among the passengers standing at the side of the plane with their leader leaning his prayer book against the emergency exit. They conducted a service in mid-Mediterranean.

9 January / *London*

Lunch party at the Stafford Hotel given by Kenneth Clark on the occasion of his coming to London *en route* to Cairo where he is making a film. Other guests: the John Pipers,* the Henry Moores,† Freddy Ashton,‡ and the Jock Murrays.¶ Jane Clark was wheeled in, looking magnificently made up, round and waxen like a large pink puppet. Henry M. sat on her right, I on her left. Henry M. arrived and left in a chauffeur-driven car. ('Oh, they're all so rich,' sighed Freddy.) Henry and I had to make heroic efforts to hear what Jane was saying. We took turns holding her plate up so she could lift the food to her mouth with her right hand, her left being paralysed. She said once or twice that she was very unhappy, but Henry said she had never looked better, braving untruth. Jock Murray told me it had always been his

---

* John Piper, the painter, and his wife Myfanwy, writer and librettist for Benjamin Britten.
† The sculptor and his wife, Irene.
‡ Sir Frederick Ashton, dancer and choreographer.
¶ John Murray, publisher, whose ancestor was Byron's publisher.

ambition to atone for the house of Murray having burned Byron's memoirs by publishing a complete edition of his letters. This he is doing.

At the end of the lunch Jane was wheeled out and there was some general conversation about abstract art, particularly that of Victor Pasmore. Henry got rather excited and talked about the time when Ben Nicholson, Barbara Hepworth and he had done abstractions in the early thirties when they had adjoining studios in Hampstead. All the artists felt that a long discussion was going to ensue but the waiter announced a telephone call from Jane to K, who left the room, saying: 'This sounds serious.' He came back a few minutes later saying it wasn't serious. All the same, the mood had been broken – we realized we were all expected to go. Henry said, 'Jane looks very well.' K. said stiffly: 'That's completely wrong. Things are very bad.'

14 January

The usual rush in which days go by scarcely noticed. Friday, lunched with Karl Miller,* who, discussing his own gloom, said: 'Why do you always seem so serene and happy?' I found it difficult to answer this question. Partly on some kind of Goethean philosophic principle that one ought to be positive, count one's blessings – and also avoid being got down either by one's own imaginary or even other people's real misery. Partly because I live too much in the day and therefore on the surface. Lack of self-pity combined with selfishness. Also gratitude for my family, for my children. Yet it rather surprises me that people see me as happy. Whenever I see myself (as in photos) I look miserable.

22 January

Have spent the past four days correcting proofs of my Eliot book. In doing so am maddened by the fact that the printers have become so expensive that the publishers send page proofs in which one can make only minimal corrections. Have become adept at making small operations in page proofs, taking out a clumsy paragraph and replacing it by one containing the same number of words or a sentence with one of the same number of letters. But this does not permit making fairly extensive cuts or injecting new material where there are hiatuses. And certainly, reading proofs, sometimes I see a place where something

* Professor of English Literature at University College, London; editor, *London Review of Books*.

added would enormously improve the book. For instance I mention that in his *Criterion* commentaries, Eliot criticizes supporters of fascism and communism, on purely intellectual grounds: e.g., that the British fascists have nothing to offer which in any way adds to the conservative authoritarian ideas put forward by Charles Maurras in about 1912; and that the young support communism on grounds of ideologies which, intellectually, are inferior to those of Christian theology. In doing this, he seems to overlook the reasons for extremism which are present in the surrounding life at that time: mass unemployment, the political violence of the police state – the life as it is suffered in the real circumstances of the time. What I forgot to suggest is that this indifference to the circumstances may have been the result of a certain indifference to human life altogether which Eliot felt at this time of great unhappiness for him.

Chester Kallman* died in Athens. I don't know anything about this except that Charles Monteith† rang me on Saturday to say he had died that morning. Sense of the inevitability of his death.

Chester was warm, witty, genuine, but completely a 'slob' with his endless 'camp', his hopeless self-indulgence. A scene that comes to my mind is (1950?) Venice, having drinks at Florian's with Chester, Wystan, Cecil Day Lewis (I think). In the middle of the conversation Chester got up and followed a sailor across the square, Wystan carried on with the conversation but as he did so his eyes were on Chester and tears were running down his cheeks.

Chester and Wystan most certainly adored and understood each other. They were by no means incompatible. (Wystan once said to me that Chester was far cleverer than he, Wystan. When I demurred, he said: 'I don't mean intellectually clever, I mean, intuitively, as my opposite.' So the idea that Chester, as an intelligence, was not 'up to' Wystan is false.) Yet it was impossible for them to live, except intermittently, together. Although Wystan enjoyed 'camp' and did not make moral judgements about sexual promiscuity, he suffered from Chester's infidelities, and he could not tolerate unpunctuality and not sticking to timetables. He had an open mind about sex but a closed one about clocks.

* Auden's friend.
† Publisher, of Faber and Faber, and friend of Auden.

Bob Silvers* rang from New York, and told me among other things that Chester had died intestate. Chester had a brother and an ancient father who has a wife many years younger than he who will inherit. For the fifth or sixth time I felt very resentful at the memory of Chester's slobbishness – that the entire estate goes to his father and step-mother seems altogether depressing. Wystan told us often that he wished it to go to his brother John Auden's children – his nieces – after Chester's death.

23 January

Memory of Wystan. He would like to have given evidence at the Lady Chatterley trial *supporting* the prosecution; stating that *Lady C was* pornographic! To him the test of pornography was whether reading the work produces, in the male, an erection.

29 January

Lunch yesterday with Harry Fainlight† – who is paranoid. As we walked along Tottenham Court Road, I asked him what he was doing. He said: 'Mostly street fighting.' 'Street fighting? What do you mean?' 'It's got to the stage now when they are murdering poets.' With a mad poet one may get the impression that he is simply living out metaphors which would not seem mad at all if they were expressed in his poetry. Thus the idea of a life going on today in the streets in which there are different sides who are dressed for their roles – some in business attire, some in leather jackets, and that the relation between these teams is one of running hostilities – this is a metaphor that would appear 'real' and perhaps true in a poem. To say this is to distinguish between poets who live out their metaphors before the world and in their behaviour and those who keep them below a kind of Plimsoll line. (Funny, that metaphor of the Plimsoll line has been in my mind ever since I first saw a ship with one, when I was 10, on holiday in Cornwall and my father explained its meaning to me. And I don't think I've ever used it till now. I can see an old cargo ship with a Plimsoll line on its side sailing into Fowey harbour as I write this.)

But one of Harry's views is that the distinction between the meta-phorical life and the literal one has become abolished in the minds of a whole lot of people walking in the street: those whom he refers to

---

* Editor of the *New York Review of Books*.

† A gifted, sensitive poet who ruined his health and mind through drug abuse.

vaguely as 'them'. Taking up his paper napkin he said: 'In order to communicate, they don't think it is necessary for me to write on this bit of paper and pass the written sheet on to you who then read it.' The breakdown of the conventions of communication has somehow been around a long time especially among those poets who have in their lives crossed the barrier between the metaphorical and the real. Thirty years ago after the dropping of the A-bomb a (then) young poet, David Gascoyne, who was in an extremely nervous condition, explained to me that the result of the explosion was to produce a mental or spiritual explosion inside people's heads so that there was a new unity of human consciousness caused by Hiroshima.

These ideas made sense to me. What seems unfortunate about poets living their metaphors in their lives is that they don't write them. There is I should say a new respect for the rational among poets. Since I am, I suppose, part of this rationalist establishment, poets like Harry have an odd attitude to me. He kept on saying: 'I don't understand your life.' By which he meant that he did not understand why I do not admit that I am mad.

The reason is partly that I value the parade, the show, the charm of *appearances*. I like to think of life as at least in part a non-stop festivity. If the truth of reality is (as I can well believe) the horror of today's violence, and if to be a poet is to be passionately aware of this all the time, showing that awareness in all he thinks and says and does, then I would rather not be a poet. On the whole I hate the squalor of poets at poetry readings. I prefer the poets who are reticent, who wear the uniform of a kind of life which has some non-poetic status to those who will go back to their cellars and sup off their raw and bleeding metaphors. (But reading this I feel: 'How philistine!')

6 February

Wrote my Israeli piece over the weekend. Sent it to the *New York Review of Books* on Monday. Am very dissatisfied with it.

I keep on remembering things I should have put in my Eliot book. Despite his being so influential – didactic even – there is no Eliot school. And this is because for another poet to write like Eliot he would have to have Eliot's combination of an intensely purist idea of poetry with, beyond it, a mysticism beyond poetry – separate ideas which nevertheless are always moving together until they finally join. He would also have to be able to transform in his work his personal ego into the colouration of an impersonal objective, yet extremely characteristic sensibility. But this also is impossible. Another poet could write poetry like Eliot's if he only knew what Eliot was like in his poetry. But this is withheld.

It would not be very difficult to imitate late Auden. For in his late poetry there is a rather crotchety persona into whose carpet slippers some ambitious young man with a technique as accomplished could slip. But it would be very difficult to imitate the early Auden – 'This lunar beauty/Has no history,/Is complete and early.' The reason for this is that, influenced by Eliot, though not imitating him, Auden in his early poetry has an idiosyncratic sensibility but no centre of his own personality.

7 February

Thoughts while shaving. A thing I am very ashamed of: that I find suggested confirmation of my 'identity' by reading my name in the newspapers. My heart really does do something journalistic – stop a beat, give a jump – if my eye hooks on to the printed word 'Spender' or even – now I am getting a bit astigmatic – any conformation of letters like it. ('Spring', for example.)

I really admire people who regard any publicity attached to them as vulgar and odious. I think of them in their cottage gardens with old-fashioned claustral red and white roses, enclosed by hedges, no act of theirs is in the slightest degree influenced by any wish for publicity. To them, for a television crew to arrive one day and do a film of them in their gardens would be a terrible obscenity.

11 February

Lunch with secretary of the PEN Club. Asked me whether I would be President in 1976 of the English branch. Said I would agree in principle. On Tuesday I rang V. S. Pritchett who said it would give him much pleasure if I'd accept.

17 February / (*Staying with Ann Fleming at Sevenhampton*)

Roy and Jennifer Jenkins* and Paul Channon† and his wife came to lunch. Talk about Mrs Thatcher being Shadow Conservative Leader.

---

* The Rt Hon Roy Jenkins PC, MP, politician and writer. Former Labour Minister; First Leader, Social Democratic Party.

† The Rt Hon Paul Channon PC, MP, Conservative Minister.

Also about Dick Crossman's funeral. I told malicious stories about Dick at Oxford, remembering, all the time that I was doing so, a reading party at Crackington Manor when I had a slight 'affair' with Dick which was compounded of passion and lust on both sides, and was not in the least serious. It was partly Dick's influence, contempt and perversity into whose focus I came at one moment – half an hour, let's say.

All these memories are now overweighed though by the news on the wireless that Dick's only son Patrick, aged 17, has hanged himself. In the announcement they seem to have connected his death with some remarks in the extracts from Crossman's journals published in the *Sunday Times* last week, which were reflections on his reasons for giving his son public education at a comprehensive, rather than the private education at Winchester, which Dick himself had.

I don't know whether the suicide was connected with the publication of Dick's journals, but if it is, it is the third or fourth recent example of the influence of the actions of the dead on the living. One: Cyril's debts which both leave his family in great difficulties and make claims on his friends beyond the grave; second, Chester's dying intestate with the result that all Wystan's money, royalties, etc., will go to an 83-year-old dentist – Chester's father – whose girlfriend married him recently.

I don't see any moral to be drawn from these things. Only a Hardy-esque irony, especially evident in what happened about Auden's money.

23 February

I am writing four sonnets about sculpture. They are really about Michelangelo and I've been reading Michelangelo's poems. Also writing the poem about Romanticism and the Industrial Revolution. Directly I start writing poetry I develop a resistance to doing so. I feel this could be a great poem – the poem I've always wanted to write, the great subject left over from the Romantic movement and the nineteenth century.

26 February

Yesterday lunched in the University College refectory. Bill Cold-stream* joined us. Rather red in the face and extremely funny. He

---

* Sir William Coldstream, painter, Slade Professor of Fine Art 1949-75.

started talking about Wystan. He said he had first met him when he (Bill) was 17. They had both been taken to see a play called *White Cargo* by a journalist who was queer, called Michael Davidson. After this he had met Wystan frequently and they had gone to films, theatres, etc. His pockets were always stuffed with papers on which there were poems. He remembered a line from one: 'The midwife seen against the curtain.' Bill also went to Wystan's home. His father was a very nice, rather subdued, man with the kind of voice of someone you overhear talking behind a hedge. But his mother was upright and downright, the kind of High Church which goes with near-upper-classness. Wystan asked Bill to go to bed with him 'in the nicest way possible, so that it was easy to refuse'.

His early friendship with Wystan must have been in 1925. Then they met again in the early thirties when they worked together with John Grierson on the Post Office Film Unit. J. Grierson was a tremendous admirer of the proletariat and used to do films in which workers appeared undressed to the waist, covered in sweat, while the voice of a background narrator described in heroic terms what they were doing. The best effect was produced if an enormous white-hot steel girder was shedding its strip of light on their upturned faces. Wystan and Bill were very irreverent about the pieties of Grierson and used to leave their office and go to the pub saying how much they hated the British worker. In a run-through of a film on a factory they heard the voice of the narrator say: 'Ever on the alert, this worker lubricates his tool with soap.' Grierson was furious when they told him he ought to cut this line. Bill said it was a pity it had not been left in. It would have been much appreciated in the north of England.

Recollections: Auden saying to me, late in life: 'I'm glad you've become a gourmet.'

After he walked out of the dramatization by Nevill Coghill of *The Canterbury Tales*, objecting to the coarse humour, he said it showed the difference between action and the written or spoken word without the action. Reading, or listening to it read, you would find this funny, because you were not confronted by the brutal fact – but to see enacted someone having a poker shoved up his arse or being thrown down a latrine was merely nauseating.

6 March

Mary McCarthy rang in the morning saying she was in London for a day. Could we lunch with her? We did so at the Ritz. In quite a businesslike way, as though to deal with matters in hand, she explained that she had not at all liked my piece about Israel in the *New York Review of Books*. She did not believe in the method of conveying information through reported interviews. If the interviewers are not named they became mere ghosts. I agreed with much of this, though found it spoiled my lunch by filling my mind with misgivings – fears that I had let down Bob Silvers, that the whole thing was a mistake, etc. Feelings I had already had when writing the piece and which I had in fact communicated to Bob when I sent the article in.

After lunch I happened to buy the *New Statesman*, and there read a review by Paul Theroux of Mary's book of reports on Vietnam which contained the following paragraph:

> The low point of her efforts, though she does not say this, was her desperate list of famous people who might be willing to go to Hanoi in 1972 in order to provoke Nixon to stop the Christmas 'carpet bombing'. There is certainly something creepy about Stephen Spender agreeing to go 'without hesitation' and then worrying about who would pay his air fare.

I was very annoyed when I read this. What seems wrong is to care what is written. The fear is that readers will have a wrong impression of one's behaviour. There is also the deeper fear that one will see it oneself in that distorted mirror of their opinion (or of what one imagines to be their opinion). My worrying about how to pay the fare to Hanoi was quite real. I didn't have the fare and would have had to obtain it in order to go there. I did not wish to be paid for by the North Vietnamese government or any similar organization (if there was a question of that). So why worry about Mr Paul Theroux saying my behaviour was 'creepy'? Well, because his readers would not know the facts. But then they will not care very much anyway. Well, because being the object of spiteful attack is worrying. But then, that is the world. Natasha wrote the following anagram: 'STEPHEN HAROLD SPENDER: Pen holds tender phrase.'

12 March

Francis Bacon writes about the 'frustration and despair' he feels when painting. I think that for him there is no exaggeration here, the feeling must be real.

Despair occurs when the artist does not work with a pre-prepared or a preconceived structure, such as a drawing, a model or object before him, in other words when he has not predecided his ideas and efforts. Everything – ideas and means – the paint itself – surrounds him with its swarm of potentialities threatening to engulf him. Creativity is a struggle to control this rush of ideas and means. Despair is almost a necessary condition in such circumstances. It is the measurable point in time and place at which the force he is trying to control almost overwhelms him, the point at which victory and defeat are in balance. It is either the moment of defeat, or of breakthrough.

In writing poetry I have to go through the stage of despair when I have mentally and quite convincingly abandoned the thing. But in a task as seemingly simple as writing a review for instance – certainly writing the *TLS* piece two months ago about Cyril Connolly. I also experience despair as the result of not having a disciplined mind (terrible defects in my education) and feeling overwhelmed by the material and the uncontrollable rush of my own ideas.

12–13 March

Matthew's birthday.
Worked. Dined with Rodrigo Moynihan.* Sonia (Orwell) was there and we spent the whole evening discussing Cyril's finances. We were each of us supposed to send appeals to various people. I must say I find this humiliating and pray that when I die no one will need to raise money for my widow, etc. Many suggestions were made, those by Natasha very helpful.

15 March / *Paris*

Rain. Taxi to Hilton Hotel. Left my things there. Then took taxi to Danton's statue. Boulevard St-Germain, direction given me by Lizzie for finding David Hockney's studio. This is in a little courtyard called Cour en Robson where Bonnard lived (David told me, pointing out as we left a view of the courtyard exactly as it is in a Bonnard painting). David said he greatly preferred Paris to London, that London was dull and lifeless, nothing was open after midnight, in order to enjoy yourself there you had to spend a great deal of money at expensive nightclubs,

* Rodrigo Moynihan, painter. Member of the London Group. Joint editor, with his wife Anne Dunn, John Ashbery and Sonia Orwell, of the magazine *Art and Literature* 1963-8.

there were no cafés, etc. And the worst of London was that no one protested. If he came back he would protest. He also talked rather angrily about the state of art in England. And about art schools, and said he now dared to say he hated modern art.

I went home thinking David has superb gifts both as an artist and as a character (he is honest and clear and decent). But he has always been divided between fashionability and vision, and his attacks on modern art, etc., though often justified are not relevant to what is right or wrong about his own art. For there was never any question of his being a 'modern'. What is required of him is that he should have vision acquired through critical acerbity and original idiosyncrasy. At present he seems lost.

16 March

A whole day of meetings about the UNESCO discrimination against Israel. Long speeches. Finally quite a good resolution, drafted mostly by Raymond Aron. I sat next to Aron at lunch. He seemed less gloomy about Israel than I thought he might be. Believes Sadat really does not want war and wants to come to an understanding with Israel. There is something very trying about the state of excitement people get into at conferences. Isaac Stern got into a terrific state of excitement about the protest artists should be making. He got covered in perspiration and kept on dashing to his room for an aspirin. The pianist Rubinstein was at this meeting. After studying his face for the entire session, I said: 'Mr Rubinstein, you look like a cross between Bertrand Russell and Chopin.' He replied: 'Bertrand Russell – good. But anyone can look like Chopin.'

23 March / *Oxford*

To do television programme for BBC TV *Book Programme* based on interview about Wystan in his undergraduate rooms, on the first floor of Peckwater Quad at Christchurch. They looked much smaller than I had remembered – and shabbier. I suppose that mentally I was back in undergraduate days, which accounts for my having some vivid memories – having for the first time heard Schnabel play Beethoven Opus 111 in the Town Hall. By the time it came to my being televised my memories were so vivid they thought they should make them the whole programme – excising John Wain (to my momentary mean and jealous satisfaction, I'm afraid) and two undergraduates. PS. Later I was very glad to hear that they did not cut the others out.

27 March / *Newfoundland*

An oblong of water apparently a natural harbour wedged between long horizontal hills, now covered with dirty snow through which dirtier rocks show. The harbour could – if it were like the old harbour at Marseilles for example – be very nice. One imagines clapboard houses, clean restaurants beyond a pleasant quayside framing the water. Actually there is a huge Esso oil refinery and several factories on the side opposite the town; on the town side a jumble of filling stations, large impersonal office blocks, a half-finished multistorey hotel, with, apparently, no windows in it. Outside the window of the room in the hotel where I am staying there is a gravel-covered balcony on which repose a dead seagull, a weather-soaked newspaper, two empty bottles and some chicken bones.

28 March / *New York*

My last evening at St John's was a faculty party, very much according to form. Various people told me that there would be a fog, a snowstorm or an Air Canada strike. They added to the claustrophobic feeling of St John's – so many squalid buildings crowding down the oblong pocket handkerchief of the harbour. A woman told me that St John's was the dirtiest town she knew and that the people there never cleaned up anything. When I got back to my hotel it was a crowded scene of Good Friday eve festivity. I went to my room and read *Wuthering Heights* listening to sounds of an orgiastic party along the corridor. The mixture of mechanical music, phoney female voices, growling masculine ones, emanated a vision of fat blondes and swelling businessmen – caricature images which motels give off.

Got up at five. Apart from anxiety about taxis the journey went quite smoothly to New York. Took a taxi to 166 East 68th (Muriel Buttinger's apartment). Put down my things and then went straight to the Metropolitan Museum to see the Francis Bacon show.

3 April / *Memphis*

Something happens in America which is like the change when water reaches freezing point or boiling point – and there is a total transformation of the atomic structure – and I suddenly see Americans in a warm and sympathetic light, which makes their furnishing of their houses, their conformism by which one might so easily judge them, irrelevant. If they are unimaginatively conventional in one respect, in quite another respect – their generous sympathies – they are magnificently conventional. I hear on TV about the thousands of Americans pleading to adopt Vietnamese war orphans and one sees the creative conscientious side of the country again – as though Americans had stopped reckoning the gain or loss of S.E. Asia and were concentrating entirely on a salvaging operation which would do practical good and in so doing to some extent atone for the price to the Vietnamese themselves of American failure in Vietnam. When America was bombing the North on such an unprecedented scale one heard very little of the victims (except from those who opposed the war). Now all Americans are united in wanting to help the victims, and to commit themselves to doing so for as long as it takes to bring up and educate a Vietnamese child.

4 April / *New Orleans*

Wonderful flights from Little Rock to Memphis and from Memphis to New Orleans. Seen from the air, the Mississippi is like a glittering Roman army, a force occupying the whole countryside. It looks as though, apart from the main army and its tributaries, it spreads out hidden under trees and grass of swamps, with shields and swords that reflect the sun's rays, and are visible through leaves and grass-blades.

From the air, the earth has the look of some recent art. It is its own full-scale replica composed of elements of earth, air, light and water and worked upon – formed – by those very elements. A river is a line drawn by its water across a plain. A dust storm or bowl is how the wind sculpts in dust. The hand of man seems that of an instinctive modeller using different materials: carving a house out of wood and bricks, making roads and railways, factories and slums out of their materials. He makes his habitat tracks his tracks like any other animal – like ants.

Landing at New Orleans we flew over Lake Pontchartrain (which I mistook for the mouth of the Mississippi). From the air, its expanse is seen bisected by a thin pure line – some artist has bisected it with this thread, like the wire down the length of a musical instrument. It is the longest causeway in the world – or so they tell you in New Orleans.

16–18 April / *New York*

Went with Ed Mendelson* to see Peter Matson† and discuss the Auden book. PM first of all seemed to think the publishers would want their money's worth in the form of scandal, gossip, etc. But we said we were not going to do this and I think I convinced him of our idea that we should write a book about the life leading into the poetry, not the poetry into the life, and that we need not discuss facts if they were not relevant to the work of the intellectual and moral development of Auden.

A flood of interviews of various kinds with journalists, broadcasters and TV on account of the idea for the Auden book.

Over these two days I decided to resign at once from UCL.‡ If I don't do so I shall not be able to get going with the Auden book till June 1976 – since it's very difficult to work in the summer.

I read a review by Anthony Quinton of my Eliot book, in the *Observer*. It is of the kind which I always bring down on myself and which is the result of the bad phraseology and lack of organization in my books. This gives a reviewer like Quinton the opportunity to misrepresent completely what I have written – which he certainly did. He sneers at me for calling Eliot a 'gentleman'. I felt humiliated and furious – with myself above all – perhaps this was a good thing in view of all the attention I was getting from the media – attention which is really a tribute to Auden.

Walking down Madison Avenue I saw a woebegone man with a look on his face which combined suffering with gentleness and sympathy, sitting on a trash can at the edge of the sidewalk. The bright sun made a halo of his white hair, his head was leaning sideways. I was reminded of a self-portrait, all anguish and wry humour, by Goya. It was Robert Lowell. For a moment I thought I'd pass him by, but something sweet and touching about his appearance made me decide to risk talking to him. (I had been told that he had had a breakdown.) So I went up and said: 'I hear you've taken an overdose of your pills and that you are in hospital.' He smiled affectionately and said: 'Yes, I'm better

---

* Professor Edward Mendelson, literary executor, editor and writer about Auden. Mendelson and I planned to write an Auden biography and then abandoned the project.

† Literary agent.

‡ From my professorship at University College, London. I was due to retire in a year's time.

now. I'll be out in a few days.' We talked a bit and he didn't seem to be under any strain, put me at my ease. I was just thinking we looked like two down-and-outs in a photo by Stieglitz, when two quite smartly dressed women started staring at us with a look of recognition. 'They're my nurses,' said RL. 'I'll have to rejoin them' and he walked along a few paces behind them as they crossed the street.

18 April

Caught the Boston 'shuttle' from La Guardia. Really, really tired after getting up at 5.30 and all those interviews. Also still undermined by the feeling that the Eliot book is a flop. To add to the mild torture of this I have the proofs for the US edition, which I must correct at Yale. Tea and dinner with Pauline de Rothschild.* Talked about my TV and radio advertising the Auden book and she said: 'One has the feeling that no one any longer reads books because they want to do so. They buy certain ones because they think some virtue is attached to them, as in the Middle Ages when they used to buy indulgences.' I agreed with this because it reaffirmed the view I've already been form-ing that even the young at the university take it for granted that they read in time paid for by their parents and/or the universities do so. They press to read very modern literature. But without their being paid to do so it is doubtful whether they would even read work of their own generation.

Pauline also talked about Glenway Westcott telling her that his journal was the first completely candid one ever written about the life and loves of a homosexual. 'He keeps on saying this, but I can hardly think it isn't a gross exaggeration.' I agreed it must be. There was Gide's journal for example. She asked me whether I was totally candid in my journal and I said I did not feel impelled to be (or rather, I felt impelled not to be – that is what I meant). I told her about one or two things in my life I could not write about because I did not understand them myself; for instance, experiences of falling in love which seemed almost hallucinatory, perhaps a shared hallucination with some other person – and did not seem to touch reality at any point. I said I sometimes had the experience of loving someone as though we shared each other's dreams.

People I meet sometimes say: 'I've read your books.' Secretly I do

* Baroness Philippe de Rothschild.

not believe that anyone has read anything (apart from a few anthologized poems) I have written. When I was young I was so convinced of this that I used to write unkind things thinking they would never be read. I do now realize that arrows, if they are tipped with venom, have a tendency to reach their target.

15 July / *St Jérôme*

The Bayleys* were ideal guests, so thoughtful and always pleasant and amusing. Iris† was reading Plato. To them, this place is an enchantment and they fill it with their love – the black wasps flying in and out of the morning glory, the hidden valley, the secret copse. Every afternoon they walk down to the water and take their swim. Douglas Cooper‡ in his castle – known to Iris as the Monster and therefore much tolerated in all his roles – is part of the legend. We went over to lunch there. There was Renée Laporte, author of a book describing her affair with Picasso at the age of 17. Also a French novelist who is a homosexual in the manner of someone always fighting on the barricades, and whose novels are apparently about this. He complained that his last novel had only sold 10,000 copies and had received almost no reviews. He was intense, handsome in a somewhat bony way, consciously a bit diabolical. I pointed out that until she had a success with *The Waves*, Virginia Woolf had not sold more than a few thousand of her novels, but this did not seem to impress him.

Douglas's walls have almost no pictures on them, but no one referred to the burglary¶ – a subject about which rumours are rife. Douglas himself seemed in better form this summer than I have ever seen him. He adores the Bayleys ... After lunch we went to the Pont du Gard, where the Bayleys swam in the river.

---

* John Bayley, Professor of English Literature at Oxford since 1974.

† Iris Murdoch (Mrs John Bayley). Novelist and philosopher. Fellow of St Anne's College, Oxford.

‡ Douglas Cooper (1911–84). Art historian, critic and collector. At this time he was the owner of the Château de Castille, Argilliers, near the Pont du Gard. His highly polemical reviews were often written to cause unassuageable anguish. His book on Graham Sutherland, with whom he later quarrelled, was used by him as a stick to beat other English artists.

¶ There had recently been a break-in and some of the smaller works were stolen.

8-10 August

Richard and Day Wollheim and Bruno Wollheim* came to stay *en route* to Sylvia Guiry† near Toulon, David Plante‡ near Cortona, and the Berlins at Portofino. They arrived utterly exhausted having had three flat tyres on the autoroute. Their old Mini was weighed down with luggage and – they complained – books for Sylvia, pillows for David. On the evening of the 7th Douglas Cooper arrived for dinner to meet the Wollheims and, especially, his godson, Bruno. He asked Bruno what he was going to do, and he said study art history in Boston at the Fogg Museum. This gave Douglas a tremendous opening to say what he thought of art historians at the Fogg and at Harvard. He then branched out laying into art historians generally, Anthony Blunt at the Courtauld Institute, next Francis Haskell at Oxford. He extended his blasts to critics. He said the only intelligent and interesting art historian in England was Michael Jaffé, but that MJ had been given no support by Cambridge University. This led to a general attack on England where no one was now interested in anything but Lady Antonia Fraser and her affair with 'a Mr Harold Pootler'. Then there was 'Lord Clark of Trivialization' who lived at Saltmarsh Cussle (he managed to rhyme castle with arsehole). From time to time Richard and I interrupted to make what could be only token defence of friends attacked. Douglas did not draw breath. He drank a good deal and was plastered by the time he left – which was at 2 a.m. Getting into his car he made a speech in favour of his godson Bruno who had improved immensely since two years ago, when he had resembled a pudgy puppy – who now had a structure to his face, which had excellent bones – who seemed intelligent and very sympathetic. I was glad Douglas had not noticed that towards the end of the evening Bruno had fallen asleep for intervals of two or three minutes – as Natasha had also done. I decided that Douglas is like one of those birds on whom ornithologists have made experiments showing that if a piece of cardboard painted with the colours of its mate is stuck in front of it, it will immediately start up its love-making ritual. Given some blobs stuck round him in chairs, Douglas will strike up a monologue of malicious

* Richard Wollheim, Professor of Philosophy, Columbia University, and Grote Professor of Philosophy of Mind and Logic at University College, London, his wife Mary Day (*née* Lanier), and his son Bruno by a previous marriage.

† Painter.

‡ Novelist; author of a memoir *Difficult Women* (about Sonia Orwell, Jean Rhys and Germaine Greer).

wit for the audience of blobs, interspersed with mating calls to the handsome-youth blob. It struck me as odd that as the evening progressed he became more amicable, less spiteful and destructive. Perhaps this was the effect of Bruno, perhaps it was that some warm and friendly side of his nature emerged ... His appearance combines energy and ebullience with something precarious – especially about his stomach, which billows like a balloon in front of him, independent of the rest – a kind of Achilles heel of a stomach – which certainly seems most vulnerable to attack. Drunk, he totters, sways, seems top-heavy. Richard told me that in 1936 or so Douglas had an appalling motor accident in which his face was terribly damaged. Refusing the attentions of the English doctors, he had himself bandaged up, got into an aeroplane and went to Switzerland where he put himself in the hands of a plastic surgeon who constructed for him the face with one artificial eye which he has now. The surgeon was a sadist and was extremely cruel to Douglas.

11 August

It rained intermittently very lightly during the night. The plants in the garden have now a relieved, gratified look. Last night before the rain there was a quite prolonged dry thunderstorm, with thunder, sheet lightning and occasional forked lightning. The flashes floodlit the rocks making them look like snow floes or icebergs. Then there was this light rain. The lack of water is what frustrates us most here. I am not a Pisces in vain. All poets are Piscean regardless of the month when they were born.

During an excellent dinner I suddenly and overpoweringly started thinking about concentration camps. Did once-elegant inmates talk about the society they had once frequented? 'Of course, she was a Balfour related to the English prime minister. Her brother's wife was a Delahaye.'

12 August

Dined with Douglas Cooper. An assistant of his, Margaret Potter, was there. Douglas seemed a bit restless and, under everything, lonely. He seems to get like this at this time of year. His vindictive remarks about Peter Watson lacked conviction. His politics seem to have changed since the death of Picasso. He is now anti-communist. He said he thought that after the death of Franco there would be a revolution in

Catalonia, the Catalans joining forces with the Portuguese communists. He said he thought that within ten years the whole of Europe would be communist.

He described his last meeting with Berenson, nine days (he said) before BB's death. They had a conversation during which, said Douglas, 'I saw him, I saw him with my own eyes, leave himself, go away, over there, while he was sitting in his chair. We talked about Caravaggio. Every sentence BB said was in a different language, English, Italian, French and German mostly and I tried to make up sentences in the language he had last spoken in.'

I noticed that when Douglas reclines in his chair and his stomach is horizontal it assumed an independent personality from his face – as though it too were a face that laughed, frowned, shrugged, burped, agreed and disagreed violently.

20 August

Noel and Gabriele Annan here. Much conversation in intense heat. Shortage of water. Noel is truthful and has independent views. He gives a private and personal view of public people, which is always interesting. He is self-critical – perhaps deeply so. He said, 'Let there be no doubt about it, any kind of creative work or real literary task is immensely harder than directing, organizing or doing public work.' Noel keeps alive his intense interest in people's sex lives in a way that surely goes back to his Cambridge days. This forms quite a part of his uninhibited conversation. He is a character in an unwritten novel by E. M. Forster and I sometimes feel he is conscious of being so.

22 August

Terrific storm most of the night. About four inches of rain fell. While N. was going to Marignane Airport to fetch Lizzie, whose plane was two hours late, Sylvia Guirey and Keith Milow lunched with me here. After lunch Sylvia had a siesta. Keith and I went for a walk up our little mountain to see the view from this extreme edge of the Alpilles across the huge plain of the Camargues. K. got tremendously excited by the rocks, which were of an extraordinary whiteness after being washed all night by the rain. They are cut out in shapes of scallops, pyramids or crystal superimposed on one another. I could quite see how these forms should fascinate Keith, who makes constructions. We climbed up a miniature peak beyond which there is a small shallow valley, high up, with flowers and shrubs of the *maquis*. Then we walked across to the further miniature range, beyond which one looks down on the dragon-like tail of the Alpilles, which finally disappears into the plain far below. We were both elated and I had an almost Nietzschean feeling of the heights I haven't had here before.

23 August

Philippe de Rothschild appeared. With him his daughter Philippine. He is staying with an old friend, Madame Delbée, who has a small chateau near Fontvieille.

We had invited Douglas Cooper to dinner, for the return of the Wollheims here on Saturday. The Wollheims had sent a telegram on Friday, cancelling, from Portofino, where they were staying with the Berlins. So as Philippe was so bored and longing to be asked out, we asked him. He said he would have to bring his hostess, Mme Delbée, which delighted us. When we mentioned Douglas, he said, 'that terrible man' and recalled that Douglas, bludgeoning his way into Mouton when he and Pauline were away, declaring that he was a close friend of theirs, was literally thrown out by the *maître de chai*.

The first part of the evening was subdued. But then the conversation got on to the Royal Family. Douglas declared that he was a republican; all the royals were cretins – the Queen Mother in particular was not even royal but a fat Scottish bourgeois. Lizzie stood up for Prince Charles who had been her fellow house-guest at some weekend party. She said he was modest, witty, friendly and helped with the washing up, etc. D. brushed all this aside saying the P. of W. was a repeat performance of the previous P. of W., Edward VIII, a Nazi. I said they were really hard-working conscientious people and a devoted family. Mme Delbée looked at her plate, too proud to speak out of her personal acquaintance with the Queen Mother who had been her guest. Douglas said – astoundingly enough – he had passed two hours with the Queen Mother, when, to oblige his friend Charles de Noailles he had shown her his collecton. (Mme D. later told Philippe this was quite untrue; it had been carefully arranged that the Queen Mother saw the collection when D. was away.) Douglas was now galloping ahead attacking the royal equerries and everyone who had anything to do with the Royal Family. He moved on to other European royalties and said the only decent and intelligent one – a brilliant man – was Léopold of the Belgians. I asked, 'Do you mean the Léopold who killed a million people in the Belgian Congo, or the Léopold who betrayed his allies in 1940?' D. said that Léopold was quite right to stay with his people in their darkest hour, etc. Philippe asked, 'What about his relations with the Nazis?' D. said they were very limited. Philippe said, 'All I ask is that you don't tell that to a Belgian Jew.' Then he said resoundingly, 'Now we shall speak no more on the subject.' Douglas stopped short. N. introduced a new subject. The temperature sank from fury to cordial mutual dislike. The evening ended early and when I saw Douglas off there were no ecstatic embraces as there had been when the Wollheims brought Bruno.

Lizzie had arrived Friday the 22nd, happy at the prospect of her theatre school. Very sweet and helpful. She must have had a bad evening on Saturday because she has a simple reaction to D. – which is that 'he is wicked'.

26 August

Lizzie made me a big speech to the effect that Matthew and she were agreed I could write anything about them in my diary. She is quietly excited about starting her training at Theatre Presentation next week. Does her meditation and also sits playing her guitar and singing, quietly – I was going to write – and quietly is really the word – with a sweet absorption and seriousness. I can't stop reading Proust. *Le côté de Guermantes*, and Andreas Mayor's translation of *Le temps retrouvé*. I wake up every day feeling liberated – not to be at UCL.

22 September / *New York*

We left St Jérôme Sunday, 30 August, about the worst weekend of the year for travelling in France. Stayed the week in London at the Dufferins. We went one night to dinner at Lizzie's. She has just had her first week at her theatre school where she is made to work tremendously hard. Also lunched with Alan Ross who seemed pleased with my *London Magazine* piece about Matthew's and my trip to Venice.

N. and I went on Saturday (5 September) to Sussex to see Mrs Ventner (aged 80), a cousin of Wystan's, and I interviewed her. She hated Wystan's mother.

Sunday, 7 September, I flew to Hartford (Connecticut). No distraction, I work almost uninterruptedly.

26 September / *Storrs*

Exceedingly rainy in New York, with sensational news stories about storms. I lunched at the Frick with Everett Fahy and colleagues. After lunch to the Richard Avedon exhibition of photographs at the Marlborough Gallery. They are all in black-and-white, uncompromising photos at once fashionable and unflattering of fashion – a consistent show-up – of all his models. There is a projection of realism about them yet they are often extremely unlike their subjects. They even make nude young men look completely serious as though gloomily entering into a role. One, in which he seemed to have forgotten everything except poignant drama, was of Ezra Pound, looking like a statue of Sophocles. Another was of Andy Warhol, after being shot, opening his leather jacket to expose the stitches in his chest and stomach. The Ecce Homo of modern exhibitionism.

At three drove from New York through frightful rain and flood conditions. An agonizing journey down tunnels, across bridges, through partly flooded roads, in scarcely moving traffic.

29 September

Worked with great excitement on *Trial of a Judge*, which I have now decided to call *The Death of Freedom* (*1933*). While I am writing the first act lines from the second and last act come running into my head. When I go out for a walk I feel so many words going on in my mind, it is a kind of seizure.

30 September

At dinner alone I drank a bottle of Soave. This did not affect me at the time but I woke at 2 a.m. Read Boswell. His life with Johnson a very sensible affair. Their circle of friends attached supreme importance to correctness of manners plus an extreme preoccupation with the game of wit. How much discussion there is of Goldsmith's desire to shine, and his misery if he doesn't do so. Johnson himself isn't as witty as all that. It seems to me that Cyril Connolly was often much funnier. What appeals is the man who suffers and the strange desire of the society, despite the competitiveness and malice, to stay together. Reading Johnson one can feel that one belongs to this company, that it is better than no company, no conversation – that works of literature and scholarship emerge from a community, and not from isolation.

The hatred of Scotland is really because it is a place of 'loners' despising one another and everyone else, no real warmth.

Does one love Dr Johnson? I think that by a narrow margin one does, but I think the most lovable Englishman is what might be called a New Testament Conservative. (I am thinking of Christopher Glenconner.)

7-11 October / *Kansas City*

Rilke seminar at Kansas City. I gave a poetry reading, also a discussion about literature and politics, also took a class on Eliot and Pound.

Gave lecture comparing Rilke and TSE – *Duineser Elegien* and *Four Quartets*. Attended various lectures on Rilke. A young German who is at the University of Colorado told me how utterly out of touch with the rest of the world he feels America to be. It is true that there is a pall of bored disillusionment here.

11 October / *Tucson*

Arrived Tucson. Extraordinary to think of this South-west of America, the continental underbelly which always rolls over into the sun and knows nothing of the dark, icy winters of the great plains, New England and the North-West and Canada.

At night beyond the little gardens of small houses at the edge of the desert, like the one where I am staying, their lights glitter sapphire and pink like cheap jewellery in the expanse of some great shop window.

14 October / *Las Cruces*

As soon as I got up to give my lecture, I was seized with violent diarrhoea pains – a nightmare situation come true! It seemed to me that I kept on saying confused sentences, though luckily some of the lecture hung together. No one seemed to have noticed. I even pulled myself together sufficiently to do well in answering questions after the talk. Then of course everything delayed my getting to a lavatory. People asking for autographs, the ones too shy to get up in front of the audience asking their little private questions. There was some difficulty in finding a lavatory. Then when the chairman did take me to one, NOT IN USE was written across MEN on the door. We found another and as soon as I got into it an elderly gentleman emerged from one of its stalls and said, 'Didn't I meet you twenty years ago? Now where was it? What did you speak about, etc.' I said, 'Excuse me, I'll speak to you afterwards, outside' and dashed into the place he had left.

Have been busier than is good for work or health or seriousness or anything except earning money. And have not kept this journal for five weeks. Much of this time was spent lecturing in remote places.

20 November / *New York*

Went to Jane Gunther's* where I found Maro and Matthew. Played with my granddaughter Cosima who is the most smiling contented little starlet. M, M. and I then went to dinner with Mrs Reynal, who was a friend of Arshile Gorky. Harold Rosenberg† and his wife were there, also Niko Callas, the Trotskyite art critic and his wife. All these were friends of Arshile Gorky and therefore of great interest to Maro.

I had not met Callas since 1937 or 1938 when, as he had recalled, he used to lecture me about the Stalinism of the Spanish Republic and put forward a Trotskyite position. He is a tall bird-like man with beaky nose and piercing black eyes. He and I have always been allergic to one another. Maybe I am completely prejudiced. Matthew thought he looked marvellous and was intelligent.

I had not seen Callas for thirty-eight years, Rosenberg for ten. For me, the evening was a bit like the last part of Proust. Time had turned Niko Callas into a bird ossified except for his grey-black plumage of hair.

28 November

I rang Christopher (Isherwood) to consult with him about the exhibition to be held in London of writers of the 1930s at the National Portrait Gallery. I asked whether he didn't think that to limit it to Auden, MacNeice, Isherwood, Day Lewis and myself was rather too narrow. There were other writers, four of whom had been killed in Spain – John Cornford, Julian Bell, Ralph Fox, Christopher Caudwell. I said that limiting the exhibition to these five would lend force to the idea that we were a thirties racket. What really mattered anyway was whether the display gave a true picture of the thirties. He said that he thought John Lehmann, who was a central figure in encouraging the writers of the thirties, should be represented (we should also suggest Grigson I now think). And Cyril Connolly – whatever one thought of

---

* Jane Gunther, widow of John Gunther, author of the 'Inside . . .' books.
† Art critic, author of *The Tradition of the New*.

him – was a very important figure. And William Empson, I said, to which he agreed. We had both written to the organizers suggesting names other than our own. Their difficulty I suppose is that unless they have this narrow range the floodgates are opened.

I said to Christopher that I was very impressed reading Wystan's private journal (1929), and also *The Age of Anxiety*, by how much he wanted to have a son. He replied, 'Well, it's very difficult for me not to understand that. Sons! My God, my life seems surrounded by sons! I've had more of them than anything else. Seventy at least.'

4 December

Got up at 5 a.m. Flew to Chicago. Then flew to Grinnell College – where I gave a reading. GC a place lost in the plains of Iowa. The drive across the gently rolling cornlands on this sunlit early-winter day was very beautiful. The fields a colour hesitating between silver leaf and gold leaf where the stalks and sparse leaves after harvesting still remained – shining and burnished – above chocolate-black stretches of soil.

Read Montgomery Hyde's life of Oscar Wilde. Wilde's motives for going through the tragedy were not just the arrogance, the *folie de grandeur*, the pursuit of some mysterious personal fate or even the self-destructive mad courage, generally attributed to him. There was a feeling that he was fighting the cause of a persecuted minority. His moment of real magnificence in the trial was when he spoke about the love that dared not speak its name. He may also have wished publicly to exult in his love for Lord Alfred Douglas. They were, in his mind, the tragic and heroically defiant lovers persecuted by the world. Douglas of course was carried away by the exhibitionist attraction of such a role. There was also an element of defiant support for the social riff-raff who led the adventurous criminal life of the homosexual prostitutes and adventurers. Wilde keeps on comparing the lively interest of these with the boredom of the English professional classes and of the respectable everywhere.

29 December / *Madrid*

Afternoon, went to Toledo – left Madrid at three-thirty so by the time we got to Toledo it was almost dark. Last time I was in Toledo, 1935 or 1936, it was a beautiful desolate city with beggars on the steps of the cathedral, a few tourists. It has now been cleared up, a touristic shrine, with arty wrought-iron lamps, brick walls carefully pointed, everywhere evidence of restoration. The cathedral was nearly in darkness, but when we came to the high altar it was a blaze of light; seated in front of it, enthroned, an archbishop, a cardinal or two, bishops, priests, etc., all robed. Then a man pushed forward from the congregation and rearranged the archbishop's mitre – and we realized it was a scene being shot for a film.

31 December

Flew to Malaga. Plane delayed on ground an hour because too many passengers had been allowed on board. Met by Jaimé.* Drove to Benharis. Natasha did not go out. Janetta, Jaimé and I dined at the Fonda, J. and J's hotel in Marbella. Went shopping in the market in Malaga with Janetta. Extraordinary the contrast between American shopping centres where everything looks chemical, and here where oranges, tangerines, lemons seem to have fallen into Adamic hands directly from the trees. The vegetables too have arisen fresh as blades from the loamy earth, the fish have sprung out of the sea on to marble slabs.

1976

4 January

Marriage is ultimately an agreement – or conspiracy – between two people to treat each other as having each the right to be loved absolutely. If there is not this understanding, there is no marriage; if there is this understanding all the things that are supposed to go with marriage – children, sex, etc., are secondary. For this reason, whereas marriage between two people of the opposite sex who are physically attached to one another fails if there is no such bond of understanding, marriage between two people of the same sex may be immensely binding, and marriage in which there are no children, perhaps even no sex, may be extremely real.

12 January / *London*

We returned home on our charter flight. How remote Spain seems already. The orange trees in Seville with their dark leaves and golden fruit, the vast cathedral, the semi-circular Victorian Plaza de España,

* We were guests of our friends Jaimé and Janetta Palardé.

the winding streets opening on to little squares, revealing balconied houses painted in Venetian red and emerald green.

Although all these became cut off, the moment we landed, I feel it has become part of me. Where Italy and France impress one with a history which recedes into the past, history in Spain seems a past which forces itself on to the present.

Art and even landscape are still locked in past conflict. How, in Southern Spain, can the relationship of the European and the Arabic seem so fertile and productive – in this, the country of fanatical Catholic orthodoxy, of the Inquisition, and of the savage conflict between Spanish and French, depicted in Goya's disasters of war? The landscape, the literature, art and architecture all seem to ask these questions.

13 January

Robert Lowell, who is now living in London, rang Sunday evening. He asked me to go and see him, which I did. He had flu and was in bed, with a temperature, wearing his pyjama bottoms but no top. He looked hot and dishevelled. He asked me whether I would like to look at some of his poems. I said yes. He produced typewritten pages of about thirty unrhymed sonnets, about Hitler, de Gaulle, China, etc. They were obscure but all have his tone of voice, and moving lines. He had worked at various versions of most of them over ten years he said. He kept on asking me as I read: 'Which one are you up to?'

He told me he had ideas for rewriting my poem, 'I think continually'. He said it should begin with, 'I *would* think continually of those who are truly great' because one cannot think of the great all the time, though one may wish to do so.

17 March / *New York*

A gap of two months.

Came to New York two days ago. Had dinner with Nicky Nabokov, who told me he was to be given the Légion d'Honneur and asked me to the ceremony at the French Consulate today. Atmosphere of comedy as the Consul made a speech, going through his whole life drawing throughout it a distinction between what he called 'creation' and 'career'. Although the festivals he had organized were listed, the Congress for Cultural Freedom was skirted adroitly. The hollowness of French rhetoric on such occasions is so transparent that it acquires a kind of sincerity.

Before this I visited Philippe de Rothschild. It is a week since Pauline's death. He told me about the last day of her life when they were at a hotel in Santa Barbara. She had been exceptionally happy (having had a miserable winter following an operation for breast cancer). She had spent the morning and afternoon making long telephone calls to friends and had got very late for their walk that they had planned to take on the beach. He said he had made a slight scene about her losing the sunshine of the afternoon through her lateness. She said, 'Don't worry, I'll come out without putting on my make-up. That will save time.' So she came out almost at once. They had a pleasant relaxed stroll on the shore. They talked about plans for the future. She said extremely nice things – 'I feel we have been through a difficult time but now we are reconciled and drawing closer together.' They went back to the hotel. He waited for her by the swimming pool while she went to the hotel lobby. People came running out after him to come at once. She had fallen down in the lobby, striking her head against the porter's desk and bruising her face. She was unconscious and did not regain consciousness, though her heart continued beating for some hours in the hospital. Philippe cannot bear to go to Mouton, to the flat at the Albany, anywhere which carries so much the mark of her style. 'I can see my way through till the Vendange this year but after October there's nothing but the abyss.' I said that by October things would look quite different.

19 March

Went to Swarthmore with Ed Mendelson. I gave talk on the young Auden. We spent much time studying the transcription of a long poem which Auden wrote when he was teaching at Swarthmore (in 1939) called simply 'Cantos'. It is a kind of 'Triumph of Life', voyage of a traveller through the world of his contemporaries with diagnostic analysis of the whole course of Western Civilization. Diction very consciously recalls Dante at times. Long sustained metaphors, which, occurring in Dante and going back to Homer, are very European. Metre that which he used later in *Age of Anxiety*. Aim to write an ambitious epic. The draft is meandering, undigested. Bits of it proved a mine for sections of *Dogskin* and *The Chase*.

Saturday. Was driven back to New York by the painter Robert

Motherwell who has the air of being a highly successful prince of art with a wide culture, great courtesy; he said he thought that after the war there had been a complete collapse of European art and all that were left were a few 'decadents like Francis Bacon and Dubuffet'.

He talked about the 'squareness', officialism, of Henry Moore. Said he thought it was the peculiar temptation of the English artist to become attached to the English society whose standards had nothing to do with art. The American artist had no such society, outside the values of art, to which to become attached. The successful American artists formed a special American élite who had no reason to become detached from their world of fellow artists. He himself lives in a town of presidents and vice-presidents of corporations but he had never gone into any of their homes.

I said to him that he and I were survivors. He seemed a bit worried at this. Said that in old age he regretted not having the body of his youth. (I said how much more fun I would have had with mine if I had been young among the young today.)

Where was it they told me they gave a faculty party for Auden? He came padding into the room, looked round blandly and said, 'Oh' – and then – 'Well, I have to go to bed. Goodnight.'

Commentary
1976-9

After becoming Professor Emeritus at University College, London (from which as I had started teaching after my sixtieth birthday I received only the smallest of golden handshakes in lieu of pension), I resumed my freelance teaching at American universities. In May 1976 I was at Gainesville, Florida (the University of Florida), where thanks to my colleagues Richard Eberhart and – much younger than either of us – the enthusiastic poet and teacher Robert Dana – there was an excellent poetry course, with a few exceptional students.

At the instigation of Robert Dana, who taught there, I went for a month in 1977 to Cornell College, Iowa, and for another month to its neighbouring college Grinnell. From January to May of 1979 I was at Vanderbilt University, Nashville. Much of my journal there was written during my first two weeks when I felt both ill-housed and neglected. What is not recorded here is that after that time I was befriended by Robert Hunter and his wife Anne, who were most kind to me. A trouble about journals is that one has time to write grumbles: after which one is too taken up to have equal time to record gratitude.

As a consequence of my having been President and host (together with the International President, Sir Victor Pritchett) of the PEN Conference held in London in 1975, Natasha and I were invited by the PEN Club in Seoul to visit Korea in September 1977, which we did. On the homeward journey we also visited Japan, for the British Council, and after that Tehrān, where we were much looked after by our friend Cyrus Ghani and his American wife, Caroline. In Japan we spent as much time as possible looking at the gardens of Kyōto, and in Tehrān we had the great good luck, at this late stage of Iranian history, of going to Isfahan, as well as to Persepolis.

In 1978 I collected some of my essays and fragments of journals, which were published under the title The Thirties and After.

10

Journal
1976-9

1976 (*continued*)

I taught in May and June at the University of Florida in Gainesville. I had an apartment nine storeys up. One looked down from its balcony at a bright-green level plain with yellowish jungly forest on either side of a highway down which cars rushed. To the right of the highway there was a swampy lake, dotted with little triple points just above the water like periscopes, which were the snouts of alligators. There were wonderful birds – at one side of the lake the brilliant green trees were white with ospreys, and looked like green hats dripping with ostrich feathers.

Gainesville itself is the most perfect non-place I have ever seen even in America, a town apparently planned according to a curious American assumption that since what General Motors wants is good for America then Americans are motors wanting only to drive through cities that have stopping places but no centres.

One moved from air-conditioned apartment into air-conditioned car then into air-conditioned classroom. Furnace blasts of the real Gainesville atmosphere, as experienced by its poorer inhabitants and its fauna and flora, assailed me, stepping from car to classroom. But one was not troubled by reality of this kind too much. I had about fifty students divided into two classes. They were all supposed to be learning to write poetry. The senior class had been taught by my distinguished predecessors, who included Richard Eberhart and Robert Dana and it must be thanks to them that three of the students had learned to hand in interesting work.

(In 1976 I was writing a verse play finished in 1978, which subsequently I set aside.)

21 June / *St Jérôme*

Poetry – and, indeed, perhaps all art – is always about the idea that there is another reality than that of the society in which the poet lives – and we live – imagined by him in his poetry. This other reality, the life of the imagination, inevitably runs parallel with his societal life, because he inevitably lives both lives, that of the society and that of the imagination. Sometimes, in experiences of love, or of nature, the two realities coincide. The life in the world provides occasions for celebration, the 'spots of time' of Wordsworth, the 'moments of vision', and of love, junketings, picnics in Thomas Hardy. Wordsworth's 'the sense of something far more deeply interfused' – the world of poetry penetrating the societal world.

In the work and the lives of certain poets – Vaughan and Herbert, Shelley and Blake – there is a kind of reversal of idea of the lived-in reality. The societal world becomes as it were faint because the world created by their imaginations is so strong in the minds of these poets. The societal world becomes merely a storehouse of metaphors, symbols and images for describing 'the world of light'. Vaughan and Herbert, and Blake, often seem as though they are writing poetry about an alternate world which they see entirely as poetry – poetry about poetry. But if poetry is a second world, alternate to the societal world, they are also writing about a third world, which is their religion, where poetry enters into an imagined reality beyond poetry (in the case of Herbert this is, of course, the Church).

Dramatic Poetry in the Modern Theatre

Eliot's achievement in 'putting poetry on the stage' is remarkable – but nevertheless it has about it the feel of a duty to poetry fulfilled by putting this Cinderella upon the West End stage. Eliot's strategy was to write plays acceptable to an audience that could regard what was happening on the stage as drawing-room comedy with a twist. This is rather like a bishop selling Christianity by introducing something of its message into a speech at a garden party. Eliot came to think that his audience had only a limited tolerance for poetry. So as he went on in each of his plays he reduced the 'dosage' as he called it.

At his best Samuel Beckett employs a concrete language dense with imagery with prose rhythms based on that of people who, as 'charac-ters', speak rhythmically, and nudging towards rhythms perhaps more formal. In this, of course, he is like Joyce, essentially a poet, the massiveness of whose material breaks down the riverbanks of formal poetry, and spreads out as an ocean of language in which tides and currents flow, which is nevertheless more poetry than prose. Eliot's achievement as poetic dramatist remains isolated, perhaps because he tried to adapt himself too much to his audience. But the achievement of Beckett points to a future for poetic drama, because, in Beckett's idiom, the poetry comes out of the truth of his characters in their situations. Harold Pinter has learned this.

29 July / *St Jérôme*

I neglect this journal because every moment for writing that is not devoted to my play seems wasted. But reading through essays I have written over the past forty years, I think: 'You should never have written anything except poetry, stories, plays (perhaps) and journals or autobiography.' In writing criticism I was always trying to relate my own ideas to those of critics I respected. Well, perhaps that is not altogether bad; what is bad is not to start out from a position which is one's own, based on one's own immediate response to a work, and not with that response tailored by other critics – or rather by one's idea of the views of other critics – schoolmasters in the classroom of one's mind.

I have been reading the *Journal* of Jules Renard, which Glenway Westcott gave me for Christmas. It contains the following passage: 'Le récompense des grands hommes, c'est que, longtemps après leur mort, on n'est pas bien sûr qu'ils sont morts.'

It occurs to me, reading this, that one's relationship with most of one's contemporaries is bodiless, invisible, like one's relationship with the reputations of those who are dead but one might suppose to be still living. They do not have to be great men to achieve this. I read in this morning's *Times* a letter from the vicar of a church in a Cornish village. For all I know he may have dropped dead in the interval between his mailing the letter and its being published in *The Times*. And, even if he hasn't dropped dead, he exists in my mind only as a few hundred words and his name and his address. Apart from this, and whatever interest I attach to his letter, he might just as well be buried in his own churchyard. The point I am making is that communication between people when they are not actually present to each other is like that between disembodied spirits. Renard asserts that the difference between great men and the others is that with great men, long after their deaths, one might believe them to be alive. One could reverse this by saying that if one knows of someone only through his fame, or through having read his works, while he is alive one might well suppose him to be dead. Renard is reflecting on a truism, the one I have stated above: that communication between people who are not present to each other is like that between disembodied spirits. An important result of this is that since, while we are alive, the majority of people with whom we are concerned are invisible to us – and even those who are close to us invisible much of the time – we do not really draw as clear and hard a distinction between the embodied and the bodiless as we certainly suppose ourselves to do. And I think it is for this reason that when we hear or read about great figures from the past the thing that strikes us most immediately about them is not that they are dead but that they are living. As far as their impact on us is concerned, so long as they have lived and done their bit or had their say, it makes very little difference whether they are alive or dead. We regard them simply as invisible presences, which is also how we regard most of our contemporaries.

15 October / *Mount Vernon, Iowa*

I have been at this place for nearly two weeks. The time has gone by quickly yet it seems much longer. This is a small campus, Cornell College, in the very small town of Mount Vernon, which has an air of waiting to be filmed in some movie illustrative of a life where the clergy, doctor, policeman, firemen, all live in the same street and doors need never be locked.

One feels incredibly remote in this place, which, despite some square miles of rolling hills on which there are white barns shaped like meat covers and cigar-shaped silos, seems unendingly flat. The fields are full of corn, baked brown by the unrelentingly rainless summer. Crops look metallic, brittle, as though you could hear them tinkle. They draw in the light from the wide sky as though to bury it in trenches between the lines of grain.

It seems to me incredible that only two weeks ago Natasha and I were at Mouton for a week, with Raymond Mortimer as a fellow guest. Other guests who arrived for a day or two were Nico Henderson, the British Ambassador, and Mary, his wife, and the poet and high Communist

Party functionary, former editor of *Lettres Françaises*, Louis Aragon, always known simply as Aragon.

I had seen Aragon last ten years ago when I had sat next to him at a party given by Pauline in Paris for him, his wife, Elsa Triolet, and, come from Moscow, her sister Lilian Brik (famed as having been the mistress of the poet Mayakovsky) and Professor Brik, Lilian's husband. In the course of dinner, Aragon told me that that very day he had received a terrible insult: a letter, he said, from Ezra Pound, asking for permission to publish letters that Aragon had written to him in the 1920s (when Aragon was in Venice, and in love with Nancy Cunard). I realized that it was extremely unlikely that he would have received such a request from Pound himself, but supposed it was from some American scholar doing research into Pound, so I asked him why he regarded it as such an insult. 'A fascist,' said Aragon, 'a terrible fascist.' 'All the same,' I said, 'Pound is a very good poet and has behaved with the greatest generosity to other poets whom he supported.' At this, Aragon got up from the table and started shouting at me. No one took this very seriously, and Elsa pulled him down.

Ten years ago, at that dinner, Aragon was still bristling, aggressive, *prétentieux*. At Mouton two weeks ago, he was a *vieux monsieur*. His features had at once softened and narrowed, so that he had quite the look of a 'colonel' retired from Algeria. He had grown deaf, a fact he acknowledged from time to time by cupping his ears with both hands. He was, however, extremely elegant, wearing a beautifully cut suit made of what looked like very fine wool, and when he went outdoors, a large-rimmed, beautiful hat. I shouted to him my admiration of his suit and asked him where he got it. He answered, 'Like all my clothes – except my hats, which are from Dior – it is designed by St Laurent.'

(A remark he made at Mouton was that he detested the communists. Since he was France's most famous communist intellectual, this surprised me, and I asked him why. He replied, 'Ils sont tellement menteurs.' I asked him how long he had felt like this and he said since 1937, explaining that since he was married to Elsa, whose sister and brother-in-law lived in Moscow, it was impossible for him to express his views about the communists.)

1979

5 January / *Nashville, Holiday Inn*

This morning it is snowing, and I sit here watching the snow, which seems not quite like the snow in England. During the past few days in England it has been exceptionally cold. A cold spell is always totally unanticipated in England: a blow struck by a god with a javelin, causing shrieking disasters – three drowned in the pond on Hampstead Heath, rashly trying to walk on the ice – you cannot even trust the ice to freeze properly in an English winter.

American snow gives one a dense, broad, opaque vision of the continent, bright at the Californian edge, but frozen above, in Portland and Seattle, with the Midwest one immense muffling blanket of endlessly soft-falling icy snow.

I think of the last few weeks in London – of concentric circles of people.

'People' to me more and more means a span of at least fifty years, at one end of which are the children and at the other the old. Between these are the young who have ceased to be children – Matthew, Maro, Lizzie, David* and Nikos,† for example. Beyond the perimeter of the old are the dead with whom one feels an increasing intimacy.

One's own immediate contemporaries – at any rate those of them whom one has known all one's life – become the special band, the crew of voyagers, who have lived through so much and who carry on; but in the very high-up territory we have reached some of us fall abruptly off precipices, some of us – more distressingly – are shut away in the almost incommunicable chambers of the senile, sick, dying. But on the whole we carry on, going to parties, meeting each other frequently, travelling, working, joking, feeling young when we don't remember we're old. We have not changed. However, there are changes, external ones – wrinkles, white hair, false teeth, defective eyesight, etc.; some of them – though due to the same physical causes – internal ones, mental, and seemingly of a different order. The most obvious is loss of memory, which is like something lapsing inside you, in your mind, as distinct from collapsing outside you, the wrinkles and white hair.

---

* David Plante, American novelist.
† Nikos Stangos. Greek poet, critic and publisher (Thames and Hudson).

But although remaining so much the same, one is conscious of being at the edge of irreversible detrimental changes, which people ten or fifteen years – or even five years younger – are not aware of. I seem to myself a very different person from even five years ago. Because five years ago, though conscious some of the time of my age – a lot of the time I was not conscious of it. If I bought a diary for 1975 I felt that I would be the same person at the end of it – 31 December – as I was at the beginning – 1 January. Now I can just about feel I'll be the same at the end of 1979 – but to look at a diary for this year haunts me with the idea of another diary – ten years hence perhaps – at the end of which I shall be, in one or another way, finished.

We went to visit my uncle George Schuster at Nether Worton. He is now 97. He and my aunt Gwen were sitting together in an oak-panelled room, formerly, I think, their dining room. She was in an upright chair, smiling, receiving us graciously, always the hostess. The only thing is she did not know who we were or who anyone was. She just made polite noises. And when we were leaving she said not to us but to her nurse, hovering in the background, who had been in the house for months, 'It has been so delightful to see you, I do hope you will come again.'

Uncle George, in a reclining chair, was very arthritic. His mind was active but imprisoned by his body. He was delighted to see us and asked me, as he has always done whenever I have met him over the past thirty years, 'Tell me what you think of the state of the world.' I did what I have always done over the past thirty years – passed the question back to him – after I had mumbled a few commonplaces. He told me that he thought it was very depressing and that for England the only hope would be that which was impossible to hope for – a national government. He had, from his point of view, a perfectly realistic view of the situation. He had just finished his autobiography and said quite modestly that he had been involved in several interesting things in his life – the First War, the Milner Commission, Financial Minister of the Indian government when Lord Halifax was Viceroy, etc., etc.

Then he said, 'Here am I, scarcely able to move, my sight gone with the last year, unable to read. I'd hoped to spend the end of my life reading Gibbon and other great masterpieces.' He had some kind of reading machine but complained that the available books read out on it were not what he wanted to read. Here I was able to be helpful in suggesting that he could get cassettes of Shakespeare, etc., etc., and that he could also get volunteers to record their readings on cassettes for him.

When we said goodbye he said we could not possibly have any idea how much our visit meant to him, cut off from most human contact as he was.

All this gives me a feeling like that of Keats's about the chambers of life – though I don't see them quite in the way that Keats did. But it is as though people's lives are compartmentalized into boxes like different sections on a stage in which one sees – for example – all the rooms of a house. One of the impressions of my particular stage of old age is this sense of simultaneity – thus my uncle is in my mind, the son of whom my grandmother was so proud: when he excelled at Charterhouse; when he rode to hounds at Exmoor (where they had a farmhouse); when he was a staff officer during the First World War. He married my aunt Gwen, a sister of the Lord Chief Justice Parker. Aunt Gwen had something of the dash, flashing brilliance and candour (while being the most unabashed snob) of a heroine in a Meredith novel. Indeed she quoted Meredith to me when I was a crazy adolescent undergraduate – a rather despised intellectual – in love with her son, my cousin John, saying apropos of life in general, 'More brain, o lord, more brain.' My uncle was made KCMG; and my grandmother, in her old age, was so infatuated by this, that in a moment of aberration she signed a cheque 'Sir George Schuster'.

With my uncle imprisoned in his physical decrepitude but his mind quite clear and separate from it, this sense of the life being simultaneous at all phases in which it has attained special consciousness of achievement, the situation is very clear. With my aunt less so, because her mind has been taken over, been victimized, by her physical condition. But if one says he is what he always was, though incarcerated in his tiresome body, but she is not what she was because her mind has gone – what does one mean by mind except that it is the real personality, the real life? Sitting side by side with her, he seemed to accept her condition. 'I'm afraid Gwen won't be able to make sense of what you say,' he smiled when I made some remark to her – a kind of ambiguity – that it was I who did not make sense – not she who had lost her sense, which emphasized the feeling that she was not gone but only partly present, and that the real Gwen remained completely real to him.

I thought how his uncle Parkes Weber – my great uncle – perhaps the most famous diagnostician of rare diseases in his time, had become physically a log at the end of his life – but had a microphone through which he was able to whisper his own symptoms – a Parkes Weber bulletin in which these were transcribed to his colleagues.

Afterwards we went to supper with my cousin John and his wife Lorna, who have a house on George's estate. John was the cousin whom I loved passionately when we were both boys of 13 or 14 and whom I continued to love when as an undergraduate I was beglamoured by the whole family (George, Gwen, John and his brother Dick who was killed in the war). What made me love John, apart from his great physical attractiveness, was his lightness, his ever-bubbling humour. He seemed to treat everything I took seriously as a joke – my love of art, my socialism. He loved shooting, riding, every kind of sport. He wasn't a swot, yet had natural intelligence, which was part of his gaiety. All this came from his Meredithian mother. They were the side of the family who looked on us – the Spenders – as children to whom all sorts of misfortunes had occurred – a neurotic mother, an absurd father – both of them dead – and thrown into the hands of my Quakerish grandmother and two servants who ran our lives. Clumsy, awkward, I must have seemed a complete joke to them. However in spite of these deficiencies I had been unaccountably successful, and they respected success. My uncle respected more than this – in his half-Jewish-English-countryman way he had a profound seriousness mixed up with his self-importance and he was deeply impressed by my play *Trial of a Judge* when he saw it.

Now, at the age of nearly 70 – both of us – my cousin John suddenly showed himself almost the person I would have wished him at the age of 20. He seemed not to have lost any of his gaiety and yet to have stopped making that division between the elegant sporting unserious things, behind barriers of which his side of the family protected themselves, and our world of 'highbrow' preoccupation. In fact he told me something which amazed me – how, when he was 18 or so, Granny had taken him to visit our cousin Adela Schuster (who had given £1,000 to Oscar Wilde when he came out of prison) and how beautiful she was.

Saskia, our granddaughter, came to stay over Christmas. She is 9. She is rather thin and a bit intense-looking. She speaks English beautifully with precision and a very slight Italian accent. It's the English of a child who speaks English almost entirely with grown-ups and contains turns of phrase she has got from Matthew and Maro (such as 'yes, yes' from Matthew and 'rumbustious' from Maro). She looked for a long time at Coldstream's portrait of me, aged 25, and asked, 'Who did that portrait of Matthew?'

7 January / *Nashville, Holiday Inn*

Sitting at the window of my tenth-storey room, I look over a large parking lot and beyond it the side of a baseball stadium, and, to the right of that, the redbrick longitudinal block of a church surmounted by a diminutive tower which looks like a little triangular hat. Then dull snow with wiry branches of trees interrupting it, posts trailing wires, and in the background a woody hillside. The weather looks as if it will stay the same for at least three months. I think I should buy galoshes. No one has communicated with me for two days. I think with equal dread of going on like this and of the classes, the academic invitations, the interviews which lie ahead of me, and I remember really far worse days at Charlottesville where I had an apartment in a tiny house that seemed made of matchwood and which was stifling with the smell of talcum powder and deodorants; and Houston where I stayed at the University Hotel on the campus looking out on an immense area of buildings like railway sheds, with beyond them, miles away, a view of some immensely expensive-looking skyscrapers, sprouting like a ring of toadstools out of the plain. It seems to me quite ridiculous I should spend so much of my life in such desultory circumstances, at my age when I ought to be surrounded by family, troops of friends, and a little honour. One can fill a blank time like this with some self-realization. But I think I have learned my lesson already: that I simply have to try, in the little time left me, to do work which will make up for the waste of so many years.

I am reading David Jones's *The Dying Gaul*. David Jones is different from other modern writers in that he is not really to be reckoned as a writer writing out of a literary situation. He writes firstly out of his own life which is that of a private soldier among other soldiers in the First War, a Welshman not quite fitting into Wales, but passionately identifying with his Welshness, an artist who feels that to be a modern artist is to be a kind of outcast from a time to which he in his most intimate being feels he belongs, when all men were creative. He is also a religious man, a devout Catholic, who feels that his every action should be sacramental, depriving himself of worldly goods not just because he is unworldly but because he has nothing to do with the utilities of the manufacturing world (well, he did have, I think, a creaky old gramophone on which he played very old and worn recordings of plainsong).

In one of his essays he writes that a real object is worth any number of descriptions of it. His contact with the past – of Rome, of Wales and of Ireland chiefly – is through objects, is archaeological rather than literary. This gives his self-identification as artist with the past a kind of authority which is questionable in Eliot and other modern writers whose connection with the past is through literature, the works of the tradition.

I was standing in the corridor outside my room hoping that someone would come to make my bed, and was encouraged when a maid came along wheeling a trolley. What was my astonishment to see that it was full of black-bound books, Gideon Bibles of the kind left in motel rooms. Later I went downstairs into the lobby. There in the hallway near the desk were several containers heaped on top of one another. Dark-suited men stood around, looking like burly undertakers. Then the largest one slit open the top container, which revealed its contents – brand-new Gideon Bibles in shiny metallic binding. Then the solemn men stood round in a circle, with heads bowed and serious expressions, while their chief pronounced a blessing on the Bibles and then delivered a little homily, full of statistics, about the greatness of their Gideon, the number of languages (fourteen, I think) into which Gideon Bibles had been translated and the quantity distributed. This seemed to me the kind of scene which gives one a sense of the foreignness of America. One cannot imagine anything like it happening anywhere else.

David Jones's analysis of the effects of technocracy and what he calls its 'utile' values on the arts is more impressive than that of writers like Eliot because Eliot seems mostly concerned with the predicament of the poet, an exceptional person. DJ does not regard the poet (whom he would term *poeta*) and artist as a special case.

He distinguished between 'culture' and 'civilization'. 'Culture' is local, particular, traditional, the communication of people who live in particular places with the past through objects made by remote an-

cestors in traditional ways that continue undisturbed. 'Culture' is
essentially provincial; 'civilization' is urban, central and centralizing
and a great deal of human history is that of the urban centralizing
forces imposing themselves on the local ones and making them
part of the larger civilization. This of course is the whole tendency
of modern civilization where the mass-produced, factory-made object,
with specifications based on market research from which the
generalized needs of human beings are deduced, replaces the one made
by the individual who satisfies the maker in himself by making it,
and who regards the made object as a sign or symbol connecting him
with past makers.

Jones's despair about the modern world derives from his conviction
that 'the visible, material, plastic forms of everyday life' are those
'where man most commonly conjoined matter and spirit, which most
naturally and of necessity have borne the stamp of locality and displayed the whole inner feeling of corporate ways of life. In places
where the culture has not become disintegrated, body and spirit become infused as it were within made objects. In such a past man
maintained 'the balance of his dual nature ... more easily and more
normally'. He is protected 'from becoming subhuman on the one hand
and disembodied on the other'.

9 January

The weather suddenly bright but very cold. Yesterday morning I
walked to the English Department, was shown my room and introduced to two or three members of the faculty. All very friendly. Wrote
to Natasha, Lizzie. Read Bergonzi's book on the thirties.* In it he
adopts the method of exploring themes. It does not seem to be a very
good way of discussing the thirties, partly because it seems so arbitrary,
partly because it leaves so much out. It gives the impression that the
thirties started with these themes and gives very little idea of where in
past literature they came from. We are told that Auden, Day Lewis,
Isherwood, myself, etc., all went to public schools (I didn't go to one)
but not what we read. The Great War is considered part of our
background, but there is no mention of Wilfred Owen. The many
influences that went into Auden – such as Owen, Eliot, Robert Bridges,
Laura Riding and even, as I recently discovered, Gertrude Stein – are

* *The Thirties*, by Bernard Bergonzi.

not considered. All the same he is very interesting about Graham Greene and I enjoyed what he wrote about Edward Upward.

10 January

Took my first class in writing poetry. Read out the list of students and asked each if I had his name correctly. All affirmed that I had the official name but corrected by supplying a familiar one. Rick for Frederick, Nick for Nicholson, etc. I asked each in turn what work in poetry he or she had done, what he or she expected of the class, had written, had read, etc. Was favourably impressed by their reading – Shakespeare, Yeats, Eliot, Proust, Pound, etc. They mentioned subjects such as 'The Fugitives'. They were amazingly better read than the students at Florida, all but a very notable and exceptional three of whom seemed to have read little except Bob Dylan and Rod McKuen. I did not overcome my shyness at this class, also had the depressing feeling that I would never do so completely, would never know the students' names, etc., yet I felt quite warmly towards them. One student at the back of the class said that poetry was religion. When asked who his favourite poets were he said, 'Rimbaud and Blake'. He wanted the class to read *Une Saison en Enfer*, to which I had no objection. He seemed a bit wild, of course, but sympathetic.

I wondered if my shyness, which was really a feeling of being locked into myself as though, like Papageno, I went round with a padlock on my mouth, was something to do with the cold. I can't get away from the feeling of the whole northern and middle section of America held in a vice of winter. Memories of terrible winters in Chicago and of deadening ones in Connecticut close in on me, and all merge into this winter (which is less bad, of course).

Rewrote a lot of the Prelude of my play.

11 January

Moved from Holiday Inn (what an inappropriate name!) to the guest room of Continental Apartments. As there is nothing to do in the evenings here, I go to bed terribly early.

I had my first seminar of graduate students, about the thirties. Asked each student in turn about his reading and interest in the subject. Some had no background about it or any other literature almost, but they all seemed interested. Also I saw as we talked that if we managed to conduct the seminar so that while it centred on Auden, etc., it could radiate outwards with each student pursuing what specially interested him or her (e.g., the novel, memoirs, sociology, American parallels with the English) this could be lively, and I myself could learn something from it. We drew up a bibliography which covered an awful lot of things.

I thought about form and music and poetry. A form is really a contraption like a flying machine with struts and stays, etc., constructed so that if provided with an engine, or set into wind currents, it will leave the ground, fly. The dynamics of the condition which the machine is designed to meet are those of sound or of language. The composer or the poet is the pilot who, while fulfilling the demands of the machine, can also dominate it. Essentially the relation of the artist to the form is a marriage and in this sense the artist always plays the masculine role. (May this be why historically there have been so few women artists?)

I am not sure whether the last paragraph works out. I write it down so as to look at it later.

Another thing I noticed recently, which I have been wondering about, is that the role of memory in music is different from that in poetry. Playing records it struck me that in music (classical music at any rate) quite apart from the question of whether one knows it by heart one has a kind of anticipating memory. Even after one has heard a work a very few times, one always knows what is going to come next in a symphony or quartet of Beethoven or Mozart – even I think with Stravinsky. Perhaps one knows the next few bars following because of the rules of composition, one is always a bit ahead, like the conductor. But I do not understand why the whole work including surprises of development, changes of key, etc., is somehow contained in one's memory. With poetry – at any rate with Shakespeare – it seems quite different. Reading *King Lear* recently I kept on being shocked by awareness of how little I remembered. And by this I mean that I didn't remember it in two different senses – sometimes (of which I am ashamed) I simply didn't remember that such and such, in, for example, a speech of Edgar on the heath, was in the text. But also, where I did remember, meanings occurred to me which had not done so before. And this happens with other poetry. Recently reading Shelley's *Ariel to Miranda* a continuous development of the imagery struck me which I had never noticed before.

12 January

The difficulty of poetry – why it never will be a popular art in the manner of paintings or music. Reading a poem in a foreign language which one knows explains part of it. One may get the utmost pleasure out of the sensuousness of the words, but one has to translate them – one has to understand what they mean.

Poetry has always this doubleness – it is both transformed into the medium peculiar to it and it still has meaning as everyday speech. One has to translate the poetic meaning into the everyday use of language. For many people this is tedious, irritating even. This is perhaps not true of verse drama, at any rate not with Shakespeare's – which large numbers of people can enjoy – because the illusion is produced that what is being said is ordinary speech heightened by the situation of the characters. Shakespeare's characters say what they would say if only they could say it. If you dragged Hamlet off the stage and asked him to explain how he felt about his father, the best way in which he could explain this would still be in poetry.

18 January

Still here after ten days without anyone in Nashville having invited me even for a drink, except the lady along the corridor who gave me a general invitation to breakfast each day and did give me breakfast yesterday. Realizing this morning I should not count on this, I did not knock at her door. She rang at ten and explained that she was now going to travel in Europe earlier than expected, so every table in her room was covered in income-tax papers. This cancelled all breakfasts and also the prospect of dinner one night, which she had held out. However, would I like her to send her son along with a pot of tea and toast? I said I would be glad of this and a bespectacled spotty boy with an incipient moustache arrived with tea and hung around till I asked him to sit down. He then explained he was interested in me because I was a poet. He did not like poetry which had metre and rhythm to it but nevertheless he had been moved by the poetry of Sylvia Plath, which made him think that perhaps if he was a poet it would help him to solve the problems he was having with his identity.

He said that next time he came he would bring along some of his poems for me to look at.

A thing about the room I now have is that it has a kind of grating

near the ceiling through which voices in the next room come magni-
fied.

At four today a man visited the old lady in the next apartment. (She
is hard of hearing.) For a time I thought the voice of the man, interrupted by inaudible gurgles from the old lady, was of a character in a
TV soap opera. He had a horribly unpleasant voice raised to a shout
to penetrate the old lady's deafness, and rising to a scream at times.
As this stopped me working, I started writing down odd sentences:

'Tell me who you trust. Is there anyone you trust?'

'The first law is my survival – unless you want me to kill myself.'

'You never once slapped your father's face? Did you ever once slap
your father's face?'

'If you can choose an easy or a hard way to do it, you'll choose the
hard way.'

'You're an old woman. Why should anyone love you?'

'You make a federal case out of being a mother.'

'I never did want my mother around. If I did want my mother
around I'd be sick. Sick, sick, sick, sick.'

I tried to visualize the man, but I could not do so. His sentences
seemed to spring up like brown water from some underground pipe in
cities where people speak with an undisguised brutality, which is the
ugly side of intimacy. There is a kind of basic unkindness, lack of
charity here, and I recognize something of myself in it, wondering at
the same time whether this kind of callousness towards others is not
peculiar to some Americans. It links up with something Frank Kermode wrote to me, that in this country the really nice people (and they
are extraordinarily nice) have an air of being dazed and lost, as though
they did not know how they got here.

14 January

More of what they call here in the news bulletins 'precipitation' – in
this case, snow. A vague sun filtering through it. I dreamed what
seemed a long dream about Cecil Day Lewis. (Funny how much I
dream here about the dead: the other night I dreamed about Harold
Nicolson.) It was a great pleasure to be with Cecil as in fact it had
always been when he was alive – though I never felt that I knew him
and was somehow vaguely suspicious of him. In my dream I very
much wanted to play him a recording of a pianist (Clifford Curzon?)
playing the 'Eroica' Variations. I could anticipate the pleasure this

would give him. But I could not find the record, though I had just been playing it before I saw him. Also there was no plug at the end of the wire connecting the gramophone with the wall plug. It was just a frayed end. When I woke, I remembered in the winter of 1941, when I was teaching at Blundell's, playing Cecil recordings of Haydn quartets when he came to stay with me once. He burst out laughing with pleasure at the scherzo of one quartet. Some of the boys teased me after Cecil's visit, 'We wish you were like him, sir.'

When Auden and I were undergraduates, one day he recited me a poem of Cecil's – I must look it up – and said, 'That is beautiful poetry' – and for the moment, transformed in Wystan's voice to language cold and clear, it seemed the most beautiful crystal in the world.

I feel mildly sorry for myself in this room, knowing no one here, with no one calling, and yet I also enjoy it with a kind of amused malice against the people who are neglecting me. I rather hope that no one will *ever* invite me – and that people will say, ten years hence, 'They had SS for three months and no one took the slightest notice of him.' I know perfectly well that in two weeks' time I will be in Philadelphia staying a day with Henry McIlhenny and next month I shall meet B. somewhere. It gives one a taste though of what must be the real loneliness of – say – the old lady in the apartment next door.

15 January

Mrs L. – the lady along the corridor whose apartment I'm going to rent – invited me to drinks. Then I asked her to dine.

B.* rang and told me about his teaching in Dixie County, Florida. He gave a course on fossils, trying to draw attention to the extreme oldness of some fossilized species and to the comparative recentness of man on earth. 'The awkward thing is', he said, 'that at some point I had to mention evolution. When I did that the children howled at me. Evolution is still a dirty word in the Bible Belt.' He consulted other teachers – his colleagues – and all said he should not mention evolution. 'But most of them, I discovered, are Bible Belters themselves.'

He was so clear and obviously so interested in interesting the kids, I suggested he should write a textbook. 'What happens', he said, 'is that the educational committee meet with the directors of the school and lay down the lines of courses. Then some teachers rush out and

---

* B. An ornithologist, who also took my writing course at Gainesville.

write textbooks along these lines. Then when the courses start, lo and behold their textbooks appear at just that moment and are used for the courses.'

21 January

Horrible snow and sleet. Impossible to go out. I spent the day working – not well – and transferring my things and myself into Mrs L's apartment, which I'm renting from her. Mrs L. is an interesting woman though conversation with her always seems to teeter on the edge of some frightful revelation about her divorce. She is going to Cambridge in relation to her studies, which seem to have to do with the rhetorical structure of political oratory. She said to me this morning, apologetically, that she had now read one or two of my poems (in anthologies) and found them 'opaque' – more so than Auden and others.

I feel very dissatisfied with myself. When I'm working I constantly interrupt myself, listening compulsively to music on the FM radio. My powers of concentration really seem weak though, by writing things many many times, I seem sometimes to arrive at a result which I could have arrived at much more easily if I could really concentrate. When I eat out at restaurants, I nearly always choose an expensive dish. This is partly self-indulgence, partly just a neurotic wish to get rid of money.

Telephoned Natasha and Lizzie in London.

22 January

Finished review of David Jones and mailed it together with a dozen more letters, which took all morning to write. DJ and people who think like him are doubtless right that local cultures have been destroyed irrevocably and that the civilization destroying them is global. It is hopeless pretending that there will be any future in which people can attach sacramental importance to places where every building and store can be regarded as a 'sign'. But people like DJ tend to think that since no one can exist within the old 'Natural' conditions, everyone is conditioned by the 'utile' civilization. This I think is simply untrue. Many people are *not* conditioned by the 'civilization', even if they are unable to get back into the culture – because they ask questions about life and are serious. It is very easy to suppose that all the young, for example, must be spiritually and mentally the products of the civilization. But in fact they aren't because the scene it provides does not satisfy their own sense of vitality or answer their questions about life. It may seem miraculous but teachers are always coming up against this kind of miracle. Mostly the children reflect the 'scene' – drugs, sex, etc. – which the 'utile' now presents, but some of them simply ignore it – or it does not affect them – and read books and have a real sense of literature or love learning or are really interested in scientific truth. This happens because it is part of human nature that it should happen. The Happy Few exist and recognize one another. In the past they were the people who, in the Dark Ages, went into the monastery. Why should they have done so? Because they really liked religion, poetry, music, art and those things which always seem on the point of disappearing but never quite do. Beyond social conditioning there's life itself. Consciousness of life lifts one out of one's time into all history. This does not answer DJ but it is a challenge to his insistent nostalgic depressiveness, to his feeling that to care about the lost values of the lost culture dooms one to live in a religious, moral and aesthetic diaspora.

24 January

I feel extremely pessimistic about politics, pessimistic about humanity (given the political conditions within which it exists), but optimistic about the irrepressible intelligence, affection, sensibility, industry and seriousness of certain individuals.

26 January

Got my pay cheque today. Thought I would celebrate by taking myself to a good restaurant. Walked home; thought about so many things. One of them was how some weeks ago in London I walked along Long Acre from Covent Garden where I had seen *Götterdämmerung* – alone as I thought, along the street I farted. It was much louder, after five hours of Wagner, than I had dreamed it could possibly be! Some boys and girls, rather charming, whom I had scarcely noticed, overheard me, or it, and started cheering. In the darkness I was more amused than embarrassed. Then a self-important thought came in my mind. Supposing they knew that this old man walking along Long Acre and farting was Stephen Spender? What would they think? Anyway, for some reason a bit difficult for me to analyse, it would be embarrassing. Then I saw how an incident like this divides people one knows into categories – those who would laugh and those who would be shocked

(shocked anyway at me writing this down). I don't think F. R. Leavis would have been amused. But Forster, Auden, Isherwood, Connolly, Ackerley, and Matthew, my son, would be.

A memory of Wystan comes to me, as an Oxford undergraduate. He thought that Shakespeare's characters should not be thought of as having a history or personality apart from that which existed in their lines. To talk about Ophelia's relation with Hamlet before the play started was wrong – because H. and O. existed only within the context of the play. They were the poetry, the lines, everything outside the lines was the fantasy of the reader or the spectator.

31 January

On Monday two people from a community college fetched me. They appeared an hour late. They seemed a knockabout pair, like Laurel and Hardy. The one who drove was rather silent, his companion was extremely lively, bouncing up and down in the back seat, and talking a great deal. When we got to the community centre, three-quarters of an hour late, half the audience (it had been packed) had left.

I had to give two performances, one immediately, the second one in the evening. In the afternoon the two knockabouts took me to my hotel room where I rested an hour while they drank in the bar. We then drove to a restaurant where about six ladies joined us, the no-nonsense, fuzzy-haired schoolmistress type. There was also an intense-looking greasy-skinned girl, with a nose which seemed knocked to one side, who sat herself down next to me, and, producing a large block of yellow-lined writing paper, proceeded to ask me questions such as 'Where did you come from yesterday? Where were you the day before that? Where are you going tomorrow?'

X. took me to dinner together with a pupil of his, a young man from Connecticut of rather sullen sulky upper-class appearance with very thick hair brushed down sideways over his forehead like the sweeping curve of hair that conceals a wig (but his certainly was not a wig). From the in-talk between them, I formed the impression that X. was trying to persuade the youth to relax his sexual morals. The youth however took a moralistic line. X. pointed out that this was not consistent with what he had said a month ago. 'No,' said the youth, 'but I have thought a lot about it since then.' He then, rather self-importantly, started citing his own short stories as illustrating this hardening of his attitude. In the story he was 'presently' writing a couple, who had been previously cohabiting for two years, failed to achieve satisfaction on their wedding night. 'Why?' I asked. 'The husband was impotent,' the youth said unblinkingly. This he evidently regarded as some kind of judgement by nature on them for their two years of immorality.

1 February / *Philadelphia*

Sunday with Henry McIlhenny. It was delightful to be in his house for twenty-four hours, with a really comfortable bed, servants, excellent food and Henry's exhilarating conversation and gossip. I suppose the key to H.'s personality is that he counts his prodigious blessings every day, is enormously grateful for them, and lives up to them. He gives life and spirit and lessons in tolerance to the people in Philadelphia with whom he consorts. They all seem covered in gold plate and one never knows what he thinks of them. Completely sceptical, he is also not in the least disillusioned. He sees illusions as illusions and thoroughly enjoys them for being that. Someone told me this weekend that the painter who did the portrait of Henry as a languid young man dominated by an enormous piece of furniture, which fills up most of the canvas, had meant to convey that H. was overwhelmed by his possessions. Many years later he said, 'I was wrong. He is completely in possession of his possessions.'

At one of my readings a feminist asked me: 'Mr Spender, why did you write the line "Bare like nude giant girls that have no secret" and not "Bare like nude giant men that have no secret"?'

Read *Lions and Shadows** in plane today. The relationship of Christopher (Isherwood) and Edward Upward at Cambridge seems to me to come across more strongly than ever before. Also the extraordinary imaginative consistency of the Mortmere world, which they invented between them, which became a kind of medium of their communication.

3 February

I dreamed about Geoffrey Grigson (quite convivially) and woke up thinking of Edwin Muir whose name seems to have faded out of the anthologies. I thought anthologies are like night skies in which some stars – from edition to edition or collection to collection – shine more

* Isherwood's early book of reminiscences.

brightly while some fade away. Looked up Edwin Muir in *The Norton Anthology of Poetry*. There's no poem by him.

Took the Davies* to dinner at the best restaurant in Nashville. I think the idea of the expensive ceremonious meal goes back to Cyril Connolly in the mid-thirties. One of the things we talked about (*I* talked about) was the Stravinskys and how they treated life as a banquet - a tradition, in their case, going back to Liszt and Wagner. We thought it didn't quite apply to the Romantics - not in England at all events. They fed on bread and tears (all except Byron - and sometimes Shelley).

Looking back on the evening it seems to me I did most of the talking. Boasted. Was falsely modest about my own writing - difficult for me not to be falsely modest - because it is rubbed into me by every stroke of my pen that my lack of natural talent, facility, concentration is something to be modest about. Name dropping. But this is different. Donald mentioned he had read about the Stravinskys meeting David Jones. Who was I not to tell him that we had taken them to this meeting? And then went on to tell about taking Eliot to meet Stravinsky at the Savoy Hotel. People want to know from me about other people, mostly dead, I have met, just as I wanted to know from the Woolfs about Henry James or George Meredith and dozens of people (they loved launching out into gossip, descriptions of characters).

7 February

I went to visit Allen Tate in hospital. He was lying in bed, extremely emaciated, with one thin arm outstretched. The skin along the length of the bone seemed like white tape. The first question he asked me was whether I had received his *Collected Poems*. Not quite remembering, I said 'yes' and then felt embarrassed lest if I said I had enjoyed them he would then ask me which I liked most and I might stumble in answering. (I don't really like his poems - they seem to me terribly self-conscious and what Lawrence calls 'would-be'.) He then asked me about MacNeice and how his reputation was doing. I said I thought students were very admiring of Louis. I must have told him I was shortly going to see E. He said E. had written two early poems praised by I. A. Richards but not much to care for since. He asked me how

---

* Professor and Mrs Donald Davie.

they were treating me at Vanderbilt. He asked about Natasha. Altogether our conversation was very normal, as it has always been, showing his interest in literary news, gossip, reputations. I thought I might be tiring him, also felt he wanted me to stay, also, ignobly, wanted to get away as soon as possible. After fifteen minutes I said I had to go, I felt guilty that I was using the convention that I really despise. If I had exhausted Allen or even killed him with shock by saying something outrageous it would not have mattered. I realized that he had only a few days to live. Outside I thought there was something wrong about the feeling of awe one has when visiting the sick and dying. I thought that if I were in his condition I would want my friends to keep away if visiting put this kind of strain on them. I would like them to feel that visiting me on my deathbed was like being with me on any other occasion. Looking at them from my pillow, I would not feel that they were extraordinary or that they had to act up in any way or even feel anything special. I think that the people I would want least to see are those I most love if they were to undergo this sense of reverence, and were unable to be natural about it. The people I love I would just want to look at, if this did not hurt them; as when I hear the voice of a friend who is 3,000 miles away, on the telephone, I feel that however much I enjoy the conversation, I would rather have him present and palpable in the room beside me, sitting in a chair and saying nothing. Hearing a loved voice, one knows how precious it is to see a loved face, let one's eyes travel over it, to read the things the voice has left unsaid.

9 February / *Gainesville*

Went to Gainesville. Tony Lombardy rang me and told me Allen had died. I said I was glad, as he had absolutely nothing to live for. B. met me at the airport. Everything about him seemed to say that nothing had changed and that in meeting again we harvested every moment of affection we had ever had together.

It seems extraordinary that at his age he should be so completely conscious of this and that our few weeks together seem for him, as well as for me, to have been put outside all the very long periods of separation.

Various people in the hotel and even in the street seemed to know me and some of them came up to say so. B. said, 'Everyone here seems to know you, from the lowest dishwasher to the highest desk boy.'

After lunch and putting my things in the hotel, we drove 50 miles to B's trailer (which is 30 miles from his school) near the Sewanee River. The country is flat with fields of stubbly grass, yellowish at this time of year, and firs, forming a screen along the roadside. Driving past them, one has flickering glimpses of cows in the fields, with the light brilliant on their flanks ... Under the wide skies these glowing fields – burnished – reflect back the light like mirrors. We drove to a camping area giving on to woods along the river. Always trees. Swampy, very dense. Jungle-like. One tree, stripped of branches, a big S-shaped silver gleaming trunk rising up from the ground like a modernist sculpture.

I worked Saturday morning, and B. went out so as not to interrupt, but otherwise we were separated only for an hour or so the whole weekend.

He said, 'You're different. You grin and show your teeth.' I did not tell him this was because Lizzie had made the dentist provide me with a new set because she thought the previous one made me look like Dracula. B. too had changed. He has a beard now, just a fringe around his chin, leaving a small space below the mouth, emphasizing its lines, and the nostrils. With his pale green-grey shining eyes and dark brown hair, he looks more than ever like a portrait of a young Frenchman by Manet.

B's purpose this weekend was to show me his life, which I certainly wanted to see. To show me his trailer, the school where he teaches (but we missed out on this) and also, as he told me, to show me off to his friends. These encounters are very risky and make him nervous – we might not get on – in fact they are a form of living dangerously.

9 March / *New York*

A gap of nearly a month between the last entry and this, a month during which I've been to London and celebrated my seventieth birthday.

Nashville seems very faint compared with my life outside it, especially as I sit here, looking out over New York. London – travelled 23 February. The journey was very long and I was knocked out by it, and can't remember much about 24–7. Matthew and Maro came to London – also all Maro's Gorky and Phillips relations. From the point of view of seeing Matthew the time was much too divided and distracted. Natasha was very philosophical about this.

I did quite a lot of work – the first week on my play, the second on an article, 'Defence of Name Dropping' for the *Observer*, reviews for *New York Times Book Review*, the *Observer* (Brecht's Journals), *Sunday Telegraph* (book about fire service). But the two weeks were dominated by social gatherings. My seventieth birthday at the Royal College of Art was wonderfully organized by Natasha. About a hundred people came. Family – Humphrey, Christine, Philip, Jason, Nancy, Matthew, Maro and Maro's mother and sisters, Lizzie. Friends – the Berlins, the Glenconners, the Wollheims, the Gowings, Angus Wilson and Tony, the Martyn Becketts, Ann Fleming (escorted by Pat Trevor-Roper), Lucian Freud, Dominique de Grunne, the Snowdons, Cyrus Ghani, Bill Coldstream, John and Myfanwy Piper, David and Nikos, Keith Milow, James Fox, Gareth Evans (with Antonia Phillips), the Longfords; the rooms proved excellent once they were full of people. Everyone could talk without being drowned in conversation. Philippe had provided Mouton Cadet claret. The food served by the common room was excellent as was the service. The party would simply have been a noisy crush if we'd had it anywhere else, I think. The impression made was that everyone was fond of everyone else and delighted to meet. It was one of those reunions in which a lot of people present realize how long they've known each other, how little perhaps they've seen of one another, how glad they now are to do so. Natasha had arranged that four students from the RCM play a fanfare (from a Gabrieli piece) when the cake was brought in. During dinner I sat at a table with Isaiah and Aline and Cyrus Ghani. I kept on getting up nervously to see whether people at other tables had enough to drink so did not take part in the conversation.

The Royal College people opened seventy bottles of Mouton Cadet. In addition to this there was champagne so we had twenty bottles of the claret left over, and arranged a drinks party on Sunday (4 March) to finish it. This was very nice also. Kingsley Amis, Elizabeth Jane Howard, Bill and Hetta Empson and their son Mogador and his wife, Matthew and Maro came. I took photographs. Bill Empson was beaming, obviously very glad to get a knighthood.

Before this, on Saturday, we drove to Oxford, called on Stuart and Renée Hampshire in the morning and then had lunch with the Berlins (Stuart came too). In the afternoon we drove to have dinner with the Pipers at Henley. He is working on stained-glass windows for a new Cambridge College – Robinson College – of which he showed us some designs.

I remember nothing of what was said on Saturday. What I remember very well was visiting Clifford Curzon at his wonderful house in Highgate, overlooking the heath, on the following Wednesday for drinks. We had not seen Clifford for two or three years. I had not written to him since the death of Lucille, his wife, but N. had done so, because he spoke of this and apologized for not having answered. He was in a rather nervous, yet welcoming, gleaming and ardent condition. A lot of his conversation was a kind of talking aloud to himself in which he showed a charming and engaging candour. He said that when he hadn't seen friends for a long time, one wondered what reason one had ever had for seeing them. Now we sat in front of him drinking sherry and eating macaroons, he seemed to recollect that he did have good reason for seeing us.

He went on talking about the past and said that he and I had been in Berlin at the same time, though we had never met. We had common friends in Roger Sessions and Christopher Isherwood. He said that the only occasion in his life on which he had fainted was when he was with Christopher, who had taken him to a very smoke-filled *Bierhalle* and then had proceeded to tell him about various forms of sexual perversion. Suddenly he found himself lying on the floor and people unbuttoning his collar.

He asked Natasha whether she found anything to admire in any living pianists. She tactfully brought him on to the subject of Schnabel. He said that when Schnabel played he made you forget the instrument and enter into a world of pure sound.

I left feeling very touched by Clifford. He may be a puritanical worker, who respects in other people only work, yet he is a visionary of music, a totally dedicated artist and a highly perceptive and intelligent man. Wish I had known him better.

11 March / *New York*

Saturday. Bill Mazzocco* and I lunched, at the Fleur du Lys, then we went for a walk in Central Park. A grey and white day in which everything looked very filmy. The only colour, that of skaters silhouetted in reds and blues, turned blackish against the paper-white surface of a miniature lake in the park. We walked past slab-like slate rocks,

---

* Robert Mazzocco. Poet and critic. Frequent contributor to the *New York Review of Books*.

which emerge bald above the grass slopes, gleaming patches of the stone on which New York, surrounding the park with towers like brandished prongs thrust into the sky, is perched. I told Bill I was keeping this journal. 'Do you fictionalize it?' he asked. 'What do you mean?' 'Do you in describing, say, the party last night, take some person, or a fragment of dialogue, as the centre round which you make a kind of story?' I said my journal always seemed to me an effort of catching up with time, loaded with people and events, rushing past and I hardly had the leisure to do more than write things down in order to keep up. We talked about casual sex. He said that he could see the point of people saying that total release of all their sexual inhibitions was the most important thing in life. He didn't agree with those who said that all values would break down in a totally permissive society. He thought that if everything were permitted most people would impose their own restrictions on themselves simply by getting bored.

As we watched the skaters (who skated surprisingly badly) I said, 'The kind of sex you're talking about is magic, the transformation scene. People who are living their routine lives in their routine world, wearing their routine clothes, go into a room and become disporting nudes in a painting. Then everything is permitted.' (Actually I didn't say this but something much more clumsily put.) 'Having achieved the transformation in which they discover themselves as pleasure incarnate, it must be difficult to relate it to their routine lives.' I did not say that either, but I did say, 'The definition of a vice is that it is an activity more interesting to the person who does it than anything else in his life.' I said when I was young I was brought up in such an atmosphere of anything to do with sex being unmentionable that it was as though all the clothes of all the people in the world were a curtain forever drawn over them.

I have to speak on the *Dick Cavett Show* on Tuesday. From some exploratory questions telephoned, it seems they may ask me about my religious views. I thought I would simply say I had none. By this I would mean I don't subscribe to any official religion, nor have I formulated for myself any private or personal religion. But simply to be negative about religion doesn't really cover my case, so in case I am asked, I should write a few notes here.

I regard Christianity as poetic myth – whether or not it contains an increment of historic truth – which expresses very important truths about life. To me the most important part of its message is that humanity can be served by love, and inseparable from this is the fact that it will not be so served on account of the innate selfishness of the individual, the group, the nation, quite apart from the fact that Christianity is not the universal religion. The crucifixion therefore expresses the truth that love is perpetually sacrificed.

Apart from this I consider Christianity takes a too limited view of human potentiality. Despite the great achievements of Christian art, there is really no room for art in the Gospels. So-called Christian art is paganism imposed on the Gospels.

I cannot accept dogmatic religion because dogma – though I see the necessity of it for some people – insists on treating poetic truth as literal truth. I see the arguments for doing so but I can't do so.

I believe that all consciousness consists of co-ordinating sense-impressions which we treat as real though, or because, apart from them we do not know any kind of reality. The colours we see, the sounds we hear, the things we touch, we apprehend through the medium of our senses. We can think of them only in terms of our senses, and our senses are subjective to us. We create the pattern of what we call reality. All life is automatic fiction.

This being so, nevertheless we do believe that certain things are good beyond dispute. Love, and truth. Truth is the extremest obligation imposed on us because as conscious sentient beings, the points of awareness in which the universe itself becomes self-aware, it is our duty to attain the utmost consciousness. We cannot believe otherwise.

Finally I agree with the passage in Proust in which the narrator says that we lead this life as though the obligation of another life were imposed on us – another life, the aims of which are truth and beauty so that a painter so little eager for fame in his time that we are scarcely certain in the attribution of his name to his pictures, can devote unending time to painting the exact yellow of a wall in a picture of his native city.

Bill Mazzocco also talked at some length about his South Sea journey* – how everything was far more commercialized, vulgarized, than he had imagined it would be. There was no local culture left. Gauguin had noted the Europeanization of Tahiti: now Americanization had been added. Moreover, in this part of the world there was a complete

*He had gone by himself on a tour of French Polynesia, Australia and New Zealand.

lack of seriousness. No one wrote or read a serious book. (I remembered having the same impression of Thailand.) I said that what we call civilization *is* extremely thinly spread. Bill talked about Wystan's view on sex. How he accepted the church's view that homosexuality was sinful. How simplistic his criteria for deciding whether someone was hetero- or homosexual – if you went to bed together with a man and woman – which would you turn to? 'That is absurd,' said Bill. We talked about his projects – a book of poems and a book of essays. He said he wanted to dedicate his poems to me – which I regard as a great honour.

12 March

Yesterday lunched with Howard Moss.* We discussed Bill and his work. He said he thought he was the best critic of poetry living, because he was not in the least academic. All his judgements came from careful reading, original thinking.

When I got home I telephoned B. Told him about the wave of salvationism which has swept his part of Florida.

Woke up early this morning feeling apprehensive about my various interviews, request that I should read 'Seascape' on the *Dick Cavett Show*. So I got out my *Collected Poems* and read it through to myself, then a few other of my poems – with much dissatisfaction. One which struck me as having virtues and faults is 'Messenger'. It is a beautiful idea bungled by my inability, shown in so many of my poems written since 1933, to expose, lay bare, the basic structure of the poem. 'Messenger' starts catastrophically by failing to establish clearly the situation of a modern messenger travelling back to the world of Greek temples and sculpture and trying to convey a message from the modern world to the past.

> Oh messenger, held back
> From your journey! walled in,
> Imagination trails leaves
> Shut from the sun!

This is obfuscated, obfuscating verbiage, and the beautiful things in the poem need clearing of all these trailing leaves, brambles, weeds.

Through writing certain speeches in *The Corporal* I have learned to work through to the clarity of the original idea in a poem. In other

* Poet, and poetry editor of the *New Yorker*.

words – more simply – I have learned how to work, to uncover from the rhetorical gesture pure sound, pure image seeking the simplest, directest apparel of words. 'The lineaments of gratified desire.'

13 March

Went to the studio for the *Dick Cavett Show*. A very long wait, made trying by the fact that I was never left alone by various ladies connected with the programme or the publishers. Cavett, a young-old man, boyish wrinkled face, wisecracking, but not offensively so, started in almost immediately with the question of religion which I struggled with. Unfortunately had not been able to look up the Proust quotation. Later there were questions about London, America, the state of the world – not boring really. I think I dealt with them adequately, though occasionally remembering things I think I said sounded either shallow or idiotic. After the interview I went to Random House to see Jason Epstein.* He was very nice. Asked me what my plans were and proposed we should renegotiate all my contracts so as to give me advances to free me from having to do things like Nashville. But I don't want to take money for books I haven't written. Besides, I don't yet know what my financial position now is. It may be better than I think when royalties come in. He invited me to stay over tonight and dine with him and Gore Vidal in NY. I at first accepted, then had an access of conscience that I ought not to leave returning to Nashville till tomorrow morning.

15 March / *Nashville*

In the morning duty bound me to go to my office for office hours. There, I answered and wrote twenty letters. Afternoon thirties class. A girl read a very good paper on Orwell – followed by one who read a diffuse one on Isherwood.

I went to hear a quartet play Mendelssohn and Beethoven (opus 127). They did so harshly, squeakily, stringily, stridently but with energy enough to give some idea of the strength of the music, though not a suggestion of corridors opening on to heaven.

16 March

A very *distrait* sort of day. Got up at 6 a.m. and worked quite well at

---

* Then my editor at Random House.

my last act. Had to go to university to be interviewed by an undergraduate for a magazine devoted to Baudelaire, on his influence on American and English poetry. At first I adopted a rather bored.attitude – 'Read T. S. Eliot', etc. Then I began to get rather interested. Cited Christopher's translation of *Mon coeur mis à nu*,* which had an introduction by TSE and which caused Christopher trouble, since the translation was criticized unfavourably (I think by Raymond Mortimer in the *New Statesman*) thus annoying Eliot and humiliating Christopher. I said Baudelaire was the great modern forerunner who fused the poetry of the industrial city with the classicist tradition of Racine. The nineties writers like Swinburne and Dowson only skimmed the froth of sin and *fleurs du mal* off Baudelaire – the decadence. Eliot himself really began from the decadence. Yeats did not know French (I suspected) any more than he knew Greek or much Latin. Verlaine was Baudelaire without tears – or, rather, with scented tears. Rimbaud derived from B. but became quite a different matter. Had lunch with the group of witty younger teachers here at the students' restaurant. Went to my apartment, tried to work, did little.

Evening, heard Stanley Kunitz† give a reading of his poems. I liked some of the poems a lot. He read with much expression but a rhythm more monotonous than might appear on the printed page. Standing ovation. A drinks party afterwards.

At dinner, which we had in the Sheraton Hotel restaurant, Kunitz said the only bearable places in America were the East Coast and the West Coast. Talking of jobs in universities, he said, 'You can find yourself in places where there is absolutely no one to talk to at all.' This seemed to me very much the judgement of an 'intellectual' – but perhaps true, as it is what I had written here about B. who did not even realize that he had no one to talk to until we met in Gainesville.

19 March / *Durham, North Carolina*

Spent two days with Reynolds.‡ It was very like old times and R. looked extremely well, successful. Sixteen years ago I stayed with him in a trailer in a field. Now he has a house with a burglar alarm. Nevertheless he does not seem in the least spoiled. Besides having total dedication to his work, he also has a fundamental austerity.

---

* Baudelaire's intimate journal, translated by Christopher Isherwood with an introduction by T. S. Eliot.

† American poet, critic and educator.

‡ Reynolds Price.

He showed me a typescript of his poems, which were an extremely pleasant surprise because I have always thought him a bit awkward when using poetic forms or writing formal verse – as happens often with writers of poetic prose. What struck me most was a longish narrative poem about a friend of his nearly getting drowned in the ocean off Key West.

Weather very beautiful. R's house is in a hollow, without much view. I walked up above it into a large field surrounded by woods – birch or beech trees, I think, not yet in leaf – like silvery veins flowing into the molten pale-blue cloud-flowering sky. There are little ponds with water that looks as though mixed with greenish-khaki paint, surrounded on one side by woods, the other by the hillside, reflecting trees, clouds and patches of pale sky.

Reynolds read my play. He said it was not only political, it gave a picture of life not unlike that of Webster, and had a surrealistic view of modern history. Was very pleased.

22 March / *Nashville*

On Wednesday dined with Chancellor Hurd and his wife. They live in a large chancellorian mansion with columns outside and inside a series of cavernous reception rooms. Towards the end of dinner the Chancellor suddenly tapped his spoon against the side of his glass and proposed a toast to me. Luckily he followed this by toasting Donald Davie. Worse was to follow, one of those questions that seem so ironic coming from administrators or scientists: 'How would poets save the world?' I tried to pass that on to Donald. People always ask this question with an air of being sheep looking up to be fed – however unsheeplike and important they themselves may be. I said something to the effect that it seemed difficult to save a society which depended for its well-being on over-production – people buying things they did not need or even want – in itself an unhealthy state of affairs – but where, if this unhealthiness ceased, everything would collapse, there would be millions of unemployed.

24 March / *New Orleans*

Almost the first person I met in the street yesterday was Allen Ginsberg.

He told me he was attending some meditation symposium at Tulane College, also giving a reading. The results of meeting him were fairly electrifying. First, I was invited to lunch with a Mrs X. She also invited B, who had come to New Orleans to meet me. We all met up with Allen Ginsberg and his friend of very long standing, Peter Orlovsky, who looks like a portrait by Géricault of one of the extremer results of the French Revolution. We went in a taxi to the Garden quarter where Mrs X. lives in a spacious house full of paintings by her husband (one of three or four). There was also some more primitive art, either by children or by Haitians, perhaps both. Mrs X. had a grand air of vagueness, wandering blue eyes, a soft voice which uttered sentences that all seemed sections of some great rambling, free-associating interior monologue. She knew everyone I almost knew – the figures of the twenties. She talked of husbands who painted or didn't paint, who were killed in the war or in accidents, or who survived to be divorced, and also children who seemed to have been conceived and brought up within the surround of some great tapestry which is her life. The luncheon arrangements were odd. There were two little tables placed at the end of her sofa in which she reclined throughout because, she explained, the doctor had told her she must eat lying down. This rather excited Ginsberg: 'Do you mean the food has to pass horizontally?' B. entered into conversation with Allen. Later he said to me, 'Of course I see that meditating is an aid to thinking, but there are other ways of doing this – just thinking, for example.'

After lunch Ginsberg asked me if I had ever heard his music for Blake's songs. I said, no, but that Auden had told me they were good. G. said rather sharply, 'Did he? Are you sure of that?' I said, yes, remembering that A. had actually said they were rather better than he expected. G, unpacking a bag which contained a keyboard harmonium, said, 'Well, he refused to hear them. As soon as I started to sing one, he said, "Won't you please stop? Hearing people sing songs they've composed embarrasses me terribly. I can't bear it."' After this Allen sang, 'Little Lamb, who made thee?' 'Tyger, Tyger' and at least six more. They were a bit like hymn tunes, but they retained something of the language, making one attend to it.

After this, Mrs X's cook-waiter changed roles and became chauffeur, driving us to our hotels. As we drove back, Ginsberg started questioning him. We had heard from Mrs X. that the waiter had been a seminarist. G. asked him about this. He answered that he had trained to be a priest. 'Does that mean you believe in God?' asked Allen. 'Oh yes, I do believe,' answered the youth rather smugly. Ginsberg then went into an explanation of his own religion, which did not seem necessarily to involve belief in God. I remarked that in some religions, ritual was more important than belief. Ginsberg said the basis of his religion was meditation, not ritual, or belief. After more of this, they started asking the waiter-chauffeur where to go in the evening. At this he underwent a further change from religious into drag queen. 'Oh,' he cried with a joyousness of a solo instrument swooping from a solemn *adagio* slow movement to a *vivace* finale. 'You must go to Jules. Not just the front room but the back room.'

Next day, there was a message for us from G. who'd arranged with a friend to show us the Garden quarter. I telephoned thanks and three of them appeared in a Volkswagen which smelled strongly of leaking petrol. The driver was a rather earnest photographer. Accompanying him was a dark-skinned jazz pianist of very lively appearance and camp manner. They all talked excitedly as we drove down a huge avenue on each side of which there were immensely swaggering nineteenth-century houses.

It was very difficult to get away from our new friends. They wanted us to dine with them but we managed to extricate ourselves.

Monday was quiet and wholly delightful.

At Mrs X's Allen gave me his volume of poems: *Mind Breaths;* and Orlovsky his - *Clean Asshole Poems* and *Smiling Vegetable Songs.*

B. and I discussed - to me an elusive topic - why people like Allen, Orlovsky and their friends who seem to be living on a level of truth - and according to values of love and charity - which are a reproach to everyone else - yet seem so sealed off into what they would call their own 'thing'. I always feel false, stuffy, stuck up, armoured in a reputation and achievements I don't at all believe in with such people. If I could not accept the kind of religious beliefs they talked about none the less I felt that as a 'life-style' theirs was truly religious whereas the life of a man of letters or an academic was in itself hollow. B. said, yes, but the trouble is that the only value for them was self-expression, they didn't really recognize anything except expressing whatever they wanted to do or be at the given moment. Afterwards I put it in a nutshell for myself by thinking: 'One respects them because they are concerned with profound questions: then one ceases to respect them because they accept superficial answers.'

28-9 March / *Nashville*

Literary conference at Vanderbilt. The speakers coming from outside were Helen Vendler, critic, Wallace Stegner, novelist, and Robert Pinsky, poet. Helen Vendler, pale, rather transparent complexion. Rimless spectacles like pince-nez giving her the appearance of a governess in a Russian play. Of course I found her immediately attractive, was longing to appear the good boy to her, at the same time to confess all my sins. Pinsky gave a very good reading of his poems. Their merit is an accuracy of observation which can be breathtaking. The material though – familial feelings mostly – a bit prosaic. The excellence of the reading emphasized this. He read a long poem about playing tennis which was wonderfully observed, but it struck me that this was poetic copy-writing. Illustrated with photographs, the poem would make a marvellous brochure for a firm selling tennis rackets. A very long poem about America was disappointing because there were so many passages which seemed just opinions. It wandered too far from the subject in trying to attain some kind of commentary on *A Winter's Tale*. All this is my superficial impression from listening to the reading. I might feel quite differently if I had read the poems in print.

Before Pinsky's reading, Donald Davie delivered a panegyric on Allen Tate whom he referred to as 'a great poet'. Orotund and at times polemical, Davie's speech was really very fine indeed, the kind of speech I imagined people making two centuries ago but which today seems altogether exceptional. He coupled Allen with Yvor Winters, praising them both as writers who maintained inflexible standards in their critical work. He contrasted them with a later generation of rhetorical, exhibitionist poets – who had driven these two masters out of fashion. He brandished words such as 'discipline', 'structure', 'severity' like tridents from his rostrum. As an example of their critical acumen and personal generosity, he singled out their patronage of Hart Crane, whom, by a combined strategy, they succeeded in putting on the map.

Listening, I agreed about Hart Crane, but thought that what DD was saying would be more convincing if he produced a complete list of poets whom Yvor Winters (I didn't know about Tate) had praised. I seem to remember an essay by Winters describing Robert Frost as a spiritual loiterer, and another interpreting *The Waste Land* as an exercise in disorder, ending, in the last twenty lines or so, in chaos.

The trouble about this insistence on the values of discipline and integrity is that the critics who insist on them make judgements that prove as fallible as those of critics who do not.

30–1 March / *Midnight*

Was rung today by a highly eccentric rich lady who asked me to dinner. Out of curiosity, I accepted. She drove me to her immense, sumptuously furnished but rather disordered-looking mansion. She prattled *en route* about her preoccupation with the Life Beyond. She showed signs of considerable snobbishness. When we arrived we found her husband, a large flabby man, like a huge flatfish, in an armchair, his legs over a table like the flatfish's tail. The TV was blazing away. The husband did not move from his chair nor turn off the TV for some moments; at the end of which he said to me in sonorous tones: 'Greatly as I appreciate the idea of it, poetry has never come my way and now I do not anticipate that it ever will do so.' He expanded on this theme – how he had ignored poetry at school – suspected it was a phase some people went through and then passed beyond, etc.

We went in to dinner. The table was laid with gold knives, forks, spoons and a golden goblet for each of us. Husband and wife talked at cross purposes throughout the meal. The husband returned to the subject of poetry, asking how it could be compared with the medical profession, which he said preoccupied him. 'At hospital,' he asked, 'ten minutes after the patient has expired under the knife and we ask ourselves whether there was something more we could have done to save his life – where does poetry come in?' I said that a poet called Keats who had himself – in the horrible conditions of operating theatres in 1818 – been a medical student, had addressed himself to this question – and had concluded that the healer was superior to the poet, and the poet justified in being a poet only if he could absorb into his imagination, and thus transcend, the real suffering of humanity. Like a sop to Cerberus, this seemed to silence him for a while.

But when we returned to the drawing room, he started up again, with renewed force, about poetry. 'Now tell me, whatever would make someone decide to be a poet? Would he wake up one morning and say, "I'm going to be a poet"? Would he say when all his contemporaries were deciding to go into the professions, "My profession is going to be poetry"? Would he say "The most useful thing I can do in the world is to be a poet"?' Suddenly I felt fed up with this insolent baiting, got up and said as abruptly and emphatically as I could manage, 'I have to leave', then, as I left the room, I said loudly, 'I hope we never meet again.' Oddly, he seemed to take this as though it was the kind of thing that had often been said to him before. Nor did his wife seem particularly disconcerted. She ran out of the room after me and drove me back to the morgue I live in, absolutely overwhelming me with the kindest offers. She said she'd already left her husband twice and saw as little of him as possible. Could she drive me to the airport tomorrow to meet Natasha? Well, if I didn't want that, could she telephone on Monday and take us anywhere we pleased then or at any other time? I didn't regret my rudeness to her husband. All I had done was to behave as madly as my host and hostess.

1 April

At 8 p.m. yesterday Natasha arrived, rather exhausted – after her long flight. Nevertheless by this morning she has transformed the apartment.

4 April

Lines from Auden's Epilogue to *Journey to a War* which struck me with unerring force:

> For what is happiness
> If not to witness joy upon the features of another?

7 April / *Indianapolis*

A flat bone-coloured plain with sparse trees growing out of it like pubic hair from brown wrinkled skin, the grey sky above it through which moved a few grey clouds like trucks along the grey road.

I have been given a book of photographs of Ottoline Morrell, compiled by her daughter Julian Vinogradoff. It contains photos of so many of the dead I knew in my youth. I have been looking at it for an hour and reading the extracts from writings relevant to Garsington and Gower Street with which it is sprinkled.

A terrible dinner in a public dining room at a U-shaped table, with thirty or forty teachers. Apparently no one reads in Indianapolis and the teachers had the discouraged air of vegetarians trying to convert to cannibalism.

8 April / *Indianapolis*

A dull rainy dreary day. Twenty-four hours gone. Only forty-eight more.

9 April

Anyway I had two mornings undisturbed in which to work. Afternoon two to four talk with students. Dinner, then my lecture on the thirties. It went well but really I was completely without confidence. Somehow I have in my own mind no contact with an audience when lecturing. It is as though I were behind a glass screen gesticulating, and everything I say somehow keeps them attentive but is almost meaningless to me. When I am reading poems I do have confidence or at any rate can become absorbed in the problem of trying to read them effectively. After half an hour I broke off and said I would answer questions. Rang B. and told him how appalling I found Indiana. He said, 'It is the most awful state in the union.'

11 April

Five a.m. Centre College, Kentucky. Met at airport by a genial Southerner. The sort of man who talks about horse racing and Jane Austen in the same breath. He showed me to the campus guest room where I slept for an hour and then worked on my lecture with autobiographical references to Auden. This was better than the one I gave in Indianapolis, but I have the same sensation of not being in touch with the audience, of feeling, and looking, frightfully unhappy. Ended by reading three poems, 'The Secret Agent', the first part of 'Consider this and in our time', and 'Look, Stranger, on this island now'. Read not badly, but feel critical of A's early poems if I read them aloud, whereas they give me pleasure if I read them on the printed page. 'Financier leaving your little room', etc., seems rather verbose and abstract read aloud, 'The Secret Agent' hopelessly obscure and the kind of pleasure I get when I come to the line, 'The street music seemed gracious now to one' - difficult to communicate. After lecture one of those faculty parties with a few students.

Someone asked me whether I really liked Wystan. This was a disconcerting question because it seemed to imply that I had drawn a picture of him which was unsympathetic. Thinking it over, I can see that I may have partly done so. I described him seeing his friends one by one in his rooms at hours he had fixed and interviewing, cross-examining them, laying down the law about the poets of whom he approved, the way poetry should be written, the personality of the poet, being very dogmatic about everything. I did insist that he was not a 'leader' or authoritarian and that he brought a touch of absurdity to his pronouncements which made them seem jokes. He did not wish to be taken altogether seriously. But this would mean nothing to a member of the audience without a sense of humour. In fact to the American who thinks that when one is serious one should be serious, and when funny, un-serious, this would make A. seem even more unsympathetic. But during sleepless patches of the night I asked myself a question I certainly did not ask at the time – *did* I really like Wystan? To attempt to answer the question I had to recall what Wystan thought of me. He thought I was a wild romantic, rather 'mad' (using the word rather loosely). To him I was, I suppose, a kind of Dostoevskian Holy Fool. I was so tall, he once told me, because I wanted to reach heaven ('The heaven-reachers'). I wanted really to be a saint. References to me in *Paid on Both Sides* and the original version of *The Orators* bear this out. He was so contemptuous of my pamphlet *Nine Experiments* (which certainly was very bad) that when this was reported back to me (of course, by Gabriel Carritt*) I destroyed every copy of it I could retrieve from friends. On the other hand, there was something about my utter vulnerability and openness which he respected. When I first knew him and told him about my plans for writing (which included writing novels, etc.) he said, 'We must save you for poetry' and I was instantly a member of an élite which was headed by Auden and Isherwood but included Day Lewis, Rex Warner and very few others. He said, 'You will be a poet because you will always be humiliated' and he felt that I had a kind of truth ('Blurting out the truth' – Isherwood). I imagine he laughed at me a lot behind my back. He also regarded me as a bit paranoid at Oxford (which I was). So, to measure my attitude to Auden, it is that of a somewhat battered observer. Moreover when a friend forms an idea of one when both he and you are very young and retains the same attitude throughout one's life, one feels a bit resentful. Finally, he came to be slightly jealous of me for reasons not indeed to do with talent or success, but because I had a family.

---

* Gabriel Carritt, son of E. F. Carritt, Professor of Aesthetics. Friend of Auden at Oxford, referred to often in his early poems. He became a Communist Party member in the thirties and later a journalist on the *Daily Worker*.

When, in May 1945, wearing GI's uniform, Auden arrived at our house in London, the first thing he said when I opened the front door was, 'You've got a son.'

The lady who asked me whether I liked Auden said I had made him sound a bit inhuman. This did ring a bell, because I remember when we were both young thinking of him as *sui generis*, not at all like other people and of an inhuman cleverness. I did not think of him as having ordinary human feelings and I felt about his early poetry the lack of any 'I' at the centre of it. If you appealed to Auden for sympathy or help he would be attentive, kind, but like a benevolent doctor or psychoanalyst whose task it was to provide a diagnosis and prescribe a treatment, more than as a friend who entered imaginatively into your situation as though it might be his own. He seemed also to have this detached 'clinical' attitude towards himself even, and this is borne out by some of his early poems. A famous poem called 'The Letter' is about the poet walking through a landscape where he takes shelter from a sudden shower by crouching behind a wall where he reads a letter from someone with whom he is in love. The contents of the letter are summed up in a line: 'Speaking of much but not to come.' The reader scarcely feels the emotion implied. The poet seems consciously to be exploiting it for the purposes of a poem in which he expresses clinical detachment even from his own hurt.

24 April / *Nashville*

I did not finish the notes above about Auden. And now I don't have the heart to read them.

4 May

Very taken up with writing essay on Venice. The usual awful misgivings about my lack of knowledge, experience of Venice, etc. I come out with a few big metaphors and then read Hugh Honour's excellent, at times scintillating, guide book and think facts are what I want and what I lack. Well, I must devote the weekend to attacking this subject from a great many different angles.

On 29 April I went to Detroit. It is a huge sprawling desolate city, but in some ways very interesting, frightening but lively.

The hotel, inside and outside, seemed stain-coloured – like the stains we used on wood as children in carpentry lessons. A great expansive view of Detroit from the window. Many oblong buildings, some of them coloured a kind of chocolate-crimson, which seems a prevalent colour. Towers and spires of a great variety of churches.

For Detroit is the most 'ethnic' of cities – ethnic is a key word here.

I was amazed at the dirtiness and shabbiness of General Motors HQ, one of the administrative centres of America.

I took Bob and Peg* out to a rather hasty dinner, then I gave my reading.

Monday a.m. there were meetings with students. Several of them told me they were excited by Detroit, and I saw the point. The clashing of all these ethnic groups, the sense of immensely powerful machines manned by grim muscular workers, the ugliness but vitality, is quite different from the impression made by Indianapolis.

On Tuesday I lunched with people at the Art Institute and looked round the magnificent collections. I had done a preliminary survey Monday afternoon. I can quite see Mexican and Latin American art becoming the art of the future in a socialized world. They also showed me the Noguchi retrospective exhibition – which I admired – this cold, pure, almost disdainful art.

I gave a lecture, with slides, on Painting and Poetry. After that went to another party from which I couldn't extricate myself until 1 a.m.

8 May / *Sewanee*

A great deal of work, making, in my usual way, draft after draft of essay on Venice. Symptom of senility that I can write a draft then put it aside and forget about it. Write a new draft and in bringing up some theme completely forget that I have written about it already (and perhaps far better).

Gave my reading in the university chapel.

12 May / *Nashville*

Pack up things at Continental apartments. Take Anne Hunter out to lunch, plane to Gainesville.

14 May / *New York*

Three days at Gainesville with B. scarcely make a dent in my memory. Yet they were entirely happy, without a shadow in them.

* Robert Dana, poet and teacher, and his wife.

22-5 May / *Paris*

My lecture at the Sorbonne. This went well. It struck me very forcibly that I do certain things like lecturing much better than I have previously. Why? Partly because I think I have learned a great deal about writing through working almost daily for three and a half hours on *The Corporal*. It must also be due to some kind of equilibrium arrived at this moment of old age – when my sight is getting bad, etc. – despite all that.

Talking about the thirties I even had new ideas, which seemed a kind of breakthrough – that the thirties marked the end of modernism and everything one means by symbolism.

3 June / *London*

Went to Much Hadham to the Henry Moores. He and Irina were alone. He was extremely lively, rubicund, a bit shrunk perhaps. He is 80. She, as usual, remained mostly in the background, but sometimes talked as it were parallel with and not across him, to Natasha. Everything with the Moores has expanded. Irina's garden seemed fuller of trees, hedgerows, a herbaceous border, a goldfish pond, two small greenhouses, one for orchids. Henry's side of things has grown still more. There is the Henry Moore Foundation in a house on his property, three storeys of it, containing files, archives, drawings, photographs, books.

Henry has become an institution and he thrives on it, radiating happiness, which Irina reflects.

He talked much more than usual – about his childhood and what a marvellous man his father was – had read the whole of Shakespeare, played classical music on the gramophone, wanted him to learn the violin. (H. hated this – when he failed his entrance exam to the secondary school he said, 'Dad, I failed because I have to do so many violin lessons, I can't study.') He and Irina talked about the incredible amount of work H's mother – a miner's wife with seven children – had to do. How his father could get angry if everything was not right. He obviously feels his father in different circumstances would have been famous.

H. talked about the First World War, how he was the youngest soldier in his regiment – only 18. The first night the other soldiers gave him all their rum and made him drunk. How he wanted to be a hero, win a medal. At first little happened in the way of fighting, then aeroplanes flew over. He asked the commander for permission to fire at them. Stood in a field doing so – of course hit nothing – 'It was as though the wall of this house flew over and you had to hit one brick in it.' On another occasion he went out with a sergeant and lay in a hole on lookout. The sergeant got dead drunk but got a medal. Henry's heroism went unrecognized.

He said a thing about his work which struck me as true for me of mine. 'I go by pleasing and not pleasing.' That is to say that when he works he knows instinctively what he does right and what wrong, and proceeds on the basis of correcting what is wrong. He showed us the HM Foundation, and gave me one of the portfolios of etchings, *The Reclining Figure*, for which I wrote an introductory poem, 'Sculptor and Statues'. He showed us the studio. His age sometimes shows in a kind of sagging of the forms in the sculpture, a blurring of the line in drawings, etching, lithos, etc. He is also repetitious. But when he has a new idea, as in making a bronze of three figures which are modelled from the small Cézanne of three women in a landscape, which he owns, he still seems completely in control of what he is doing. Also in perfectly straightforward drawings of hands, animals, trees.

After this little tour we went back to his sitting room. He got rather tipsy on three whiskies. He talked a lot again. About how his great early aesthetic experience had not been of sculpture, but of literature. The first novels he read were by Scott. He had not cared much about Dickens. Later had read Tolstoy, Flaubert, Stendhal. Could not imagine anything greater in the world than Shakespeare. Could anything be put better than the vignettes of different stages of life in the speech on the seven ages of man. 'Mewling and puking in the nurse's arms' he said, and 'creeping like snail unwillingly to school' – could anything be better? 'This wonderful world' – in spite of all its disadvantages, how beautiful to be alive – what happiness!

I mentioned that the first Moore I had seen was shown to me by Michael Sadler, the Master of University College – when I was an Oxford undergraduate. He said, yes, when he was an art student and Sadler was Chancellor of Leeds University he had invited Henry and two other students to see his collection. Henry remembered a Gauguin. It was among his earliest glimpses of modern art. Later, Sadler had bought one or two pieces from Henry. Still later, one day he received a letter from Sadler saying he wanted to tell Moore that he had always kept a sculpture of his on his mantelpiece, and how he looked at it every day and how grateful he was for this pleasure. Two days later Moore read in the newspaper that Sadler had died. 'What spiritual greatness to have thought at that time of thanking me,' Henry said.

'I always had energy,' he said. 'Tremendous energy. I would never stop doing things. Only recently have I felt less energy sometimes.'

9 June

Went to Aldeburgh Friday and Saturday. The Festival has always been dedicated to Ben Britten and now he is dead it is dedicated to his spirit.

On Saturday we went to the Gladwyns'* party. I was put next to Diana Cooper. She has aged like all of us, and she is immensely conscious of it. 'I am very old, but my spirit is the same,' she said, looking at me with her beautiful wide cornflower-blue eyes in which tragedy seems at every moment cancelled out by laughter. One adores her as one might a Greek goddess, when she gives one a long look that seems to express things from a well of centuries past, and winds up by saying, 'I'm still here! My spirit is the same.' She knows all about mortality, graves, prisons, scandals, sex.

When we were in the garden having drinks, she said, 'Two days ago I made a gaffe.' At the party for Sir Robert Mayer's† hundredth birthday, a woman came up and started to talk to her. 'I'm so blind, I hadn't the faintest idea who she was. Then I saw two enormous diamonds on her dress and I realized who it was. So I put in a lot of ma'ams, and said, "I'm so sorry I didn't recognize you, ma'am. But you see I don't recognize you when you're not wearing your crown."' The Queen explained, 'I thought it was Sir Robert Mayer's evening, so I didn't put it on.'

9 July / St Jérôme

I've finished my play and sent it off to the agents. Before they and the directors have reacted to it, I'll put down my own reactions, qualified a bit by those of Joan Littlewood to whom I showed it when she was here.

---

* Lord Gladwyn. Deputy Leader of the Liberal Party in the House of Lords since 1965. Formerly British Ambassador in Paris and Permanent British Representative to the United Nations.

† Sir Robert Mayer (born 1878). Philanthropist, founder of the Robert Mayer Concerts for Children.

Three and a half years ago, in the autumn of 1975, in Connecticut, it occurred to me that I should rewrite *Trial of a Judge*, which was one of my best ideas, but bungled, dramatizing the relationship of a judge with his son. The judge had a life that connected with that of Berlin bars, etc. (It occurs to me now, he might have had a boy.) In 1934 or whenever I wrote *TOAJ*, it seemed improbable that a judge would have a son who was a male prostitute, took drugs, etc. The events of the past years make such a situation quite feasible, almost a *sine qua non* of child–parent relations, especially if the parents are intellectually distinguished. I first had to prove to myself that I could create the character of Kolya and so I began *The Corporal* with the second act. To my surprise this went very easily. I wrote most of it, it seems, in a few days. Nor did I rewrite it much. I then wrote a version of the introductory expository scene between Herder and Shark. Shark was first of all just a cypher, a message, or some such. Like Hank and Nore II his character emerged as I wrote the play.

I had enormous difficulty in writing everything else. All I can say is that somewhere in the back of my mind the whole action existed like something that on a really unconscious level of my mind I knew already. This was helped by occasional flashes of the kind, 'This is how it has got to end.' But the great difficulty was doing several things at once: (a) retaining the story all through every line of the dialogue or rhythm, so that every line has its place in, relates to the narrative; (b) inventing a characteristic idiom for each character.

This seemed easiest with Kolya who so to speak wrote himself in imagery, idiom and rhythm. It is often actors' performances rather than playwrights' characters which I think enable one to invent a character. Thus it was the young actor, Peter Firth, as Adam in Peter Shaffer's *Equus* who showed me that there could be a performance like that of Kolya. Matthew, my son, insists on thinking Kolya is a portrait of him, but the boy I was thinking of I knew in Berlin in 1932. He was called Georg, was by origin Russian, was extremely lively, mischievous, untruthful, etc., a very nice, totally unreliable delinquent, always in need of money. The thing is one felt one knew him. On one occasion after he had been particularly dishonest about something, then repentant, I said, 'How can I know when you're not telling lies?' and he answered (I must find the correct German for this) 'Wenn Du die Expression meiner Augen studierst!' [By studying the expression of my eyes.] But of course Kolya is a very developed Georg who knows Wagner.

The greatest difficulty in *The Corporal* was expressing ideas in terms of the characters, making them absolutely clear, and also making everything fit in with what seems to me now a predetermined rhythmic pattern. I have incredible difficulty expressing ideas anyway. Writing to me is a humiliating experience (even in this journal) because it brings me up against the difficulty of being able to say anything clearly and economically. The difference between real-life conversation and dialogue is that conversation is tonal – it skips over slips, awkwardness, incompetence – by the tone in which the speaker says it, which results from the pressure of needing to say something. 'Dialogue' is conversation translated into the written, giving the illusion of the conversational.

10 July / *St Jérôme*

Hearing a girl practising for days on end one passage or phrase from one piece suddenly threw light for me on my way of writing a few lines out hundreds of times. It is as though I have to know them like the music before I acquire the freedom which is interpretation.

Ninety in the shade for several days on end – really unbearable.

13 July

So far I have heard nothing positive about *The Corporal* but already I'm getting depressed about it and am full of misgivings. Perhaps the whole thing's absurd anyway. I should have thought more about the conditions of the theatre and been more modest in my demands. I rang Peggy Ashcroft (to do so before she got in touch with me showed lack of control). She said she was thrilled by it, especially after Act II (the beginning she found a bit slow, which caused me to lie awake last night mentally rewriting it). She wanted my agent Peggy Ramsay to send it to Trevor Nunn at the Royal Shakespeare. There was lots to say about the play, which she couldn't say on the telephone.

This morning Peggy Ramsay telephoned. She said – as Peggy A. had done – that it was obviously a serious and important work. Discussing probabilities of production, she said that the National was in a terrible way. Their finances had become absolutely disastrous as the result of a series of strikes.

Joan Littlewood* and Philippe (de Rothschild). I want to write about them. They seem such an extraordinary couple. Some years ago Joan and her companion of thirty years, Gerry Raffles, were together in Vienne walking in the street when Gerry dropped dead. They were only on a visit to Vienne but Joan has lived there ever since. Gerry died at approximately the same time as Philippe's wife Pauline. Philippe knew through John Wells. He heard from John that Joan was miserably unhappy in Vienne and drove from Mouton to Vienne and brought her to Mouton. At Mouton she was a stormy guest, always saying exactly what she felt on every subject. Sometimes she would leave abruptly without informing Philippe or anyone else where she was going. She told Philippe to his face that he was an old reprobate; in good moods addressing him as 'guv'.

Joan is very small, lithe, lively, impertinent-looking. She looks like the mascot of some virile troop of Highlanders whom she keeps perpetually amused. She seems largely occupied in trying to get the Mayor of Vienne to put up some kind of memorial – a garden within a garden – to Gerry. When she talks about the theatre she reveals the bitterly disappointed side of her nature. No one is any good, they are all corrupt. Anyone off the streets could be a better actor than the best of them. One does not dare to mention names for fear of the derision. But when she talks about producing a play, suggests a movement on the stage, she suddenly becomes a different person – can make a bowing sweeping movement of extraordinary grace as though her beret had become an Elizabethan courtier's hat with a wonderful plume in it. After reading *The Corporal*, she kept coming out with ideas for it: 'First of all, abolish all those blackouts between scenes. Play it as one continuous action without breaks. No scenery. Two or three screens on which photographs can be projected which put the action into the context of the thirties. When it is at its most violent, project photographs of poignantly beautiful scenery by way of contrast.'

15 July

Nights of very little sleep here. It is too hot. Besides, ideas of what I am writing go through my head the whole time. Am doing a long essay on Auden in the thirties and have read all his poems in *The English*

---

*Theatre artist and producer. Founded Theatre Workshop with Gerry Raffles in 1945, and directed the Theatre Royal, Stratford, East London, 1953–75. Co-authored the autobiography of Baron Philippe de Rothschild, 1984.

Auden. I got up in the middle of the night – 3 a.m. – and wrote a lot of notes, having had a vision of why his early poetry strikes a younger generation of readers today as that of an extremely isolated person. Of course I could not find a pen, or, rather, found three pens, none of which would write. So I have this morning some words scrawled in different coloured inks. Useful just the same.

As reaction to the fact that I have undoubtedly written a work very difficult to produce in the conditions of the modern theatre, I keep on thinking of another play – really about D. H. Lawrence in 1916. Scenario – a house like Ottoline's run by Ottoline and Philip Morrell where pacifists are working. It must be near the coast. The guns of the battle of the Somme faintly audible. The play would in a way be the chapter in *Women in Love* which Lawrence never wrote since *WIL* encloses but skips all mention of the war. Begins with the Lawrences turning up without anyone knowing who they are – on some pretext – perhaps because their car (could they have had one in 1916? Probably!) has broken down. Characters on the farm – Ottoline, Philip, Bertrand Russell, John Middleton Murry, Katherine Mansfield, David Garnett, Dorothy Brett. Lawrence is driven mad by the war. At first this works wonderfully because they think they are all on the same side. Lawrence and Russell are going to collaborate in planning a utopia. Then this breaks down because Ottoline has (or tries to have) an affair with Lawrence as does Middleton Murry. Lawrence is the man who tells the truth. He tears down their whole world. While he is doing this, the Dorothy Brett character falls in love with him. She is a painter. Offstage she paints him in the nude. She commits suicide. This is an appalling shock and to Bertie Russell it shows that Lawrence is a fascist (what it perhaps really shows is that he is mad). Lawrence takes her death calmly since all ultimate conditions of living and dying seem options to him. Perhaps – in fact certainly – there should be introduced a man who has been fighting on the Somme – Siegfried Sassoon or Richard Aldington.

7 August / *Corfu*

We drove from St Jérôme to Mouton, spending the first night at Conques. A quite unspoiled little town in the Massif Central, between hills, with a wonderful Romanesque cathedral – that bare stone interior of very tall columns, and with cloisters down some steps below it, looking across the valley to the hillside hanging down like an immense curtain. One has the feeling here of something chiselled, chaste and virile about the French past – of lives moulded by the combination of massive forces – the scenery, the architecture, the voices singing in the choir, the harvest, the wine, the family. The France of Claudel – *L'Annonce faite à Marie*.

The next day we drove to Le Havre, stopping for two hours at Bayeux to look at the tapestries, which reminded me a bit of *Guernica*, a bit of strip cartoons. Night on the ferry then we drove to the K's house in the country where we stayed two nights.

There was a great deal of talk about their old friend Wystan, concerning whom they have many theories, some illuminating, some, I think, wrong.

About Wystan: their theory is that he was not gay. They attribute his gayness to the influence of Christopher (Isherwood) who knew Wystan from prep-school days and who demanded his loyalty to the homosexual tribe. Apart from Christopher, the other destroyer of Wystan's happiness was Chester (Kallman), a totally selfish and self-interested neurotic, concerned with ambition and utterly depraved, who used Wystan to achieve his own ends, they said.

Of course, it can be said of any homosexual that he wouldn't be one, if he hadn't been influenced by someone who was. But Auden did not see Isherwood between the time when they both left prep school and they both went to their universities. And at Gresham's Wystan fell in love with Robert Medley and was attracted by other boys. Doubtless the reunion with Christopher led quickly to the mutual revelation that each was homosexual; and this was the equivalent of an oath of *Blutbrüderschaft*. Each would know that for the other to become 'normal' would be the equivalent of a betrayal. When, soon after he left Oxford, Auden became engaged to a nurse, it was Christopher who persuaded him to break off the engagement. But before that W. had explained, to me and others, that he regarded changing his sexual disposition as a matter of will – something which he would be able to make himself do – a self-imposed cure – of which he was capable. But it was Wystan who 'discovered' Berlin by going there in 1929, staying at Magnus Hirschfield's sexual institute, going to the male brothels, taking up with Gerhardt Meyer, befriending John Layard and extracting from him the ideas of Homer Lane, etc., and it was Christopher who followed him there.

Christopher and Wystan were a club of two. This does not mean that Christopher stopped him becoming normal, though it is possible that without Christopher's influence he might, through exercising his will in which he had such confidence, have made his life fit into the pattern of imposed normality. Perhaps this would have been a success. Wystan's idea of the marital relationship which he wished to share with another man could have been transferred to a real family with children. He would have made an excellent father. In his homosexual relationships he tended to regard himself as the boy's parent (he was Gerhardt Meyer's 'father', Chester's 'mother').

Wystan, who believed so much in discipline, nevertheless came to think that he was unalterably homosexual. In 1945 he had an affair with a girl, Rhoda Klonsky, which he gave up because he could not enjoy sex with her (or with any other woman).

The women he knew best – Elizabeth Mayer, Ursula Niebuhr, Hannah Arendt – were to him priestesses like Moneta in Keats's 'The Fall of Hyperion'. He became the confidant of other women who used him as a lay psychoanalyst to whom they poured out their secrets. My friends seemed to think that he had a compulsion to thrust himself into the lives of certain married couples whose love life was not going very well, extracting from the wives their most intimate secrets, probing wounds, and driving them to desperate courses. There may be examples of his marriage-breaking, but I feel the breakdown must have been less his fault than the result of the wish of the woman to use him as the instrument for breaking up the marriage. Wystan was the born father confessor of whatever philosophy he happened to adhere to at various periods of his life. In this he was like his part-mentor, John Layard, and I suppose the predecessor of all three, Homer Lane. Part of his fascination for several women was that; as a result of their confabulations with him, each became convinced that – with her – at all events – he was not 'really queer', but merely of a sect bound to queerdom – and of course for these ladies it was easy to see Christopher as some kind of magician like Sarastro in *The Magic Flute*. The truth – but no, one can't discover the truth – but what is nearer to the truth than the idea of each of these ladies that Auden in different circumstances might have married her – is perhaps that this father confessor used women disciples who confessed their problems to him in part as substitute mothers in whom he confided. In his 1929 journal, describing a conversation with 'Margaret' (Gardiner, I suppose) who prods him about his feelings towards women, he reports himself saying,

'What I hate is the fucking.' I did not tell my friends of the existence of this diary and I think I was right not to do so, because I suppose them to have constructed their own myth about Auden, which should not be disturbed. Mrs K. said that on one occasion Auden made a conditional proposal to her. 'If anything happened to K. would you marry me?' According to Tekla Clark* he proposed to her, on condition that they adopted Chester.

An interesting idea of K's is that Auden lacked what he calls *Menschenkenntnis*. I think this may (in a way) be so. It is true that you don't really know your friends if you hold up, between them and yourself, a graph upon a transparent screen drawn on your mind, upon which their symptoms and characteristics are charted.

> Lay your sleeping head, my love,
> Human on my faithless arm.

These lines are often cited as illustrating passionate love, yet what they are like is a fever chart which on a particular night attains a peak in the poet's psyche, thus provoking his moving reflections on one-night love. The poet's arm is 'faithless' – uncommitted to repetition of the occasion and the beloved is asleep pathically contributing to those symptoms which, as the poem insists, are of a temporary nature – though undeniably true, and in harmony with other examples of human ecstasy, the hermit's, for example. How different from:

> Let me not to the marriage of true minds
> Admit impediments. Love is not love
> Which alters when it alteration finds,
> Or bends with the remover to remove ...

In Auden's love poems the lover is removed from the beloved, being more fully conscious, more responsible, more guilt-ridden than the beloved. This poet knows lovers and friends more completely than they know him. He is the analyst. They are the analysed. Love is not mutual because there is not shared knowledge of each of the other. There is an element of the arbitrary, on Auden's side, about even his closest relationships. An example of arbitrariness is his choice of Isherwood as the judge who would decide for him finally what were the good and what the bad lines in his poetry. An intelligent choice, of

---

* A friend of Auden's from Forio, Ischia, who later married John Clark, printer of fine books.

course, because it set up Isherwood's intuitive judgement against A's intellect but at the same time, however good a judge, Isherwood must have been fallible; to set him up as infallible was to give him a fixed place in Auden's constellation of his friends. One might say this was not altogether fair to Isherwood, just as one could certainly say it was unfair to Chester Kallman to set him up as an ideal. This could only show how very fallible Chester was. K. would say I suppose that Wystan's attitude to Chester showed his lack of *Menschenkenntnis*. Yet he did come to know everything about Chester and suffered greatly through doing so.

11 August / *Corfu: Rovinia**

This beautiful place. The little bay with its rocky beach and the cave shaped like a tip-tilted cathedral window, and studded in the interior with lozenge-shaped stones, and with ferns and grass tufted on ledges. Just beyond it is the headland with two hoofs of rock thrust into the bright water. It seems like the restful end of life, dreaming its way into poetry, Calypso's cave, *The Odyssey*, Byron's Canto about Haidée and her piratical father in *Don Juan*.

Harold Pinter, Antonia Fraser, her brother Tom Pakenham and three of his children to lunch here Wednesday. They all, except Natasha and Harold, went down to bathe with the Glenconners. Harold said he had read my play, which he described as 'passionate phantasmagoria'. He said the play was extremely powerful with brilliant scenes; like Peggy Ashcroft and Joan Littlewood, he thought the excitement began with the second act. Kolya was marvellous, the Corporal brilliant, but Herder was too abstract, as were his speeches and the argumentation that takes up so much of Act One. He said one thing that interested me greatly – that it's a matter of the language. Trying to analyse it in my own mind, I see that in order to get the language I have to do what I've done in the rest of the play, make the language the function of (1) situation, (2) character, (3) ideas.

22 August / *Newby Bridge*

We drove from London to Newby Bridge in the Lake District. Stayed the night at the Swan Hotel, with a beautiful view of the river. On Thursday we set out in search of the farmhouse where, when I was 6

---

* Rovinia. Home of Christopher and Elizabeth Glenconner.

or 7, the Spender family stayed in the summer of 1915 or 1916 in order to get away from Sheringham on which Zeppelins dropped occasional bombs. (This means it was 1915 rather than 1916 in which case I was only 6.) I have extremely vivid memories of these weeks in the Lake District. Of walks through rain showers which suddenly cleared – the woods gave off an exhalation of pine scent – drops of rain hung on the furled ends of fern and bracken; large black slugs, which delighted me, crawled along the paths. Sometimes we came to caves along the roadside in which I would find stone or slate encrusted with crystals. It was a landscape of jewels, the greatest of them being Lake Derwentwater below us. I remember rowing and trawling on the lake and my father catching a pike and our eating it afterwards. But the deepest memory of all was lying in my bedroom, which overlooked a garden or lawn, and hearing my father read Wordsworth to my mother, where they sat outdoors in deck chairs.

On our way up to the Lakes, I remember staying the night at a hotel in Leeds, a city which gave me the impression of being all black or caked grimy brown with a texture like sandpaper. I remember brass rods up the shafted stairwell of the hotel. I caused a mild sensation there, I was told, by scaring ladies in the lift who were horrified to see that my jacket was crawling with caterpillars, which had escaped from the match-boxes in my pocket where I kept them.

23 August / *Yester House, East Lothian*

We spent the morning going all around Ullswater in the mistaken belief that it was Derwentwater! In crannies of rocks, there were plants growing, clusters of harebells and ferns, most beautiful of them a maidenhair with stalks that look like fine black wire from which the little dots of leaves, spore-spotted at the back, spread out, flat, not curling. When we got to Keswick, looking at the map we realized our mistake, so we set out again. I had remembered that in 1915 or 1916 the very moment we arrived at the farmhouse we children, accompanied by our father, had scrambled up to the top of the little mountain (my brother Michael said it was 1,000 feet high), and that it was called Catbells: so we went along the road with its panorama of the lake below us, the name of the farm – perhaps, I thought, a false memory – sprang into my mind. It was Skelgill Farm. We came to a small mountainside hamlet where a lady was walking, and Natasha asked her, 'Is there a mountain here called Catbells?' 'Oh yes,' she said, 'it's just there.' She pointed to a hillside. 'And is there a farm-house called Skelgill?' 'Oh yes, you go along this road until you come to a hairpin bend, and then on the left you'll see a lane – rather rough – which leads up to Skelgill Farm.' All this was as she said. We drove up to SF which was one of those domino-shaped longitudinal houses with oblong windows in a stucco wall which seem to be ruled into it at regular intervals. It was framed by an immense sheltering tree. (It could not have been there in my childhood.) There was a gate leading into a yard in front of it. Dozens of trippers, mostly schoolchildren, were walking along the lane to go into it. There was a view as far as Keswick on one side and across the lake in front, and behind there were the mostly grassy slopes of the mountain we climbed as children. To establish its identity beyond doubt, in front, on the grass bank above the lane, where two pink-skinned recently shorn sheep were crouching, was a wooden sign with carved into it the name CAT-BELLS. The sheep brought me further memories of sheep being dipped and of seeing once on a walk, a sick, scabbed, flyblown sheep near the path side.

With my caterpillars in boxes, I had thought of myself, until Der-wentwater, as a naturalist who would eventually grow a long white beard like Darwin. But now this image merged into that of the nature poet – Wordsworth.

30 August / *London*

A tremendous relief to be home. Excess of travel this summer has disoriented me.

2 September

Meanwhile have chores to do immediately. Reviews of Brecht's poems in translation for *New York Times; Letters of D. H. Lawrence* for *Now*. The long Auden essay must be done by 27 September. I must finish these things so I can start on revising my play.

21 September / *Venice. A week with Matthew*

By the time we put our things in the hotel, it was eleven. We went out for dinner, but nearly every restaurant was closed. (I had always thought of Venice as nocturnal.) Finally we found a place near the Fenice which was excellent – and very expensive.

Although it was two years since Matthew and I were last in Venice together, it was as though we'd taken up just where we'd left off. Matthew even taller than I, walking ahead of me, carrying my things or most of them, looking scholarly and a bit remote when wearing his gold-rimmed spectacles, somehow with quite a different kind of smile, sweet and attentive, but at the edges lurkingly ironic, when not wearing them: beautiful at times, at other times rather lean and craggy, too keen-looking to seem entirely physical. Sometimes he'll take my arm, sometimes push me from behind up the steps of one of those Venetian bridges. Then I feel we are a comic duo, oversize the two of us. I with crumpled trousers, my legs like an elephant's, my face pushing fleshily through crevasses of red skin, my hair windswept mass of white cotton and fluffed up round the sides like a mad ecclesiastic. (I remember how some years ago at night at the lake's edge in Hamburg, in darkness when I was walking there, a boy dressed in skintight shirt and shorts came up to me out of the darkness and asked, 'Sind Sie ein Theologer?')

When we came down to breakfast at a table in front of the hotel, looking across the wide causeway crowded with people, and through sticks and mooring poles of gondoliers on to the laguna, who should we see but Charlotte Bonham Carter? Very white with her head and shoulders bowed by arthritis, the skin of her high forehead engraved with parallel wrinkled lines, sociable creases spread out at the pointed corners of each eye like rays, she extended an amicable arm to us and said, 'How perfectly delightful to see you. What a surprise!' and having ordered an egg for which she couldn't find the word *uovo* went on to describe a terribly exciting lecture she had heard at the Cini the previous day on the influence of eighteenth-century Venetian painting on English painters of the same period. It turned out that her room was actually next to our two rooms. 'Only a cupboard, but it was all the dear Ashley Clarkes* could get for me in the whole of Venice,' she cried. 'But what does it matter, it's so wonderful to be here.' She said that at the end of the war she had taken a vow to come to Venice once every year, and she had kept it. During the war she worked for Aerial Photographic Survey. She said, 'It was such a bore not being able to travel. But the RAF did make a tiny sortie over Istria which I went on. Such a marvellous view of the coliseum.'

We saw Charlotte a few days later at dinner at the Ashley Clarkes'. She looked like the bent figure of the Virgin at the Cross. At moments

* Sir Ashley Clarke, former British Ambassador to Italy, now living in Venice.

when her head had fallen to one side, I felt that she really might have passed out. This happened once during dinner. Frances Clarke got up to take away Charlotte's plate and as she did so she gently put an arm around her shoulders. Charlotte woke and immediately started saying, 'Oh, how perfectly wonderful', as though she had just been interrupted in mid-sentence.

We seemed to see quite a lot of old ladies. For at drinks with Mr and Mrs Rylands there was Olga Rudge*, to be followed a bit later by Charlotte. Olga Rudge and I talked a lot about subjects other than Ezra Pound. Later we separated and Matthew heard Mrs Rylands introduce Olga to Charlotte. 'Olga Rudge', she explained, 'was the constant companion, almost the wife of Ezra Pound.' 'On the left side of the bed as you might say,' said Olga. 'Ezra Pound? Ezra Pound?' said Charlotte. 'Was he the man who made those dreadful broadcasts during the war?' 'I didn't find them so dreadful,' said Olga. 'I thought the fuss about them greatly exaggerated.' 'I heard them myself. They were perfectly abominable,' said Charlotte. 'Moreover, I could see no merit in his poetry.' This passed by without any explosion from Olga Rudge. Perhaps she was so taken aback that she was speechless. I happened to be in Venice on the day, two years ago, when I heard the news of Robert Lowell's death. The same afternoon I went to a drinks party at the Cini Foundation. Olga Rudge was there and I told her the news of Robert's death. 'The best thing that could have happened to him,' she said. 'After what he wrote about Ezra.' Lowell had always written praisingly of Pound but had remarked somewhere that one could not ignore his anti-Semitism, but must balance it against his genius and his generosity.

For our first two days the weather was slightly foggy. Venice was seen through a yellowish golden haze, the domes of Santa Maria della Salute looking like a painting of Seurat. When on Saturday and Sunday it cleared and was windy and cooler than it had been, Venice had that look most characteristic of it, I suppose, of stone and marble objects played on and painted by reflections of lights and colours from blue sky, white or umber clouds, dancing water.

Matthew had plans that we should study Byron and Shelley in Venice. So we went to the Lazzaro Island where Byron stayed among

*Olga Rudge, American musician, Ezra Pound's companion, mother of his daughter Mary.

the Armenian monks at some time in his Venetian career. This proved dull.

The most interesting place Matthew led me to, which we had not visited before, was the Palazzo on the Grand Canal where there are the Longhi paintings – wonderful pictures of social and domestic life of Venetians. Here is that cluster of people watching a rhinoceros thinly and lightly painted, with microscopic accuracy – beautiful pink colour.

We left Venice on Thursday thinking we would visit one or two villas and then go for one day to 'Avane'* to see Maro and the grandchildren. On the way, we went to Asolo. I remembered that Freya Stark lived there and thought it would be polite at least to telephone her. There was no reply from her house. We went to the Cypriano restaurant and had already started eating our meal when a lady sat down alone at the very next table. She had very Roman, solid moulded features, under a hat which surmounted what looked like a Victorian dust cap worn in the parlour. I went to the desk and asked if this could be Freya Stark. It was. So I asked her whether she would come and join us at our table. She did so. We had a very pleasant time. She said she had given up writing – was passing the end of her life reading. At present she was studying prehistory. Then she would read the Greeks. 'What I dread is having to come to the Romans,' she said. 'They are such bores.'

Drove to 'Avane' where we were greeted first by Saskia and Cosima† running out at the sound of the car, followed by Maro, Claire Peploe‡, their house guest, who was very nice, as was Sebastian Walker¶ who arrived Saturday.

27 September/*New York*

Flew to New York and spent the weekend there. Saturday I lunched with Ed Mendelson. We talked as always about Wystan.

30 September

In the aeroplane I started having American-European feelings. Suddenly I had an insight into what is continentally boring, with an expansive

---

* Matthew's and Maro's house, which is near Siena in the Chianti country.
† Matthew's and Maro's children.
‡ A film director who was Maro's neighbour in London before her marriage.
¶ Chairman of Walker Books Ltd.

all-pervading boredom here, compared with Europe (and, I suppose, Asia). Being in an aeroplane going almost anywhere in America brings it on. (I know there are lots of qualifications to what I'm going to say, but I'll go on.) In Europe to be in an aeroplane means arriving at some place fundamentally different from the place you left. In America it means arriving at a place fundamentally the same, however different the geography. America is like school or university – there are different houses and colleges and their members try to exaggerate the difference but the enclosing atmosphere is that of the all-including institution.

When I arrived in New York I had this odd feeling of being back at school with the good boys and the naughty boys, the prefects, the bullies, the toughs, the scoundrels, the clean, the dirty, the puritanical, the pornographic, but all really moving in the same ruts between the sky-scrapers. But then I went the next night to George Plimpton's party – right after that to Bob Silvers's – and I felt quite differently. America is a place of groups and cliques amid the surrounding sameness where people try to lead distinct and individual lives – intimate, personal. It is untrue to say that Americans drop their friends. On the contrary, they hold on to them, trying to set up eccentric communities within the vast conforming community.

1 October

I am reading Virginia Woolf's letters – all about her, Vanessa, Leonard, Roger, Maynard, Morgan (Forster), etc. – a world so different that I can imagine her standing over me saying, 'What in heaven's name are you doing there?'

3 October/*Lynchburg, Virginia*

Yesterday I was supposed to have my first class with the eleven poetesses allotted to me. I was driven to Hopwood, and set down in a classroom with eleven poems and eleven copies of an anthology of poetry – one for each of them. By now there was a terrific storm going on. I read the poems, which were all of the women's magazine variety – then I started reading from the anthology. 'The Wild Swans at Coole', Book IX of *Paradise Lost*, some William Carlos Williams which made me revise my opinion of him. What incredible language, how edible, how delectable, why, I wonder, do I ever read anything but poetry? 'The Bishop Orders his Tomb'! The answer is that poetry has become a kind of battle of critics and also of poets writing about other poets, disturbing the pure springs. One comes to think of poems as the objects of abstractly prose commentaries. By now I was praying that none of the poetesses would appear. I had with me a notebook. In it was a very rough draft of the idea for a poem I'd scrawled down when we were in the Lake District. Suddenly, isolated as it were from everything in space and time, I wrote another draft in which I seemed to experience all I'd felt about Lake Derwentwater, the words trembling upon my senses, whirling round me like moths. Then I took up the anthology again, read 'The Circus Animals' Desertion'. This, Yeats's last and perhaps greatest poem, was written in 1939, when he was 74. 'I have four years then,' I thought. 'If I could start at once to write those four or five poems for which I wrote notes, then I could be reborn as a poet – an entirely different poet – in these four years.' I started thinking about a poem I had in my head when I was reading in the aeroplane VW's letters – a poem about how those who have the most tragic sense of the horrors of life are also often those who daub the outsideness of their conversation and behaviour with the brightest language of jokes and laughter. I thought of VW's relationship with Vanessa. They called themselves Dolphin (Vanessa) and Baboon (Virginia). Their interchanges, conversational or by correspondence, are gay, gossipy, joking. This is because knowing the darkness within, which is the very nature of life, they know also that they must cherish their outsideness, paint what is external in the brightest colours, like the eyes which fishermen in the Mediterranean paint on the prows of their ships. What I know is that given a subject like that I can explore the reality of it; what I can't do with confidence is fit it into, or create for it, the form. I am beginning to think that if I am able to make the situation concrete it will discover its own form, which might be something new.

I prayed my class might never arrive and my prayers went on being answered for all of two and a half hours. Then two bewildered flustered girls, very attractive in their distress, and with faces rain-wet like apples fallen into grass in orchards, appeared and repeated their excuses and apologies – a dirge of bells and wrung hands.

They were not comforted. I began to feel very guilty. I realized that in similar circumstances Natasha would have done something positive – rushed through the rain on to the campus, found someone.

4 October

Now I've moved into my apartment. It is a minute's walk from the campus. If I can overcome my fear of someone coming up and saying, 'Are you Mr Spender?', I'll be able to eat in the student cafeteria.

My first class in a room dominated (of course) by the uninterrupted stage whispering of the air-conditioning system against which I tried to hear the voices of the girls who talked as softly as just-hatched chickens. Their poems seemed all mush when I first read them. But seemed to improve in the discussion. They were searingly attentive. Nothing funny. A relief to get it over. Next time will be chattier. I feel better.

5 October

I wrote a poem about Derwentwater. One of my best, at this moment, I think. Why do I have such resistance to writing poetry? Since when I am writing it I can become very absorbed, happy, fascinated. The resistance comes first from the sense not so much of failure as of non-recognition. I can't really convince myself my poetry gives pleasure to anyone. I feel apologetic sending it to a friend, humiliated sending it to an editor, as though asking a favour. Next, writing it is a test in which all one's best qualities are brought in confrontation with all one's incapacity. Next, poetry is not 'work'. And there is always 'work' elbowing its way in and pushing poetry aside. For instance at this moment the reading I have to give tomorrow (and before I give it I can never believe a reading gives pleasure), the review I must write today of Janet Flanner, the Auden essay I have not looked at since I came here. The Heine article.

All this is what B. would call self-indulgent. In fact only yesterday I had evidence that a poem I had put out of my mind because one reviewer had attacked it – 'Judas Iscariot' – is read and discussed on this very campus. (It is not in my *Collected Poems* because I was discouraged by the reviewer. How stupid.)

Being a minor poet is like being minor royalty, and no one, as a former lady-in-waiting to Princess Margaret once explained to me, is happy as that.

8 October

Bill Smith* came at about five, so we had three hours' conversation. He talked about an attack by Clive James on Voznesensky in the *New York Review of Books*.

Bill spoke with warmth and affection of Allen Tate 'who helped me so much'. I asked him how good a writer he thought Tate was and he said certain poems, e.g., 'The Swimmers' and some of the critical writings, were wonderful. Tate was one of the great American writers – didn't I agree? I said that Tate always seemed to me terribly self-conscious and didn't have qualities which moved me in Eliot, Yeats, Lawrence. I said that when I last saw Allen, just before he died, I was slightly shocked because he was talking about literary reputations, as though he still regarded who got a Pulitzer or a National Book Award as important. 'Oh, but that was what was so marvellous about him,' said Bill. 'He cared about whether these things were used in the right way.' But can literary merit be decided by giving the right person the right award? Well, I suppose it is better than giving the wrong person the wrong award.

9 October

I gave my lecture. Up to the last moment I was troubled by the conviction that nothing I could say was of the least interest to anybody. It went very well. I wrote quite a long passage and draft of the poem about Auden's funeral. I am going to have a Final Phase.

10 October

My class, which I took last night, seems irremediable. I have really almost given up trying to discuss their poems, and just talk about poetry.

In one of their poems were the following lines:

> I seem as though from a polished ship
> Torn
> Between the anchors at the dock
> And the currents at sea.

'This doesn't work. You can't think of a ship as having an emotional

---

* William Jay Smith, poet and translator.

life divided between attachment to its anchors (anyway it doesn't have anchors at dock) and the call of the tides,' I said.

'She personalizes the ship,' a friend of the poetess said, in a just audible squeak.

'Well, even if the ship was you – I mean – if you were the ship – it would be absurd,' I argued, beginning to feel dizzy. However I could see that the class was against me. Crushed ambitions and women's lib feelings had rallied to the author's right to identify herself with a polished ship.

When I got back to my apartment I ate some ham and beans, and opened a bottle of rather rust-tasting claret. I ate much too much and drank nearly three-quarters of the bottle. I felt disgusted with myself, repelled by my heavy, aged unlovable weight of flesh.

I started wondering why, since I have tests in hospital ahead of me, I feel no dread. Perhaps the incapacity to anticipate the future anyway. Perhaps because in my mind I have always regarded the flesh as a vehicle for the spirit – a kind of aeroplane into which the pilot has been built as part of the whole apparatus though spiritually he is outside it. One accepts the fact that the machine is bound to break down, but one does not think of this as the concern of the spirit. One side of my family – the Schusters – never seem to have cared much about dying. As my cousin John said to me, 'Of course one knows one might be translated any minute.'

10 October (later)

I started working seriously on 'Auden's Funeral'. The metre seems to echo some kind of terza rima, though I would prefer the lines not to be triplets. Words like thud, dead, lid, clod, wood seem to recur as I write.

What strikes me about most elegies is that they say so little about the character of the elegized.

I went to my class expecting to be confronted by eleven girls and found one – the very nice and attractive one, who had been so apologetic last week when the class failed to turn up. I was greatly relieved and went back to my apartment where, having been given three hours, I wasted them watching TV. I rang B. and had a long conversation with him. He is very serious about trying to get out of his school teaching and was spending the evening filling in forms. There he is, teaching all day and alone in his trailer most nights on weekends, always cheerful, gentle, calm, loving to talk, full of news, amusing, intelligent. When I think of how I wasted the evening given to me, I feel ashamed.

News. The second worst day in history on the American stock market. This is disturbing partly because it brings reminders of 1929, partly for reasons which go beyond this, which I've always felt and of which economic crises are only the symptoms. We live in totally economic societies. The conditions in which we live are entirely dependent on an economy over which we have no control. But this economy, if translated into human action and behaviour, is frivolous – the gambling of operators and traders on the stock market, and beyond that the purchasing of commodities by people who do not need them. For the margin which keeps the economy buoyant is the unnecessary, not the necessary.

In a capitalist system what is solemnly called 'the collapse of the economy' is, in human terms, collapse of the frivolity – people, because they panic, no longer buying un-necessities. And if this happens on a large enough scale, there is mass unemployment.

I see I am getting into a muddle. Because it is also frivolity which produces waste. The American crisis today is caused by the wastage of oil. If waste was cut out it would not be where it now is. But what this means surely is that the same frivolity which buys unnecessary commodities to keep the economy going, when sacrifice is needed in order to save it from the results of excess, cannot make that sacrifice simply because to keep the system going it has to be wasteful.

The alternative kind of society to built-in frivolity is communist or socialist controls of the whole society, which leads to something even worse – loss of freedom. Go on with your poems and stop writing opinionated nonsense.

11 October

Went on with 'Auden's Funeral'. What I am looking for is a line which echoes terza rima (has clinching imagistic lines or a strong rhythm – a lot of internal monosyllabic rhymes) but has four- or preferably five-line stanzas with a lot of enjambment between stanzas. I am just writing down as much as I can at present in the hope that I will arrive at the desired stanza and rhyme pattern (if there is a regular pattern). I tried opening the poem with Auden's friends going from Vienna to Kirchstetten then found this didn't work. From the way I am writing it (or it is writing itself) the narrative form seems to be strong, situations (such as dropping clods of earth on the coffin then imagining W. lying in his coffin with a rather triumphant expression on his face) with parentheses which are flashbacks.

This morning I had to take an English class. I was asked what was the dividing line between poetry and prose, and I said, 'Well, if you go for a walk and when you return home you try to describe what you saw on the walk so that the important thing is that the reader sees the things you saw, that is prose description – the words you use would be replaceable by other words which described the same scene. But if you try to transform the experience into words which enable the reader to enter into the uniqueness of what you have experienced and of you experiencing it in words irreplaceable by other words, that would approach poetry.' I felt this was incoherent, that I had somehow myself caught the surrounding incomprehension.

17 October

Got up feeling rather depressed. Gradually the feeling that I ought to write off my play is overtaking me. Not three years wasted, but three years in which I could have done a great deal else.

I can now trace the depression I felt, and still feel, to an interview with a young woman reporter from the local newspaper at Hollins. She asked 'Why-do-you-write-poetry?' type questions veering on personal ones. Also she had a technique of candour: 'Do you hate being interviewed?' 'Are you always as silent as this?' She asked what had happened to poetry since 1970 – was anyone interested in it since then? Then she said, 'All my friends think poetry is passé.' This struck a terribly true note. Why is poetry the one art of which people can say things like that? I suppose because it does not have a public. It has only individuals who read it, or who don't read it, write it or don't write it. 'Jackals round an exhausted well' was how Cyril Connolly once described poets. But the poets then living and writing were Auden and Eliot. Envy, with Cyril, was a passion even stronger than his love of art. And 'beauty which is frailer than a flower' can wither under the envy, competitiveness, self-interest of the poets themselves. Anyway this to me is very existence, life itself.

> Feeling clumsy as I do.
> Every poem my Waterloo.

18 October

Lizzie rang and talked about her work. She can't make up her mind whether to go to Finland with the film they are making – *Reds* – or whether to stay in London for auditions. She seems very conscious of having to make choices in her life.

Keep on thinking of subjects for sonnets and will try to write a few.

I read again and again Goethe's unbelievably concentrated and powerful poem about seeing Schiller's skull, written in terza rima. It is perfectly regular and yet a rhythm drives through it which is organic to Goethe and his passionate feelings. Wonderful exclamatory breaks. What liquid silver language! What energy, mastery, power!

20 October

During the week I read Nicholas Blake's (C. Day Lewis's) crime story *Death of a Traveller*. This is the second N. Blake I have read in a week. Cecil told me that Nigel Strangeways, his investigator, is a portrait of Wystan but in fact NS has only the faintest resemblance to W. He is on the other hand, in the way he talks, in learning, sense of humour, love of poetry, the mixture of affection and cynicism, sly secretiveness, convivial readiness to play the role of neighbour, comrade, or colleague, strikingly like Cecil himself. Cecil had a very conscious sense of his intellectual superiority. Malice as well as affection towards others, razor-like contempt, especially for women, perhaps even for those whom he loved. He worked off the murderer in him in the secretly autobiographical passages of his crime stories. In a straight novel and even in his autobiography he can never depict character as well as he does in the crime stories, because in them he regards each character as potentially murderer or murdered. *Death of a Traveller* is really about the killing egotism of the poet who could amiably strangle everyone round him for the sake of getting on with his poem, charm them even into suicide to protect his isolation. There is deep love of poetry in it, even sympathy for murderers and murdered, and a flickering whiplash or snake-tongue humour.

What bores me about crime stories is the necessary obfuscating and congealing complexity of plot, the anti-climactic banality of the dénouement. Still this weekend I felt I had a few hours alone with Cecil. (Also am reading in a biography of this poet, that Housman was circumcised, on his father's instructions, when he was 12, and that he had a gondolier in Venice, and male prostitutes (descriptions and prices paid noted in a notebook) in Paris – how I longed to tell Wystan. One cannot telephone to the dead.)

1 November

Meanwhile I wrote notes for my talk about Henry Moore. He strikes me so much as being normal as a man that you might expect him to produce works of art which reflected one's conception of genial, sensible, brave, manly 'normality'. In fact he produces 'modern art'. But this is precisely because in our time the normal is really the exceptional. Within the dehumanizing circumstances of modern life, a completely human art must do far more than create figures which are traditional or anatomically correct. The artist who is himself an intensely vital, energetic and energizing man has to establish and realize and uphold his individuality against the environment. In order to do this he has to absorb into himself some of the machine-like, beyond-the-human-scale characteristics of the age. A mother and child, or a reclining figure, or the most primitive of figures, have to absorb into themselves the strength of machines, whereby they can fortify their own humanity. This is what Moore does in his sculpture, which is strong in the way that the painting of Léger is – combining both the human and the abstract – the abstract being in their cases not a void, an emptiness, a coloured or bare space, but a concentration of energies, drawn from the world of machinery, and able to reflect, comprehend, and resist dehumanizing forces from which they derive. The heads in HM's sculpture seem as depersonalized as, say, the top half of a pair of pliers, and yet they have a frontal gaze which seems to contemplate past and future and the universe.

8 November / *Portland, Maine*

On 6 November flew to Portland, Maine. My visit to Bates College was rather remarkable. Instead of 200 students turning up for my reading, about 700 did (out of a student body of 1,200) and the reading had to be moved from the intimacy of a lounge to the bareness of a chapel.

At the University of Maine I was banqueted in a way that I found discomforting. Before the banquet I had to stand in a line with dignitaries. This followed on my reading, which was introduced by the President of the University, who recited lines of 'I think continually' at me. (This – or some of it – was read recently by John Kennedy, son of JFK, at the opening of the Kennedy Library in Boston, and has much affected my public relations.) I then read from a brightly lit rostrum into a black void, the unseen public.

10 November / *Philadelphia*

I read at Boston College poems by Auden and MacNeice as well as my own. Read Edith Wharton – *The Age of Innocence*. She always gives me the feeling of Henry James without tears.

In Boston I bought two weeks' editions of the *New York Times Book Review*. A review of Volume 5 of Virginia Woolf's letters contained the following quotation:

> He [Stephen Spender] talks incessantly and will pan out in years to come a prodigious bore. But he's a nice poetic youth – big nosed, bright eyed, like a giant thrush ... He is writing about Henry James and has tea alone with Ottoline and is married to a Sergeant of the Guards. They have set up a new quarter in Maida Vale; I propose to call them the Lilies of the Valley. There's William Plomer with his policeman, then Stephen, then Auden and Joe Ackerley, all lodged in Maida Vale, and wearing different coloured lilies. [1933]

Oh, blessed Virginia, if you look down on me from any height where you now live, help me in my old age not to be a bore. Boredom was taking tea with Ottoline. Boredom was writing about Henry James and volume after volume of literary journalism. Boredom was being like my father and my uncle, public figures. It's impossible not to write these lines without the sense of a reader looking over my shoulder. Am I not putting the best possible face on V's remarks? But what I write is true. I'm struggling at the end to get out of the valley of hectoring youth, journalistic middle age, imposture, money making, public relations, bad writing, mental confusion.

Virginia was never boring. She was cruel in her perceptions and the cruelty was part of the price of not being boring. Insane at intervals herself, one wonders how she can write to Ottoline as she does about Vivien Eliot whom she describes as 'malodorous'.

11 November

To revert to Virginia Woolf. Reading her letters and journals, I find this justification – that in remarks that are cruel and treacherous (e.g., about Vita Sackville-West) to correspondents, what she is really doing is being candid about her own candour. She is more concerned – in her journal certainly – with showing herself (the 50-year-old Virginia who will read what the 20-year-old V. showed herself to be) as what she is at a particular moment than with anything else. There are layers of one's own truth which are deeply undermining of the lives of others – she was not afraid to show these – because they were the truth about herself.

Another memory – Auden saying when we were undergraduates that philosophy was something to study late in life.

With old age I see myself more as object and less as subject. Perhaps this is because I look back on most of my life and see it as having happened, irremediable, as though it were the life of another person. It is clear to me that I am much more like my father against whom I reacted than I have realized. What characterized him was incomplete activities enclosed by optimistic rhetoric. Writing journalistic books about subjects he hadn't really studied and hoping that feelings, intuitions, sympathies would carry him through. *Men and Mansions*, *Byron and Greece*, etc. I have done likewise. What makes me different from him is my self-distrust. Still that hasn't been sufficient to stop me.

23 November / *London*

We had lunch at the Albany with Philippe de Rothschild. This was for the Queen Mother. The other guests were Miriam Rothschild, Christopher Fry, Cecil Beaton, and the QM's lady-in-waiting, Lady Fermoy. Cecil, who has had a stroke, paralysing him on one side, did not realize perhaps that he would have to walk up two flights of stairs to Philippe's sitting room, another flight for luncheon. He was heroic about this tremendous effort. He did not show his exhaustion (as it were with the unparalysed side of him) but was his friendly charming self. To make him laugh I reminded him of the time when we both had *fou rire* at Mouton because I rather peremptorily asked Philippe to produce his gardener, famous for his beauty. Cecil leaned against a wall unable to stand for laughing. Afterwards he sent us a drawing he had made of the gardener. We stood around and talked a bit, then noises from the corridor foretold the QM. What was irresistible was that she seemed the most at ease and also the freshest guest in the world, as though she had just come in from a marvellous outing to meet old friends whom it was bliss to see. When partridges (perfectly roasted) were served, Philippe took one out of the dish by its claws and plumped it down in her plate. She giggled like a young girl. She talked to Cecil a lot of the time – as to an old friend who she was refreshed by seeing and about whose welfare she was greatly concerned. I was mostly occupied with either talking to Lady Fermoy on my left or Miriam Rothschild (right).

At one point I asked the QM whether she remembered the concerts at the National Gallery during the war. She remembered them as absolutely wonderful – reminisced how a bomb had gone off nearby in the middle of a Beethoven sonata played by Myra Hess. She said what a wonderful time the war had been – at least, in some ways – perhaps the happiest of our lives. 'Everyone was so ... so ... so, I don't know what ... so friendly with everyone else. The whole country was like one family.' Later, I said that when I was given the Gold Medal for Poetry by the Queen she asked whether people wrote letters these days, and remembered that when she was on one of her tours she always wrote every day a kind of journal-letter for her mother. 'Oh yes, she does,' she said, 'and then I give it back to her after she comes home.' She said Prince Charles was a great letter writer.

Miriam Rothschild, who is writing a memoir of her family, produced a photograph of a group of sportsmen standing in front of the house at Tring, and asked her whether she could identify them. 'Well, I'll have to find my specs,' she said, and fished them out of her bag, put them on, roared with laughter at the posed group of sportsmen taken in 1903 and said she couldn't identify the ones Miriam R. wanted to know about. 'But I tell you what, I'll take them to Aunt Alice, Princess Alice. She's 95, she may well recognize some of the faces. She'll be very pleased anyway to see them.'

There was a little talk about the theatre and what was going on. She was very glad to hear that there was a success – *Amadeus* – by Peter Shaffer at the National.

24 November

At the Writers and Scholars luncheon, Lord Longford came up to me and shouted the word 'Marx' at me. I somehow guessed that this referred to Anthony Blunt. What he wanted me to do, he explained, was write a book about the position of the Marxist today. I said I could not do this. Afterwards I thought though that I might edit a

book of essays by diverse hands, a kind of *The God that Failed* of the
1980s.* This might take the post-dated moral bankruptcy of the thirties as its starting point. Anthony Blunt in his statement said that he
had been loyal to his 'political conscience' instead of his country. This
did not seem to me quite to state the choice – which was not for a
vague abstraction (political conscience) over *patria*, but for the horizontal world of the whole of humanity viewed as one in the classless
substratum of the oppressed and the proletariat – the International –
as against the vertical segmented *patria* of England. The question this
gives rise to is whether there is any international concept of humanity
(the world) today which is represented by any political party or creed.
I think of Bill Mazzocco's remark to me in New York a few days ago
that nowhere in the world today is there any political cause to believe
in. For the unifying political cause would be that of all humanity
confronted by world problems of population, resources, relations between rich and poor countries, questions of race, etc. (Various movements even in their fragmentation somehow nevertheless yearn towards
a wider unity – Women's Lib, Gay Lib, etc. – it is forgotten that the
1930s, among other things, was a sexual revolution.)

Drove to Oxford, had lunch with the Berlins. Talked about Virginia
Woolf's letters. In her remarks about Isaiah she calls him 'a violent Jew'.
Isaiah said that her letters increased one's sense of her cleverness but left
one feeling that she was not as nice as one had thought previously. I said
that I thought that after all it was an honour to be mentioned by her at
all. 'That's what we have to say to ourselves, that's the line we have to
take,' said Isaiah.

28 November

Went last night to *Norma* with the Berlins. Beautiful, noble music in
which situation after situation of the plot based on human passion, love,
betrayal, sacrifice, freedom, memories of Druid religion and Roman
Empire give rise to architectonic forms, temples of music surging from
voices and orchestra, so melodious with its wind instruments, so struc-
tured and dynamic with its strings. It was Wystan's favourite music –
Bellini.

At the Royal Free Hospital where I go every morning for radio

---

* *The God that Failed* (1948) was edited by R. H. S. Crossman and contained essays
on their experience of communism in the thirties by Arthur Koestler, Ignazio Silone,
Louis Fischer, Richard Wright, André Gide and myself.

therapy, the past few mornings I've found myself sitting next to Bill Coldstream, who accompanies his 86-year-old sister. He is 74, I suppose. He said to me today, 'I never feel old. I think every day that perhaps tomorrow I will stop being young and get down to work that is serious.'

8 December

A week has passed since I wrote the above. Since then I have been four days in King Edward's Hospital, in a private room with what seemed a dozen nurses, sisters, matron, house doctor, all covered by BUPA. On Monday soon after I arrived I was taken down to an X-ray theatre and had X-rays taken of my kidneys, etc. The doctor making the plates informed me that I had eaten pheasant the previous day and showed the four black pellets sputtered through my intestines as though I were a shot pheasant myself.

I thought about the reception given on 29 November at the Athenaeum Club by Sir John Partridge to celebrate the publication of my Uncle George's book *Private Work and Public Causes*. Partridge made a speech in which he pointed to the main peaks of the mountain range of my Uncle's achievements, allotting them their names in continents – India – Africa – where they uprose. He was followed by Bishop Fleming (the Fleming family seem to have one of everything – a general, a bishop, an explorer, a merchant banker, a crime-story writer). Then my cousin John got up and said how delighted my uncle (who knew nothing of this celebration) would be to hear about it, and to receive all the heart-warming tributes. The strange thing is that none of his cronies ever succeeded in making my uncle sound quite human. The world of the Schusters and Spenders of that generation is the World of High Stuffiness.

The whole hospital situation makes me think of the strangeness of life. Hospital, though a miracle of organized routines, never seems ordinary. It also has the effect of making me think a lot about the past. Of childhood illnesses. When a nurse comes up to my sickbed I instinctively expect a maternal glance to which I respond with a child's smile.

I've written no poetry for a month. I am bored writing about Auden.

I found in the 'bottomless pit' where all our stuff is buried rather than stored, three typed volumes of a novel I wrote in – I surmise – 1931 (funny how one didn't date things in those days) called *The*

Temple. With my hopeless inability to read things I've put aside, I hadn't read this for over thirty years and was astonished how evocative and alive it is. An absurdity is that I've made the main character – myself – a girl. This was doubtless out of fear of censorship.

The book I did read in hospital was V. S. Pritchett's *Life of Balzac*. What an overdriven lunatic, the most obsessed of characters in his own novels, wrote those novels. I often think that creative art is, for the artist, experience of life almost unattainable by other men. But with Balzac his existence seems to have disappeared into the world he created.

10 December

Nothing gives me more a sense of chaos than tidying up masses of things. Before I undertake it, I feel helpless and hopeless – impossible to start. But when I do it I become obsessive, a hunter for treasure. Find hundreds of letters I'd forgotten about, manuscripts of poems abandoned, which after the Horatian nine years – no, thirty years! – suddenly seem workable.

20 December

Dined last night with Mervyn Stockwood, Bishop of Southwark, at his annual Christmas dinner. This was the last such dinner before his retirement. Guests included the Archbishop of Canterbury, with whom I had some pleasant talk. He said that they were going to live at Sissinghurst. I said I knew Nigel Nicolson. 'Oh yes,' he said, 'the author of that strange book about his parents' marriage. What a business.' I said, 'Nigel and his brother Ben thought it was the ideal marriage.' He said, quite twinkling, 'You mean his father having his boyfriends and the mother having her girlfriends?' 'Yes,' I said. He laughed, really amused. I told him my idea about thinking of tunes and having friends as a formula for happiness. He said, 'How strange you saying that, I was thinking something of the sort this very day.' 'I suppose you'd put religion where I put music,' I said.

'Well, yes, but I was thinking how much of one's happiness one owes to friends, and of course to one's wife,' he said, glancing benignly at Lady Coggan.

21 December / *San Sano*

Rush to answer letters, tidy house, buy presents.

After lunch to Luton, plane to Pisa. Matthew met us at Pisa.

We got to San Sano about eleven where Maro gave us an excellent dinner. Saturday, a gale and very cold. I read Elizabeth Bowen's *The Death of the Heart*. She is brilliant in the part that describes her 16-year-old heroine Portia's visit to a seaside resort, staying with her sister-in-law Anna's governess. All the members of this family and their 'gang' are flashingly described and the portrait of the young man Eddy, who makes love to Portia, must be based on Goronwy Rees who had a love affair with Elizabeth and then left her. Portia's sister-in-law, Anna, is probably ironic self-portraiture. Anna's husband Thomas seems based on Elizabeth's equally opaque husband Alan, and St Quentin has the style of William Plomer. The novel alternates between brilliant satiric observation and heavy seriousness. There is a muffled quality about her descriptions and generalizings which brings back vividly to mind a day a year or so before her death, when I drove her from Oxford where she had been staying with the Berlins. It was one of those days in which sun struggles with mist, gilding and whitening the landscape and making it difficult to see. The whole hour and a half of the journey, Elizabeth talked, a long flow of anecdotes and comment, which, owing to the weakness of her smoker's throat, was, for the most part, just below the threshold of my hearing. I had a sense of unreality, as though the car I was driving was a crayon or chalk marking a line across a landscape of paper.

She could say unforgettable things and remarks occur in her novels which sometimes strike a bull's-eye. She described Jean, the first Mrs Cyril Connolly, as a 'great soft crook'. She said of Alan her husband, that in talking with him there were 'mined areas'.

26 December

The children very excited. Before lunch we took a walk across the valley up the bosky hillside to Teddy Millington-Drake's* house. I found the climb surprisingly hard work – I was leaden and breathless. The wintry woods very beautiful here. Such brilliant emerald moss, such threaded vermilion berries, such brocade of red and olive oak

* Teddy Millington-Drake, painter, who lives partly in Tuscany and partly in Patmos.

leaves never fallen from their boughs. On the hilltop Teddy has made a discreet villa of his farmhouse, with swimming pool, which looks like a sheet of looking-glass, reflecting tangled boughs of trees, lawns of rough grass, hedges, a thyme garden, low walls, sloping gardens of irises and other plants. It is very beautiful, quietly displaying art to the sky.

When we got back to San Sano we decided to have a light lunch and postpone Christmas dinner until the evening. Stilton cheese and – our undoing – a sumptuous hot sausage made of giblets, liver, etc., of the turkey. The children were, in a quiet old-fashioned sense, very good.

I read Hugh Trevor-Roper's selection from Macaulay's *History of England*, published now as a Penguin book. The Introduction, which is more interesting than Macaulay, tells us how grotesquely, perversely and implacably unfair Macaulay was about William Pain, John Churchill and other imagined villains in his starkly caricaturist narrative, a procession of events rather like a Victorian version of the Bayeux tapestry. Macaulay, I suppose, is very readable, but I find the style repellent. It is the generalizing style of Gibbon, in which all the historical material is put through a machine which produces the triumphantly balanced lapidary sentence, but it altogether lacks Gibbon's refined worldly subtle wit.

We drove to lunch with Bill Weaver at his house near Arezzo. He showed us the new house which he's built, into which he's going to move. To get there we went through what I always think of as the 'real' Tuscan landscape with its curving hills, fields that look flat, rather shiny as though they had been planed and polished, interrupted by the exclamation marks of cypresses, black and occasionally very tall, sometimes in isolation, sometimes clustered in groups around farmhouses which consist of separate buildings for living and storing, barns. The landscape today a deep brown colour, almost golden, but greenish where there are olive trees. And scattered across this terrain of almost semi-circular hillsides, towers, with their peaked circumflex rooftops above belfries through which the country behind them gleams.

To me the earth of this landscape is a monochrome ground, reflecting light: light showing through it, light gathering in faint patches of mist, forming a background into which the objects – towers, trees, etc. – are painted with the thinnest, most meticulous of brushes, hair by hair as it were.

I dreamed about Goronwy Rees. Can remember nothing about it except that he seemed rather reproachful. (Freddie Ayer had told me that Goronwy had felt aggrieved by me. I also had a grievance against him.) I woke with that strange feeling that the dead want one to think about them.

29 December / *Mouton*

Our week with Matthew and Maro was beautiful, touching. The weather was bad throughout, their house in winter dark, cavernous; a house that makes a very strong impression on one's memory. Seen from outside it lies in the landscape like some large spread-winged bird, with its central tower the chest, neck and blunted head. People going to the country to live quiet lives in which they can pursue their vocations, develop routines (especially if they have families) that seem just as absorbing and distracting as in town.

31 December / *Mouton*

I did not sleep much and woke at intervals which were abysses. I tried to read *The Third World War*, a book which Sidgwick and Jackson sent me. The third world war is something I find I cannot read about, does not interest me; it is simply the most noisome possible development of everything horrible. Some introductory statistics given seem even more horrifying than the war. That in 1977 there were 4 billion people in the world of whom two-thirds lived in countries with a median income below $300 a head, while one-third lived in countries with median incomes above $3,000 a head. These figures are like fire.

I was brought up to have primitive Christian ideas, which I got from the New Testament and Nonconformist religion long before I had political views. Therefore I've always been conscious of the pressure of those who are starved of the means of realizing their talents – and have always felt that the deprivation and suffering, the inferno of terrible underlying realities, hollows the civilization, makes it a mockery, a wonderful empty show.

Of course I've never done anything much to deal with this realization. Yet I remain haunted by childish fantasies connected with it. And so here I am at Mouton after a dinner of delicious wines and foods thinking these thoughts, and finding myself unable to sleep, turning from *The Third World War* to read prose as delectable as the food and wine – the essays of Max Beerbohm.

This morning Natasha and I went for a walk with Guy du Mur*
along the coast, with its miles of wide deserted beach flanked by dunes.
But much of the sand is blackened by oil slicks.

After luncheon, we joined several of the household in visiting Pauline's
grave in the cemetery at Pauillac. This is a depressing place like an
enclosed asphalt playground stuffed with graves, with their cement
headstones. However, they are well cared for. Caring for their dead, Guy
told me, is a great preoccupation of people here. The Mouton staff men
and women had covered Pauline's grave with flowers. Philippe delivered
some kind of an address to the staff whom he called 'mes enfants'. He
told them that this was only the temporary resting place of Pauline. Her
remains would be removed to a site at Mouton – where exactly was still
undecided.

N. and I drove back, together with Joan Littlewood. Philippe stopped
the car at a headstone inscribed 'Mouton', got out of the car and told us
he was going to cut down a tree and put a statue here, so that people
would be struck forcibly by this being the boundary of Mouton. Natasha
protested, 'But it is a beautiful tree. You will ruin the approach if you
cut it down.' Joan supported her. I walked away. Philippe roared, 'You
always object to what I want to do.' Things quieted down and he drove
on to a part of the estate, near a pond, which he thought would be the
best site for Pauline's grave. We all agreed.

The American sculptor Richard Lippold is here. We were in the
courtyard, looking up at the steep roof of red tiles. Above the roof was
the cloud-dense sky. I said, 'It seems strange how there is a redness in
the clouds which seems an upside-down reflection of the roof.' He said,
'Most of my writer friends don't notice anything.' I said that when I was
young I had always wanted to be a painter but I could not go to art
school as my father thought it immoral to draw nudes. He laughed. Later
he said perhaps I wrote poetry because in some way I was carrying on a
dialogue with my father.

* French critic and journalist for the *Nouvel Observateur*.

Commentary
1980–1

On 14 January 1980, I had a rather sensational accident. Running out to buy some food for an unexpected guest, I fell off the slippery pavement (it was a rainy evening) outside Finchley Road station and broke the ligaments of both knees. I was in hospital for nearly three months, but managed, immediately on leaving, and looked after by Natasha, to keep a month's teaching engagement at the University of Kentucky, at Louisville, Kentucky. As this happened to be the Year of the Disabled, the university was full of equipment recently installed to deal with a case such as mine.

As I note in my journal, 1980 was a year of much worse disasters among our friends than my accident: the deaths of Renée Hampshire, Michael Astor and Ann Fleming.

In 1981 David Hockney and I went together for three weeks to China, and did a book, China Diary *(published in 1983) with paintings and photographs by him as illustrations, text by me.*

11

Journal
1980–2

1980

1 January / Mouton

The New Year's Eve party a shadow of what it used to be twenty
years ago (to think that we first came here in 1956) when Pauline was
living. It was preceded by TV news of that gloomy, doomsday kind
which has been the background music to the little society to which I
belong throughout my adult life. I found it difficult to shake off hideous thoughts about the game of musical chairs we live through. The
Ayatollah in Iran, Russian tanks in Afghanistan, President Carter, a
pale, grinning, innocuous boy who has not been invited to some party
of bloods and bullies.

   Very good wines, the third of which was a Mouton of 1879. Dinner
conversation pleasant, but rather brutally crossed by a violent altercation between Guy and Philippe about the causes of anti-Semitism.
Philippe was shouting, Guy was white and hissing. 'I tell you,' shouted
P, 'there was not the slightest trace of Christianity in the anti-Semitism of Hitler.' Guy had evidently been saying that the basis of anti-
Semitism was Christianity and that this was a constant in all anti-
Semitism. Philippe was insisting that anti-Semitism was racist, of the
same nature as hatred of Blacks by Whites, Whites by Blacks. To
provide a kind of buffer argument, I said that the cause of anti-Semitism was not that the Jews were seriously considered the crucifiers of
Christ (at any rate not since the fourteenth century) but that they were
an alien community bound together by race and religion within another
community which resented its failure to assimilate them. 'All the same
they are hated for not being Christian,' said Guy, 'as the enemies of
the Christian religion.' 'If you say that,' I said, 'I will tell you who
Auden said were the murderers of Christ.' 'Who then?' asked Guy.
'The French.' 'Why?' 'Because the person who delivered Christ to his

executioners was Pontius Pilate, the Roman Governor and the French are inheritors of the spirit of Roman thought.'

The preposterous Audenism killed the conversation.

4 January

Did very little except read Michael Holroyd's *Lytton Strachey*. Immensely long, not very well organized, sometimes merely informative. Yet after reading these 1,100 or so pages one does feel that one knows Lytton very well.

A great deal, of course, about male homosexuality. One thing that comes out very well in this biography is that for homosexuals of that period and belonging to that class, going to Cambridge or Oxford and connected with Bloomsbury, the bespectacled intellectual homosexual was put at a life-long disadvantage in his love life to the insouciant good-looker who was not an intellectual. A Lytton Strachey or a Maynard Keynes was always conscious of his physical inferiority. In the love game, he attempted to play off his mental qualities against the athletic ones of the beloved object. But the athlete or the great beauty (and sometimes – as with Rupert Brooke – dazzling looks could be accompanied by outstanding intelligence) retained the advantage over a lover who represented a Mind. Also, with that mind, the intellectual homosexual, despising his own body, fell easily into the role of victim. That any beautiful young man could make physical love to the physically unappetizing Lytton was a stupefaction to Lytton himself. Actually it did happen, of course, that men – even a heterosexual like Ralph Partridge – and certainly queers like Roger Senhouse, gave themselves to him. They did not and could not do so absolutely and unreservedly, but their doing so at all meant that for Lytton they had opened a door into a paradisal garden of intellectual and physical mutuality. When they became scared of the intensity of feeling that they had aroused in him and when they tried to set up boundaries round the relationship, an abyss opened up before him which was a life sentence to solitary confinement in his own body. He did acquire some skill in handling these relationships, and in getting pleasure out of love which was more companionship than bed, he learned to extract happiness within his circumstances of limited love, but he never found, in a man, the total love which, ironically, was offered him by Carrington, in his relationship with whom he played a role very similar to that of Senhouse to him. It is a very interesting story.

As a writer, Lytton did not have the health and energy necessary to make revolutionary interpretations of history based on research of source material. He was old-fashioned in being almost exclusively interested in the leading personalities of the historic past.

Lytton was a great reader. Holroyd tends to describe this as idleness, an attitude which Lytton himself shared. But reading is not idleness – any more than listening to music or looking at pictures – it is the passive, receptive side of civilization without which the active and creative would be meaningless. It is the immortal spirit of the dead realized within the bodies of the living. It is sacramental.

6 January / *London*

It was raining, quite a lot of traffic, how it happened I can't recall but I think my heel must have slipped off the pavement. This was followed by a cracking-whip-like sensation and I fell to the ground.

I did not feel particularly alarmed but I was immediately surrounded by people who took me across the road to the shelter of Finchley Road station. When they tried to lift me by my arms and legs I suffered almost unendurable pain – whatever that phrase means. However, the moment they got me to the station and I could stretch my legs I felt quite at ease and in a calm state of mind. Two or three people lingered suggesting ways in which they could help. One called for an ambulance. While waiting for this, another man appeared who was a New Zealander. He sat down beside me on the floor and started asking where I lived. He told me about the pleasures of Christmas in New Zealand. Although I felt calm I also felt I had behaved with extraordinary stupidity. I arrived at the Royal Free Hospital and shortly after Natasha arrived. We were taken to the casualty ward and I was examined by a surgeon.

Walking, or being rolled along hospital corridors one feels that one is in a vast modernistic stage set arranged so that scenery and characters can be transformed frequently.

I had a flash of my whole life's achievement and it seemed to me to be a succession of botched beginnings, of tasks inadequately done, few real achievements. A dozen jewels perhaps in a refuse dump of failures.

I thought how I had been planning to write a selected version of my work, which would separate the worthwhile from the junk. Perhaps the significance of the accident was that although I have this intention,

I was not seriously carrying it out, I was still continuing to live the life of a journalist.

When blows of this sort come as it were from out of the night I always think of the figure of Auden. I hear him say, 'He has to have a definite signal which will really commit him to the path which he has still not properly set himself on.'

14 April / *Louisville*

Apart from these notes, which I taped, I did not keep this journal in hospital. Being there was a gap, I felt, time (eleven weeks) that had to be lived through. N. was wonderful at organizing visits from my friends and they were extremely good.

Francis Bacon visited me. Luckily no other visitor was there and I saw him alone. After a little conversation I mentioned that nothing I was going through – the discomfort of having both legs in plaster – compared with the real suffering of certain friends of mine – which they were enduring at this very moment. Renée Hampshire* in the last stages of cancer.

After a week or ten days in a public ward, I was moved into a room by myself. I have the memory of my visitors in the vertical, myself horizontal.

James Joll† and John Golding‡ came, radiating sympathy and friendliness. Stuart Hampshire, always rather elated, wonderful. I wrote to him two days ago (from Louisville) saying it occurred to me that his visits were partly a gift from Renée who, though dying, must have pressed him to come and see me. Isaiah Berlin – conversation of one who regarded my illness as quite incidental – just went on talking as he might have at Headington House or at his club. My brother Humphrey, agitated, anxious, protective, horrified that I, of all people, should be stricken. Rosamond Lehmann, concerned, with Sean Day Lewis's biography of Cecil – but very warm and affectionate. Peggy Ashcroft. Juliette Huxley (who lives across the road from the hospital) nearly every afternoon, bright, pretty. Clifford Curzon who, rather like Isaiah, carried on with the conversation of the outside world. Philip Spender – pale and tense – rather worried, I feel, about *Index*. Lizzie very often, bringing me prunes she'd stewed, chicken she'd boiled.

* Mrs Stuart Hampshire.
† Professor of International History, University of London 1967–81.
‡ Painter and art historian.

Once I couldn't talk to her for a few minutes because I suddenly started crying, thinking about Michael Astor – like Renée, dying of cancer. (They both died before I left hospital.)

Then Matthew came to London for a week. He visited me every day and stayed for hours, with great cheerfulness till it nearly broke my heart, and I said, 'I'm sure there must be people you want to see.' He said, 'No, I just want to be with you.'

Natasha came every single day and was wonderful, though desperately tired.

Mostly my thoughts were of a summing-up kind. I thought of my life – of my work. Everything I had done – or nearly everything – seemed a failure, not that of a person who does not use his talents, but worse, does not use them enough even to discover how much talent he has.

I blame myself for not having pressed ideas to the point of proof. So often I put aside the things I most deeply want to do – the things that came from inside myself – and did things which were proposed from the outside. Wrote a book of criticism which was suggested by a publisher – instead of writing the novel I had in my head, or the poetry. Was too easily discouraged by a remark repeated to me or in a review – turned back from a vein of work which I should have continued exploring. Distracted, lazy, pleasure-seeking, frivolous, ever ready to fall in with other people's wishes, desiring to please them, fearful of losing their good will. Years wasted, slipping by hour by hour, day by day in a routine of undertakings external to my own inner tasks – reviewing, editing, party-going, travelling, attending conferences, UNESCO, *Encounter*, teaching. Thriftlessness, extravagance, folly.

12 July / *London*

A gap of three months since I last wrote in this diary. Two days after leaving hospital – in mid-April – we flew to Louisville. I went in a wheelchair, which means you get very privileged treatment – being rushed through all the formalities at the airport, cushions, etc. The very long journey did not seem nearly so tiring as I anticipated.

I was in a wheelchair for my days at the university but this really did not matter. My classes consisted simply of students producing their poems. They also attached great importance to 'interviews' – tutorials – with me, each student separately.

We saw a good deal of the Barry Binghams – a family who seem largely responsible for all that is best in Louisville – the orchestra, the ballet, local radio and TV. They took us to Shakerstown – a compound, in green countryside, of large white frame or stone buildings. This strange sect repudiated sex, adopted orphans to bring them up according to their rigid rules. However, they also indulged in orgiastic dancing.

I'll skip London and France – that is May and June – and resume with the Saturday before we went to Salisbury.* Christopher [Isherwood] and Don [Bachardy] came to dinner with Lizzie. They first of all came to Loudoun Road and we had champagne. They were both in extremely good form – Christopher seeming scarcely altered from when I first knew him – if anything sharper, clearer, more completely in command of everything. Don, being now clean-shaven, looked years younger. Their attachment to each other is wonderful. On Christopher's side it is a vast inclusiveness of Don in everything. On Don's side it is an absorption, into his own, quite undependent personality, of Christopher's way of speaking, his phrasing. I felt strangely touched by the way in which, when C. talks, Don's eyes are never off him.

C. got drunk. This makes him even more emphatic, noisy, uproarious, with a great many exclamations – 'Oh Yes!' 'Gee!' 'Oh yeah!' He has acquired an American accent – like chips with everything he says. Occasionally he speaks of Americans as 'us'. ('We're real proud of our senators,' he said about the Senate Committee enquiring into Watergate.) At the end of the evening, he uttered a cry and, flapping back his arms like flippers, advanced them and gave each one of us an all-inclusive embrace, followed by a resounding kiss on the cheek.

I had given him a proof of my essay on his *My Guru and His Disciple* which I had written for the *New York Review*. I had taken great pains with this review – but it had turned into a general essay on Isherwood with an interesting thesis – I think – but too developed for a review of this particular book – not sufficiently developed for a general essay. When I read the proof I was disappointed, realizing that it was the kind of piece one should put aside for three months and then rewrite. So I gave it to Christopher with trepidation. Next morning I rang him at his hotel. He was polite about the review, but as though he was searching for reasons not to be annoyed about it.

* On Sunday 6 July, for the BBC, to film an Introduction to *The Winter's Tale*.

The review was defensive about Isherwood and his religion as though his religious views were extremely vulnerable (which *qua* religion, I think they are) and I had to point out that what the reader must look for in this book were the portraits of the Guru and of Christopher himself. I thought that Christopher's tone of voice conveyed that I had in some way betrayed him. He had once told me (*re* a less than enthusiastic review of his last book) that one should give only rave reviews to one's friends. I found myself carrying on a dialogue with him in which I said, 'After all, no one has used his friends more extensively for copy than you, and you have often been critical of them. Myself, I am only interested in the opinions of my friends about my work; and I do not expect them to be uncritical. Besides the only books I ever want to write about are those by my friends' - etc. I relived this imaginary dialogue for several days. Then, just before we left for America, Christopher and Don both rang from Santa Monica. They were completely friendly. I felt immense relief and happiness.

We flew to America on 15 July for the Santa Fe D. H. Lawrence festival. Margaret Drabble was with us. We liked her very much.

Al Alvarez, with wife and two children, very well organized and with their own car, were at the hotel. The following day Al and I gave a joint reading at Albuquerque.

On the third day we drove to Taos, then to Lawrence's ranch, now taken over by the University of New Mexico, where there was to be a ceremony at the shrine which contains Lawrence's ashes; near it is a slab under which Frieda is buried. The ranch had changed so much since I was there in 1948 that it was scarcely recognizable. It is now built up to be a tourist centre, a showpiece, and the trees are so grown that they shut out most of the view of the landscape below the sacred mountain. We were almost the first to arrive, apart from some girls dressed entirely in white, who were practising a ballet of sylphs dancing outside the shrine. The white-attired sylphs, swaying, ran up to the shrine and then bent over, bending their right knees and raising and pointing their left legs, so that I could see right up the skirts of the one nearest me. They kept on practising this, to the accompaniment of drum taps, until it began to grow dark. We learned that the bus bringing the celebrants from Santa Fe had broken down. Finally they arrived. With them were two movie stars, Anne Baxter and ——, direct from Hollywood, come to give readings of Lawrence's poetry and prose. Anne Baxter looked incredibly crushable and artificial. The rain came pelting down. I thought how Frieda would have roared with laughter at all this (but she would have been pleased) and of the malicious pleasure Brett would have taken in it.

Next day we drove to Albuquerque Airport, from which we flew to Orono,* Maine, via Boston. I had partly prepared myself for a lecture on Pound, and had been reading books by him and about him in all my spare hours recently. But in fact what I was expected to do was talk each morning for forty minutes or so, about Eliot, Yeats, Auden and (on the last morning) myself, to a group of students. In the afternoon I had to comment on students' work. It was all quite easy. One of the students was a nun, who after a poem had been read, would make comments such as, 'I like that poem, it has so many w's in it.' At one of my morning talks she asked the question, 'Is the name of Shelley a cryptogram?'

2 and 3 August / *New York*

For the weekend we stayed with the Buttingers, Muriel and Joe.

On Sunday N. went for a drive with Joe and I was left alone with Muriel. She wanted to ask me questions about my life, work, etc., which I tried to answer. Then she said, 'I want to ask you the question which now I ask all my old friends. What do you think of life?' I answered that I thought that the people I knew were divided into those who wanted the satisfactions of fame, wealth, love or recognition, and those who simply enjoyed things that were given – beauty, for instance. That the latter had an immense advantage – unless they were very poor, ill or in some other way deprived. They simply enjoyed life with their senses. Thus, although I felt that I had failed in some important respects – I still loved life and could say I was happy. And, in a negative way, I counted my blessings and considered myself far luckier than most of the world's population. She said that on the whole she felt the same.

8 August / *London*

More notes about America. When we were with Susan (Sontag), I mentioned the name of a friend who had done many good works (Muriel). Susan said, 'Oh, I remember meeting her once. It struck me

* The University of Maine.

that she was extremely boring, and made me wonder why it is that people who do good are so boring.'

I wonder about the concept of who are boring and who are not boring. People who easily dismiss others as boring are usually judging by the standards of some small self-admiring group of friends who speak a special language of personalities and gossip. That is what members of Bloomsbury did so well, being mutually self-congratulatory. Nevertheless, it has its disadvantages – almost every member of such a group anxiously asks himself, 'Am I boring the others?' and this imposes on him a kind of inhibition. Insiders can be pushed out because life involves them in complications – work, family – which makes them bores.

The most boring thing about Virginia's *Diaries* is that she finds nearly everyone outside Bloomsbury boring. That almost defines the limitations of her fiction. Chekhov never found anyone boring.

Auden made the distinction between being boring and being a bore (a distinction I found boring). God was not boring but a bore. Beethoven's quartets a bore, but not boring (or perhaps it was the other way round). In Proust, Mme Verdurin's circle came to regard Dr Cottard as a bore – but when we discover that he is the most distinguished diagnostician of his time we realize that he is not boring. According to this classification the friend whom we were discussing – Muriel – is a bore (to Susan Sontag) but not boring.

18 August

Ian Hamilton, hatchet-faced, lively and amusing, came to interview me for the biography he is writing about Robert Lowell. I could remember best what was least useful to him – RL's appearance – far better than anything he did or said. His way of holding his head down and forward and looking up at you with penetrating eyes under the dome of a magnificent forehead, balding and with locks of somewhat greasy-looking white hair falling to his shoulders, claimed all your attention. His smile pressed his benevolence down on you. The movement of his hands was like that of some conductor who moulds a phrase of music in the air. His misfortune was that somehow he seemed to be bringing pressure on you to sympathize with (or agree with? or approve of?) him. He gave a sense of claustrophobia like that produced by a schoolmaster who wants to force knowledge upon you. Once when I was at Brandeis University during the summer of the early fifties, he visited me, and tried to persuade me to come to Boston with him and stay the night. I was panic-stricken at the thought of having to sit up with him till the small hours while he read his poetry to me or made pronouncements.

On another occasion, in New York, I was in a taxi with Lowell and Grey Gowrie.* Suddenly Cal [Lowell] leaned over, and tapped the taxi driver on the shoulder. 'Driver,' he said, 'I thought you might like to know that sitting in your cab beside me is the only surviving direct descendant of the ancient kings of Ireland.'

24 August

We visited Peter Levi† and Deirdre (ex-Connolly) at their house near Oxford. Cyril's 10-year-old son, Matthew, was there and showed me his collection of fossils, perhaps so like the snails which his grandfather, Major Connolly, collected.

After this we went to see my Uncle George and Aunt Gwen. If anything, George seemed better than last time, now that he is 100. He said that Gwen, sitting opposite him day after day, has not communicated with him for two years, but that during the last fortnight some kind of change had occurred in her and she was now attempting to do so. He said that a secretary of Prince Charles had been to consult him about Atlantic College. 'He agreed with every word I said.' (N. said afterwards that the secret of longevity was egotism.)

25 August

In order to make true metaphors one has to have precise and accurate knowledge of the mechanism or organic processes of things - machinery, games, plants.

28 August / *Bruges*

We stayed the night at Bruges, arriving 9 p.m. approximately. Most of the streets were empty by ten. I had fantasies of the *vie de provence*. All the men either at home before midnight or else at brothels. Secretive and repressed lives of girls and boys who have thoughts and

---

*Lord (Grey) Gowrie. Poet, former Lecturer on English and American Literature, University College, London. Later he entered politics as a Conservative. Minister for the Arts 1983-5.

†Peter Levi, former Jesuit, poet and classical scholar, married the widow of Cyril Connolly. Professor of Poetry at Oxford.

interests which reach to the capital. All this is nonsense, probably. When we went round Bruges the next day it seemed bustling, full of people, many tourists. We went to the Memling museum: Memling, that wonderful painter of figures with skin through which the bone is sculpture, draperies like carved ivory, necklaces and jewels painted with hair-spring precision. Figures as delicate as flies' wings, seen against backgrounds of hills, plains, cities like enamel.

We went to the great church near the Memling museum. It combines that shining pale austerity of columns and roof of churches in Belgium and Holland – the lowlands – with interrupting accents of gold or black, of altar, pulpit, figures of saints.

All the time we were there, I couldn't get it out of my head that a part of Bruges was destroyed in the First War, and that the streets with their steep-roofed houses and narrow perpendicular slits of windows, were – all except the hotel – a scrupulous reconstruction.

We went to Brussels. I went to the Musée des Beaux Arts. More Memlings and other miraculous Flemish paintings. Also a Tintoretto of *The Transportation of the Body of St Mark*, like the one in the Academia in Venice but smaller. The Brueghel of *The Fall of Icarus* about which Auden wrote his famous poem, 'Musée des Beaux Arts'. It works wonderfully as a poem but misinterprets the picture in which the figure of Icarus is only an accent in a visionary Turneresque land-and-seascape: a field in the foreground where a ploughman is ploughing furrows in long parallel S-shaped lines; ship on the sea below; beyond, headlands, the sun rising (or setting). Wystan created a new work of art from his immediate impression of another work of art.

How many of these early Flemish paintings are about sadistic events. Bodies of saints lie on the ground beneath the straight shadow of the sword which has just decapitated them. The severed neck shows in a circle like a section of an asparagus stalk or a sapling. The taut buttocks of a virile, bristle-bearded young man, tense and springy with gloating malevolence, override the palely recumbent figure of Christ, in a *Flagellation*. Flemish painters – even the gentle-seeming Memling – seem to delight in the tools and machinery of crucifixion – the hammer and nails, the ropes that haul up the Cross.

I go on thinking about the structure of metaphors in poetry which enclose within them the logic of the structure of nature or machinery. Painting much more directly models itself upon the real structure –

anatomy, horticulture, machines. But ignorance of how things work – how processes proceed – is a fundamental weakness in a poet. The metaphysical poets turned such imitation into dogma and caricature, but they fascinate because they had got hold of one of the basic truths about poetry – much truer than the imagist idea – that what is called the 'logic' of poetry is imitation of a structure of things which in the poem perhaps becomes invisible, yet is present, and felt.

2 September / *St Jérôme*

A new notebook. The accident which put us in dirty rooms for two nights at Fontoy* had the effect of projecting another self, a spectator, standing above me who asked, 'Where shall we be tomorrow?' For mishaps have a way of making one see oneself as a character in a drama written by someone or something outside oneself (perhaps the origin of fiction is mishap).

A voice told me that tomorrow we'd probably be in St Jérôme, though another voice said we'd be still here at Fontoy for the rest of our lives. Fate having landed us here it seemed such an effort to get out ... I began to wonder whether this room would not seem tolerable after a time. Dirty, with one much peed-in wash basin, torn sheets, a view from the window of a yard full of cans and building material – fifty years ago I would not have thought anything of this. I remembered the room I occupied in Hamburg in 1929 – just such an interior looking out on darkness, where I was happy. And whatever I felt about Albacete† – the hideous town that seemed to belong to some quite other Spain than the touristic one I had previously been to – the room with the bed and discoloured walls and the smell of vegetables being cooked in rancid olive oil, which provided its pervasive atmosphere – was what I least cared about. The car was patched together by the local *garagiste* in one day.

We got up early and drove all the way to Avignon where we had lunch. Then we proceeded to St Jérôme – where the electricity kept turning itself off. This not only meant candlelight but no water.

A lot of plants have died in the garden.

While in France I must rewrite and complete the Auden essay for Ed Mendelson, also write my lecture for New York University on the 23rd.

But what I want above all to do is complete 'Auden's Funeral'.

* A small town in Alsace.
† Headquarters of the International Brigade during the Spanish Civil War.

5 September

A strange nightmare. That I was made Pope. I sat in a large room, waiting to deliver my first sermon before about a million people. I had about two hours in which to prepare it. From numerous flunkeys, autograph hunters, etc., who kept on interrupting me while I tried to put my thoughts in order, I asked for paper on which I could write notes. They brought me only torn-up sheets of newspaper, impossible to write on. I scrawled a few notes, between lines of typography, and, in looking at them, my writing was illegible. I had a faint hope, belied though by past experience, that when it came to making my sermon, my illegible handwriting might stimulate me to inspired improvisation. My sermon was intended to bring the full weight of starvation, preparations for nuclear war, etc., into the consciousness of people so they would change the world. If I had armed myself with only a few telling examples and statistics I could do this, I was sure. But I knew my sermon would be a humiliating failure. Then I thought that after all it could be very short. Everyone would be grateful if I spoke, say, for five or ten minutes - delivered some brief tremendously moving exhortation. But I knew I could not do this. Now I started thinking of ways of getting out of being Pope. After all, I was married and in every way totally unqualified to be the Catholic God's representative on earth. I convinced myself that in fact it was inconceivable that I should be Pope, and proved, by pure argument, that this must be a dream. Then, having succeeded in this, I woke up.

COMMENTS: (1) Thinking that perhaps the accident we had last week was only a dream and I would wake up.

(2) The fact that I have not yet written a line of my lecture.

(3) The only recurrent dreams I have are of having to perform in public and being unprepared.

(4) Illegibility of notes, owing to my bad eyesight.

(5) The poem I am writing about Auden's funeral of which the ending is only a cloudy vision at present.

(6) The Pope - Polish - concern with great issues of Third World - my own feelings about Poland - material about Poland in Iris Murdoch's *Nuns and Soldiers* which I was reading till 2 a.m.

7 September

I finished reading Iris's *Nuns and Soldiers*. She is extremely gifted yet doesn't seem quite a novelist. She can do certain things very well – passages of dialogue between cliff-hanging characters; set pieces of adventure-story fiction. The atmosphere of the countryside here wonderfully evoked. At the same time, she exaggerates. There are centipedes and lizards on the walls in a Provençal house. Well, yes, occasionally one or two centipedes but never lizards. The mistral is made to sound and behave like a hurricane. Well, it often does. She treats her characters as pieces in a game, invented by herself, which she shifts about arbitrarily; thus removing from her fiction the inevitability of plot and behaviour of 'real' characters. But obviously she doesn't want them to be realistic. She can describe very well the surface behaviour of characters – particularly sleazy ones. Incredibly funny about the modish young – students, beatniks, etc. She goes in extensively for describing her effects – long passages in which she tells us not only of the history of her characters but how intensely they are feeling. Perhaps she is trying to put across a view of life – 'people do behave in this abstract way – the only pattern is that which is imposed, there is no real underlying pattern', etc. We are pieces played in a game.

Writing 'Auden's Funeral' gives me ideas for how I could complete other poems of which I have the sketches I wrote in hospital and of which I have drafts in notebooks, etc. I realize that I have so many notes that I could be working on poems every day. In a sense they are all one poem, one *oeuvre*. I have the feeling when writing one poem of chipping away at a corner of a big work.

10 September

Last night we went out to a restaurant called the Regalido, in Font-vieille, one of those places where they have *specialités*, select dishes with a main course served with excellent sauces.

At the end though, as nearly always with meals where there are specialities and sauces, I felt depressed. To put it precisely, I felt like Cyril Connolly *looked* once when I happened to meet him one day about 3 p.m. in Leicester Square. I asked him to luncheon the following day. He glowered at me and said, 'I can't bear to be invited to lunch when I've just had lunch' and walked off in the opposite direction, greatly offended.

Fearful of not sleeping, I read Edmund Wilson's *Thirties Journal*. It is journalism of a high quality – informative, intelligent, crammed with facts. Wilson was a man of great brain power. One felt his brain revving behind the great frontal box of his forehead. This machine ran very largely on alcohol – enormous quantities of it. At the Princeton Club he would order six Martinis at a time and drink them one after another. In his journals he reports on everything including himself, his wife, her body, his body, his sexual activities, people he meets, the workers at Ford's during the Depression, with great precision. It all remains very external, however, like an account of life in a factory.

I read through a volume of my journal after leafing through Wilson's. It gave me the sense of myself rushing (a brutal hurry).

I have worked through to the stage of despair about 'Auden's Funeral'. What I have written is articulate without being articulated. The stuff is there but not the movement, which is clogged and hampered. The point is to write it as though one was there – at the graveside – dropping the clod of earth on the coffin lid – thinking of Wystan in that box – his grinning – his thinking he had scored over us – his companions – got ahead in a game. While grinning at us – he is also sufficiently still of this world to be sharing the joke – like a child in a game of hide-and-seek. But he has stolen a march on us. We are left alone on a star (a planet) growing cold as we walk along the path to the village. There, sitting on benches outside the inn, we toast his ghost. Each of us becomes totemistic, a local habitation of A's spirit to enter at the last feast. Thus one becomes a ventriloquist's doll through whom the voice of Wystan speaks, recounting anecdotes. Then Chester puts Wagner – *Siegfried's Funeral March* – on the record player. That music is like a bier on which the corpse of Siegfried is borne. Underneath it we feel Auden's spirit carried out – the loss of one to us who made his life an instrument for expressing experiences in language, where each of us loses his loneliness, and becomes part of a spiritual community.

20 September

Have read the *Ides of March* by Thornton Wilder. I enjoy reading invented letters and documents by Julius Caesar, Clodia and Catullus, but got more and more bored by Thornton Wilder who is a soft old tabby cat, as I read on. But it did make me reread Catullus by which I'm overwhelmed. He is a whizz-kid of poetry – a whizz-kid with a very powerful mind and wonderful technical gifts. There is nothing quite so controlled and direct except certain of Shakespeare's sonnets ('The expense of spirit in a waste of shame'), some of Byron's most hectic letters, and parts of *Don Juan*. The rhetoric of a furious statement which sweeps everything subsidiary into its course and never loses direction.

I more and more think that beneath everything one writes, there is a model of thought, feeling and rhetoric, bones over which language is flesh. Unfortunately, one can very easily make flesh which is bulging, flabby, and unrelated to the bones.

23 September / *St Jérôme*

On Monday PD, his wife, a babysitter and baby and a dog all arrived. They are going to take over the house.

PD, who has worked for CBS in Canada, now has an astonishing and apparently very recent independence. He said that he'd written a novel which was just appearing in America. He had no ideas about writing or publishing novels, but did have some kind of idea about what made for popular reading. So he put ingredients of the eminently saleable into the book, and then sent it to an agent – now his agent. Rather to his surprise, the agent, instead of sending it to one publisher after another, had Xeroxes made and sent them all at the same time to ten publishers who then had the privilege of bidding against each other for it. The result is that PD comes to France, buys a wonderful car, two bicycles with ten gears each, and has a wonderful smile on his face. I reflected that I simply can't take pleasure in writing if I am doing so with the thought of money – that I can write the unpublishable with great facility and ease, whereas anything I write for a market I always have to write six or seven times. I don't mean that I want to be like PD, or him to be like me, but I would like such a lively and aware person to be writing with an eye on the truth, not on the market. Better then not view him as a writer at all – in any sense in which I understand the term – and be happy in the thoughts of his baby, who crawls over our tiled floors like a lizard, his car and his dog, and his very great amiability to us.

24 September / *Mouton*

I rang Lizzie who is going to New York tomorrow, and a week later to Los Angeles.

We went round the garden at Mouton with Philippe. Building the Mouton of the future has absolutely gone to his head. N's little contributions to planning the garden are just bulldozed by his great plans. Looking at a shrub, Natasha says, 'I'm glad the ceanothus we planted is doing so well.' 'Yes,' he says, 'all that will be done away. There will be a drive for charabancs.' 'Oh, those have done so much better than mine in Provence.' 'Yes, yes, all that will be filled in.' We walk into what remains of the village impinging on his estate. 'The mayor did not want us to pull down this house, but by private treaty with the owner I have arranged with him to build another one. We found that we already own these houses just beyond the one I have bought, so here we will make a public garden.'

As we walked back towards the original park of Mouton he said, 'This is going to be the driveway to the parking place with trees along it to provide shade, and on the further side of it there will be a great lake. And on the further side of the lake is the plot of land for Pauline's grave.' We walked through the projected lake to the other side of the park where there is a large nineteenth-century house. 'This will be partly torn down and then extended for a banqueting hall for up to 450 people,' P. said. 'That is what Mouton has always needed – a banqueting hall.' As we walked back, he added, 'All the vines, the vines will be extended everywhere.'

This is how old age should be – bursting all bounds, expanding into futurity.

Meanwhile Joan Littlewood had been making a terrific scene with P. and he had completely lost his temper with her.

Just before luncheon I met Joan on the stairs, as I came out of the house – she said she was going to disappear, hide. She never took lunch anyway. However, she did appear and immediately started laying into P. He didn't hear what she said – he is getting deaf – or pretended not to. She went on and on saying he knew nothing about architecture, ought to read a manual on architecture, had no aesthetic sense, etc., etc. We tried in vain to change the subject.

I felt furious with Joan who sometimes acts as though she were a character in the *Ring*. But this evening after my walk in the vineyards

I felt differently. She was with Raoul, the old man responsible for all the cellars and wine. He was describing to us how he'd got up early in the morning and seen – across the vineyards – the moon rising. 'Now that's the most beautiful thing in the world, La Nature.' 'Everything else is destruction, war, pollution, cruelty, terror,' he said. Joan listened to all this with the most wide-eyed appreciation. 'Monsieur le Baron n'apprécie pas la nature,' went on Raoul, 'he has never seen the moon rise. Now Madame la Baronne saw everything. She used to get up in the middle of the night and walk in the vineyards. She knew nature. C'était une femme extraordinaire. Le baron a eu de la chance en se mariant avec une telle femme.' I marvelled at the legend of Pauline, la Baronne, among the employees, but I can well believe that she had a very understanding relationship with them. She talked to each separately and with sympathy. But one hardly sees her as a nature-lover. A woman who lay awake all night reading books into which she inserted scraps of paper, sometimes with comments on them, who took two hours to dress and arrange herself in her unique style – with those pipe trousers, strange cloaks and hair in long plaits, like some elongated magical girl in a fairy story; who lunched at 4 p.m. and dined at 10 p.m., who wrote long letters to John Huston, and some Russian prince – and I don't know who else – which were full of novelistic romantic passion; who thought the Soviet Union was the ideal place to live, wrote a book saying so and almost did a deal with the Russians to let Philippe and her have a place there; agreed with Furtseva, the Russian Minister of Culture, that censorship was inevitable in a country which needed discipline; who, towards the end of her life, left Mouton and Paris and was happy living only in the Ritz Carlton Hotel in Boston – there is a potent mixture of the sympathetic and the frightening here, but little that seems 'natural'. But she made Mouton what it is – a place of original and faultless taste. Each room has its own consistent style, all the objects in it are displayed for what they are, and the vineyards on the great plain outside, like a green ocean in spring, summer and autumn – and like a brown bare infinitely stretched-out Dutch landscape in the winter, reflected through the large port-hole windows of the great salon.

I can never really work at Mouton, apart from writing this and a few letters. But I read a lot from Pauline's very random and ill-arranged library. I've been reading a life of Henry VIII. Reading history in old age can easily become a passion, something that one seizes on. It gives an odd sense of *déjà vu*; also, of discovering, at the end of a journey on some island upon which one has done servitude, the documents which explain everything about its past and why one has been put there. In the futility of history lies so much of the explanation – that the people whose lives were anonymous and the rare individuals whose thoughts and aims were universal and of no time – the artists, poets, philosophers – were always in the hands of the powerful. The aims of the men of power, scarcely changing from generation to generation, give reality to concepts which would otherwise be senseless – the Empire, England, France, Italy, Venice, the Papacy, etc.

Reading history, one has a glimpse into the tangled forces which have conditioned our own lives today, one understands why there are still entities called nations dominated by men who identify all the activities of their lives with the nation's 'interests', which are the materialist, aggressive, or defensive, all of them expressions not of love or beauty, but of brute force.

When I was young I couldn't read history because I had absolutely no grasp of the motivations of rulers. I saw the world as run by people older than myself, whose behaviour realized certain principles. Later I thought societies were divided into rich and poor, haves and have-nots. Let lovers of justice take from the rich and give to the poor, and rule the world, retaining both their power and at the same time remaining faithful to their love of justice, and the world would be a place of happy and enlightened equals. I did not see that the world is run by a special race of monsters – those who understand the reality of power, so that even when a social system is changed, it is the power-mongers of whatever side who take over.

27 September

Reading the above it occurs to me that the reason poetry, fiction and other forms of art are durable, whereas the preoccupations of the powerful date, is because power-mongers are concerned with externals, which change entirely as situations alter, whereas art is concerned with the feelings of individuals within an unchanging situation, the life experience.

Nevertheless the great man – the ruler – holds our interest when in him the machinery of office and the human person coincide, as they are bound, at some point in his consciousness, to do. We are interested in someone like Wolsey because although he is a person who has successfully transformed himself into an instrument of power, there is also, hidden inside the formidable chancellor, cardinal and papal legate, the child and youth and grown man who willed himself to become these things.

Read Somerset Maugham's *A Writer's Notebook*. An excellently commonplace mind writing in an excellently commonplace style. He writes notes for himself which are really only journalism, or with some philosophizing which one takes on trust (since he says that reading philosophy is one of his chief interests), and some criticism. The reflections on old age – written when he was 70 – are sympathetic. There is nothing to indicate that he is homosexual. I don't mean simply that he doesn't tell us, but that his style is so lacking in nuance that there is no hint of the androgynous, as there is in D. H. Lawrence – even in Ernest Hemingway. Taste but no sensibility.

30 September / *London*

Gordon MacDougall from the Oxford Playhouse came to see me about the version of the Oedipus plays (including *Antigone*) it is suggested I should do for them (I am mad – in both senses of the term – to do it). And I spent the last day at Mouton reading the Jebb version, which is very good. The girl who is going to provide me with a literal translation arrived – about an hour and a half late. I can't quite see what her function is, as I can work quite well on the Jebb translation. She is plump, rather pretty, and reminded me very much of some undergraduate of Inez's generation. 'Shall we go and have a bit of supper? Is there a restaurant near here?' asked GM. 'I haven't been very well. I don't want to eat anything.' 'Well, do you mind if Stephen and I eat something and you watch us?' 'There is quite a good Chinese restaurant down the road,' I said. 'I don't like Chinese food.' 'But I thought you weren't going to eat.' 'Well, after all, I might eat some cheese.' We went to a rather poor Chinese restaurant in the Finchley Road.

This evening I dined with Maud Russell.* Richard and Day Wollheim were there, also Nikos. Richard got talking about his war experiences. He was an officer in the British army at the time when the

---

* Mrs Gilbert Russell. Former owner of Mottisfont Abbey, Hampshire, which she gave to the National Trust.

occupying forces were not allowed to have any social contact with the Germans, especially with German girls. After a time, it occurred to the authorities that the soldiers were getting frustrated. So someone had the idea that there were girls at Belsen who did not come under the ban. So a group of emaciated girls were brought along to the English quarters and given a party. They were like terrified animals, huddled in a corner, not knowing what was going to happen. The soldiers tried to make friends. All the girls would do was point, with scratching fingers, at the only identification they had: the numbers tattooed on their wrists.

2 October

Together with Laurie Lee and P. J. Kavanagh, gave a poetry reading at St Paul's Church, Hammersmith Broadway. As usual, I cursed whatever weakness it is that makes me accept such invitations. I arrived too early and walked in the Hammersmith neighbourhood for a bit – past the end of Brook Green where Inez and I used to live. It has not changed much and brought back so many memories. The passage from past to present – like opening a door and going from one room into another. The threshold is forty-five years wide.

Laurie told the audience that one of his poems had been written between two bus stops and that the fare at the time had been a penny; today it would be 50p. Paddy displayed his book to the audience to show the shape of the poems on the page. He read a long sympathetic poem of childhood – reminiscences of the wartime comedian Ted Kavanagh – his father. When I stepped on to the stage, I suddenly felt reassured, and read to a responsive silence. Most poetry – when read in public – after all, is the poet's self-delusion projected, which he can – if he puts on a fair show – make the audience share. Since it is self-delusion it is very difficult for the poet to know its worth – all he can say is that the hallucination holds. True poetry is fact transformed. It's the truth which reaches beyond the lines to the human condition. Why one admires poets like Frost and Edward Thomas is because one sees so clearly their images have an inside, which relates to their interior darkness, and an outside, which turns towards nature and human beings.

3 October

Lunch in Soho with Nikos and Harry Fainlight, who is clinically mad.

With his lustrous curly black hair pressed to the sides of his skull and coming down almost to his shoulders, his thin white intense features – a good forehead, a nose that looks as if it has been carved into its distinguished distinctive hook, small bird-black eyes – he is someone whose searching glance is perpetually analytical.

I asked him where he found some lines he had quoted to me in a letter.

> Those who opposed the walls of our advancing sea
> Are crushed to pebbles. Their minds faded and failed
> O failed and faded like flowers before our enormous tide.

He looked – in his sidelong way – at Nikos and said, 'Now isn't that extraordinary? He doesn't know his own best lines.'

Then I remembered they came from *Trial of a Judge*. Harry said, 'Well, you see, that's what's happened. Minds are crushed before the advancing tide which is like an electric field sending out rays which burn up everything that intercepts its path.' He said that 'they' – the advancing forces – especially wished to destroy poets because poetry was a source of energy that resisted them.

I asked him where he lived now. He said he had a cottage in the depths of the Welsh countryside. Nikos said, 'You're so much better there, Harry, better than you've been for years.' 'Yes,' he said, 'but even there the forces follow me.' 'What forces?' 'The complete silence I need in which to work is incessantly invaded by aeroplanes directed by rays.' 'I understand what you mean,' said Nikos, 'but that happens everywhere. You must accept that it does. You mustn't allow yourself to think like that or you'll be completely unable to do anything.' 'Oh, I know I have paranoia,' said Harry, 'and I do try to correct it. I used to think that the noise was directed specially at me by people sitting at some centre with maps in front of them, but now I realize the forces are directed against all civilization. But nothing is done. No one protests. No one resists.'

I said I knew very well what he meant, because I had been reading Wordsworth's Preface to *Lyrical Ballads* that morning. Wordsworth wrote in 1800: 'A Multitude of causes, unknown to former times, are now acting with a combined force to blunt the discriminating powers of the mind, and, unfitting it for all voluntary exertion, to reduce it to a state of almost savage torpor.' Wordsworth felt as Harry does.

Harry is at the centre of things. Paranoia means that he thinks incessantly about the outward forces that are destroying inner peace. His 'madness' consists (a) of thinking that the disturbance of the world is all directed at one person – him, and (b) of taking what is really poetic metaphor as poetic truth. If poets are associated with madness it is because some poets have inhabited a world of their own metaphors, taking them quite literally. Perhaps, in ancient times, poets were holy madmen.

I found the conversation tiring, because I understood it so well. Harry was talking about the realities I know and run away from. There are inhibitions which make it very exhausting to pursue a line of thinking which is not only a verbal metaphor but which coincides with literal truth. For one thing – one thinks, 'If this is true, it is more important than anything else, then I should think of nothing else' – the way to a kind of secular religious mania.

I got up and said I had to catch a train to Oxford – and arrived at Paddington an hour and a half early and caught the 3 p.m. instead of the three fifty.

I changed at University where I have a room. The University College banquet was enormous but made pleasant by the company. Lord Perth discussed with me, our (David Hockney's and my) prospective visit to China. I sat next to a young physiologist who is doing a study of the brain. He wanted to know whether my memory was stimulated more by visual or by auditory impressions. For the dessert and port part of the meal I sat at another table next to Herbert Hart* and opposite Lord Goodman, the Master. A don talked about *Private Eye* and its editor, Richard Ingrams, who had been his pupil and whom he thought clever, a throwback to Belloc and Chesterton. The chief targets of *Private Eye* were homosexuals and Jews.

6 November / *Potsdam, New York*

Over a month has passed since my last entry. I was terribly busy clearing things up before going to Toronto on 17 October.

I'll begin with today and work backwards. I'm at a place called Potsdam, NY, the landscape is flat wintry grey – or rather white for it is snowing lightly – with few leaves left on the trees. The steadily falling snow makes me apprehensive that I shall wake tomorrow and find the landscape a foot deep in it and the little aeroplane not going

* Principal of Brasenose College, Oxford; former Professor of Jurisprudence, Oxford.

to Syracuse on the first step of my complicated journey to Tulsa, Oklahoma, where I'll meet David Plante. Still, I do lead a life of transformation scenes. Tomorrows so often transform my circumstances.

Yesterday at Plattenburg, Vermont. I was met at the airport by the most conscientious and serious of Jewish professors. The moment we got in the car, he started the kind of conversation which is tormenting. 'You cannot imagine', he began, 'what a tremendous moment in my life this is' and so on.

He was in fact immensely considerate; but he made me think all the time that I did not deserve all this consideration.

I got to like him more during the next twenty-four hours. Perhaps his goodwill and kindness won through, perhaps he became less pressing, having got to know me better. But our attitude towards each other was typically Jewish, I thought, and I remembered passages in Christopher's autobiographical books in which he describes me when we were young. How I irritated him with my attentions, my presents, my considerateness, which made him by contrast seem inconsiderate. Underneath I have felt with people I admire that my very presence with them is a demand on their time and I am always apologizing to them about this – knowing too that the apologizing is a worse, because more irritating, claim on their attention.

9 November / *Tulsa*

Characteristically, two days later, I can't – without greater effort than I want to make – remember anything about Plattenburg.

To go back to New York, Tuesday, 4 November, election day.

I went to 920 Fifth Avenue to visit Vera Stravinsky, who, I had been told, was in a bad way. Her nurse-companion took me into her large drawing room, lined with books, most of which seemed enormous, and full of large sofas and armchairs. An effect of untidy opulence. Vera was sitting in an armchair at a table on which there were, I think, some painting things. 'Here is Stephen,' said her nurse. Vera looked up at me, not recognizing me but seeming to realize I was a friend and not a stranger. Her face, beautiful, soft and round, with the enormous brilliant eyes and the sumptuous Titianesque hair, seemed to have shrunk. The skin, red and white, drawn back like a scarf over the bones, wrinkled, heavily painted. Still she smiled in her indulgent way. 'I don't know what this room is,' she said, looking round her. 'I am sure these are not my things. Anyway I don't want them. One ought not to have any things. One should give them all away.'

She wondered where we were. The nurse suggested New York. 'No, I don't think we are in New York,' she said, 'and it's not Paris either. I have been to so many places. I know so many languages. Let's see (as though she were playing a game) how many languages do I know? – English, French, German, Italian –' 'Russian,' I put in. 'No, I don't know Russian. No one anywhere knows any Russian any more. It is not spoken,' she said firmly.

At this point I stupidly allowed tears to trickle down my face. If she had noticed, which fortunately she didn't – this would have been fatal. For once having indulged myself in this way, I couldn't stop and was quietly crying for the rest of the meeting. There was plenty to cry about, if one thought about the wonderful festive life, like an endless succession of gifts, borne in on concert platforms, gondolas, good company, fame, wit, laughter, rage, passion, wine; of the life of Igor Stravinsky, Vera and Bob Craft. I remembered the first night of *The Rake's Progress* at the Fenice, and afterwards walking through the Piazza. People at café tables stood up and started clapping Stravinsky. I remembered visiting them in Hamburg or Paris or in their Hollywood house, a life lit by Igor's glinting humours.

The nurse brought in a large framed photograph of a ballerina of a pure boy-like beauty. 'Do you recognize this?' she asked. 'No,' said Vera. 'That is you,' she said. 'That's me?' cried Vera, quite in her old enraptured voice and with smiling eyes like those of a girl in a painting by Greuze. 'No, I do not believe that; it is too beautiful.' I said something to the effect that it was her and she was beautiful. She smiled, half flattered, half uncomprehending. I left soon after this.

Another reason for crying, I thought, as I walked down Fifth Avenue, was that the whole scene was operatic. Even things Vera said – her 'Where am I?' 'What is this place?' 'I speak these languages', above all, 'No one speaks Russian any longer' – were the kind of things a librettist might have written for music by Verdi or Puccini. The tableau of pathos is supremely that in which one sees the life before one frozen into the gestures in which it will be hurried away into the galleries of death. Stravinsky and Vera – while their American lover, worshipper, and amanuensis Bob Craft remains in the world, like Horatio at the end of *Hamlet*, to record the scene – wheeled off to join the other festive princes of the art of music – Liszt, Wagner, Mozart.

Journal / 1980-2

I was in Toronto 17 to 21 October. On 21st gave a reading together with a Portuguese poet, whose English was almost incomprehensible. On 22nd went to University of New York at Buffalo.

New York

On the 26th Stuart Hampshire and I dined, and next day, Sunday, went to the concert of late Beethoven sonatas given by Charles Rosen. Rosen plays with ice-cold precision, cutting up the phrases as though with a knife. At the same time in interpreting the music he communicates a kind of intellectual passion.

On Monday, 27 October, I went to a place called Oneonta, a branch of NYU. I was met by a pleasant young man who told me that this was one of the very rare days in the year (averaging 67) in which it is fine in Oneonta. It was clear and sunny and very beautiful. He took me to a hotel where I had a room overlooking a churchyard, with its stones and crosses going up the hillside and with trees that were now bare except for a few large transparent leaves – daubs of yellow. He said that Joseph Brodsky had stayed in this room when he gave a reading here and had adored the graveyard.

I gave my reading. Next morning, he called for me at the hotel, took me out to breakfast and then on to the airport. When we got to it, there was the tiny little plane, and a family of father, mother and son, and a big cloud which sat like a large cushion over the landing ground. We were told the plane could not take off unless there was visibility of at least a mile. The man was in a state of agitation because he had to make some public performance. He had no violin, but from his conversation with his wife it sounded as though he was a member of a quartet and if he could not appear that evening they had to find a substitute. After an hour he rang someone to say that he could not get to New York, and then settled down quite calmly. After three hours I became even more agitated because in NY I had (1) to go to the opening of Rodrigo Moynihan's exhibition, (2) to attend Rosamund Russell's lecture at the Met and (3) to join her, John Russell, and Jacqueline Onassis and her daughter Caroline Kennedy, to dine at a restaurant. I had not seen Jacqueline for twenty years or so (before JFK became President), the Russells had taken a great deal of trouble about arranging the dinner. There was no means of telling them I was delayed. I simply had to get there. I enquired about taxis and found that Oneonta had just one. So I said I would take it. After an hour, an octogenarian taxi driver appeared in his octogenarian taxi, and as the cloud had scarcely shifted I decided to wait no longer. The drive was indeed interesting, through the Catskills, wooded hills, brilliant colours, winding roads, old wooden houses, derelict-looking little towns, signs of the decay of upper state New York. After 100 miles or so, the driver said he wanted to eat a sandwich, and his car to drink some gas. We went to a diner. Then we started out again on the highway and made very good progress. After going 50 miles, we came to a pay booth and I felt for my wallet. It, together with my credit card, on which I was totally dependent, had gone. We hunted through the car but it was not there. Finally we drove 50 miles back to the diner. As soon as we walked in the owner said, 'How much money is there in this wallet?' waving it in our faces. I said, 'Twenty dollars.' He said that I'd had amazing luck. The wallet had been found in the road outside the diner by the only honest man in the district. He gave me the honest man's name and address so I could write and thank him (unfortunately I have lost this). I've also lost the wallet again – this time irretrievably – through the same hole in my pocket.

Everything now became nightmarish. The octogenarian made it clear that he did not want to drive me to NY. A hundred miles having been added to our journey – he said he would drive me to Albany – which was on his way home – and there I could get an aeroplane to NY. He went into a phone booth and started telephoning airlines – but there were no flights from Albany that would get me to NY in time. Then he drove to a town and started to look for bus terminals – but their schedules would have made me late. Finally I said the only thing was to find me another taxi. At last we found an immense grey-bearded Black driver who turned his car radio on to stations that had religious revivalist programmes. He listened to these, occasionally joining in a chorus of 'Praise the Lord' or 'So be it' or 'God is your salvation' in a deep bass voice. He tried to draw me into a conversation about theology. Despite his theology he charged me $118 instead of the $100 he said he was going to charge. I got to Rosamund Russell's lecture just as it was about to begin. After the lecture Jacqueline Onassis, Caroline Kennedy, the Russells and I dined in a restaurant. I sat next to JO. Her face is an enamelled mask, squarish, with large dark eyes. She is beautiful like some piece of sculpture. She talks in a way that suggests she is marvelling at everything. She was beautifully polite and seemed to want to talk seriously.

I asked Caroline how many young Kennedys were prospective politicians. 'Sixteen boys,' she said, 'and they are very annoyed with me because I am the only one who has political office,' she laughed, adding that she was a town councillor, or something of that kind. I asked why they were all going into politics, all so ambitious. 'It's not that they're ambitious so much,' she replied, 'as that it would never occur to any of them to go into anything else.' I asked Jacqueline what she considered her greatest achievement in life. 'Oh,' she said, 'I think it is that after going through a rather difficult time, I consider myself comparatively sane. I am proud of that.' I felt humiliated at ever having asked the question, by this answer. We went on like this, having real conversation or keeping up the pretence of having one – at any rate playing a game of good manners which I enjoyed.

I spent four days – Friday to Tuesday – at Tulsa staying with David Plante. Tulsa – or what I saw of it – seemed quite surprising – rather elegant, stylish people, talking and looking almost as if they came out of a movie, something between *Dallas* and *Oklahoma*. Immensely rich people live here. D. said it had more millionaires than any city in America. I doubt that.

D. is popular with his students whom he teaches fiction writing.

Germaine Greer also teaches at Tulsa, sharing an office with David. We went out to dinner with her. She has the look of an overgrown schoolgirl who has won all the prizes and has never quite got round to tidying herself up. Nor does she want to. Lively descriptions of walking through Central Park and men emerging from the dark and flashing their dicks at her. She says she is too hefty to be mugged.

David told me that she is dedicated to her students, and I can quite believe it. If she has any complaints against the university, she communicates them through interviews with the newspaper.

13 November / *Los Angeles*

Lizzie met me at the airport. She gave me fruit to put in the fridge of my suite at the Tropicana. She took me there and then went on to one of the interviews with agents and directors with which she fills her days.

B. turned up, looking the same as always, smiling in the same expectant way, as though he'd walked into the room after an absence of ten minutes. He still loves LA and defends it against criticism.

Dick (Sylbert)* and Lizzie gave me a party. Old friends like Christopher and Don, and new faces including Albert Finney, who was extremely cordial.

On Thursday, Christopher Isherwood gave a dinner for me. David Hockney and his friend, Gregory, Gore Vidal, Edward Albee, Don Bachardy – of course – B. and myself. Gore had just returned from two weeks' health care, which had completely changed his appearance. David looked round-faced, pudgy, cheerful, the gold rims of his spectacles glinting. Edward Albee has long moustachios, which look as if they are waxed, those of a melancholy drum-major. Before Albee arrived, Gore said he was concerned whether he'd written anything particularly acid about him lately. Towards the end of the evening, Gore and Albee got together and sang a duet of hate against the theatre critic of the *New York Times* who can kill a play in three days. Albee's and perhaps one of Gore's seems to have suffered this demise.

Christopher was rather silent, and sometimes appeared not to hear what was said to him. The next day I asked David whether C. was a little deaf, or perhaps preoccupied – and if so was it with his being 75? David said, 'A little bit of both, and I think there's a third thing. He is much affected by the fact that Don is now the same age (48 or 49) as Christopher was when he first met Don, who was then 18.'

20 November / *London*

Flew home from LA on night of 15 November. The journey was frightful. I took two sleeping pills but could not sleep a wink all night. My legs kept twitching as though they had acquired an independent life of their own. What was marvellous was the dawn, a burning beam of light like a red-hot strut of metal emanating from the glowing hub of the sun, intersected by the wing of the plane, on which the real sky was reflected. At London Airport N. met me.

In my mail there was a letter from George Plimpton† enclosing letters from Martha Gellhorn‡ and Laura Riding¶ attacking remarks I had made in my interview in the *Paris Review* some months ago. Laura Riding was indignant because I had said that Yeats, who loved

---

*Richard Sylbert. Art director of films such as *Who's Afraid of Virginia Woolf*, *Chinatown*, *Shampoo*, *Reds*.
† Editor of the *Paris Review*.
‡ Journalist, once married to Ernest Hemingway.
¶ Poet and essayist, once collaborator with Robert Graves.

gossip, was much amused by the Laura Riding-Robert Graves saga, including the story about Laura throwing herself from a fourth-storey window. Martha Gellhorn was even more incensed by my description of a luncheon with Hemingway, her and Inez in a Paris brasserie in 1936, in which Hemingway had said Inez was 'yeller' because, while he and Martha ate steak, Inez ordered sweetbread and drank only water. Hemingway remarked that Martha had been like that when he first knew her so he had taken her every morning to the morgue in Madrid to toughen her up. On the same occasion he had shown me photographs of murders in Spain, which he thought I ought to see to overcome my squeamishness. Martha professed to believe that I had invented all this.

I answered that it had happened. It took two days to deal with Gellhorn and Riding – not really a waste because there is nothing much else I can do in my present jet-lagged state – also controversy is good for my prose.

The 'situation' of being accused of inventing a luncheon forty years ago has fascinated me, suggesting possibilities for fiction.

Put it like this. There was a meal at a restaurant for four people. H, I, G. and S. H. and I. (Hemingway and Inez) are dead. The only survivors are G. and S. (Gellhorn and myself). G. denies that the occasion ever took place. She may genuinely think so, because it is completely obliterated from her memory. To her, meeting I. and S. was completely unimportant – one tiny episode in the glamorous, mutually self-dramatizing life of Hemingway and herself carrying on like characters in a Hemingway novel. The reason that S. remembers is because meeting Hemingway was an important event in his life. I. and S. were spectators of the performance put on by H. and G, which was like a scene in a play – G. calling Hemingway 'Hem' and 'Hemmingstein'. Hemingway acting up to his tough role for his butch journalist girlfriend. Preoccupied in their drama, H. and G. of course scarcely notice the spectators.

But what I remembered is my re-enactment of the scene in my own mind for my pleasure. I don't really remember the original, I remember only these repeat performances going on in my mind. At least I think this is so. I search in my mind for some fragment of the original scene. I don't remember anything 'new' about the luncheon itself, and I can't place the restaurant. It sounds like the Brasserie Lipp, but I don't see it on the boulevard. The only thing I do remember is collateral – that at about the same time Hemingway and I jointly gave a reading at Shakespeare & Co., Sylvia Beach's bookshop in the rue de l'Odéon. I have not thought about this for many years – though it is rather memorable – Hemingway ordering drinks and reading a passage which I think I would recognize (its vapid violence made Inez laugh) if I reread that book. Also James Joyce was there. Again, I cannot think of anyone alive today in that audience from whom I would obtain confirmation of it – but in fact there must be surviving witnesses, and there must be some record of the talks and readings at Shakespeare & Co., which someone is working on at this moment.*

On Tuesday, we had a very lively dinner party with Paddy and Joan Leigh Fermor, John Wells and Theresa, Philippe de Rothschild. The Leigh Fermors and John W. had spent the weekend at Ann Fleming's so for them the conversation was a continuation of the weekend. They raced along. N. and I managed to catch up after a while. Philippe was rather left out, though N. gave him special attention. He looked worn and melancholy, a bit left out but resigned and rather sweet about it.

Thursday. They played the Schubert Octet on the wireless and I stopped writing this and listened to it. Oboes, flutes, clarinets always bring to mind a day in 1929 when Erich Alport took me to visit friends of his – a young man called Lothar – and his wife Ilse – in the flat sandy pine forests among dunes near the sea not far from Hamburg. The small square modern concrete house had a large central room with a staircase along one side of it, leading to the bedroom on the upper floor. We lay on cushions in the dusk and someone put on a record player – a movement from Mozart's Clarinet Quintet. The liquid voice of the solo instrument played through the semi-darkness of those hollow walls within the pine-filled forest, like a white waterfall through darkness. Then Lothar, our host, a young man with a flap of yellow hair falling down over his face, through which his amber eyes resembled an animal's looking through iron bars, lit the fire and threw pine logs on to it. It blazed – the only bright thing in the dark, occasionally throwing out sparks. Then, wearing a dress with a full skirt which extended the bulge of her pregnant body with a bow-like curve down to her feet, Ilse came out of the bedroom and stood looking down at us from the head of the stairs. Splashes of light reflected on her dress from the fire and made her

* My memory is confirmed by the published photograph of the invitation to the Hemingway–Spender reading, and by Muriel Gardiner's recall of our telling her, on the following day, of our lunch with Hemingway. See *Paris Review*, vol. 79, p. 304.

bronzed young German face with the shining smiling eyes seem burning in their flame. Lothar, sitting beside me, said he could not bear to be home when his wife was having a baby, so he was going to leave early next day and bicycle to Holland. I imagined him in the grey dawn leaning over handlebars, tyres leaving tracks in the white sandy path, his eyes looking straight ahead, through the green flat country, all the way to Amsterdam.

In the past week we gave a dinner for Alan Pryce-Jones. Rosamond Lehmann, Claire Tomalin and V. S. Pritchett. Pritchett at 80 was really my great impression of the evening. He arrived early so asked me about Vanderbilt, where he is going to teach. He is completely alert, smiling, attentive with an authentic light in his eyes. At the end of the evening when everyone had gone we talked about the brilliant loquaciousness of Alan P-J. Victor's theory is that there is a kind of pool of rhetoric and story-telling fantasy in Wales which a great many Welshmen draw on. They all produce an unending stream of anecdote, wit, sentiment which derives from this shared source. Never particularly truthful, sometimes they are political, sometimes poetical, sometimes devout, sometimes frivolous. But it is always the same flow.

VSP is very English. There is something circumscribed yet inspired about him and conversation with him in Hampstead makes one think of the kind of talk that must have gone on between Hazlitt, Leigh Hunt, Benjamin Robert Haydon and Keats in the early 1800s.

28 November / *Cambridge*

Two undergraduates met me at the station. One of them wore a kind of wreath around his head and trailing garments. He looked a bit like Ophelia. Throughout the reading I kept catching the eye of a stalwart elderly gentleman in the fifth row who nodded encouragement more to himself than me – he was horribly bored. Next morning, in a snowstorm, joined Dadie Rylands, Frank and Anita Kermode, Helen Vendler and Natasha – who'd driven from London – at the lodge of King's College. We took them to lunch at some kind of university restaurant. Dadie, who took my arm in case I should fall in the snow, was all sweetness and concern and affection. I thought back over all the years I've known him, back to Ipsden staying with Rosamond and Wogan Philipps in 1930 or so. Wogan did a painting of him with two heads like a king on a playing card. He painted it on wood, put a nail through the middle, hammered it into a wall and made it spin like a catherine wheel. In those days Dadie was the golden-haired, blue-eyed boy favoured by Lytton Strachey. He had acted as the Duchess in *The Duchess of Malfi* (Isherwood as an undergraduate had seen him perform). He had written a charming book about Shakespeare's words.

Dadie loved L. as no one else did. Affection is his nature. And here he was guiding me over the ice (and I was thinking that if I did fall, I would be like a tower of bricks crushing this smiling, frail, delicate octogenarian). I thought how I had missed a life of friendship with him, because his clever mocking brittle manner made me think that affection – for someone as gauche as I have been all my life – was only an act, but I was wrong.

1 December

We stayed the weekend with the Giffords in Aldeburgh, in their new house. The other guests were the Beekman-Cannons from Newhaven, Connecticut. The weekend was largely devoted to the affairs of the Aldeburgh Festival. At the back of everything, I sense that there is a kind of selected revolt following on the death of Ben, comically like the reaction against Mao after his death.

Everyone is loyal to the memory of Ben – his photograph is up everywhere – but it is admitted he had his faults. He suddenly took against people in the Festival and either made their lives intolerable or had them fired. He was extremely open to flattery.

We decided not to go to Italy but to stay at home over Christmas. This gives me a clear run of work till 12 January.

10 December

Went to house-warming at Veronica Wedgwood and Jacqueline Hope-Wallace's new flat.

I saw a familiar, much photographed face, and it was Dr David Owen. We talked about the Labour Party. He surprised me by talking very frankly about his wish to see a social democrat party established. He said he thought the prospects for this would begin to come clear in January or February. I asked him whether he thought the third party should declare itself then. He seemed to think nothing should happen openly for a year at the end of which the impossibility of the Thatcher or Foot alternatives would become evident. I said I thought that the National government of 1931 was – fifty years later – a precedent which made it extremely difficult to think of any alternative coalition. He said, 'No, I'm not thinking in terms of a government of all the talents – Heath, Callaghan, Shirley – that kind of thing. I'm thinking of a social democratic party.' I said, 'I suppose they might do well in by-elections.' He said he thought by-elections were too much of a gamble. The idea seems to be to wait a year then declare themselves then fight the next Election as a third party. We talked a bit of non-political subjects. He said that the writer who had most influenced him in his life was Isaiah Berlin.

14 December / *Oxford*

Went to the New College banquet, as the guest of Richard Ellmann. I sat between Freddie Ayer and Dick.

Freddie is writing a continuation of Bertrand Russell's popular *History of Western Philosophy*, which solved all Russell's financial problems. Freddie said he sometimes felt now that he would like to stop working, put his feet up, and read. He asked me whether I felt this. I said I thought it was a noble aspiration – that it was a prevalent current heresy to think that everyone should be a writer and no one a reader, but I felt I had not begun to write yet. I was like Bill Coldstream who, at the age of 75, tells me that whenever he takes up his paint brushes, he feels, 'Well, one day perhaps this promising young painter will produce something worthwhile.'

'But do you really think you've produced nothing that will last? Don't you think that in your whole life you have produced twelve poems?' 'Well, perhaps twelve,' I said, mentally trying to count them on invisible fingers. There were a few younger people at the banquet, but really it was a parade of the old. Dick Ellmann told me it was also a test set for the cook who had been rebuked for failure at some earlier festivity. So we commented on the *melon con prosciutto* (well, the cook had nothing to do with that) followed by oyster soup (just a faint taste of oyster, after one had been told) followed by a dry leg of *pintadeau* (peahen) followed by a slice of beef, followed by a sorbet, followed by fruit. We ploughed through all this industriously like examiners vivaing students, some of whom failed, some of whom scraped through. Nearly all of us seemed the same age, with sides like those of old walls crumbling, and sparse almost colourless grass growing out of the tops of our heads.

15 December / *Oxford*

I saw more of Isaiah and Aline Berlin on Sunday than for many years. On Sunday morning we breakfasted, then sat in his study. Asked him about Wittgenstein. He said that once, before the war, he had gone to Cambridge to read a paper to a philosophy society. There were a lot of people there, some sitting on the floor. Suddenly he realized that a man with an open-neck shirt and wearing a jacket with leather patches on the elbows must be W. Isaiah read his paper, which he said went on much too long. At the end of it, after a pause, Wittgenstein asked a question. Isaiah was terrified but answered just as he would any other questioner, to the best of his ability. Then Wittgenstein went on questioning him for an hour. At the end of the meeting he was surrounded by young philosophers congratulating him at having had a dialogue with the great man, as though he had won an award. He thought Wittgenstein must have thought he was sincere, confused, but worth conversing with. Talked about the brother of W, a pianist who had lost an arm during the war, for whom Ravel had written a concerto.

Isaiah said that what Wittgenstein stood for and cared about most was morality, but since he had no language for this it could never be discussed or explained.

Left Isaiah and sitting in my guest room overlooking the beautiful walled garden with its tall burnt-out-looking tree trunks, a few last leaves and the metallic-looking grass reflecting the filtered golden sunlight, wrote this journal. Natasha and Day Wollheim arrived, having driven from London. Alfred Brendel, a tall, scholarly, very upright man with an expression on his face of extreme sensitiveness to things going on outside, a slow meticulous fastidiousness. I felt he was a bit dazed amongst us frivolous descendants of Bloomsbury who make a game of passing the ball of conversation from one to the other, feeling the cuff of rebuke if anyone tries to introduce a note of world-suffering into the conversation.

However, after lunch Isaiah started talking about the Greeks and how strange it is, with all our knowledge, we still have no idea of what they looked like, how they lived, etc.

We got on to the subject of the future. Isaiah said he didn't mind very much about everything coming to an end. If there were a choice between human beings surviving in conditions of utter poverty and misery, and the extinction of the human race, he would prefer extinction.

I said I did care – meaning that what I cared about was the civilization the world produced. Images of Renaissance achievement rushed before my eyes. Brendel, to my relief, said he cared also – and I could see that this man who transmits through his fingers the great invisible stored-up bank of great music meant what he said.

16 December / *London*

Went to a large luncheon given by George Weidenfeld. Mostly people from the press there. They all had the too-busy-to-discuss-anything-but-the-most-important-subjects look. The guest of honour was Gaston Thorn, the new President of EEC. When he answered questions he seemed imaginative, good-humoured, intelligent and human. In fact he made a good impression. But everyone else seemed utterly bored by the Common Market. Their interest in being there was to look at one another.

17 December

Had lunch with a young man who is writing a book about me. I wish I had more confidence in people who are trying to support my reputation. What has really happened is that of our group – Auden, Day Lewis, MacNeice, myself – Auden has activated teams of scholars and research workers and a few biographers. The biographers have been second-rate diggers up of personal anecdotes so far, the scholars and research workers heavy-industry exegetes. Still they have been far better quality than the biographers of Day Lewis and of Louis MacNeice – and of Isherwood for that matter. One wishes one could escape from it all.

Christmas Eve

Time hurtling by and I have been trying to work, and just keep up with letters, engagements, dinners. Two nights ago I mended fences with Peter Porter, poet and reviewer. In the *Evening Standard* he wrote how delighted Auden would have been with Charles Osborne's biography of him. As the book was totally against A's expressed wish that no biography should be written and his still more vehement wish that nothing confidential and private about the poet's life should be published, I felt this was outrageous. I said something to the feeble effect that I had a bone to pick with him, and explained (very mildly) why. He said he felt Charles had been attacked by other reviewers, and he wanted to defend him. Even as I spoke, I began wondering what right I had to think that Auden would stick to his declared objections. He would probably have forgiven Charles, whom he was fond of, straight away (as he did me for passages about him in *World Within World*) having wagged a finger at him and said, 'Naughty, naughty', corrected him on one or two points, then got drunk and told him worse scandal, which Charles would then have gone away and published, to be told again he was naughty, and so on, *ad infinitum*. Did he not say, 'Naughty, naughty' to me, on several occasions, and then forgive me? He had a forgiving, benevolent nature.

On Thursday (17 December) there was Sonia Orwell's funeral at a rather beautiful Roman Catholic church in Cadogan Street. Nineteenth-century Gothic, cold, grey, stony, unornamented, or almost so, the simplicity of its columns and arches like those in a Dutch painting. Ann, Rodrigo and Dan Moynihan, Diana Witherby, Janetta Palardé, among old friends there; Bill Coldstream darting to and fro with a distracted air; Michael Pitt-Rivers looking grave. A whole contingent of old ladies like all the charwomen Sonia had ever employed. The service in Latin – I thought I heard the priest say, 'At the request of Mrs Orwell' – Sonia's last assertion of the *comme il faut* … Of course I thought about Sonia, 'the Venus of Euston Road' of 1937, when I used sometimes to paint at the Euston Road Art School. With a round Renoir face, limpid eyes, cupid mouth, fair hair, a bit pale perhaps. She had a look of someone always struggling to go beyond herself, to escape from her social background, the convent where she was educated, into some pagan paradise of artists and 'geniuses' who would save her. Cyril Connolly provided her intellectual ideal.

All the time I knew her – which was from the early thirties – people discussed whether she was frigid, lesbian – what. Undoubtedly she had passionate loyalties – loyalty of some kind was ingrained in her deepest nature – and her quite spectacular disloyalty, on occasions, was the expression of her frustration that none of those who were the objects of her devotion quite came up to her expectations – it was they who were disloyal to the idea she had formed of them. She had a feeling, perhaps, with some people, that she'd invented them, and they'd jolly well better recognize this. She wanted her friends – particularly her women friends – to be not just people but causes that she supported with passionate generosity and defended from persecutors who were, if they were women, their men. 'The first port of call of any woman friend of hers who's left her husband is Sonia's spare bed,' said Cyril.

Under a veneer of sophistication she was not at all sophisticated – in fact, utterly innocent. This all who knew her understood, but at the deepest level of all they did not know what lay below the innocence. What, people wondered, did Sonia really want? And no one ever found out: though the likeliest answer was the love of a great and maligned genius – a great philosopher perhaps – whom she defended from all opponents. At any rate, that is what she thought she wanted.

In early *Horizon* days the person she most loved was Peter Watson, who was not a genius. However, in his beauty, his intelligence, his quite unostentatious chic – like that of the young hero in a Henry James novella – his openness and friendliness, his idealism and devotion to art, he was a knight in shining armour: something which the painter Tchelitchev had realized when he painted him exactly as this. Peter, as so many of her friends did, began by laughing at Sonia – there was always some absurd Sonia story floating around. What amused him being, of course, the extraordinary mixture of sophistication and *naïveté* in many things she said – her transparent longing to be in the intellectual aesthetic swim. But very soon, when she was working for *Horizon*, he became very fond of her, whilst she of course adored him. Cyril told me that when he went to the office of *Horizon*, if Sonia opened the door, he always knew whether Peter was there: for if he was, Cyril got only 30 per cent of her smile, 70 per cent being reserved for Peter.

Peter, being homosexual, was unobtainable. I don't think that Sonia switched from Peter to Cyril, but Cyril was *there* and Peter, in an important sense, was absent (absence, anyway, for men as well as for women, was part of Peter's character). Cyril fascinated her with his brilliance, funniness and non-stop need for sympathy. No one could enter more enthusiastically into the idea that he was the cause of creative genius personified, and frustrated, than Cyril. The fact that his genius was not realized was the fault of the society which did not give him a tax-free income equal to his expensive needs. Understanding the many ways in which Cyril was misunderstood provided Sonia with a tremendous brief, which took up much time and energy. Understanding Cyril increased her pretentiousness, her lofty dismissal of all those whom he (and therefore she) considered inferior: though she still remained underneath the warm-hearted generous spontaneous person she was all her life.

A story told by Peter Quennell, besides being funny, throws light on Sonia in *Horizon* days. In the summer of 1940, Sonia was one of a house party at the house at Uckfield in Sussex of Richard Wyndham, the painter, a man of notoriously sadistic character. Dick Wyndham got rather drunk and started chasing Sonia, who ran out of the house into the garden, and when he followed her there and would not leave her alone, threw herself into a pond. Quennell followed, and came to her assistance. As he dragged her on land, shivering, soaking and splashed with mud, she gasped, 'It isn't his trying to rape me that I mind, but that he doesn't seem to realize what Cyril stands for.'

Sonia remained devoted to Cyril, and perhaps her faith was justified. He was a wonderful editor of *Horizon* and he wrote two books, *Enemies of Promise* and *The Unquiet Grave*, which are minor masterpieces. And he never wrote a line of bad prose.

1981

15 January / *Columbia, South Carolina*

I've broken off this diary for a month. And now, in Columbia, and still affected by jet-lag from my ten hours' flight on Monday, I can't continue where I left off. The interruption at least shows how quickly a month goes by – I want the next months to rush. But being nearly 72 makes me think how restless I am with time. I shall be away from London in effect for six months, since in May, when I leave here, I go with David Hockney to China. Six months is now a palpable fraction of the remainder of my life.

There were good enough reasons why I could not write here. Firstly I was very taken up with translating (or, rather, making the stage version) for the Oxford Theatre, *Oedipus Trilogy*. This is nerve-racking and obsessive. Then there were engagements, which clustered around Christmas. Then there was Christmas itself followed by New Year and Matthew's visit.

Christmas was very quiet. In fact Natasha and I spent Christmas Day quite alone, as Lizzie was staying with friends. We ate a capon and mince pies, and looked at TV and went on working. There were convivial parties over the season. Karl and Jane Miller's, an excellent buffet dinner, everyone getting drunk except for Jonathan Miller who never drinks, and who, throughout the evening, was surrounded by shifting groups of people whom he entertained instructively on various subjects.

18 January

I have now been here just on a week (five days really, but it seems like a week). People could not possibly be more helpful. Also my students were welcoming, and seemed, most of them, to have read more than most other students in most other places. Yet, waking up in the morning, I have the sense of an underlying depression like a large squid lying at the bottom of a tank, which, if I don't act with resolution, will come up from the depths and embrace me in its tentacles.

Yesterday (Saturday) I read *Vanity Fair* all day and a volume of wonderful essays on European literature by Curtius. *VF* is vivacious trash, most interesting as vivid journalism, with hypnotic dialogue. It is newsreel stuff, with an elaborate system of sentimentalized and falsified values imposed on it. Although very readable, Thackeray isn't compulsive reading (like Tolstoy or George Eliot or Dickens) because one knows that nothing by which one can live better or breathe more freely is going to be told. It is morally as vain as its title. Curtius on the other hand is compulsive reading in being revelation – revelation firstly of the extraordinary character of Goethe, his intellect, his passion, his vision, his outer worldliness, and his inner withdrawnness, his sense of awe and mystery, his grasp of present and past, and his power to relate the two, his Byronically joyful mastery of form, which he controls and breaks through when expressing his vibrant ideas (ideas of course which Byron never had).

Nearly all yesterday went into reading and this in itself depressed me, because I thought I ought to be writing. I ought to be, it is true, but reading books better than any I could write (e.g., Curtius on Goethe) is better than writing. What matters is exploring one's soul, not putting oneself on show and in competition. Everything I'm doing here – reading, writing poetry, teaching, writing this diary – is good, and it doesn't matter which I'm doing at any particular moment. It wouldn't matter to the world and it might be better for myself if I never wrote another line but read lines better than mine own. Still to overcome depression I do have to prove to myself that I can go on writing. I got up this morning and worked on 'Auden's Funeral' (which I think is approaching the stage of desperate breakthrough) and the poem about the Lake District when we were children.

The great joy of London was M's stay, from 3 to 9 December. He showed us photographs of his recent paintings. One of the most interesting was a painting in which Richard Wollheim is seated in the background, gesturing with his hands, his dome-like skull and face seen in profile. In the foreground, staring rather distractedly in front of her, is a wild-looking Day; to the side are two of M's exotic Italian friends, a father and daughter in a compromising embrace. This is the world of people, many of them experiencing horrifying dramas, some of them crazy, amid whom Matthew, Maro and their children, are, with a certain bewilderment and fascinated curiosity, enisled.

One evening in late December – I have forgotten the exact date – when Matthew was with us, N. and he and I had late dinner at Bianchi. The main room of the restaurant was taken up by a large table at which were seated about a dozen people, among them Seamus Heaney, Ted Hughes and Melvyn Bragg. When we went past their table, Heaney got up, came over to me, and thanked me for nominating his *Selected Poems* as one of the three best books of the year, in the *Observer*. He said he had not written to me because he thought to do so might be to cross some boundary which divides silent gratitude from sycophancy. I said he was quite right not to have written. When we sat at our table in the next room another poet came over. He was Charles Causley. He said that on the way from Cornwall he'd been reading my *Letters to Christopher*, and was very much entertained by them. Still later, the waiter arrived with a bottle of champagne from the next table. I put these things down because I felt far more pleasure than I did by public recognition – like getting the CBE. This was a gesture from fellow poets. Instead of feeling worse than neglected – doomed, whatever I write – to be ignored – I suddenly felt the will to write something worthy of the attention of colleagues – to finish poems – to get out of my solitary state.

21 January

Reagan inaugurated as President, the hostages left Iran. I took my classes. Everyone is polite, amiable and helpful here, but very much of a level. Impression of moving along a straight road on a day of white mist reducing everything to solid oblong forms. The element through which I move being time. At night dreams about the dead.

Last night Day Lewis. Read Curtius on European history, Thackeray. Worlds through which far more powerful, sonorous, colourful, virile forces move than this one, which is threatened at every moment with what amounts to an appalling traffic accident, the introduction by machinery of fire and metal into the soft flesh of every person in the world.

[Undated] / *London*

Today I had lunch with Frank Auerbach. We met at his studio in George Street, Camden Town. The floor consists of paint accumulated over the years in an abstraction that looks like Tapies. The studio has a skylight, diagonal beams of sun which make objects they pick out seem contrasting like a black-and-white photo. While Frank talked to me, one side of his face was in a darkness which seemed to have Venetian red in it, the other lit white. He has a weight and seriousness which are Central European, and his expression changes abruptly from serious to smiling. He has a way of laughing which asks you to join in.

He makes me feel humble when he treats me respectfully. One thing that interests me very much with painters as well as poets is what idea they have in their heads before they embark on a work. My own feeling is that I have a strong but vague idea of the work before I write, and that the actual writing is an effort to recall an impression. Instead of 'Ripeness is all' I'd say 'Recollecting is all.' He said that for him his starting point was only a sketchy idea that he altered as he went on painting, discovering what was new. I asked him whether he thought at the end the completed picture was the realization of the original idea when he first started. He said, no, what he ended up with was pure discovery. At most he would admit that the finished picture contained the ghost of the idea he had started with.

He said he didn't see Francis Bacon much – perhaps they had quarrelled? he asked himself – but answered he didn't think so. 'Friendships wear out,' he said. He accepted that. I suppose I do too, but it is the last thing I'd want to admit.

Frank strikes one as unworldly and perhaps it is on account of this that he is someone totally without malice.

1982

21 March

Apart from the China trip when I kept travel notes, I haven't kept the journal for a year. Wrote nothing when I was in South Carolina last year. Now I have been reading the latest volume of Virginia Woolf's *Diary* – Volume IV – and feel fascinated again. First of all, I looked myself up in the index and found I was Wednesday, 2 November 1932, 'a rattle-headed, bolt-eyed young man, raw-boned, loose-jointed who thinks himself the greatest poet of all time'. Did I ever think this? In the context of the whole diary I don't mind what VW writes about me. If one reads the whole thing one ceases to care what V. thought about any but her own family and a few intimate friends. She lives in a hostile world in which everyone is outside her looking at her. The young are not 'us' to Bloomsbury – but a new generation, and she dislikes the whole lot of them. There is something about her of the bitter-tongued spinster alien to the world of buggers and fuckers who discuss each other's sexual parts. She can be perfectly candid about this but remains outside.

Anyway her suspicion of me was fundamentally justified. Too much of a journalist really, too impressed by the broad generalizations of public reasons and considerations for things, not having at the centre a core of unassailable private values, wanting to justify myself before a court of public evaluation and success.

We were in Venice last week – guests of the Gritti Palace Hotel. I had to give two 'talks' as the price of our holiday. On Friday, 12 March, Matthew, Saskia, Cosima joined us. They stayed at a hotel looking over the whole lagoon, near the naval museum, where all three of them shared a room. Saskia said it was a tourist-class hotel but, she pointed out, their room had the advantage of having three bidets.

They accompanied us everywhere, sight-seeing, enjoyed all we saw, were very gay. During the weekdays Venice was very empty – a dozen or so people in the piazza – the *calle* deserted. Usually sound runs along the gulleys of streets – sound of water in the canals. Now the streets seemed positively filled with silence.

Saskia is a curiously ironic child, perhaps because, though born in Italy, she feels a bit of a spectator. She suddenly started singing, with great liveliness, a song which she said was that of the villagers in San

Sano, then another one about Siena – all rather satirically acting them up – and making them very amusing.

Venice was wonderfully beautiful, quite unlike it is in the summer when it has the quality of painting with dark fissures, keyholes, patterns of clover, chimneys like halberds thrust into the sky, marble in the *palazzi* of the Grand Canal, which looks like stained leather. Last week it looked more drawn than painted, and geometrical: the vertical lines of *palazzi* windows, triangles, circles, semicircles, oblongs, squares. Buildings shone, subdued in colour as in a glow of dawn or sunset. Venice in bud, in spring, not the blown flowers, all pink and green of summer – the water a steely undulating mirror in which the reflections of buildings were strong and clear. The *calle* cool and shadowy in their near emptiness with light clear colour that cut like knives into the darkness above – and, overtopping all, the lid of blue sky.

There were very few people in the hotel. Among them, for the first three days, were Richard Burton and various assistants. He is making a film of Wagner and every day turned up at the bar of the Gritti Palace in different costume, according to the phase of Wagner's life he happened to be playing. He said that for each scene they produced great stars playing roles, which he had to measure himself against – Gielgud, Olivier, etc. He was friendly, quiet, curiously assured, as I've always found him – so much in contrast with his drunken public image.

22 March / *Williamsburg, Virginia*

I flew here from London by way of Washington. Today read and wrote and telephoned – trying to get my affairs in order.

27 March

Everything was so strange after this that it is difficult to piece together. On Tuesday (23 March) I lunched early, thinking I would rest before my next appointment, which was at three. At about two thirty I had violent abdominal pains and vomiting. I lay down, thinking the pain would pass off but when someone arrived to take me to my appointment, I was in too precarious a state to go. He asked me if I would like to go to the hospital. I said, yes, thinking it a good idea to try and find out what was wrong in view of the fact that I have a month's travelling in front of me.

At the hospital they discovered that I had a kidney stone on the right-hand side, which had moved from the kidney down into the urethrum, partly blocking it. By the time I had been through their tests I felt better.

On the following day I took an English class at eleven. They sent in prepared questions, which I answered. Then I went on to lunch with the College Review staff. They were all very nice – in fact at Williamsburg one gets an impression of genuine amiability. I got back to the hotel at two where Jack Willis, the professor who so kindly looked after me, asked me questions about my relations with Leonard and Virginia Woolf at the time when I did the translation of the *Duiner Elegien* with John Leishman. He showed me correspondence I had with Leonard, which was amusing – brought back memories of living with Inez in Queen's Mansions, Hammersmith. Apparently I kept on putting off meetings with Leishman. Although (I think) a Yorkshireman, he had a grim Germanic character of total seriousness – the kind of man who can exhaust a subject like a Hoover taking dust out of a carpet. He wrote a book about Shakespeare's sonnets in which he quotes so many sources in Ovid, etc., and so many examples of friendship being a convention of sonnet sequences, and of men calling each other their true loves, that nothing original is left but convention in the expressions of friendship. Anyway I remember meeting this grey mountaineer attired in pepper-and-salt tweed (solitary rock-climbing seemed to be his substitute for sex) and sidetracking him into listening to a recording of Beethoven's Ninth.

Suddenly, during Jack Willis's interview with me, I had exactly the same pain as the previous day. I asked him whether he minded going to my room where I could lie down, but the pain got worse. He took me back to the hospital where they suggested I stay the night, and I embarked on a nightmarish twenty-four hours of further X-rays, and a barium check involving one enema followed by another. In the underworld seabed of my intestines they had already found a polyp. On those great transparent sheets of film, produced at amazing speed, and while a moving picture of my insides being filmed also appeared on a TV screen – I felt anything might appear – the wreck of a ship sunk in the Armada, a shark, a coral branch attached to a drainpipe which proved to be cancer. I felt in myself the utter passivity that proves to me, at the end of my life, that I am nothing that I would wish myself to be, no fighting genius but an ideal patient merely, who has passed his life being operated on by other people and never really acted upon his own initiative.

However, as often happens when everything seems hopeless, I was let out, all in a rush, at about five. I was even able to go to a party of my co-conferenciers and members of the faculty.

I did not go to the reading but back to the hotel and rewrote the short piece I'd been doing on the poetry of Karol Wojtyla who happens to be the Pope.

28–9 March

Weekend at Washington. I did not go out but read Andrew Boyle's book *The Climate of Treason* about Burgess, Maclean and Philby. The career of Burgess seems incredible – that a person who could scarcely have been let into, say, Leonard and Virginia's drawing room should have had the run of the Foreign Office, the BBC, etc., and ended up, when he was considered too outrageous for anywhere else, at the British Embassy in Washington. Blunt, Burgess and Maclean all treated me with near contempt when I met them. I don't know whether this was because I was an ex-communist, or a liberal, or an innocent – what they all had was the arrogance of manipulators who thought they could manage other people. Perhaps this was in part because they had voluntarily put themselves at the service of their Russian manipulators. As a matter of fact their faith in a creed whose mixture of sanctity, bloodiness and snobbery gave them a sense of great personal superiority has parallels in the arrogance of English Catholic converts: Graham Greene combines Catholic and communistic bloody-mindedness. The drunken Catholic priests who are made sacred by their office meet the alcoholic dedicated upper-class English communist in the figure of Philby.

4 April / *Vancouver*

Morning, I write about half (I suppose) of my lecture for Ann Arbor about how writers write. Wasted a lot of the afternoon looking with cow-like imbecility at TV.

But when I looked at the rough drafts of poems, which I carry around with me in a notebook, I had a lot of ideas. They seemed to be moving forward into life, and I crossed out, added, rewrote – especially 'The Mythical Life of David Herbert Lawrence'. It would be nice to do potted memoirs of a few poets. Altogether poems seem to be growing under my hands, which spasmodically have green fingers.

In the evening, dinner with Wayne Holder, his wife, and the poet Robert Bringhurst, and – to ruin the whole evening – a former acquaintance of mine, Y.

Few sensations can be more mutually disagreeable than remeeting former friends after twenty-five years and I daresay Y. felt the same. From what he said (and he made numerous over-the-head-of-the-others references to this) we must have met in Berkeley. His voice booms and he pontificates. He talked across the others at me, 'I agreed with you so much, Stephen, when we last met at Berkeley and Natasha was there – and Matthew – how is Matthew by the way? – and you said . . .'

There was nothing really to be done. Y. stroked and stroked and stroked with all his fingers every hair of his beard. Nothing is more lascivious than long fingers combing up and down and in and out of a gingery beard. Bringhurst, who also has a beard – but quite a short one – abstained from touching his, which I took to be a kind of message that he understood my exasperation. He leaned his face on his hand, asked me once whether I would add a third volume to *The Destructive Element* and *The Creative Element*, to which I could only say that I would never write any more critical books – and said very little else.

In bed, as soon as I woke (at six) this morning I read the volume of poetry Bringhurst had given me and was bowled over. They were poems about ice and stone and light – of a dazzling purity – something so elusive and yet so controlled – and linking up the Arctic continent and the North Canadian experience with ancient Greek mystical philosophy and Pythagorean geometry – pure form yet given the precision of mathematics. The work of a mind dwelling on great geographical and historical heights, completely unlike anything else, showing the utter commonplaceness of the confessional writing fashionable now.

Reminds me of how I once spent weeks trying to write a poem about a glass of water – with no success. To read Bringhurst was to enjoy his work for its own sake and yet to glimpse (I thought) new possibilities in my own writing.

7 April

A large upper room called 'The Bookstore' in Vancouver where I was asked to reminisce about literary life. It was the excitement of provincials for whom I represented a world from which they felt cut off. But they aren't so cut off as to know nothing about it, in fact perhaps not really cut off, only feeling they don't have enough from outside. There was a kind of excitement which, with some of the young, was erotic in a platonic way. One young writer gave me poems he had written for me the night before when he was drunk.

The 'Store' set out to emulate Sylvia Beach's Shakespeare & Co., of which there were photographs on the wall, and of Sylvia Beach, Joyce, Pound. The crowd were anxious for every crumb of information I could give them about Sylvia Beach, Adrienne Monnier, etc. It was a strange evening.

9 April

Left Vancouver 7 April. At Seattle Airport the man at the desk asked, when to pay the bill I produced my credit card, whether I was related to the poet Stephen Spender. So I said, 'That's me.' He looked pleased and said, 'Gee, a near-celebrity.'

Arrived Los Angeles and took a taxi to David's (Hockney). My fellow guests were David's friend Celia* (married once to Ossie Clark) and Ian, David's pupil.

David was in a great state of excitement. He has invented a way of juxtaposing multiple Polaroid photographs as part of a subject (which may be a portrait, still life or landscape) so that they produce an effect of many superimposed images of the subject taken from different angles, as with cubism. The remarkable achievement is that the spectator seeing a face which has perhaps three noses and four eyes nevertheless makes a sum in his head of the multiple images and sees a single face correcting the distortion. That D. can produce such unity out of multiple images is due to his unerring eye, which one can judge from seeing him at work making one of these compositions.

He tells me that he has put into photography the dimension of passing through time which it lacks. He attaches importance to the fact that it takes up to three hours for him to make one of these pictures. The three hours through minute transitions in the lighting as well as the observation of things from different angles go into the picture, as they would with a drawing that took the same amount of

---

* Celia Birtwell, fabric designer and model for many of Hockney's portraits.

time. He calls it 'Drawing with Photography' and is having an exhibition of his results in New York by that title – though he is tempted also to call the exhibition 'Today Photography is Dead'. Actually thinking of it now, I wonder whether what he is doing is not nearer futurism than cubism. The futurists tried to give the idea of movement through multiple images of the same subject. But perhaps what they did was borrowed from the cinema.

Staying at D's was disturbing because one felt that one was one of a number of people, all of whom were *de trop*. I was perhaps in a physical sense the most *de trop* of the lot.

People kept wandering in and out of the apartment the whole time I was there. David seemed utterly indifferent to them, neutral perhaps, welcoming them as spectators of his new photographs, and listeners to his spiel about them. Usually David and I got up before anyone else, and David would say mildly: 'You would think that someone would have noticed there is no bread and no milk in the house' and I would accompany him to the store.

David, Ian, Gregory,* Celia and I all had dinner with Christopher and Don one evening. There were no other guests. This was very much as usual. Don greatly preoccupied with the meal, which was excellent. Christopher has become a bit like the weather, sometimes bright, sometimes silent. He was sort of average that evening, talked a bit about memoirs he is writing of his early days in America.

B. came on Friday evening. We dined out. He was very much himself and told me his plans. He is going to write, together with a woman he knows, a book on seagulls. He was affectionate, intelligent, informative, concerned as always. He said he was beginning to forget some of the details of the trips we went on together at Gainesville. I said it was quite right that he should forget, and, also, that I couldn't help remembering. We went to a famous restaurant where there are booths. Gore Vidal was there and after we had eaten we joined him for a bit. He talked about his candidature for the Senate and said he now seemed favourite in the polls out of five. Afterwards, B. said he didn't really understand why anyone should want to vote for Gore in preference to Jerry Brown.

We talked about David and I said I couldn't understand why he was always so surrounded with people. B. said, 'He has people like my parents have TV on all day.'†

* David's assistant. † When he read this later David commented, 'Oh, but I always thought they were my family.'

Occasionally, David delivers a terrific speech – not at all a lecture – about some subject such as modern art. This may occur in his studio, his car, the swimming pool, anywhere. It is said with utter conviction, is interesting, but contains no opening for any answer or contribution to be made to it. It's often followed by the announcement: 'I know I'm right. Absolutely right.' No one, David said, can draw today. This is the result of the criminal neglect and cowardice of the art schools. It means much more than might appear. It means that people can't see either. It leads to a general diminution of truth. Obviously this has some universal application for him – bad drawing is indicative of the decline of standards in everything everywhere. On the whole I say yes to all this. Once I said that all the same I met young people who seemed not at all in decline but alive and interested. B. had told me that his students were amazingly aware and intelligent, so much so that it was difficult to give anyone a mark lower than C. David said, 'Yes, but they're not art students.'

He wants me to tell Isaiah that he wants to do one of his photo-drawings of him. 'It doesn't matter – he can talk as much as he likes when I'm photographing him.' I said that unless he objected, I'd like to be there when he 'did' Isaiah. He said that would be all right. Then he added: 'Not that it's necessary to make him talk. He'll talk with anyone. Nothing will stop him talking. If the charlady comes in, he'll talk about detergents with her. What I like about him is he has humility' – how true, I said.

29 April / *Minneapolis*

Now, writing this on the grim campus of Gustavus Adolphus where I'm stranded for two days, I feel happy about David. On the last day I was there, I made shepherd's pie for everyone – David didn't seem to object to my doing so. Someone said something about being successful and David suddenly burst out: 'As though that isn't the most terrible thing that can happen to you.'

Apart from meetings with B, the visit to LA was disturbing. One symptom of this is that I was not able to write a line of this journal or the lecture I have to give here about Raoul Wallenberg.*

---

*Raoul Wallenberg, the former Swedish diplomat in Budapest, was arrested 40 years ago by the Red Army. He saved the lives of hundreds of thousands of Jews during the war. His fate is still unknown. The Soviet Government claims that he died in 1947.

I sometimes think that the reason David, always surrounded by people, has a curious indifference to any point of view other than his own must lie in his Bradford childhood. I think of him surrounded by a family fond of and admiring him but amazed at his wonders of art and experience and dress and speech so utterly unrelated to what they are used to – yes, his originality, for he is nothing if not original. At the Royal College of Art he was also a spectacle and I can't believe that he and Ron Kitaj really exchanged ideas, were anything more than a mutual admiration society. What David wants to do is stun admirers.

David said to me: 'One never gets away from the first years of one's life. I never get away from those dark streets and the dark atmosphere of Bradford. The colours of Los Angeles are stronger to me, the night more shining because I always see Bradford behind them.'

15 May / *London*

So it's nearly a month since my last entry in this journal. Nothing much has happened except that I have read everything about the Falkland Islands.

On 2 May Philippe de Rothschild, the Annans, Nin Ryan* and Rodrigo (Moynihan) dined here. Philippe told me how on his eightieth birthday he gave a party at Mouton. Joan Littlewood was of course invited and said she would not come. However, when everyone was seated for luncheon suddenly the door was flung open and it was Joan. Philippe was touched and delighted. She had flown all the way from Vienne to get there. Towards the end of luncheon she left the table. Philippe thought she would be back in a moment but she did not reappear. Finally he asked one of the domestics where she was. He said she was gone – on her way back to Vienne. She had persuaded Philippe's chauffeur to drive her to the airport. Philippe said he had had to close all the residential part of Mouton. Owing to taxation under Mitterrand he could no longer afford to live there.

The Falkland Islands. At the back of everything else, this goes on, like sickness – the seasickness never written about or photographed of the soldiers on their ships.

These operations are an automatic function of the capacity to perform them, just as the war in Vietnam was a function of American

* Mrs John Barry Ryan.

power. If we didn't have the ships and weapons and men we would never have set off on this expedition. Given the fact that we do have them, we use them; they demand to be used. It is the automatism of power. They demand to become a task force and to sail 8,000 miles. Having got there they demand to be used. When they have gone into battle they will demand a victory. If they don't win and win quickly then they will demand an extension of the war – to bomb the mainland. That is the ground-swell of our lives.

16 May

Oxford, dinner at All Souls – one of their annual banquets – as Isaiah's guest. I sat next to Sir Keith Joseph, a worried-looking man with whom it was very difficult to talk and whom I thought I ought to attack on the subject of English universities as he is Minister of Education. I did not do so, however. He said at some point that he thought it would be healthy for English universities to be largely private and supported by big business as they were in America. I said that University College, London, was trying to raise money from big business, but with little success.

21 May

Went to Oxford to see an American professor who has made a computerized concordance of my poems. It lists all the nouns and how many lines each occurs in, giving those lines. He told me about this first two years ago. I cannot have understood what he was talking about or, surely, I would have managed to stop him. I hate bibliographies, concordances, etc., applied to my own work. But it would seem masochistic – or rather, to show a complete lack of faith in myself – to say, 'I'm not deserving of such treatment. Try it on someone else.'

He wants my publishers to produce a new volume of my *Collected Poems* (which I had told him I was planning to do) together with a companion volume, which would be the concordance. He says this will make literary history. It will also, I think, make me ridiculous – but if I were to tell him this, I would be saying that he had wasted a year of his life – more, in fact – computerizing me. So instead I feebly said I would send him copies of my new poems, for him to ask the computer questions about. Again – to say that all this had nothing to do with poetry would be to insult him.

25. Chuck Turner, Hansi Lambert, Lucy Lambert, the author, Nicolas Nabokov, Samuel Barber (Photograph Natasha Spender)

26. Cyril Connolly with lemur

27. Peter Watson, 1942

28. Auden and Spender at a Faber party in 24 Russell Square, 1963
(Photograph Mark Gerson)

29. Louis MacNeice, Ted Hughes, T. S. Eliot, Auden and Spender
at the Faber party, 1963 (Photograph Mark Gerson)

31. Julian Huxley
at UNESCO, 1946

30. Isherwood, Spender and Don Bachardy in
New York, 1975 (Photograph Eva Rubinstein)

32. Rodrigo Moynihan, 1983

33. Angus Wilson at
Mrs Ian Fleming's house, 1980

34. Natasha Spender
(Photograph C. A. de Barry)

35. Matthew Spender in his
Roman uniform, aged 7

36. Family group, 1950: Matthew, Natasha, Lizzie, Stephen
(Photograph Lucilla Sherrard)

37. Corfu, Rovinia, the bay with the cave

38. Painting of the cave by the author

39. Matthew painting, 1981
(Photograph Humphrey Spender)

40. The author with his grandchildren, Saskia
and Cosima (Photograph Matthew Spender)

41. Lizzie (Photograph Bee Gilbert)

42. Stephen Spender and Francis Bacon,
Montmajour, 1966 (Photograph David Plante)

43. Giving the Address at Auden's memorial service, Westminster Abbey, October 1974 (Photograph Mark Gerson)

44. David Hockney caricature of the author

45. Poetry reading, Collegiate Theatre, Bloomsbury, 1973; Ted Hughes, Stephen Spender holding up Auden's *Poems 1928*, Seamus Heaney (Photograph Frances Charteris)

46. The eye of the poet (Photograph Michael Astor)

4 June

On Tuesday we went to see Lizzie in a play about Queen Christina of
Sweden by Pam Gems. A very small theatre called The Tricycle in
Kilburn High Road. I felt a sudden pang for Lizzie, wishing that she
was appearing as a lead in some wonderful play, her name in lights.

Inside, the theatre was a bit like a tent with tiers of chairs round
three sides of it. The play was centred entirely on Queen Christina,
played by an actress who looked like a land worker digging for victory.
She acted with a great deal of energy, man-handling the role and not
letting go of it for a moment, as though it was a dangerous wild beast.
At the beginning of the play she seemed to be a lesbian and spent her
time making passes at Lizzie who was some kind of lady-in-waiting.
Lizzie also had a male lover who kissed her, much to the annoyance
of Queen Christina, who was beside herself with rage when she discovered Lizzie was pregnant. Later Queen Christina seemed to undergo a change of sex, wore female clothing and had a lover who soon
proved to be involved in some kind of plot against her – so she had
him murdered in front of her (and – unfortunately – our) eyes. She
shouted so much that one could scarcely understand a word of what
she said. Lizzie had three different roles, the last of them as a nurse,
towards the end of the play. The pope appeared shortly before the
murder (which took place in Rome) – Queen C. had abdicated and
gone to live in Rome. She was invited to be Queen of Naples. She
refused, but one had the impression that she would have accepted if
the handsome young cardinal who made the offer had agreed to sleep
with her. He would not, and this seemed to lead to QC's final breakdown. One had the impression that the cardinal was gay and perhaps
having an affair with the young man – QC's corrupt young lover –
who was murdered. But this may have been due to the fact that the
producer, directing a scene in which the condemned man pleads for
his life with the cardinal, could not resist displaying the two of them
in what looked like some scene of love in an S/M bar in New York.

Lizzie came back and had supper with us afterwards. She was so
funny about it all, partly very serious, partly giving hilarious accounts
of the rehearsals. I felt sad thinking of her doing this – looking so
gentle and beautiful on the stage – but having only a two-dimensional
supporting part, night after night. Just before I sit down to write this
the telephone rings and she tells me she has a TV part with a comedian

who does what is essentially a one-man show, for which she is the foil. It is not important but very encouraging, and the great thing is continuity.

7 June

John Schuster rang at ten or so to say that Uncle George had died. The funeral, he told me, would be on Friday – could I inform Christine and Humphrey and then let him know how many to expect. It would be at three. We were all invited to drinks afterwards.

It is curious, the gap between death and burial. If there is a love bond, or blood bond between me and the person who has died, I feel a very heightened mutual awareness during this interval. The ghost is hovering at the back of my consciousness (someone read on the wireless yesterday Thomas Hardy's 'Who's in the next room – who?' which gave the feeling I'm trying to locate). I do feel the ghost needs my loving prayers – which are more a state of feeling than of words. More than this I feel as though the spirit of the dead is watching me. I have to be careful for a few days to do nothing in word or deed or thought to offend it. What the dead must be searching for during this interval is love in the hearts of those they loved.

Woke up at six, read poems by Goethe in the Penguin *Anthology of German Verse*. My uncle, like the best and most human public men, always made the impression of redeeming and wanting to be redeemed. He was always charitable, imaginative, liberal, liked by people with whom he worked, but of course he could not in middle life escape from having an air of self-importance. He was involved in public affairs. 'Men improve with the years' – this is a dubious generalization but it is probably true of certain people who have gone into public life for honourable reasons and then become enlarged beyond the scale of private personal relations – they return, the public importance drops away from them, they shrink back into being ordinary human beings, they think that they will soon be less even than this, they are lonely, they need love; physically they are their own husks. Something like this happened to my uncle.

The last thing he said to me was: 'You can't realize how much it means that a few people come and talk to me. That is all I have.' There were tears in his eyes, but not of weakness or senility.

A Hollander called Peerbohm lunched with me at Loudoun Road to interview me for a Rotterdam newspaper in connection with the international meeting of poets in Rotterdam next week. I now have a list of all the poets who are to read, in all their languages. This makes no sense. But I have to go because, very generously, the Dutch have made *Index* the theme of their meeting – and I must try to raise money for *Index*.

10 June

We seem to have a lot of social life suddenly. Tuesday the annual party given by Nin Ryan at her flat overlooking Green Park. So many famous faces, a good bit older than one's idea of them, clean as wax-works, and very difficult to put names to more than a few of them – Harold Macmillan in a wheelchair, rather desiccated, and slumped at one side – in the crowded room fashionable ladies taking turns to kneel or crouch down on the floor beside him, making little speeches, one in the left, one in the right ear.

And on Wednesday, one of those luncheons at George Weidenfeld's where one is lucky even to be introduced to the guest of honour one has been invited to meet. This time it was Franklin Murphy, President (or Chancellor) of Un LA (I think) and president of a lot of banks. I sat next to his wife and worked rather hard at being polite. After a bit, she said: 'I didn't hear your name, I am afraid. Are you a professor?' I said I had been a professor and my name was Spender. She said, 'I'm afraid I've only heard of one Spender – Stephen Spender – and he's dead I believe.' 'Well, I'm Stephen Spender.' She took this in good part, repeated it to everyone at the end of the meal, with relish, so we won't forget each other.

11 June

Uncle George's funeral was at three at Nether Worton in the little church, which is much more like a Schuster chapel. There my grand-mother, my aunt Gwen (George's wife) and my cousin Dick have memorial tablets.

The coffin, very expensive-looking, with the finest oak panelling, seemed to fill the whole chapel. We found places near the door, but just as I was taking my seat, John appeared and said, 'Stephen sit here' and took me near the front. John very efficiently took charge of the proceedings, reading the lesson, which was a psalm about work (this certainly being an important part of Uncle George's credo) and a very sweet poem written in 1645 about marriage, which John had chosen, he said, because it described so exactly his parents' relationship. He had his usual buoyancy in doing this together with a kind of command, which was moving. He read extremely well; I thought how strange it was that we cousins who had started out so far apart (with us the children of parents who died when we were young, and brought up by my grandmother and two servants, and they so conventional and respected with all their foxes and hounds and grand social life and the City and administration of Empire) should have ended up together with John reading poetry. The congregation recited with fervour (I thought) the Lord's Prayer and I thought that if it wasn't anchored to a religion, it would be pure poetry.

The service seemed very short. The pall bearers shouldered the coffin, which looked enormous and heavy. While they did this John put on a concealed gramophone: the choir of King's College, Cambridge. As the coffin passed me, music seemed to be coming from inside it, as from a concealed loudspeaker. When we left the church the coffin had been lowered into the grave. People walked past the cleft in the earth, some of them threw flowers down on to the coffin, which had a brass plate on it, engraved, I suppose, with George Schuster's name.

After this there was a tea party in the dining and drawing room at John's and Lorna's house. Their children, Joanna, Peter and Dick, formed a separate Kensington group – the rest of the party, some very consciously gentrified Jewish people, distinguished and culture-respecting, like descendants of the union between Wilcoxes and Schlegels in E. M. Forster's *Howards End*.

I have always thought I was half-Wilcox, half-Schlegel. We said goodbye and walked back to our car, past the churchyard. Gravediggers were spading the heaps of clay earth into the open grave. So that was the last of Uncle George. Or perhaps not.

12 June / *Rotterdam Central Hotel*

I had rather grandiose expectations since the organizers had made such a fuss about me. In my imagination I consigned myself to a comfortable hotel. Actually this is a third-rate hotel, a poky little room, no bath, just a shower, a stuffy smell along the corridors like that of Berlin rooms in 1930. It must be the only building in Rotterdam that survived the German Blitz, and I can't help wishing it hadn't.

Went to meet the other poets at a Greek restaurant. I sat next to

Journal / 1980-2

Alberto de Lacerda.* Talked with the scowling contemptuous-looking Israeli delegate, A. He complained to Alberto - within an hour of his arrival - that he had not yet found a girl with whom to spend the night. He wanted to know whether there were discos in Rotterdam where he could pick girls up. Alberto, of course, knew nothing of all this. The Israeli said he had a good mind to leave Rotterdam at once. Later in the evening I saw him and he lectured me about the British in Argentina. In the first place, he said, they should have told no one they were raising a task force. The whole thing should have been done in complete secrecy while carrying on negotiations with Argentina. Then they should have had a great many more infantry. Then they should have made a sudden attack with all their forces, etc., etc. The conversation reminded me unpleasantly of something I could not quite identify. Then I realized it was hearing Germans talk in the thirties. The same arrogant tone, the same assumption that everything he said was incontrovertible.

14 June

Our hosts, the Dutch, are charming, though, and do everything to please. Yesterday there was a poetry reading, diversified with songs and music on strange instruments from Africa and Indonesia, a fair and children's games, all outdoors in the park. Alberto and I escaped in the afternoon and went to the Boysmann museum which is magnificent, especially the early rooms of Flemish paintings, also wonderful Dutch landscapes, interiors of houses and churches. Dutch painting is really the purest, most painterly, least theatrical of all the schools. There is a wonderful portrait by Rembrandt of Titus as a child, his cheek leaning on a pudgy hand. The paint looks like impasto from a distance but when you scan closely the flesh of forehead and eyes, it is in what look like very long-drawn threads of colour thin as the hairs on a violin bow, interrupted by almost imperceptible dots. I liked very much the small Cuyp landscapes, paintings of light almost like Turners, with a few cattle just shadows standing in pools of light, as of air. The modern art is not so interesting. There was an immense exhibition of young modern German artists, large pictures very loosely painted, rather garish, expressionist subjects, often pornographic.

In the afternoon there was a larger meeting in a hall, which I had

* Portuguese poet.

[453]

to address about *Index on Censorship*. This was followed by a quite lengthy discussion. One or two people – notably a Latin American poet called Cisneros – said I was talking very much from a Western bourgeois point of view, in a society where there were writers and a literate public. But in South America the public is censored by not being able to read the work of writers, etc. There was an extremely long speech by an Indonesian poet, who had been seven years in prison, most of which I could not understand. I did, however, hear him say that when he was in prison, knowing that people in the world outside were remembering him and agitating for him to be released was more than encouraging, it was life-giving.

After this, there were radio interviews in the bar of the hotel. People talking all round, muzak in the background, very distracting. But there is something about the Dutch which is endearing. They seem like toy people going through the motions of public occasion, as though they were pulled by strings, but warm and pleasant underneath.

Christopher Reid, Richard Murphy and I escaped after this and dined together in an Indonesian restaurant.

15 June

Christopher Reid is like some charming miniature, with delicate features, a complexion of pink Dresden china, limpid, slightly protruding eyes, a faint look of a famous portrait of Shelley. He is serious and amusing, explains his feelings about things, paintings we saw in the art galleries, poems read at the meetings.

Richard Murphy is tall, lean, very distinguished. He reminds me in several ways of Cecil Day Lewis, especially a white paperiness of the handsome rumpled features almost like a Japanese lantern, and falling into curves and lines, expressive of a rather lofty humour, a hovering arrogance. Like Cecil, he has a beautiful reading voice, though he modulates it so as to isolate and underline expressive words, not to melt the language into song as Cecil did.

I began by not caring for him much, thinking he was rather aloof – too literary and not fitting in anywhere. Towards the end I got to like him very much. Altogether this Dutch conference was made agreeable by the poets assembled here. I also liked Christopher Merkel from West Germany, and having been slightly put off by the appearance of the East German poetess, who looks like a hockey mistress in a Ronald Searle cartoon, I found her rather sweet. Merkel told me that the Israeli, in spite of his mephistophelean appearance was really a decent fellow. I came to feel a certain affection for him, too, deciding that he was not so much arrogant as eccentric. He seemed to have some structuralist view that poetry by inventing language could make the language used by politicians masochistic. He said that what a few poets in Israel were doing with Hebrew would make the language of Begin incomprehensible within a few years. It is a nice idea – that poets should so undermine the language of political leaders that their rhetoric would quite literally turn to ashes in their mouths. I had reason as an English writer to feel apologetic towards Alberto L. because I did understand from things he told me that he had been badly hurt by the English. When he was in London, during and after the war, he was taken up by Edith Sitwell. Then Edith seems to have turned against him. He told me that Elizabeth Salter in her book on Edith described him as a servile lackey. All this seems to exemplify the way the Sitwells could lavish attention on a friend they made their courtier, and then drop him. From what he told me he understood very well Edith's mixture of compassion and paranoia. He spoke with dignity about this.

20 June

I'm now in King Edward's Hospital to have my stone in the urethrum and my polyp in the intestine dealt with. Natasha brought me here and sweetly stayed for a time. I regard all this as routine and am completely passive about things doctors do to me. I read, in the *Sunday Telegraph*, in an extract from Frances Donaldson's book about P. G. Wodehouse, that, after the war, Malcolm Muggeridge had to break the news to Wodehouse that his daughter Leonora had died unexpectedly after a minor operation. Then I turn on the TV to see the programme about Stravinsky's *Les Noces* and there on the screen is Nicolas Nabokov who also died after a minor operation.

I do not in the least expect to die, but I think how grateful I am to Natasha for her care of me, of which I am quite undeserving. I think of how my father and mother both died after operations. Anaesthetics are rather strange and solemn occurrences, when the body becomes a sacrificial victim upon an altar, on which priestly surgeons perform blood-streaked rituals while one is blank.

On Thursday last, in Amsterdam, I went alone to the van Gogh museum. Van Gogh's vision is of the rhythm of organic growth, which he follows with brush strokes throughout his landscapes, portraits, still lives. Looking at his trees, fields of grass, mountains, I can quite believe that the lines of energy moving through every object, animal, vegetable or mineral are essentially as van Gogh sees them and that some scientific scanning instrument could demonstrate this. But van Gogh has not just a hallucinatory vision of atomic dynamism. His own feelings are a force among these forces; feelings about men who labour and suffer; about the animation of terrestrial nature by the sun; feelings too about himself, his 'madness', his sexual frustration, his poverty. His letters are the counterpart in language to his painting, letters and painting are both autobiographical but always reaching outwards beyond himself.

When I see VG's paintings – as when I read Lawrence's prose – these russet-bearded geniuses have a lot in common – I wonder why one does not see nature as they do.

One usually sees it, I think, as frozen, static coloured photographs with proportions, and rhythms measurable but not as dance. VG and DHL see a universe like Nietzsche's 'dancing star'.

29 June

Thursday I felt very low. Fortunately had cancelled lunches Thursday and Friday. Thursday evening we gave a dinner party. Clarissa Eden,* the David Astors, James Joll. I opened two bottles of the '71 Rothschild Lafite claret Francis Bacon had given me, to Natasha's horror. The dinner went at a snail's pace, I felt, longing for it to end, because I was by now so ill, with a high fever.

For the next twenty-four hours or so I was in a state of mental passivity, a prey to fantasies, memories, thoughts that pressed down on me, and which I could not control. My ordinary active thinking self was reduced to the role of spectator of my passive self. Damnation must be the sensation, throughout eternity, of being 'thought' not thinking. The thoughts that weighed on me were ones that are always on the edges of my existence, that my talents have been wasted, that I have done nothing with my life, this, despite the fact that I have known with exceptional clarity what my obligations are: work (poetry), love (marriage) and human responsibility. In the kind of despair I felt, these thoughts took over, and they weren't in my style either, they were couched in the

* The Countess of Avon, widow of Anthony Eden.

language of speakers at congresses or articles in newspapers. These formed a barrier dividing me from customary personal language. My existence fell behind this barrier. During the night I had a very bad attack of shuddering, a kind of seizure, while I went to the bathroom and vomited. The next day when I struggled to read a novel, the words took off from the printed page and began a quite different story of their own, disjointed and incoherent, about evil and demons. All this was shot through with guilt-ridden memories mostly to do with my family, memories of frightful mistakes, the self-reproach of parents thinking: 'If I had acted differently my children might have been happier.'

1 July

The Wollheims and Karl Miller came to lunch; also David Hockney and his friend and pupil Ian Faulkner. David and Ian, scrubbed, gleaming, smiling, seemed like gold from California.

After lunch, David took us to the show of his Polaroids at Knoedler. The photos, by splintering their subjects, then reassembling the fragments within grids, really are extraordinary, because of David's control of their explosions – a kind of prismatic effect.

After that, I got David and Ian to drop me at the Serpentine Gallery where there is an exhibition of Adrian Stokes – landscapes, nudes, still lifes, bottles. He was certainly a painter of visions, and visions are what I most look for in painting. An iridescent palette of pearly colours – azures, pinks, emeralds, applied to all subjects whether a nude, a landscape or a bottle. He is a painter of trees in landscape, great castellated chestnut trees looking like immense crumbling ochre-coloured towers.

The trouble is that he does not have the talent of his considerable genius. The drawing is tentative, the whole effect thin and dim and transparent as drizzling rain. One is reminded though, of Turner – of the greatest effort to see and record the sublime – that is where we are – the sublime – oh, what a relief.

3 July / *St Jérôme*

We got off at last after a terribly distracting day. All went remarkably well. We had a cabin with four berths all to ourselves on the ferry to Le Havre. We had decided to make ourselves spend the night at some place *en route* – in order not to get too tired.

However, we did not stay anywhere overnight. We got up at seven and drove straight here, stopping off for croissants. During the last part of the journey I thought a lot about Julian Huxley, remembering how wonderful it was to walk with him in Wales, while he identified the song of every bird, discovered flora totally unfamiliar to that region, and talked of his plans and his philosophy. Very Victorian, except that he flouted respectability by talking about sex. Once he told me that J. B. S. Haldane had confided in him that he had a diminutive penis. 'He wanted to show it to me,' said Julian, slapping his thigh, 'but I declined the honour.'

Julian had a very affectionate nature, was witty, cultivated, tolerant – how is it that with all these qualities he was so shut off from other people? He was also self-centred, self-willed, brusque, impatient, sometimes ill-tempered and unlistening. At the centre of all this was some deep dissatisfaction with himself, and some repressed religious instinct. In Wales, where for some days I once went to stay with him and his family, off the puffin-populated island of Skoda, he came down to breakfast, rather shaken one morning, and related an extraordinary dream he had had about meeting a young man who said to him, 'I know who you are, but you do not know me.' 'Who are you?' asked Julian. 'I am Jesus Christ,' was the answer. Julian was simply amazed, incredulous, almost outraged that he, Julian Huxley, should have had this dream. The core of his 'failure' (he thought himself a failure, I'm certain) was lack of self-knowledge. He was an object of astonishment to himself, and because he knew so little about himself, was constantly hurt by the attitude of other people to him.

His French colleagues at UNESCO had a formula for describing him: 'Il est improvisateur. Il improvise toujours.' He was always coming up with projects for UNESCO but they were not, in his own mind, organized with a coherent overall plan. He was out on his own with no real gift for communicating with colleagues. He had, to a self-destructive extent, the idea that what colleagures care about is scientific accuracy in discourse. That mistakes should always be immediately corrected regardless of the sensibilities of those who made them. Thus, chairing a UNESCO meeting, he would interrupt and correct the interpreters – on at least one occasion causing a lady interpreter to burst into tears and rush from the room. In this way he provided his opponents with a ready-made argument against him – that he was inconsiderate, whereas in fact he was the kindest of men.

When there was the General Meeting of UNESCO at which the Americans decided to set Julian aside, Julian could not understand why he had so many opponents. 'What amazes me', he said to me, 'is that there are so many people here who really seem to hate me.' He was quite right of course to feel that there was nothing hateful about him; he simply failed to realize that he sometimes behaved to colleagues in ways that made them fear and hate him. He was always consistently kind and forbearing and sweet to me. Even so, I once had an experience with him which, if I had been ambitious for promotion in UNESCO, might have upset me. I had come back from a UNESCO-sponsored meeting in Venice, and went to a party of UNESCO officials. Beaming, Julian said, 'How was Venice?' I started to tell him that the curator of San Marco (which is in a perpetual state of disintegration) had asked me whether UNESCO could do anything to help save it (subsequently UNESCO has done so). In front of all our colleagues Julian exploded, 'How could you be so stupid as to think we could support such a proposal? Don't you realize that because we are an international organization if we proposed that, we would have to support Santa Sofia and a dozen other mosques and temples all over the world?' I thought this was funny (I somehow felt impervious to Julian's snubs) but my colleagues felt resentful on my behalf (or pretended they did) and did not notice that within ten minutes Julian was explaining he did not mean what he had said, perhaps we could do something about St Mark's, etc.

At the UNESCO Conference of 1948 at which the American Delegation, led by Archibald MacLeish, under the impression that he was 'soft on commies', used all its influence to remove Julian from the post of Director General, that humbug Archibald MacLeish told me that we were participating in a Greek tragedy in which Julian Huxley, much as Archie loved him, had to play the role of sacrificial hero. As head of the American Delegation, MacLeish himself assumed the role of Creon.

When I think of Julian I think of him when he was head of the Zoo and took us to look at camels on heat – their swollen tongues covered with spittle lolling from their opened mouths. Or again, of staying with him and Juliette and the two boys in Wales. Once Julian and I were alone together in a boat, trawling. We caught a mackerel just outside the harbour, rushed into the house, which was empty, grilled it and ate it then and there, just the two of us, within half an hour of catching it. Julian was delighted. I think I liked him so much because I was always aware of this happy and suffering childish Julian under all the armature which had formed over him, and despite the demons which possessed him.

It has been over 90 degrees by midday every day since we've been here. If only it would get cool I would do a lot of work. Have reread *World Within World* and have a lot of ideas for the new edition.

Have read the typescript draft of PB's book about me. I dread its being published because the excessive praise the author lavishes on my work would bring both him and me into contempt. I have written suggesting he wait a year or so before publishing. By then I shall have published a *Collected Poems* with new poems in it and also the new edition of *WWW*. The extraordinary thing about his book – which made sections of it very valuable to me personally – is that although he has almost no sense of my limitations, he has very great insight into my intentions. Again and again, he described what I intended to do in a poem (or in *Trial of a Judge*), which makes clear to me why I failed to achieve it. After reading his description of six or so poems, I took up *The Still Centre* and more or less rewrote six poems. In fact I now intend to base the new *Collected Poems* on critical insights based on his analysis of my intentions.

I now have an idea of what I should write in the Introduction and should set it down before I forget. I should divide my poems into categories of those (a) that I consider finished, (b) that have been so widely anthologized that they are no longer my property to play around with, (c) that are ideas for poems incomplete in the writing but which are still in my own mind in the process of being written, even if I drafted them (and published the drafts) forty years ago. In respect to certain autobiographical memories I have 'total recall', and these include what I wanted to do when I set out to write a poem. Certain poems in my books remain botched sketches or drafts – notably 'The Marginal Field', 'The Past Value', 'Exiles from Their Land', 'History Their Domicile'. I can simply take these up, remembering what I intended, and have another attempt at doing it. And the strange thing is that I feel very much as if I had the power to do this now.

Other poems, e.g., 'The Uncreating Chaos' are obfuscated by irrelevant imagery. Still others suffer from what I'd call 'unreleased rhythmic energy' and often this critic in praising something puts his finger on what is to me precisely the weakness. Altogether these poems are full of energies, ideas, simplicities of lines, rhythms and images, crying to be let out. If only I could release them they might be positive instead of being, so many of them, the negative lumpish efforts which weigh down my *Collected Poems* of 1955.

14 November / *London*

The past week has been terribly busy – which means I've done far too little work, and time is running out, running out. Every morning since Tuesday I've been to the Royal Free Hospital having radiation for a patch of skin cancer. One hardly ever sees a really scared or suffering face, scarcely ever a happy uncaring one. Patients look as if they are occupied in some particular business – an office job, or the routine of living which has terminated in the routine of dying (perhaps).

On Tuesday had lunch with Karl Miller. With his rimless or very thin rimmed spectacles, his thin face, his tall, slightly hunched body, he looked a bit like a medical specialist. He told me I was looking remarkably well. I told him he was looking all right too. He looked as if he was thinking, 'What an unperceptive fool' when I said this. He said insistently, 'You do look well' (as though he were saying, 'Well you are stupid') and added, 'I've always thought of you as the perfect example of *mens sana in corpore sano*'!

Karl is ironic. We dined that night with the Bonham Carters* who were giving a farewell dinner to Hugh Lunghi who is leaving *Index*. Mark has behaved with great responsibility and conscientiousness as Director of Writers and Scholars – a position for which he receives nothing and which he might well have treated as a token one. He has strong views about everything, talks a lot about his family. I feel very sympathetic to him.

18 November / *London*

The day before this Philip Spender and I lunched with Ronald Dworkin† at the Garrick and discussed the fund-raising I propose to do in America in March for *Index* and Writers and Scholars. Dworkin very helpful. He had the amused air of a highly intelligent and enlightened man who treats serious things in a smiling way, which lightens them.

---

* Mark Bonham Carter, Chairman Writers and Scholars Educational Trust since 1977.

† Ronald Dworkin, Professor of Jurisprudence at Oxford since 1969. Council of Writers and Scholars Educational Trust.

21 November

Time rushes by, I write reviews and essays. I have got into a habit which may be bad. If I am writing something – even a review – I find it very difficult even to think of finishing it – I have to force myself to do so. Writing seems a kind of state of mind I get into – rather a befogged one. Any piece of writing which is worth doing could expand indefinitely. For instance, in reviewing Ian Hamilton's book about Robert Lowell, which is rather bare and factual, ideally I would have liked to have given a full and just account of what Hamilton's book contains and then enclosed this within my own thoughts about Lowell.

I have an entirely different experience when writing journals or letters. I can sit down and write straightaway whatever is in, or on, my mind. It is like digging directly into the life around one – a spadeful of soil is flung down upon the page. Thoughts are plucked from the air where they are on the wing and all that matters is to catch them.

Joe Ackerley, when he was literary editor of the *Listener*, once told me that he was worried about one of his reviewers, Geoffrey Grigson. To send G. a book to review was an act of hostility against the author of the book.

All my life there have been critics who set out to be the 'terrors of the earth' and who make their editors fellow conspirators in this. Usually they are scholarship boys with a strong sense of inferiority, who hook on to the older universities, perhaps become dons. The *don terrible* is a blown-up version of the *enfant terrible*. Having got his economic claws into Oxford or Cambridge, he can redeem himself in his own eyes only by attacking the university that nourishes him, which he sees as a vast establishment Rock of Ages into which he bores holes that will finally bring it crashing down.

In my lifetime, F. R. Leavis was the type of such a don and Cambridge University – particularly its English School – was the fortress – or perhaps I should say great mountain of Roquefort cheese – which he chose to batten on and bore into. Of course, there were some particularly rotten senior members of the university who opposed his efforts, greatly aiding him by doing so, because his followers could claim with some justice that they were persecuting their declared enemy.

Commentary
1983

In the spring of 1983 I went to America with Lois Sieff, a director of Writers and Scholars International, trying to raise money for Index. *I was completely inexperienced in fund-raising, and my journal becomes concerned with my amateurish attempts to do so. A few hundred dollars were raised by speaking and handing out leaflets at cocktail parties in Washington and Chicago. But we would hardly have done more than cover our expenses had it not been for the enterprise and generosity of Anne Cox Chambers in Atlanta, who organized a reading given by Joseph Brodsky and myself at the Historical Society in that city, the benefit of which went to* Index. *Six months later a similar reading at the Metropolitan Museum in New York was organized by Mrs Samuel Reed and Mrs John Fairchild. This time, in addition to Brodsky and me, Derek Walcott and John Ashbery read poems.*

12

Journal
1983

I rang the editor of *GEO* who had commissioned me to interview
Henry Moore. He said, 'There's a lot of disagreement in this office
about your article. It's unorthodox by our standards.' I felt upset by
this but hung on to the fact that N. thought it good – so I shouldn't
care a fuck about the editor. I should say to him, in effect, all I care
about is the $2,000 you contracted to pay. I ought to do this but won't.
I'll offer to revise the article. I'll accept $1,000, $500, nothing – just
to forget about it. I've never been able to think big (if $2,000 is big)
about money.

I rang the Department of Biology at UCLA. I thought to myself,
'He dialled the number of the Biology Department and B. answered
the phone.' This was so unlikely – considering that I hadn't the faintest
idea where B. (who had last sent me a postcard from Argentina on his
way back from a scientific expedition in the South Atlantic) was – that
I invented it as fiction, but it gave me a bit the sense of the miraculous.
In fact the person who answered the phone had never heard of B. So
I asked for his professor, got on to him at once and asked if he knew
anything of his whereabouts. He said, 'Yes, I've just been talking to
him. He must still be outside in the corridor, I'll see if I can find him'
and a moment later B. was talking to me. His voice had a kind of
springiness about it. He kept laughing, chortling, as he did when I
first knew him six years ago in Gainesville.

Woke up this morning unhappy about my mission for *Index*. Lizzie
had said to me two days ago that T. had said to her: 'Who wants to
support *Index*? It contains nothing but gloomy news about repression,
and who would want to read it?' I see her point. Lois told me at
drinks before our dinner that some other possible sponsor had said
much the same to her, adding that the name *Index* should be changed.
He suggested what seemed to me an equally gloomy name – 'Censored'

– with a large X half crossing it out. I woke this morning with the name 'Voice' in my head, and, at the moment, find that good – good for its obviousness and, imagining the cover, think the image of Munch's picture *The Cry* should be in it. Why not, 'Shout' or 'The Shout'?

13 April

Lunch at the Century Club with Herbert Mitgang of the *New York Times* Book Section. Before lunch he interviewed me, nominally about *China Diary* but really over my whole career. I told him about Writers and Scholars. He said he was head of an organization called 'The Writers' League' and suggested that they might be helpful particularly in cases of refugee writers.

At five-thirty drinks at the Westbury Hotel with Mort Zuckerman and Mrs O. who cross-examined Michael Scammell,* Lois and me about helping us. Discussion of the form the meeting is going to take in Washington next week.

14 April

Lunch at a restaurant called Quo Vadis with an elderly interviewer, a cultivated bon-viveur type. Find set interviews tiring. Read. Then dinner at Sardi's.

Telephoned Christopher who was delighted to be called and wanted to go on talking for hours. We did in fact talk for half an hour. Discussed loss of memory in old age. Later he asked for my number, and writing it down at his end, in Santa Monica, he said: 'A horrible old wizened claw writes crooked letters.' I said: 'All the same that's exactly the kind of thing you'd say if it was fifty years ago and I was telephoning you in Berlin.' 'Yes,' he said. 'What could be more untrue than that remark someone made – "If things are not getting better, they're getting worse?"' 'Who said that?' I asked. 'Oh some awful old nineteenth-century bore. Gladstone perhaps. What a shit.' After we put down receivers I thought: 'Perhaps it was Tolstoy.'

Dinner at the Russian Tea Room with Bill Mazzocco. He talked a lot about politics and questioned me about the thirties. Said they were difficult to understand. How could people then be anti-fascist and at the

* First editor of *Index on Censorship*; biographer of Solzhenitsyn.

same time support disarmament? I said it was unrealistic but we tried to believe in the myth of Collective Security. I said after all it was not dissimilar from the attitude of people today who support nuclear disarmament in the face of Russian nuclear forces. He said it was dissimilar because today what was involved was total destruction of the world. I said, well, in those days we did imagine that cities would be totally destroyed by the new bombs of that time. Still, I admit there was a difference.

After dinner we walked along 57th Street to Madison Avenue. Wonderful reflection of the golden skyscraper in the black-mirror glass walls of the Avon building across the road. The golden skyscraper seemed painted in livid shimmering van Gogh yellow on the matt black surface on which it was reflected. We walked along our side of the street watching that image, which suddenly inexplicably disappeared and left nothing but an intense almost roaring blackness reminding me of that incredible black produced by some modern print-makers. I went back to my hotel, rang B, to whom I relayed my conversation with Christopher and told him that I was going to go out again and look at that New York vision. He laughed. 'Well, if you walk in New York at midnight, put all your money in your shoes.' Then I went out again and walked down Madison Avenue, turned into 58th Street and walked on the pavement (where there were two or three dangerous-looking figures lingering) opposite the black-glass skyscraper. For a long time nothing appeared, then suddenly I saw what was a milk-white pale reflection of the golden skyscraper, seeming much smaller than before. The lower storeys of the building were divided by a gulf of darkness from the golden ball at the top, floating above them like a hovering crown.

I phoned Christopher again in order to tell him what the Immigration Officer said to me when I arrived in NY four mornings ago. He seemed rather an intelligent friendly man and rather welcoming. Then, looking at my visa, from the fifties or sixties, he said: 'There's something odd about this, I'd better find out.' He took the passport and disappeared through a door at the end of the hall. Returning a few minutes later, he said, 'Something arcane, from the far past. Two "i"s with special dots on them, meaning socialist or some shit, we don't have that now.' I had told that story to Herbert Mitgang when he interviewed me. He said: 'We still can't print the word "shit" in the *New York Times*.'

This morning I worked at the Fairchilds'* apartment in Gracie Square. It overlooks the East River, swirling dark grey and white waters seen on the far side of the road and lashing around a little island opposite with a miniature lighthouse at the end of it. I typed out part of an article. Just as I was about to leave, Jill Fairchild came in. They had been at Washington overnight dining at the White House. I asked how Reagan looked. 'He looks as if he hasn't a care in the world. Usually they look a bit furrowed or worn down by the time they've been this long in office. But he looks younger than any of us.' I commented on a still life of oranges and a bottle of Vichy water against a pale blue background, standing on an easel. 'Oh, I don't know anything about painting. I just try to teach myself, maybe I'd be better if I took classes but it just doesn't seem worth it.' She said this with her throwaway lightness and charm, which goes with a sort of wildness in her features.

In the afternoon Lois and I went to see a Miss F. at her skyscraper office. She was very tall and white with blonde hair loose over her shoulders, quite the collegiate Valkyrie, but for a faint yet formidable touch of austerity under her friendliness. 'I have all the time in the world for you,' her look seemed to say, but a tautness of her neck said *sotto voce*, 'You'd better make it snappy.' The room was vast with immense armchairs set so far apart that they seemed built for giants with voices like megaphones. A few modern abstract paintings of the sort that seem to come in all sizes punctuated the great spaces of the walls.

Miss F. listened with the utmost attention while Lois explained about *Index* to her, then she said thoughtfully, 'The thing is to get these things started. What you want is to interest a few people and then get them to talk to a few more people. After a time everything suddenly comes together. Now how much money would you be wanting?'

Lois hesitated, then she said: 'We were thinking of something in the neighbourhood of $100,000.' Miss F. seemed to think this quite reasonable. 'Well, if you put on an entertainment for 1,000 people, and each person paid $100 you'd get your $100,000. Or you get ten people each to provide ten thousand. It depends who you ask – I could ask Alexandra Schlesinger about Norman Mailer.'

---

*John and Jill Fairchild. John Fairchild is publisher of *Women's Wear Daily* and other magazines.

I said I had seen Alexandra only yesterday – at drinks with Jo Alsop. She warmed perceptibly, 'Well, Alexandra's about my best friend.' I thought Americans are really wonderful – not just that they give money – but that they are capable of such seriousness in asking their friends. It's really more the time-giving than the money-giving which seems admirable.

Afterwards, Lois said: 'Raising money's such a strange game. You go on asking, nothing happens, then suddenly you seem to strike it rich.' I said that Miss F's strangely precise cold/warm manner, her great precision of utterance, controlled friendliness, reserved intelligence, reminded me of someone – who was it? Mrs Graham of the *Washington Post*.

The editor of *GEO* wrote saying that my Henry Moore piece was unacceptable by their standards. 'Our "conversation" features in a conventional Q-and-A format, while your article is most unconventional, combining interview with diary entries, poetry and third-person narrative. You are perhaps too creative for us.

'Also what we were looking for ... were the philosophical musings or reflections of an artist on the subjects of art, life and creativity. Instead of addressing these topics, Moore dwells primarily on his schooldays. What he has to say, unfortunately, is not very interesting.'

The letter ends, 'Although this project did not "work out" we hope that – not just now perhaps, but some day in the near future – you will consider writing something else for us.'

His name was Boreham, or something like that. He enclosed a copy of the current number of his boring magazine, which contains a lot of photographs of hideous centenarians. I wrote back answering his final paragraph. 'Thank you for your kind suggestion that I should consider writing for you in the future. Doubtless when I am as old and hideous as the centenarians who fill up so much space in the particularly boring new number of *GEO* which you enclosed, I shall take up this offer.'

19 April / *Washington*

I'm staying with Mrs M. in Georgetown. We went to a very high-powered party given by Mort Zuckerman,* which included Senator Kennedy. I spoke for about ten minutes. Apparently several cheques have been, or will be, produced.

* Proprietor of *Atlantic Monthly*.

I went to the Library of Congress twice these two days – in the poetry room where I worked thirteen years ago. Nancy, the Poetry Consultant's assistant, was still there, looking completely unchanged – she was very attentive and affectionate and everyone welcomed me. Tony Hecht is now poetry consultant.

He introduced me nicely before my lecture this evening at the Library of Congress.

But one must never take American applause too seriously. Americans are pleased not to be disappointed by a reading or lecture. They thank you for not letting them down and don't mind being a bit excessive about it. I said in my lecture, speaking of *The Waste Land*: 'The poetry is images wrapped up in rhythm.' A young man came up to me at the party afterwards and thanked me for this.

20 April

A rather discouraging day from the point of view of fund-raising. This afternoon Lois and I met a professional fund-raiser, obviously quite a decent person, not going to take us on unless it was both in his interest and ours, quite sympathetic. He said candidly that no rich person was going to give us money unless doing so brought him something. Mr X supported us because, by inviting people to meet me, he – a new arrival here – could meet a whole crowd of rich people. I had – and have – no idea that I am such a social asset. I can't really believe it. And it is utterly confusing to attempt to understand it. Lois said, after he had left, that it made us into prostitutes. I don't really mind that, I mind the confusion, and I want the money for *Index*.

This evening Mrs O. provided a meal for people in government. One of the ladies gave me a look of leering hatred. Mrs O. had arranged her sitting room with many tables, only three people sitting at each. I had two ladies who talked about how they were both crazy about tombstones, a vice they were thrilled to find they shared. When we had finished eating Mrs O. suddenly stood up, tinkled a little bell and introduced me, 'the great poet', etc. I did my spiel. I think people gave me credit for trying hard. The grey solemn men listened attentively. Mrs O. asked if there were any questions. The lady who had given me the leering look of hatred got up and asked why we supported communism in Latin America. I said we did not support it, we simply reported cases of censorship, etc. The senior members of the State Department and the ambassadorial contingent took my side. Someone asked me why people were romantic about revolutionaries all over the world and hence anti-American. I said that I thought there were two reasons. (1) In the nuclear debate America was attacked because the CND people knew America would respond. Russia not attacked fundamentally because they would get no response from the Kremlin. (2) I thought that the guilt European powers had formerly had about their own empires was now transferred to America, which was felt to have inherited the imperialist role.

Lois had said after our meeting this afternoon that it was sickening to ask people to help who did not really care about the cause one was begging for. I do have a certain respect for the State Department people. They are conscientious, much maligned. Ultimately it is simply embarrassing to meet them because poetry strikes them as a kind of hypochondria, an imaginary illness compelling them to show a sympathy they do not really feel. And anyway, with them, I do not feel I am a poet, which adds further falsity to the situation.

22 April / *Boston*

Television programme about *China Diary*. My interviewer, enthusiastic about the book, was so pleased with our interview, which was live on their breakfast AM programme, that she asked me to go on after the ads, and to extend the programme. All the interviewers have been extremely pleasant and have taken the trouble to read the book – much more than the English ones have done.

I went to the Boston Museum of Fine Arts. The picture that fascinates me today is the Sargent of a family with children in the foreground, and behind, figures beside enormous porcelain jars (shows how atrocious my visual memory is that I can't retain all this). There is a curtain of abstract triangular shape to one side and the shapes throughout the picture are so silhouetted that they might be cut-outs. The composition obviously refers to Velázquez's *Las Meninas*. With all this, the picture has the virtuoso flourish of Sargent. I walked through the Chinese and Indian rooms. The wonderful collection of Oriental art is what this museum is famous for. I feel – almost with a stunned dread – the influence of that calm dignity – perfection of pose, elaboration of detail, all contained within a form controlled as a drawn circle – there seems a lifetime of study.

I left my luggage at the Ritz Carlton, and had lunch there. Thoughts of Pauline (de Rothschild). How she went to a Boston hospital for examination, before being flown to Auckland, New Zealand, for open-heart surgery. Faced with this terrific operation, she seemed completely calm. In fact, relieved. While I was visiting her in hospital she had some forms to fill in with the usual question about what racial group you belong to. 'I suppose I'd better put "Aryan",' she said, 'though it might be different next week.'

Perhaps after all the fund-raising has not been a complete failure. Lois writes that 'Teddy Kennedy will be making a contribution'* and that others would probably send something.

She sent the list of members of the Administration we met at Mrs O's.

Copying out the names, it struck me as extraordinary that these people should – not just one or two, but all of them – have gone to the dinner. They were not, it seems, going just to see Mrs O. They must have been for some reason interested in *Index*. In no other country would a dozen members of the government turn up to meet a poet. The answer must partly be in the smallness (comparatively) of Washington and the strange compounding of political with social life. At breakfast at Mrs O's I opened the *Washington Post* and it suddenly struck me as being like a magazine of some large English public school in which conventions of politeness were observed. Editors, columnists, senators, congressmen all met in the drawing rooms and knew each other very well so that there was some artificiality about editorials and attacks on one another.

24 April / *New York*

Tremendous downpour and gale during the night and continuing until about 11 a.m. New York, much more than London, can seem a rocky outpost in the Atlantic – like Land's End – or the Giant's Causeway – all these skyscrapers lashed by the elements, water pouring down their sides.

Lunch with Dick Sennett.† We exchanged impressions of fund-raising in Washington. He said the awful thing about people in public life is that they never stop flattering one another. They were doomed to do so.

A man appeared, who looked like a cross between Wystan and Chester. Very camp manner. He said he had neither eaten meat nor

---

* Senator Kennedy did send a contribution to *Index*.
† Richard Sennett. Social psychologist and novelist.

had sex for eight years. I liked him. He explained arrangements about celebrations for tenth anniversary of Wystan's death, 18 October 1983. I signed a document saying I would participate in this. Joseph Brodsky arrived with another large man – evidently a scholar. Joseph very warm. A lot of questions. 'Stephen, now there is a question I must ask you. When did T. S. Eliot first get to read the poems of Thomas Hardy?' He suggested that Eliot was influenced in his modernism by Hardy who wrote poetry on modern themes, unlike most of his contemporaries. I said Eliot disliked H's poetry, thought it amateurish (so did Hardy himself, who didn't really consider himself a pro, comparable with Tennyson, Browning, Swinburne). The point about 'modernism' is that it was extremely self-conscious. Also it was influenced by French continental models – whereas Hardy was totally English. There was something of 1880s French-influenced Symbolist poetry in Eliot and Pound. We asked about modernism in Russia, Joseph was not very forthcoming because he wanted to discuss his theories about modern English poetry. He produced a few quips of the outrageous kind.

Susan Sontag and David Rieff appeared. Susan very sweet and cosy. We talked again about the Auden memorial service. A plaque is to be put up at 77 St Mark's Place, etc.

25 April

Lunch at Century Club with Ronald Dworkin – always very sympathetic with his wide schoolboy grin. Discussed ways and means of promoting *Index*. Arthur Schlesinger (who also has a wide schoolboy grin) came over from another table and joined us for coffee. He said that *Index* was a noble cause – there could not be a better – and that he would help. There are obviously people of good will who we could call on – but the question is how – apart from asking them to subscribe. George Plimpton, Jean Stein and others would doubtless give parties but there is not much point in soliciting their help and kindness unless we have some idea what the follow-up would be. Ronnie thought it a good idea that I should go and see Bob Bernstein – which I shall do on Monday at three. He also agreed with Lois that I should discuss the possibility of someone fund-raising on a semi-professional basis.

I forgot to go to Ambassador Thompson's party on Friday last. Lady Thompson very kindly got Janet Adam Smith to ring and explain that they quite understood. I live in a panic about engagements.

27 April

Evening dinner chez Ambassador (to the UN) Thompson and his wife. Very forgiving about my having completely forgotten to dine there last week – a thing that when I realized it made me sweat all over. He is the nephew of Janet Adam Smith* (ex-Mrs Michael Roberts) who was there and very charming. Somehow looks more attractive than she did in her twenties, when I first knew her, when she was literary editor of the *Listener*. Helpful and kind as she was then, she looked a bit forbidding, now she is all sweetness.

28 April

Lunch with Richard Wollheim. Called for him first at his apartment at East 57th, which seems rather nice for New York (New Yorkers have to be very rich to live in what by English standards are pleasant apartments and houses). Anyway the room was illuminated by the sight of beautiful Day and her beautiful baby. Richard and I went out to lunch, Richard saying as soon as we got into the street, 'I'm afraid I haven't given much thought to the difficult question of where we shall eat. In this district where every shop turns out, on inspection, to be some kind of boutique, it's difficult to come to a decision.' We put our noses into a boutique which was somehow also a salad bar full of old ladies seated at small square tables, and with whatever volume knob that controls the sound made by old ladies turned on to loudest – and decided we would not be able to talk there. We left the shop, ran into John Richardson, who was with a cousin of the Queen, had a few moments' conversation in which one or two indiscretions of mine may have done us all permanent injury, and walked on.

We found a restaurant recommended by John Richardson. Richard talked about being at Columbia and living in New York. He said it was different from the impression one gets by just visiting. I supposed that he was referring to that strange feeling one can have here of being both made a lot of and neglected.

Went to Random House and called on the President, Bob Bernstein. Someone had told me that he is the most natural, sincere, well-disposed person to be found anywhere. At our meeting he certainly showed himself as this. His general attitude to me was that I was a 9-year-old

---

* Later Mrs John Carleton. In the 1930s, as literary editor of the *Listener*, she gave much encouragement to young poets.

plunged into the purgatory of fund-raising, and innocently counting on the good will of people. It did strike me that I have been quite wrong to think that Americans identify with situations outside America. It is no use saying to them, 'Imagine yourself a prisoner in Omsk, Krakow, Bratislava, Johannesburg' – they cannot imagine any such thing.

In the evening I read poems at Long Island.

When I came into the bar at the communal centre I was confronted by a man with a large beard and a larger nose, who shouted, 'Why, he even looks like a poet!' and asked me if I wanted a drink. I said I'd like a bourbon on the rocks. He got it for me, saying, 'That will stir the embers of creativity.' An Indian lady in a sari and many bangles who seemed to be chairwoman of the English Department said that unfortunately my appearance at the centre coincided with two other events. 'What are they?' I asked another lady. She said there was a banquet for honours students and, somewhere else, a meeting of female law students who were to entertain six lady judges. There was also to be a lecture entitled, 'How to wear judicial robes on the bench'. The Indian chairwoman clasped her hands and exclaimed, 'But our meeting will be the sublimest of the three.'

After that there was a dinner for about thirty-five of us at two or three tables in the communal dining hall. Another large-bearded man appeared and started reminiscing in a solemn voice about how we had met in Constantinople and gone to look at some newly revealed wall paintings. For this he went on to talk about the Muslim revival. 'I have a theory about this,' he said, 'that everyone longs to belong to something and if he cannot belong to the nation itself, then to something larger, the Race.' He then said he had a theory as to who were the two greatest image-making geniuses of the century, one of them an American unparalleled in the history of America. 'Now who is that American, the greatest-but-one maker of images in this century?' 'Roosevelt,' said someone. This was pooh-poohed. 'Eliot,' I whispered – this was ignored. 'Walt Disney.' The second large beard roared triumphantly.

After the reading I was driven home by the people who had fetched me, Mr and Mrs N. From the back of the car Mrs N. started needling me about Virginia Woolf, about whom she is writing a thesis. 'Do you consider that Woolf was able to have the quiet she needed to write her novels as a result of being married to Leonard Woolf?' 'Certainly,' I said. 'Then you think that if she'd been left alone without him, Woolf would not have been able to write so well?' 'Yes.' 'Do you think that Leonard Woolf appreciated Woolf's talents, or do you think he prevented them from flowering in a way they might have done, had he not enforced his personality on Woolf?' There was so much Woolf this and Woolf that; finally I got annoyed and said, 'Anyone who calls Woolf Woolf can't possibly understand Woolf.' 'Then what would you call her?' 'Virginia Woolf. That's what everyone called her. That's how she signed her books. No one ever called her or thought of her as just Woolf.' Silence from the back of the car. Then I said: 'Do you call Jane Austen, Austen, George Eliot, Eliot?' 'I only call Eliot George Eliot if I wish to distinguish her from T. S. Eliot. Certainly I call Jane Austen, Austen. After all you call John Keats, Keats, and P. B. Shelley, Shelley.' Quite true. Why should women writers be deprived of the male writers' privilege of being deprived of their Christian names?

29 April

On fine days, after the winter, New York comes out like torrents of spring, cascading swollen, golden, muddy, frothing. The Fairchild apartment where I am staying looks on to pools – playgrounds into which children of all colours congregate, darting, leaping, zig-zagging like minnows.

Wrote, read, made phone calls this morning. Trying to keep up.

Go with Jill (Fairchild) to the Steven Buckley show in a 57th Street gallery thinking there is going to be a party. The gallery is totally empty. The party took place on Wednesday. A pang. I miss my English artist friends in the empty gallery, under the harsh light.

Back to Gracie Square. Stand on the balcony. Watch joggers on the riverside path below. I said to Jill I thought that with a telescopic lens and a movie camera she could make a wonderful film just from this balcony. She said it would all be from the same angle.

Dinner at a Chinese restaurant with Barbara Epstein,* Dominique Nabokov,† Elizabeth Lowell.‡ Dominique is admirable, indomitable. She said, with her usual candour, that she would like to marry again

---

* Barbara Epstein, co-editor of the *New York Review of Books*.

† Dominique Nabokov, widow of Nicolas Nabokov.

‡ Elizabeth Hardwick, novelist and critic, was married to Robert Lowell. A founder of the *New York Review of Books*.

but that all the men she had met proved, after a few weeks, too dull. She has drunk of Honey Dew, the fatal curse of having lived with a man so crazy, amusing, egotistic and demanding as Nicolas Nabokov. (Women who had affairs with Cyril Connolly used to say: 'After Cyril, everyone is boring.')

1 May / *Chicago*

Arrival at Chicago by air can be one of the most sensationally beautiful experiences of flying. It was so yesterday – suddenly there was the immense shining shield of the lake, a wide curve on the horizon, held up against the sky and flecked with clouds along the base near the shore. As we descended, scattered pools and rivulets of water against the dark earth, silver-shining, seemed to bulge and swell out above the soil, like drops of quicksilver on a tray. Then in the rapidly nearing distance, main roads and highways overlapped lesser roads like tape running across them. The perfect clover-patterns of the highway interchanges looked like the ritualistic signs of some religion hewn into the landscape. And as the outskirts of the city appeared, the net of criss-crossing roads seemed delicate as spiders' webs, the organic work of pure nature, instead of the manmade grid between ramshackle hideous houses, which I knew it to be.

I remembered one long-ago winter when I had flown to Chicago and against the frozen lake the skyscrapers had looked like huge rock crystals.

From the air, at a certain distance, the works of man can seem like natural encrustations, beautiful parasitic growths like mistletoe on bark or lichen or coral. One can imagine them to be the cellular product of minute animals, toiling endlessly, unconscious of purpose, like the insects that built the Great Barrier Reef.

At O'Hare slight panic on realizing that I had left behind my diary and had no idea where I was going. Luckily I did remember the name Len Manilow* (having spoken to him several times on the phone). The Manilows are friendly, on-the-mark people.

I retreated into what seems a kind of stupor. Then it poured with rain and there was a fog. These effects came to a climax at about five, just at the time of the *Index* party, preventing a lot of people from

---

* Art collector and businessman.

coming. But about thirty or forty did come and were very concerned about *Index*, very cordial, something about them less distrait than in NY. Mrs Manilow spoke very well, then I spoke – rather bumblingly I thought, still stupefied – then Mr Manilow spoke much to the point – telling people to take our promissory gift forms.

I woke at six, left the house at six forty-five and flew to NY, arriving there at ten forty-five.

Lunch at the Four Seasons Restaurant with Mort Zuckerman. He reminded me of Len Manilow, more intense perhaps. They are both alert, concentrated, seeing their respective businesses as completely absorbing all their interests – as what Americans mean by the word 'creative'. After we'd discussed the prospects for *Index*, our conversation became wide-ranging. He said his main interest now is the *Atlantic Monthly*, which he had bought when it was run down and which he had completely changed. 'How did you go about that?' I asked. 'Well, first I redesigned the whole magazine; then I quintupled expenditure on articles, staff, everything; then I hired a new editor and new assistant editors. Then I cleared out and interfered in nothing.'

When he bought the *AM* he went to the editor of the *New Yorker* and asked his advice on how to go about changing it. The editor said, 'My advice is – whatever you do, do quickly.' An exhilarating man.

3 May / *New York*

Jill (Fairchild) was amusing about the Prokosch book.* We both agreed that for the most part it was sad, but funny about Emerald Cunard and in one or two other places. I told her when I was 21 or so Prokosch had sent me a little pamphlet of his poems. Out of it fluttered a photograph of him, naked. Wystan, to whom I showed it, was rather intrigued (which may throw light on the Turkish bath scene in Prokosch's book). Strange how Prokosch, on the basis of one successful novel, but really on his good looks, walked into and out of people's lives, asking them pointed questions, and extracting their secrets from them, which he proceeded to write down. Prokosch claims that he has perfect verbal memory, but in fact a lot of the things he records as having been said by his victims do not sound convincing. Auden never talked in that 'my dear boy' kind of way.

* *Voices: A Memoir* by Frederic Prokosch.

5 May

Read and wrote letters. This diary. Went to the Mayflower Hotel and picked up David (Hockney) who was in the lobby being photographed by some Japanese fan. We took a taxi to the Century Club. In the taxi David told me straightaway of his latest ideas about photography as an extension of cubism. He said it was no coincidence that black-and-white movies began at the same time as cubism and that no one had ever remarked on this before. I have forgotten what followed on from this. He told me that a month ago he had been in NY visiting the sick bed of his friend Jo, a male model who had died of the mysterious sexual disease, AIDS. David visited him three times daily in hospital. I asked whether Jo had had a lot of sex. 'Yes, more than anyone I've ever known. He was completely promiscuous. He'd go with people five or six times a day. He'd had every single sexual disease.' All this seemed inexplicable, baffling, terrifying.

6 May / *London*

Back in London after a hectic day in New York.

At 10 a.m. I went with Jill Fairchild, Dominique Nabokov and Keith Milow to the exhibition *Holbein and the Court of Henry VIII* at the Morgan Library. These wonderfully clear faces, with eyes fixed so that the artist can catch in them the expression of the soul, seem very familiar to us - queens, princes, aristocrats, statesmen, poets, courtiers, gentlemen - a good number of whom had their heads chopped off. Writers of two of the most beautiful poems in English, Surrey's poem about his childhood and youth in Windsor, written in prison, Wyatt's 'They flee from me, that sometime did me seek'. One can imagine this court well, so very English, snobbish, poeticizing, rhyming, gossiping, laughing and weeping, obsequious yet not at all inhibited, still human - not frozen into the stiff machinery of politeness, wit and rank of the French court. I could imagine conversing with and moving among all but the most exalted of these, more easily than with many of the New Yorkers walking in the street outside.

After that I went to the FFE* offices. They seemed very open about everything, perfectly friendly, and not obstructing us at *Index*.

I had lunch with Fred S. - who is intensely interested in my anecdotes about people and things and has a way of leading me on which I fall for.

* Fund for Freedom of Expression.

After lunch we walked across Central Park to the Metropolitan Museum and looked at the exhibition from the Vatican. Completely new to me were the Roman sarcophagi with bas-reliefs in shining white marble, so pure in their hewn lights and shadows, flattened out under the perhaps too bright museum lighting so that at first I thought they were enlarged photographs.

9 May

Yesterday we went to the University of Kent at Canterbury, for a celebration in honour of T. S. Eliot. First there was a showing of a film about him. Interviews with people, also selections from *Murder in the Cathedral* and *The Family Reunion*, etc. These were extremely good, I thought, bringing out the desolation on which his religion was based. Reminiscences, chiefly by Hope Mirrlees, of Vivien, his first wife. (Although Tom's declared aim in his writing was to be impersonal, the impression I had from knowing him was of personality, his asceticism, the union of the physical man with some mystical self invisibly striving towards God, rejecting the society (mostly Bloomsbury) in which he lived, in order to exist in his poetry and his religion.

The speeches and papers read were something of a caricature. There was an ex-British Council type, very popular with the audience – who gave examples of Eliot's wit and humour – for the most part less witty or genuinely funny than the despised Cyril Connolly. There was a strong strain of the facetious about E, and an endlessly drawn-out example of this was an interminable letter – read out by Tom Faber (son of Geoffrey and Enid Faber) – in which Eliot responded to some equally facetious letter written to him by some member of the Board of Directors of Faber – perhaps Frank Morley – and provoked by the fact that there was an advertisement for a nightclub in London called Eliot something or other.*

There was a good speech by Denis Donoghue – something by me about the effect of *The Waste Land* on 'our' generation. I could see why Eliot liked the bland clubman, the British Council type. Valerie sat there discreet, knowing, sensible, really humorous – more so than Tom – and intelligent, loving, lovable and utterly devoted, a goddess in a temple more than Christian perhaps. I would burn incense to her. The deepest thing in Tom Eliot was perhaps a kind of loving irony.

* Eliot's Club, proprietor Arthur Eliot.

I was a terrible fool with him, and certainly provoked the irony, but Valerie somehow reassures me that he also sent in my direction some love. It is nice of her to feel that I deserved some love – and I suspect she knows all the reasons for irony. Forgiveness.

10 May

A letter from the PM's office saying she was recommending me to the Queen for a knighthood. Although I've all too often said I would never accept this, when I got the letter I realized at once that I would do so, both for myself and for Natasha. There are those I respect for despising such things – they are the best. But there are many who don't despise them, and in their eyes this will be the equivalent of five or ten years taken off my age. Also there comes a time when one craves for recognition – not to be always at the mercy of the spite, malice, contempt – and perhaps even the just dismissal – of one's rivals. I feel pegged up in some way, given a shot in the arm. I've always felt some saving angel does guard me from the worst – sometimes thinking it a good sometimes a bad angel. Probably it's an in-between angel. Many of those I most respect have refused honours, and that they have done so is their supreme honour.

On a channel crossing when I was 17 I sat on a deckchair next to Sir Henry Newbolt.* He was very kind to a seasick schoolboy and we discussed poets we admired. He mentioned the name of some poet – I forget whose – and I said, 'Well, I can't like the work of a poet who has a title.' A gaffe with the power to raise a ghost.

11 May / *Venice*

The PEN. The subject is 'Venice in various literatures'. The smaller and more insignificant the literature the longer the speeches. François Bondy is here and was very informative about Venice in German literature. After his speech, I asked him whether Thomas Mann, in addition to having homosexual inclinations, actually had sex with men, and he said, quite definitely, yes. The conference arrangements are hilariously Italian … The great joy, apart from that of being in Venice, is that Mary McCarthy, her husband, Jim West, Francis King, and a few other old friends are here.

---

* Sir Henry Newbolt (1862–1938). Poet, barrister and naval historian.

15 May / *Venice*

Last night Mary, Jim, the Bondys and I skipped an official invitation to some palazzo (it was not a palazzo at all, the Polish delegate told me later, but an apartment so small that PEN could scarcely crowd into it) and went to Torcello, arriving there about seven thirty. In the past I've always gone there in the middle of the day and been slightly bored by those scattered buildings of brick and grey stone: the Romanesque church tower and the church with the great Byzantine mosaics and a few monuments among the parched fields and little vineyards, reached at the end of a canal path leading to a small quayside. But in the dusk it was magical and enchanting. Every detail stood out, the Byzantine capitals on top of their round columns, each of them different; a sarcophagus with straight clear chiselled lettering; a bishop's stone throne lying on its side in a courtyard. Behind some railings one saw statuary of pagan subjects: a nymph, a grape-crowned Bacchus: and, beyond these, a brick wall, vermilion contrast to the surrounding greyness and stoniness. Then there was a pathway leading through a small vineyard to a section of the canal with no path along it, its water like khaki-coloured glass. There were a few roses and some other flowers whose hot colours, through the fading light, pressed upon one's eyes. Seen from the stone yard in front of the restaurant, along the side of the canal, a little cluster of houses forming a deep magenta cleft cut out against hedges with, beyond them, fields.

While I was in Venice, I read Muriel Gardiner's (Buttinger's) book *Code Name Mary*, describing her early life in Chicago and how, in her late twenties, she lived in Vienna, studying medicine, and being psycho-analysed by an analyst recommended to her by Freud. This was the time of the socialist rising in Vienna against the authoritarian government of Dollfuss, and the shelling by the military of the workers' tenements, the Karl Marx Hof, built by the Austrian socialists in the twenties. Muriel's sympathies were with the workers and socialists and she describes in her book the often very dangerous missions she undertook in order to get socialists who were being pursued by the police across the frontier. Having considerable means she also gave money to the underground socialists, and later she married one of the socialist leaders, Joseph Buttinger.

Lillian Hellman's long story 'Julia' is fiction written in autobiographical form with a narrator who purports to be Hellman, who has a friend from college days – Julia – who adores Hellman and who later goes to Vienna and does all the things that Muriel did, except that at the end of the story she is killed. When a movie was made of 'Julia', friends of Muriel who saw it kept on ringing Muriel to ask her whether she was Julia. This aroused her curiosity, though she never claimed to be Julia. She had reason to think that Hellman must know about her because they had a friend and lawyer in common, called Schwabacher. Dr Schwabacher, who had a house on the estate of the Buttingers, near Princeton, had told Muriel a great deal about Lillian Hellman and the colourful world of theatrical celebrities in which she moved. It was reasonable to suppose that he had also talked to Hellman about her. So Muriel wrote to Lillian Hellman asking, 'Am I Julia?', a letter which remained unanswered and which, later on, Hellman denied ever having received.

However, Muriel's curiosity was aroused, and through Viennese connections, she had a search made into the Austrian archives of the thirties. They found there was no record of any rich young American woman having played a role in helping the Austrian socialists, apart from Muriel. On being informed of this, Hellman retorted that underground socialist workers don't keep archives. However, whatever the truth about Julia, everything points to the character being based on Muriel. In Hellman's story Julia is purportedly being analysed by Freud. Muriel, as I have pointed out, was analysed by someone recommended by Freud, and she was a close friend of Anna Freud (who wrote the introduction to Code Name Mary.) Presumably the Freud family would have known if there had been another rich American young woman giving heroic aid to the underground socialists, for this would have been the woman who (according to Hellman) Freud was analysing.

I went to the London Library and got Lillian Hellman's book Pentimento containing the story 'Julia', which I read. I can't think why she has any reputation as a writer of prose. The actual writing seems to be done with a blunt instrument. She impersonates the manners of the group of writers acting tough in which she moves, but never gets beyond this in her writing. The heroism of Julia is partly a device for flattering herself since she portrays herself as Julia's dearest friend, in fact lover. Some of the events described and the general idea of a rich American girl who lives in Vienna and becomes a member of the anti-fascist socialist underground are presumably taken from Muriel's life, but the character bears little resemblance to Muriel.

18 May / *London*

We arrived late for the memorial service to Clifford Curzon.* A tall, beautiful interior with innocuous nineteenth- or early twentieth-century stained-glass windows, very bad acoustics. It could scarcely have been more impersonal. A concert, a reading of a long, interesting statement by Clifford about piano playing, a couple of prayers but no personal tribute. The whole thing was as bleak as the unseasonably cold day outside. I kept on remembering irrelevant things about Clifford. How I first heard of him from an Italian count, Alberto de la Marmora, an attractive and interesting dilettante of the early thirties. Later when I asked Clifford about Alberto, he characteristically said he wasn't serious. Clifford worshipped at a piano-shaped altar of work, and there was very little else he valued in life. When one did meet him though, he was always friendly, an excellent talker. In New York once he told me that pianos on which he played in America either had gremlins or were damaged by agents of rival pianists.

(As I write these lines an old lady walking along the pavement plucks a rose from our garden. I rap on the window and wonder whether I should rush out and shout at her – then think – well, why shouldn't she have a rose?)

Clifford's soul went into his music – and if he really wanted to express himself, he sat down and played. He had the highest standards in everything and, with his beautiful house, garden, pictures, furniture, seemed the best possible product – redeemed and purified by work – of a very high remote remnant of civilization. Often the great musicians seem like this. They are the orchids of culture, hot-house flowers of the European nineteenth century.

19 May

I went to the Cranium Club dinner at Bianchi's. John Lehmann arrived and said almost at once to Lawrence Gowing, 'I went to your exhibition at the Serpentine Gallery. I thought the pictures were very well hung.' Pause. Expectant look on Gowing's face. 'I thought whoever arranges the pictures did so extremely well,' J. went on. 'But what did you think of the pictures?' put in Coldstream. J. pursed his

* Clifford Curzon died on 1 September 1982.

lips and said, 'I thought it a very great pity that the picture that I had lent to the exhibition had been reframed.' 'But it hadn't been reframed,' protested Gowing. 'I thought it a great pity,' said J. 'I was greatly attached to that frame.'

During dinner John leaned across the table and said: 'I am writing the fifth volume of my autobiography.' 'Oh,' I said. 'It contains things about you that I thought at the time but do not necessarily think now. I wonder whether we should change past impressions in view of later reassessments.' 'Don't change anything on my account,' I said. 'Don't let that consideration enter into your decision at all.' He looked relieved.

22 May

Nothing seems to have happened except that we are hounded by work, Natasha especially. I feel depressed by not getting on top of things. A review is by now just as much effort to write as a short story. I do reviews because I am asked to do them, and I can never say no. Money nags also. Time. I live in the present, grappling with it, trying to pour the work into the moment, yet always, even at this late stage of my life, I think about that mysterious unfolding thing, the future. I don't think enough of what I will do to it, in it, but of what it will bring.

When I think about dying I have only one question in mind – will my immortal work be written? If I say to myself, 'Well, it would be the same to have died twenty – thirty – years ago, as ten years hence,' I think, yes, but if I had died twenty or thirty years ago I would not have achieved my ambition to write an immortal work, which I also will not have done if I die tomorrow – and which I am beginning to think I will not have done ten years hence.

Lizzie rushed in, said, 'Why are you not in the garden? It's a marvellous day.' We had not noticed.

29 May

I kept on thinking of writing poems about time. One would be about past, present, and future. The present is a fixed point where one is. The future is written in invisible ink, which is made visible only when it becomes the present. It mocks us with its uncertainties. The future moves across the page from left to right, the past from right to left as in looking-glass writing. I see the past as in a looking-glass.

Appendix

Harold Spender (1864-1926). Father of Michael, Christine, Stephen and Humphrey. Liberal journalist and author. Wrote books on Byron, Home Rule and mountaineering, as well as biographies of Herbert Asquith and Lloyd George. Contested Bath as a United Liberal candidate in the general election of 1922. Son of a well-known Victorian novelist, Mrs J. K. Spender, who had paid for the education of five sons on the proceeds of her books, and of Dr John Kent-Spender. He married *Violet Schuster* (1877-1920) whose father was *Ernest Schuster* K.C. (1850-1924) and whose mother Hilda Schuster was the very eccentric grandmother of Stephen, described at length in *World Within World*. Violet Spender was beautiful, sensitive and gifted. She died at the age of 43 after an operation. A volume of her poems, *The Path to Caister*, was published posthumously in 1923.

The father of Hilda Schuster (great-grandfather of Stephen) was a well-known Victorian doctor, *Sir Hermann Weber* (1823-1918) and her brother *F. Parkes Weber* (1863-1962) became a distinguished diagnostician and specialist in rare diseases, author of *Rare Diseases and Some Debatable Subjects* (1947), *Further Rare Diseases* (1949) and *Medical Teleology and Miscellaneous Subjects* (1958). He was the great-uncle who used to take Stephen for holidays in Switzerland described in *World Within World*. Both Sir Hermann and Parkes Weber made a notable collection of Greek coins and bequeathed them to the British Museum.

Sir George Schuster (1881-1983), uncle of Stephen and father of his cousin John, and Richard, who was killed in the Second World War. Sir George was in the city and in government – a public servant of great distinction who served on the Milner Commission and set up the financial systems of the governments of the Sudan, Malta and India, where he worked with Mountbatten. He wrote his autobiography at the age of 99, and in the last twenty years of his life his great interest was the foundation and development of Atlantic World Colleges.

J. A. Spender (1862-1942), brother of Harold and uncle of Stephen. Liberal journalist and editor: *Eastern Morning News* 1886-90, *Pall Mall Gazette* 1892, and the outstanding editor of *The Westminster Gazette* 1896-1922. When the split between Lloyd George and Asquith occurred Spender was an outspoken supporter of Asquith and resigned the editorship. (Harold Spender, a life-long friend of Lloyd George, remained his close supporter, and anti-Asquithian.) J. A. Spender served on the Royal Commission on Divorce and on Armaments, and also on Lord Milner's Mission to Egypt 1921-2. He wrote biographies of Sir Campbell Bannerman (1925), the first Lord Cowdray (1930) and Lord Asquith (1932). He wrote histories: *Fifty Years of Europe* (1933), *A Short History of Our Times* (1934), *Great Britain, Empire and Commonwealth 1886-1935* (1936), and a personal history *The Public Life* (1925).

Index

Index

Index

Berns, Walter, 94
Bernstein, Bertie, 94
Bernstein, Robert (Bob), 473, 474-5
Bernstein, Leonard, 94
Berryman, John, 96, 119, 262
'Best Christmas, The' (SS), 253
Bethlehem, 284
Betjeman, John, 51, 96
Bevin, Ernest, 102
Biéville, Ann de, 107
Billy Budd (Britten), 106
Bingham, Barry, 402
Birth of Tragedy, The (Nietzsche), 115
Birtwell, Celia, 444, 445
Bismarck, Klaus von, 86, 88
Black Forest, 36
Blaikie (Kahn), Derek, 174-5, 213
Blake, Nicholas, *see* Day Lewis, Cecil
Blake, William, 161n, 319, 330, 350
Blakiston, Noel, 281
'Blanche, Anthony', 53n
Blok, Alexander, 218
Blundell's School, 57, 334
Blunden, Edmund, 193
Blunt, Anthony, 304, 386, 387, 442
Bochum, 85
Bologna, 171
Bombay, 143
Bondy, François, 133, 481, 482
Bonham Carter, Charlotte, 372-3
Bonham Carter, Mark, 14, 461
Bonnard, Pierre, 204, 297
Bonn, 38, 39, 40, 59, 62, 63, 64, 65, 74, 76, 77, 78, 84, 88, 162, 165, 166
Bonn University, 35n, 59, 63, 66, 74
Boodah movement, 143
Book Programme, 298
Book Society, 95
Booth, George, 148n
Bosham, 148
Boston, 112, 226, 302, 304, 384, 404, 406, 471
Boston College, 384
Boswell, James, 309
Botticelli, Sandro, 115, 174
Boulez, Pierre, 227
Bowen, Elizabeth, 58, 243, 390
Bower, Tony, 59
Bowra, Maurice, 111, 154, 155, 174, 213, 258
Boyle, Andrew, 442

Boysmans Museum, 178, 453
Boy's Own Paper, 80
Bradford, 447
Bragg, Melvyn, 437
Brains Trust, 159
Brandeis University, 405
Brandon, Henry, 264
Brasenose College, Oxford, 419n
Brecht, Bertolt, 232, 342, 371
Breit, Harvey, 111
Breitbach, Joseph, 87n
Brendel, Alfred, 431, 432
Breton, André, 111
Brett, Hon. Dorothy, 94, 365, 404
Brideshead Revisited (Waugh), 53n
Bridges, Robert, 165, 329
Brik, Professor, 322
Brik, Lilian, 322
Bringhurst, Robert, 443
British Council, 138, 141, 189n, 216, 219, 228, 317
Britten, Benjamin, 58, 106, 288n, 361, 429
Brodsky, Joseph, 422, 463, 473
'Brook, The' (Tennyson), 200, 202
Brooke, Rupert, 398
Brow, Major, 74
Brown, Harry, 176
Brown, Jerry, 445
Brownell, Sonia, *see* Orwell, Sonia
Browning, Robert, 473
Brueghel, Pieter, 407
Bruern, 130-1, 226, 228, 230, 232, 233, 235, 252, 254
Bruges, 406, 407
Buchenwald, 70, 77
Buckenburg, 69
Buckley, Steven, 476
Buffalo, 422
Buhler, Eve, 50
Buhler, Robert, 41, 48, 50
Burford, 235
Burgess, Guy, 57, 62n, 95, 96, 173, 210-16, 442
Burton, Richard, 440
Bush House, 58
Butler, R. A., 215-16
Buttinger, Joseph, 181, 182, 267, 404, 482
Buttinger, Muriel, *see* Gardiner, Muriel
Byron, Lord (George Gordon), 29n, 116, 218, 288n, 289, 339, 369, 373, 412, 436

Index

Calder-Marshall, Arthur, 165
California University, 131, 225n, 465
Callaghan, Rt Hon. James, 430
Callas, Niko, 311
Cambridge, 253, 257, 304, 306, 335, 338, 398, 431, 462
Campaign for Nuclear Disarmament (CND), 471
Campbell, Joseph, 94
Campbell, Roy, 126
Canterbury, 480
Canterbury Tales, The (Chaucer), 295
'Cantos' (Auden), 315
Capel, June, *see* Osborn, June
Capri, 180
Capriccio (Stravinsky), 226
Caravaggio, 306
Carleton, Mrs John, *see* Adam Smith, Janet
Carlyle, Thomas, 198
Carrington, Dora, 398
Carritt, Gabriel, 356
Carter, President Jimmy, 397
Castle, The (Kafka), 89
Caudwell, Christopher, 311
Causley, Charles, 437
CBE (Commander of the Order of the British Empire), 233, 437
'Central Heating' (SS), 269
Central Intelligence Agency (CIA), 97, 257, 258
Centre College, Kentucky, 355
Cézanne, Paul, 144, 149, 179, 204, 360
Chagall, Marc, 214
Chamberlain, Neville, 24
Chambers, Anne Cox, 214
Chandler, Raymond, 144-5
Channon, Professor (English department chairman), 101
Channon, Paul, 293
Chaplin, Charlie, 242
Charles, Prince of Wales, 307, 386, 406
Charlottesville, 95, 327
Charterhouse School, 325
Chase, The (Auden), 315
Chekhov, Anton, 405
Chesterton, G.K., 419
Chicago, 95, 221, 330, 463, 477, 482
Chicago University, 94
Chidambaram, 139
Chilver, Richard, 53n

China Diary (SS–Hockney), 395, 466, 471
Chinatown (film), 425n
Chipping Norton, 252
Chips with Everything (Wesker), 228-9
Chirico, Giorgio de', 171, 282
Chopin, Frédéric, 298
Christ Church, Oxford, 152, 158
Christiansen, Arthur, 96, 172-3
Christie's, 249
Churchill, John, 391
Churchill, Winston, 58, 214, 215, 265
Cincinnati, 97, 111, 112, 113, 115, 120, 122, 123, 125
Cincinnati Enquirer, 114
Cincinnati University, 96, 113, 125n
Cini Foundation, 373
'Circus Animals' Desertion, The' (Yeats), 376
Cisneros (poet), 454
Citizen Kane (Orson Welles), 72
Civilian Military Forces, *see* Control Commission
Civilization of France, The (Curtius), 29n
Clark, Lord Kenneth, 106, 224, 242, 288, 289, 304
Clark, Lady (Jane), 106, 242, 288, 289
Clark, John, 368n
Clark, Mrs John (Tekla), 368
Clark, Ossie, 444
Clark, Professor William, 114, 117, 118, 124
Clarke, Ashley, 372-3
Clarke, Frances, 372-3
Claudel, Paul, 151, 164, 366
Clayre, Alasdair, 245
Clean Asshole Poems (Orlovsky), 351
Clerk-Kerr, Archibald (Lord Inverchapel), 264
Climate of Treason, The (Boyle), 442
Clos, Professor, 65
Cochin, 139
Cocteau, Jean, 87n, 158, 159, 227, 230
Code Name Mary (Muriel Gardiner), 181n, 482, 483
Cocktail Party, The (Eliot), 268
Coggan, Donald, Archbishop of Canterbury, 389
Coghill, Nevill, 295
Coldstream, Nancy (later Mrs Michael Spender), 57

Index

Index

Index

Index

Index

Index

'Horst Wessel Lied', 168
House, Humphry, 165
Houseman, A.E., 155, 382-3
Howard, Brian, 53
Howard, Elizabeth Jane, 342
Howards End (Forster), 452
'Hugh Selwyn Mauberley' (Pound), 112
Hughes, Ted, 225-6, 437
Hunt, Leigh, 428
Hunter, Anne, 317, 358
Hunter, Robert, 317
Hurd, Chancellor, 349
Huston, John, 414
Hutchinson, Lord (Jeremy), 108*n*
Huxley, Sir Julian, 93, 111, 258, 458-60
Huxley, Lady (Juliette), 400, 459
Hyde, Montgomery, 312
Hyndman, Tony, 21

I am a Camera (Isherwood–Van Druten), 109
Idea Systems Group, 111
Ides of March (Wilder), 411
Importance of Being Earnest, The (Wilde), 247
Index on Censorship, 254*n*, 259, 400, 451, 454, 461, 463, 465-6, 468, 470, 472, 473, 477-8, 479
Information, Ministry of, 34, 35, 44
Ingrams, Richard, 419
In Parenthesis (Jones), 279
Insel Ruegen, 28
Institute of Contemporary Arts (ICA), 153, 171, 228
International Brigade, 21, 102*n*, 215*n*, 408
Intourist, 209, 213, 218
Inverchapel, Lord, *see* Clerk-Kerr, Archibald
Ipsden, 428
Isfahan, 317
Ischia, 95, 96, 160, 180, 212, 368*n*
Ise, 192
Isherwood, Christopher, 28, 35, 49, 94, 109, 111, 145, 153-4, 162, 186, 214, 230, 311-12, 329, 337, 338, 343, 347, 348, 356, 366-7, 369, 402-3, 420, 429, 432, 466, 467
Ishihara, Hoki, 187
Iwaszkiewicz, Jaroslav, 130

Jaffé, Michael, 304

Jagger, Chris, 269, 270
Jagger, Mick, 269
James, Clive, 378
James, Henry, 128, 152, 339, 384, 434
Jarrell, Randall, 94, 261, 262
Jaspers, Karl, 93
Jebb, Julian, 416
Jenkins, Mrs Roy (Jennifer), 293
Jenkins, Roy, 293
Jennings, Humphrey, 71-2, 90
Jerusalem, 283, 284, 285
John, Augustus, 157, 158
John, Henry, 157
John, Poppet, 157
Johnson, Basil, 41
Johnson, President Lyndon Baines, 264, 265-7
Johnson, Samuel, 309-10
Johnstone, Archibald R., 102
Joll, James, 400, 456
Jones, David, 153, 279-80, 327-9, 335-6, 339
Joseph, Keith, 448
Josselson, Michael, 257
Jostin, Walter, 66
Jouhandeau, Marcel, 87*n*, 165
Journal (Renard), 320
Journey to a War (Auden–Isherwood), 354
Journey to the Frontier (Stansky-Abrahams), 213*n*
Joyce, James, 45, 64, 128, 319, 427, 444
Jozankei, 199
'Judas Iscariot' (SS), 377
'Julia' (Hellman), 482, 483
Jünger, Ernst, 83-4, 86-8
Jünger, Frau, 86
Jurinac, Sena, 150

Kabuki theatre, 197, 204-5
Kafka, Franz, 89, 138
Kahn, Derek, *see* Blaikie, Derek
Kaito, Takikawa, 192
Kallin, Anna, 245
Kallman, Chester, 183, 290, 291, 294, 366, 368, 369, 411, 472
Kamakura, 190
Kampf um Berlin (Goebbels), 80
Kandy, 137
Kanran-tei, 198
Kansas City, 101, 310

Index

Index

Index

Index

Index

Index

Index

Index

Spender, Violet, 52, 253, 487

Spiral Ascent, The (Upward), 233n

Spiritual Explorations (SS), 66, 75

Squire, J. C., 267

Spring-Hall, D. F., 215

Stalin, Joseph, 37, 43, 207, 212, 230, 265, 286

Stampa, Gaspara, 239

Stangos, Nikos, 323, 416, 417, 418

Stansky, Peter, 213n

Stark, Freya, 374

Starkie, Enid, 111, 159

State Department (USA), 211, 470, 471

Stauffenberg rising, 21

Stegner, Wallace, 352

Stein, Gertrude, 329

Stein, Jean, 473

Stendhal, 164, 214, 360

Stern, Isaac, 298

Stern, James, 59, 230

Stern, Tania, 230

Stieglitz, Walter, 302

Still Centre, The (SS), 460

Stockwood, Mervyn, 389

Stokes, Adrian, 457

Storrs, 269, 272

Stowe School, 213n

Strachey, Lytton, 75, 198, 398-9, 429

Stratford-upon-Avon, 173

Strauss, Richard, 239, 242

Stravinsky, Igor, 106, 109, 183-4, 226, 227-8, 230, 237, 238, 239, 258, 331, 339, 421, 455

Stravinsky, Vera, 183-4, 239, 339, 420-1

Strings are False, The (MacNeice), 263

Struggle of the Modern, The (SS), 221

Suck magazine, 270

Suez, 182

Sunday Express, 214, 249

Sunday Telegraph, 253, 342, 455

Sunday Times, 228, 248-9, 264, 281n, 294

Sunion, 116, 119

Surrey, Henry Howard, 479

Sutherland, Graham, 234, 235, 242, 245, 303n

Swami, Narayan, 138

Swift, Jonathan, 233n

'Swimmers, The' (Tate), 378

Swinburne, Algernon Charles, 348, 473

Sydney, 270

Sydney University, 135-6

Sylbert, Richard, 425

'Symbolic Imagination, The' (Tate), 127

Syracuse, 420

Taft, Robert, 96

Tahiti, 345

Taikan (watercolourist), 203

Taos, 94, 403

Tate, Allen, 95, 100, 101-2, 125, 127-8, 248, 280, 339-40, 352, 378

Tate, Caroline, *see* Gordon, Caroline

Tate Gallery, 172, 229

Tchelitchev, Pavel, 434

Tehrān, 317

Temple, The (SS), 388-9

temps retrouvé, Le (Proust), 308

Tennyson, Alfred, Lord, 136, 200, 473

Tewkesbury, 173, 174

Thackeray, William Makepeace, 436, 438

Thatcher, Margaret, 293, 429, 481

Theatre Royal, Stratford East, 364n

Theroux, Paul, 296

Third Programme (BBC), 108n

Third World War, The, 392

Thirties, The (Bergonzi), 329n

Thirties Journal (Wilson), 411

Thomas, Caitlin, 192

Thomas, Dylan, 36, 135, 158, 187, 191-2

Thomas, Edward, 417

Thompson, Ambassador, 473, 474

Thorberg, Friedrich, 150

Thorn, Gaston, 432

Time magazine, 184

Times, The, 244, 258, 320

Times Literary Supplement, 126, 280, 297

Tintoretto, Jacopo, 407

Tippett, Michael, 236

Toad, Leo, 87n

Todd, Ruthven, 187

Tokunaga, Shozo, 131, 189, 190, 198, 199, 200, 201, 202, 204, 205

Tokyo, 131, 187, 188, 190, 197, 198, 202, 203

Toledo, 312-13

Tolson, M. R., 262-3

Tolstoy, Leo, 217, 360, 436, 466

Tomalin, Claire, 428

Tom Jones (Henry Fielding), 75

Torcello, 482

Toronto, 422

Torri del Benaco, 95

Index

Index

Index